COMMANDO GALLANTRY AWARDS OF WORLD WAR II

DEDICATED TO 'M'

THE COMMANDO MEMORIAL
SPEAN BRIDGE
INVERNESS-SHIRE, SCOTLAND

Commando Gallantry Awards of World War II

George A. Brown
A.I.I.C., F.C.G.A.

By the same author:

The Fenian Raids 1866–70
The Northwest Rebellion 1885
Conspicuous Gallantry Medal
Those Who Dared
Canadian Wing Commanders 1984
Canadian Welcome Home Medals

© G. A. Brown 1991

All rights reserved. The use of any part of this publication reproduced, transmitted in any form or by any means, electronic, mechanical, photocopying, recording or otherwise, or stored in a retrieval system, without the prior consent of the publisher is an infringement of the copyright law.

The Maps on Pages 8, 14, 16, 22, 110, 112 & 114 are Crown Copyright and are reproduced with the permission of the Controller of Her Majesty's Stationery Office.

Printed & bound by Antony Rowe Ltd, Eastbourne

ISBN 0 948130 09 1

Acknowledgements

The production of this book has been exciting and rewarding.

I have wanted, for some time, to tell the stories of these brave men and their unbelievable feats of arms, for they are examples of extreme courage, often in the face of great dangers and overwhelming odds.

The citations for the awards are from the official war records and for his considerable assistance in researching these I wish to record my sincere appreciation to Mr. David A. E. Morris. My appreciation for their good counsel and support is also extended to Chris Buckland of the London Stamp Exchange, Ron Penhall, Jack Boddington and Charles Bainbridge, good friends and knowledgeable members of various historical and numismatic societies.

I sincerely hope this tribute to all Commando forces will prove not only interesting to the general reader but also as a reference source for fellow collectors and historians.

George A. Brown.

They shall grow not old
  As we that are left grow old.

Age shall not weary them,
  Nor the years condemn.

At the going down of the sun
  And in the morning

We will remember them.

Contents

ACKNOWLEDGEMENTS	5
INTRODUCTION	9
NORTH WEST EUROPE BEFORE D DAY	13
Bruneval, France, 27 February 1942	13
St. Nazaire, France, 26/27 March 1942	17
Dieppe–Bernaval, France, 17 August 1942	20
NORTH AFRICA AND THE WESTERN MEDITERRANEAN	55
Tobruk, Libya, 17/18 July 1941	55
The Raid on Rommel's H.Q., 17/18 November 1941	56
THE EASTERN MEDITERRANEAN AND THE BALKANS	79
NORWAY	109
Lofoten Islands, 4 March 1941	109
Second Raid on Lofoten Islands, 26 December 1941	111
Vaagsö and Maaloy, 26 December 1941	111
SICILY	119
Primasole Bridge and the Ponte Dei Malati Bridge, 10/15 July 1943	119
ITALY	131
Termoli, 2/3 October 1943	131
D DAY AND THE NORMANDY BREAK-OUT	191
WALCHEREN	211
Walcheren Island, Holland, 1/8 November 1944	211
NORTH WEST EUROPE AFTER D DAY	225
THE FAR EAST	263
MISCELLANEOUS AWARDS	287
ESCAPES	295
BIBLIOGRAPHY	323
INDEX	325

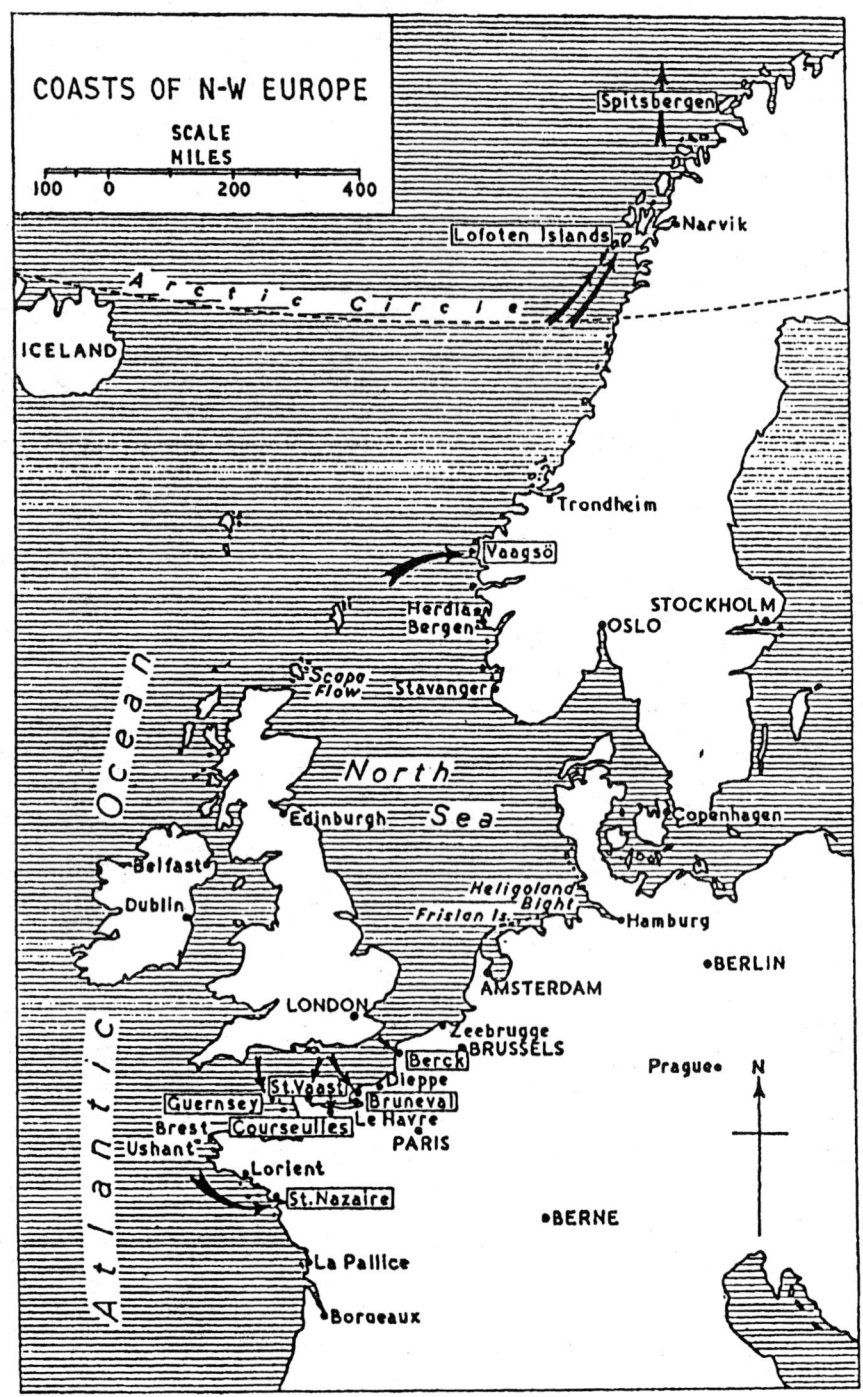

Introduction

ON THE NIGHT of June 24th 1940, a small flotilla slipped out from the harbours of Dover, Folkestone and Newhaven to rendezvous in the English Channel. The sea was calm, the skies dark and overcast. Aboard the small craft were volunteer soldiers from a newly conceived unit with the rather foreign-sounding name of Commandos. They were embarking on a strange new kind of warfare.

During the Boer War in South Africa at the turn of the century the Boers, descendants of early Dutch settlers, employed small units called Commandos—a word derived from the Portuguese language meaning 'under command.' These units were expert at hit and run tactics and able to live off the land for long periods. They were deadly marksmen and the British troops, familiar with more conventional tactics, were often ambushed suffering casualties disproportionate to the size of the attacking force.

T. E. Lawrence of Arabian fame and his Arab allies had employed similar tactics with great success during the Middle East campaigns during World War One but his experiences and those of the Boers lay dormant until World War Two.

It was Col Dudley Clarke, a Staff Officer in the War Office, who developed the concept of Commandos and their application to modern warfare. Col Clarke, known as the 'Grandfather' of the Commandos took his idea to Sir John Dill, Chief of the Imperial General Staff who, after reviewing it, enthusiastically presented the idea to the Prime Minister. Awaiting the Prime Minister's decision, Col Clarke was confronted by opposition from senior staff officers, some taking strong exception to the name and recommending they be called Special Service. Clarke opposed this, basing his argument on the fact that the initials S.S. were identical to Hitler's infamous Storm Troopers or Schütz Staffel. Happily, Sir Winston Churchill, then Prime Minister was enthusiastic about the concept for, as a prisoner of war during the Boer War, he was familiar with Boer tactics. He gave his approval with two restrictions. First, no unit could be diverted from its primary role, the defence of Britain, for a German invasion was imminent. Secondly, that the Commandos had to operate with only a minimum of weapons. All but stripped of its weapons at Dunkirk, the Army needed every weapon available to combat the impending invasion.

Col Clarke set forth the standards for the Commandos and these were the training objectives:
1. To turn out a soldier as physically fit as the finest athlete.
2. To train him in the use of all infantry weapons.
3. To teach him that darkness is not a hindrance but a help.
4. To give him the techniques for killing or capturing quickly and silently.
5. To train him to think for himself and to operate independently or in a small group.
6. To make him familiar with ships and the sea, for his operations would be sea-borne and his life would depend on working intelligently with the Royal Navy.
7 To teach him to think of warfare solely in terms of attack.
8. All Commandos were to be volunteers.

In order to recruit the Commandos, the Commander in Chief and the War Office first selected ten Commando leaders. These, in turn, selected ten Officer Troop leaders who, in turn, selected their men. After some trial and error the final strength of each Commando unit was fixed at:

1 Lieutenant Colonel
1 Major
10 Captains
24 Subalterns
2 Warrant Officers
42 Sergeants
81 Corporals
122 Lance Corporals
250 Privates

—a total strength of just over 500 Officers and men.

The War Office was swamped with volunteers from various units. Thousands applied but few were selected. They had to be unusually agile, able to think quickly and logically and respond faster than the average soldier. They also had to be willing and able to endure longer hours, harder work and less rest. Such physical and mental stamina was critical, as they were required to travel light and strike hard.

The Command training centre was established in a remote glen in the Scottish Highlands on the grounds of and in the castle of Achnacarry. Few temptations were within easy reach and, since the training was vigorous to say the least, sleep at day's end was the priority. Only one trainee in four was able to meet the demanding standards. Little wonder then that Commandos achieved so much!

Introduction

Gradually, the first Commando unit was born, followed soon by others, many of which included men from countries occupied by the Germans, men from Colonial units and from other countries opposed to Nazi philosophy. Men fluent in German were valuable beyond measure.

Commandos went on to fight in virtually every theatre of operations, either small engagements or those where thousands of troops were involved. Their total strength numbered about 10,000 and they were drawn from eighty-eight different units. Proportionate to their numbers they earned a remarkable ratio of Orders and Decorations as the following illustrates.

    10 Victoria Crosses
    32 Distinguished Service Order admissions
    7 Bars to the Distinguished Service Order (Second award)
    135 Military Crosses
    10 Bars to the Military Cross (Second award)
    46 Distinguished Conduct Medals
    289 Military Medals, and 10 Bars
—plus many other British and foreign awards.

A tribute must be made to the members of the Royal Navy, Royal Naval Reserve, Royal Naval Volunteer Reserve and Royal Air Force who, often at extreme risk bravely carried the Commandos to their destinations or supported them in other ways. They too gained many awards, richly deserved.

Rarely in the history of the British Army has one word, Commando, meant so much. In the clubs and pubs of Great Britain even now, men no longer young or agile talk of the days when the Commandos gloriously and courageously did brave deeds and often lost their lives for their country and the freedom of occupied lands.

Commandos, supported by the other services, participated in scores of actions large and small during World War II. To outline the strategy behind each action and describe them in definitive detail would occupy several volumes.

Since this book is a record of awards to these men, only a few illustrative actions are given. These may encourage the reader to go beyond this volume and study in more detail other fine books available regarding the events herein. To this end, examination of the bibliography might be useful.

Insofar as is possible (and some citations for the most secret of operations reveal a minimum of detail), recipients of awards are listed under the theatre of operations for which the award was bestowed. In the majority of instances, the original citation is given, from the form (Army Form W. 3121 or the Admiralty equivalent W.A. Form 6—Recommendation for Honours or Awards) actually submitted at the time, which normally give considerably more detail than the subsequent *London Gazette* entry. Where these are not available, the *London Gazette* entry is given, which sometimes gives a brief account of the action. For gallantry awards, where the information is very brief or no location is indicated it may be assumed that the secret nature of the action may have precluded its disclosure in the *Gazette*.

Editorial Note

The text faithfully follows the original citations, except that, in order not to tire the reader, minor spelling mistakes have been corrected, many abbreviations have been given in full and the military use of capitals for proper nouns has been suppressed.

Where dates are given at the end of an entry, they have the following significance:—

(L.G. 8.6.44) The citation is from the original Army or Navy form. The *London Gazette* date is that of the corresponding *L.G.* entry.

[L.G. 8.6.44] The citation is from the original Army or Navy form. The date is that recorded on the form by M.S. Branch for publication in the *London Gazette* (the actual publication date may be several weeks later).

L.G. 8.6.44 The original is not available and the entry is from the *London Gazette* of that date.

8.6.44 The citation is from the original Army or Navy form. No *London Gazette* date has been recorded on the form, the date given being the last approval date, normally by M.S. Branch.

North West Europe before D Day

BRUNEVAL, FRANCE – 27 FEBRUARY 1942

BY LATE 1941 the Germans had made substantial advances in radar technology and had installed a number of large Wurzburg units along the Atlantic wall. These giant 'dishes' were up to 20 feet in diameter and had the capability of locating ships and aircraft, then 'locking' the guns on the target. It was therefore vital that the secret of these units be determined so that appropriate counter measures could be taken. At the suggestion of R. V. Jones of British Scientific Intelligence, a raid on the installation at Bruneval, twelve miles north of Le Havre was planned.

Air reconnaissance had revealed that the radar unit was 100 feet back from the cliff face, the cliff being from 300 to 400 feet high at that point. There was a narrow passage up the cliff face but it was well defended by machine-gun emplacements, barbed wire and a 'pill box' at sea-level. A frontal attack up such a hazardous course was considered but rejected. The final plan evolved as follows:

a. A naval force (Lt-Cdr F. N. Cook) of two destroyers, gun-boats and landing craft with 32 men of the Royal Fusiliers and South Wales Borderers would lie off-shore. Then, at a signal from the Commandos, who would return via the gap in the cliff face, move in to take them and their captured equipment back to England.

b. The recently formed 1st Airborne Division would form the main party of Commandos and would be flown inland behind the objective, dropped, then forming into four groups proceed as follows.

Group 1: (Major J. D. Frost) would attack the house near the radar site which was the operational Headquarters and billet for the crew.

Group 2: (Lieut P. Young) accompanied by Flight Sgt E. W. Cox, a RAF radar specialist, would remove vital components from the Wurzburg.

Group 3: would cover parties one and two should the Germans launch an attack from the nearby village of Presbytère.

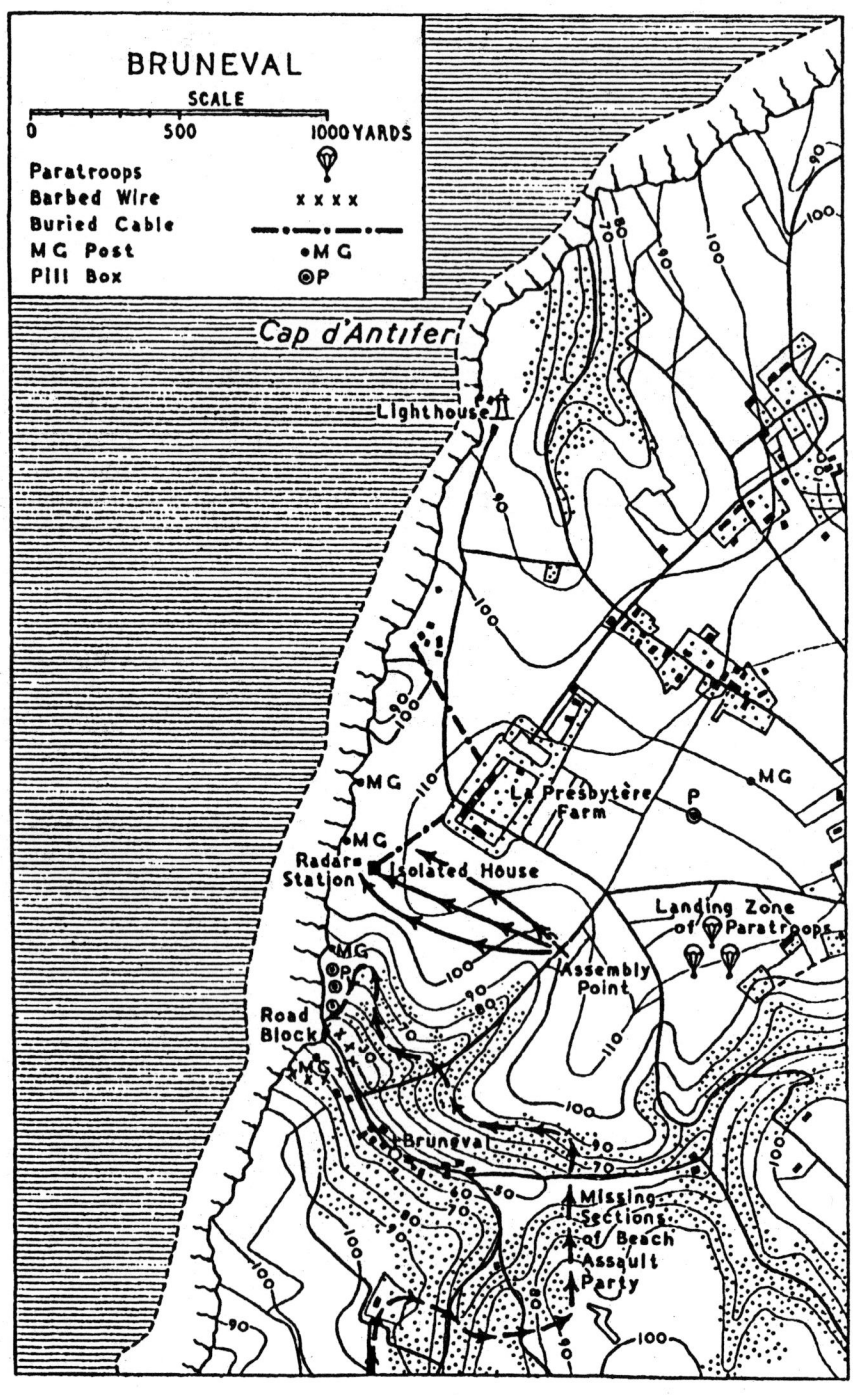

Group 4: (Lieut E. C. B. Charteris) was to attack and subdue the German emplacements in the cliff passage down which the force would withdraw to rendezvous with the RN flotilla following the operation.

The attack was to take place on the night of February 27th–28th and, boarding twelve Whitley bombers under the command of the legendary Wing Commander Pickard, the force took off. With the exception of Lieut Charteris and his men whose aircraft were forced off course by anti-aircraft fire, all other were dropped in the correct area. Charteris and his group were over a mile away.

Groups 1 and 2 (Frost and Young) immediately headed for the house and radar installation. The house, with only a minimum force present, was quickly taken and Major Frost then joined Lieut Young's party which, under fire, were busy dismantling the Wurzburg unit. The German resistance was soon overcome and Flt Sgt Cox and the Sappers removed the radar components then blew up the site.

The time had come to quickly move down to the beach, for German reinforcements were on their way from Presbytère. The passage down the cliff was over 600 yards away and as the Commandos approached it they were joined by Lieut Charteris and his men who had covered the mile and a half in record time. Thus reinforced they fought their way down to the beach. It was now 2.30 a.m. and the Commandos signalled the naval force offshore that they were ready to re-embark. Under fire from a pillbox they successfully got their wounded comrades, the radar parts and prisoners aboard the craft.

The raid was considered almost perfect and, considering the severe conditions during the withdrawal, casualties were relatively low with two killed, six wounded and six missing. Happily the latter six became prisoners of war and survived the war.

The excellent intelligence gleaned by the scientists who examined the radar resulted in the development of 'window'—long strips of aluminized paper which, when dropped by allied aircraft, resulted in distorted radar images, creating in the German's minds the illusion of larger numbers of aircraft or creating control problems for their fighters aloft, whose own radar suffered similarly.

Additionally the success of the neophyte 1st Airborne Division ensured the future of paratroops. The 1st Parachute Brigade was quickly formed and 'Bruneval' became the first Battle Honour of the Parachute Regiment.

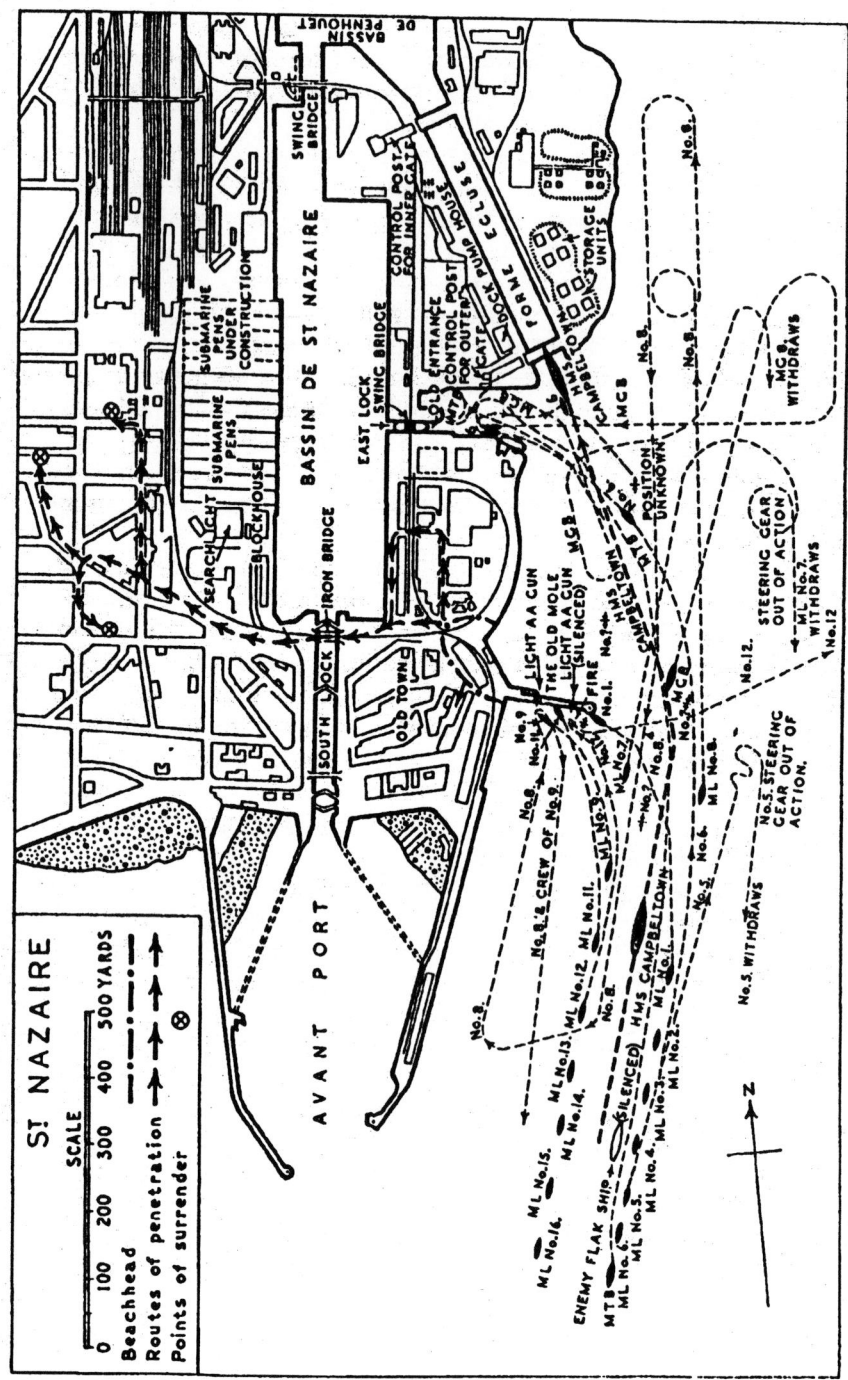

North-West Europe before D-Day

OPERATION 'CHARIOT,' ST. NAZAIRE – 26/27 MARCH 1942

The port of St. Nazaire lies six miles upstream from the mouth of the river Loire on France's Atlantic seaboard. In 1942 its famous dry dock measuring 1,500 by 165 feet was then the world's largest and noted as the 'birthplace' of the great French liner *Normandie*. As France was occupied by the Germans, St. Nazaire's facilities were being enlarged to create a base from which the Germans could launch their attacks on allied shipping in the Atlantic, thus avoiding the long and hazardous route via the Denmark Straits to German ports.

Intelligence reports reaching Combined Operations Headquarters in England indicated the battleship *Tirpitz*, although still in Norwegian waters, was planning a foray into the Atlantic. If successful she would undoubtedly make for St. Nazaire, the only dry dock outside Germany capable of accommodating her should she require repairs. If St. Nazaire could be denied her she would, given Hitler's reluctance to subject his capital ships to risk, remain where she was.

Agreeing that St. Nazaire had a a high priority, planning proceeded and by March 26th the force was ready to sail. The plan was as follows:—

Attack St. Nazaire with a force of 611 Naval and Military personnel. Destroy or damage the docking facilities, submarine pens, power station, pumping station and gun emplacements. A destroyer, HMS *Campbeltown* (ex USS *Buchanan*) loaded with 8,000 pounds of timed explosives would ram the Normandie dock gates. The Commandos she carried, along with others aboard the Motor Launches, would attack other targets. As their objectives had been achieved, the men would board the Motor Launches and withdraw.

Prior to the arrival of the force, 60 Royal Air Force aircraft would bomb St. Nazaire as a diversionary tactic.

Lt-Col A. C. Newman (Essex Regt.) was appointed to command the 265 Commandos who had been drawn from Commando units Nos. 1, 2, 3, 4, 5, 6, 9 and 12. From these, 90 men had been specially trained in demolition tactics.

Commander R. E. D. Ryder, RN, was appointed to command the naval forces, using Motor Gun Boat 314 as a Headquarters vessel during and after the attack.

The attack:
The force left Falmouth, England, on 26th March 1942 and began the 250 mile journey escorted by two destroyers, HMS *Atherstone*

Commando Gallantry Awards of World War II

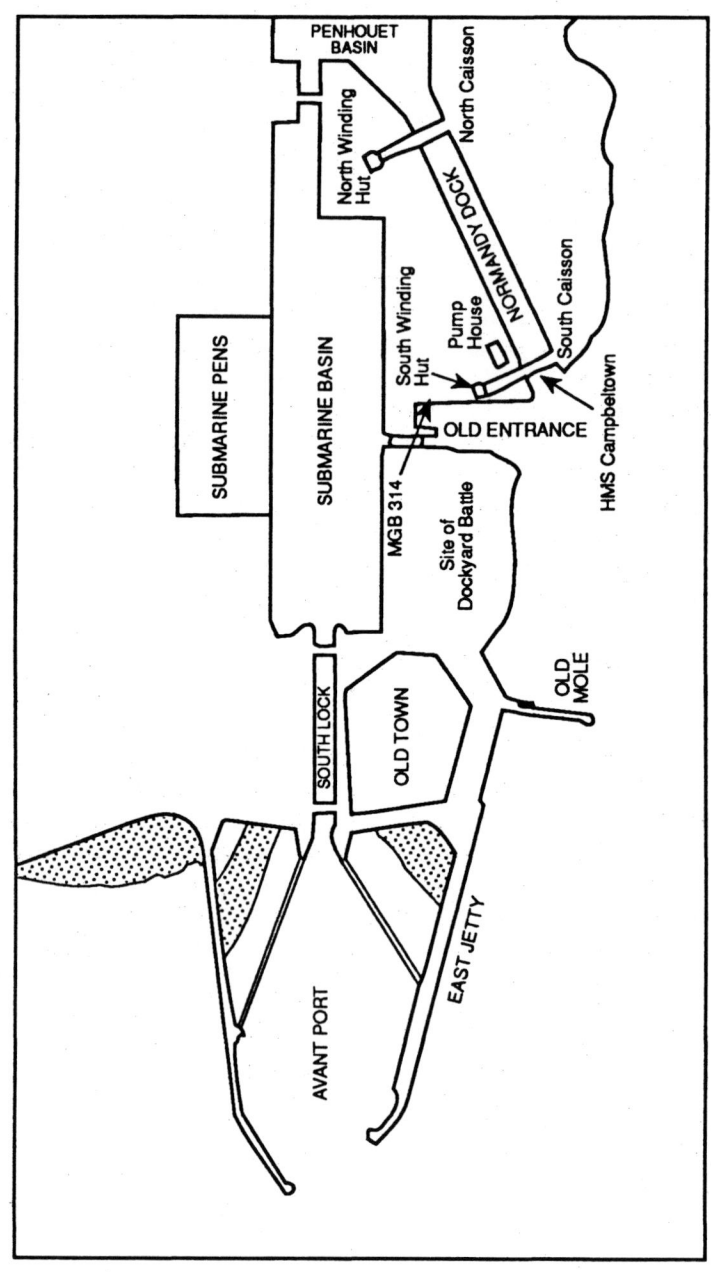

and HMS *Tynedale*, in a three column formation headed by MGB 314 (Lieut D. M. C. Curtis, RNVR) carrying Cdr. Ryder and Lt-Col Newman, HMS *Campbeltown* (Lt-Cdr S. H. Beattie, RN), followed by sixteen Motor Launches and one Motor Torpedo Boat.

Once in the river, the vessels, flying German flags and with HMS *Campbeltown* altered to resemble a German destroyer, were challenged and fired on. However, due to clever signalling ruses, ably assisted by German-speaking Signalman Pike on MGB 314, valuable time was gained and the force, still under sporadic fire proceeded to within a mile of their objective before the ruse was realized. The German flags were hauled down, and replaced by the White Ensign—the Royal Navy's battle flag. The German shelling became intense and many aboard each of the vessels were killed or wounded. MGB 314 swung aside to enable *Campbeltown* to speed up and, only four minutes later than planned, she struck the lock gates with immense force, damaging them severely, then settled down, her bows crushed.

Under heavy fire, the Commandos aboard *Campbeltown*, some severely wounded, quickly disembarked and sped toward their assigned objectives, as did those who were leaving the Motor Launches.

MGB 314 docked next to Lieut Wynn in MTB 74 and put Lt-Col Newman ashore to rendezvous with other members of his Headquarters staff, and Cdr. Ryder with L/S Pike went ashore to check on the progress of the raid. Returning to his MGB he instructed Lieut Wynn to torpedo the lock gates leading to the submarine pens, which he did with time delayed torpedoes. Later, these exploded and the pen basin flooded.

Motor launches awaiting the return of the Commandos were being struck, their crews killed and many were on fire and sinking. If the carnage continued it would be difficult to find sufficient craft to effect the withdrawal.

The seven groups of Commandos went about their difficult task at high speed, under fire and suffering many casualties. Some destroyed gun emplacements, others the caissons at each end of the dock. Those assigned the pump house and generator station climbed 40 feet down ladders to place their charges. Those charged with demolishing the winding mechanisms in the great lock gates, badly wounded, blew them up.

By now the entire area was ablaze with craft sinking, wounded and dead about, installations blowing up and a deadly cross fire between remaining German installations, the soldiers and launches. The time for withdrawal had arrived. In the circumstances it is difficult to identify individuals with specific actions since men assigned to objectives died in the attempt and others replaced them. All were heroes.

Let us examine their achievements.
1. The principal objective—demolition of the lock gates, and winding houses was achieved.
2. The pumping station and power station were demolished.
3. Many gun emplacements were demolished.
4. The submarine pen lock gates were sufficiently damaged and the basin flooded, keeping them out of action for the duration of the war.
5. When HMS *Campbeltown* blew up, nearly 400 German military personnel were aboard and died in the explosion.
6. The *Tirpitz* remained in Norway and was later sunk by RAF aircraft.
7. The Germans were denied a strategic port.

The Commandos, their numbers reduced by casualties and those who were taken prisoner, boarded the remaining naval vessels, MGB 314 being the last to leave—without the brave Newman, wounded and a prisoner. Fighting its way out of the river, the battered force was joined by HM ships *Atherstone*, *Tynedale*, *Cleveland* and *Brocklesby*. Under attack by enemy aircraft, but also defended by Royal Air Force fighters, they reached the safety of England.

Of the 611 men engaged in the operation, 169 (28%) were killed and 200 (33%), most wounded, were taken prisoner. Only three Motor Launches of the 16 that left England returned. Three others, with MGB 314, made an attempt but were in such damaged condition their crews and Commandos were taken aboard the escort vessels and the gallant trio were sunk.

The ratio of awards granted men of the force was quite probably among the war's highest—135 awards to the 611 men engaged, 22%.

Dieppe–Berneval – 17 August 1942

The raid on Dieppe–Berneval took place on 17th August and, at the time, was viewed by the general public as an incredibly brave action but, because of the large number of casualties, a military disaster. From the Canadian standpoint this was understandable, for the Canadian 2nd Division had provided 4,963 men and 3,367 were killed, wounded or captured; a casualty rate of 68%. The other forces engaged suffered casualties as follows:

Naval	15%	3875 engaged
Air	13%	1179 engaged
Commandos	23%	1075 engaged
US Rangers (attached to No. 3 Commando)	26%	50 engaged

The plan called for an attack on five objectives: Dieppe, Berneval, Puits (Puys), Pourville and Varengeville. The Canadian 2nd Division would carry out attacks on Dieppe, Puits and Pourville. The overall objectives of the raid were to:

Destroy enemy defences in the Dieppe area

Destroy any installation of value to the enemy, *e.g.* radar, coastal guns, power stations

Capture prisoners.

The force would attack at dawn, remain ashore approximately eight hours, then effect a withdrawal.

The Commandos were given the critical task of silencing the heavy batteries on the cliff tops near Varengeville and Berneval. These batteries commanded a large field of fire from their ten 150-mm (5.9-inch) guns with a range of twelve miles.

Unless silenced, naval support activities, especially the withdrawals, would be extremely hazardous. No. 3 Commando (Brig J. F. Durnford-Slater) would land near Berneval at two points: Yellow Beach 1 and Yellow Beach 2. No. 4 Commando (Lt-Col The Lord Lovat) at Orange Beach 1 and Orange Beach 2, near Varengeville, each Commando unit carrying out flanking movements to reach their objectives.

No. 3 Commando's run in to the beach was met by intense resistance and the Germans, fully alerted, succeeded in scattering 23 landing craft, only seven reaching shore. Casualties were heavy and the force assigned to Yellow Beach 1, fired on from the cliffs above, suffered heavy casualties, were dispersed and lost 120 men killed, wounded or missing.

Inexplicably undetected by the enemy, one Landing Craft carrying Major Peter Young and 19 men landed and, climbing up through a narrow defile in the cliffs, reached the top. They then started for the battery and just before reaching it several Hurricanes attacked it with cannon and machine-gun fire. Such a small group could not charge and take the battery, so, making the best of their small arsenal of two mortars, bren guns and rifles, they kept up an intense fire on the soldiers in the battery, thus preventing them, for over two hours, from firing on the ships below.

With remarkable coolness and discipline, the small group, now short of ammunition, covered the half mile to the break in the cliff, descended and boarded the Landing Craft which the brave

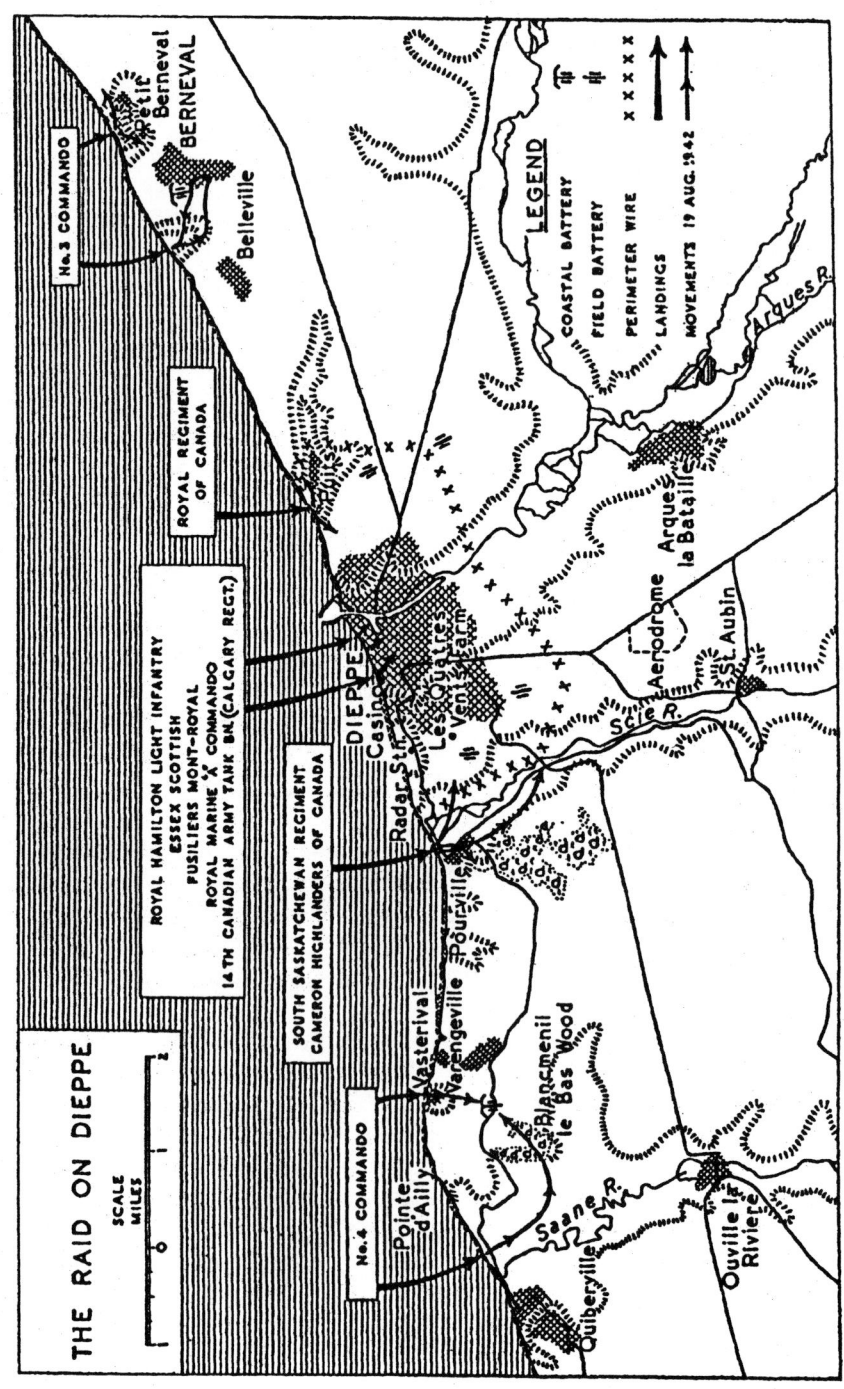

Lieut Buckee, RN, under fire, had kept inshore awaiting their arrival. By 8:10 a.m. they were safely away.

No. 4 Commando (Lord Lovat) consisted of 250 men. Major Derek Mills-Roberts with 70 men landed on Orange Beach 1 and, meeting little resistance, proceeded up a gully in the cliff face, dislodging the barbed wire with Bangalore torpedos.

Reaching the top, they managed to get within 100 yards of the battery which was firing at the ships. They attacked the battery with mortars and small arms fire and were pinning down the soldiers in the battery when a mortar shell struck the German ammunition dump and blew it up. This stopped any activity in the battery and the German soldiers attempting to extinguish the flames were picked off by Commando snipers.

Lord Lovat with the other 180 men of No. 4 had landed precisely on time and, silencing two pillboxes made quick headway in a flanking movement past the village of Quiberville to arrive behind the battery under assault by Major Mills-Roberts's men.

An aerial attack on the battery took place by cannon-firing aircraft of 129 Squadron, following which the pincers began closing on the battery. Under a bayonet attack the defending force of 112 was reduced to four prisoners, the six guns of the battery were blown up and Lovat and his Commandos effected an orderly withdrawal to the beach and the waiting Landing Craft.

Under Lord Lovat's direction, No. 4 Commando conducted a set piece action in every respect. Disembarking with three minutes of the 4:30 a.m. schedule, they completed their missions, returned to the assigned beach and Landing Craft and re-embarked on schedule at 7:30 a.m. Twenty-three brave men remained behind, twelve killed and thirteen missing.

Among the many awards given those who took part in the Dieppe operations were two Victoria Crosses. One, to Major John Foote, Chaplain of the Royal Hamilton Light Infantry, exemplifies the manner in which Major Foote viewed his calling. The planned withdrawal from the terrible beaches of Dieppe was about to take place. Men lay about wounded, many near death, many more already so. Major Foote could have left, but elected to remain giving last rites to the dying, comforting in other ways the wounded. Later they became prisoners, but Foote, in the prison camp, remained a tower of strength to the men until war's end.

Lt-Col Cecil Merritt, commanding the South Saskatchewan Regiment was also a recipient of the Victoria Cross, awarded for his dashing leadership when he and his men, attempting to cross a small bridge, were held down by enemy fire from the other side.

Lt-Col Merritt, with complete disregard for his own safety, helmet in hand, ran to the centre of the 100 foot long bridge, turned toward his men and called out 'come on over, they can't hit anything.' Some joined him and he led them toward the German pillboxes. Recognizing that a larger force was required to capture them, he again crossed the bridge, rallied the remaining men and led them against the German positions which were quickly taken.

The Dieppe Raid has been a controversial topic for nearly half a century by the survivors and others. Was it a 'D' Day rehearsal? One will never find total agreement, but expert military strategists with the benefit of retrospective analysis now appear to agree that the lessons learned at Dieppe reduced very substantially the casualties on the 6th June 1944.

SERGEANT THOMAS FRANK DURRANT, R.E.
1874047, Corps of Royal Engineers (attached Commandos)

Victoria Cross

War Office – 19th June 1945.
The KING has been graciously pleased to approve the posthumous award of the VICTORIA CROSS to:—
No. 1874047 Sergeant Thomas Frank DURRANT, Corps of Royal Engineers (attached Commandos) (Green Street Green, Farnborough, Kent).

For great gallantry, skill and devotion to duty when in charge of a Lewis gun in H.M. Motor Launch 306 in the St. Nazaire raid on the 28th March, 1942. Motor Launch 306 came under heavy fire while proceeding up the river Loire towards the port. Sergeant Durrant in his position abaft the bridge, where he had no cover or protection, engaged enemy gun positions and searchlights on shore. During this engagement he was severely wounded in the arm but refused to leave his gun.

The Motor Launch subsequently went down the river and was attached by a German destroyer at 50–60 yards range, and often closer. In this action Sergeant Durrant continued to fire at the destroyer's bridge with the greatest coolness and with complete disregard of the enemy's fire. The Motor Launch was illuminated by the enemy searchlight and Sergeant Durrant drew on himself the individual attention of the enemy guns, and was again wounded, in many places. Despite these further wounds he stayed in his exposed position, still firing his gun, although after a time only able to support himself by holding on to the gun mounting. After a running fight, the Commander of the German destroyer called on the Motor Launch to surrender.

Sergeant Durrant's answer was a further burst of fire at the destroyer's bridge. Although now very weak he went on firing, using drums of ammunition as fast as they could be replaced. A renewed attack by the enemy vessel eventually silenced the fire of the Motor Launch, but Sergeant Durrant refused to give up until the destroyer came alongside, grappled the Motor Launch and took prisoner those who remained alive.

Sergeant Durrant's gallant fight was commended by the German officers on boarding the Motor Launch.

This very gallant Non-Commissioned Officer later died of the many wounds received in action. *L.G. 19.6.45*

HONORARY CAPTAIN JOHN WEIR FOOTE
Canadian Chaplain Services Royal Hamilton Light Infantry

Victoria Cross

Department of National Defence, Ottawa.
14th February, 1946

THE CANADIAN ARMY

The KING has been graciously pleased to approve the award of the VICTORIA CROSS to:—

Honorary Captain John Weir FOOTE, Canadian Chaplain Services.

At Dieppe, on 19th August, 1942, Honorary Captain Foote, Canadian Chaplain Services, was Regimental Chaplain with the Royal Hamilton Light Infantry. Upon landing on the beach under heavy fire he attached himself to the Regimental Aid Post which had been set up in a slight depression on the beach, but which was only sufficient to give cover to men lying down. During the subsequent period of approximately eight hours, while the action continued, this officer not only assisted the Regimental Medical Officer in ministering to the wounded in the Regimental Aid Post, but time and again left this shelter to inject morphine, give first-aid and carry wounded personnel from the open beach to the Regimental Aid Post. On these occasions, with utter disregard for his personal safety, Honorary Captain Foote exposed himself to an inferno of fire and saved many lives by his gallant efforts. During the action, as the tide went out, the Regimental Aid post was moved to the shelter of a stranded landing craft. Honorary Captain Foote continued tirelessly and courageously to carry wounded men from the exposed beach to the cover of the landing craft. He also removed wounded from inside the landing craft when ammunition had been set on fire by enemy shells. When landing craft appeared he carried wounded from the Regimental Aid Post to the landing craft through very heavy fire.

On several occasions this officer had the opportunity to embark but returned to the beach as his chief concern was the care and evacuation of the wounded. He refused a final opportunity to leave the shore, choosing to suffer the fate of the men he had ministered to for over three years.

Honorary Captain Foote personally saved many lives by his efforts and his example inspired all around him. Those who observed him state that the calmness of this heroic officer as he walked about, collecting the wounded on the fire-swept beach will never be forgotten. *L.G. 14.2.46*

LIEUT.-COL. CHARLES CECIL INGERSOLL MERRITT
South Saskatchewan Regiment

Victoria Cross

Department of National Defence, Ottawa.
2nd October, 1942.

THE CANADIAN ARMY

The KING has been graciously pleased to approve the award of The VICTORIA CROSS to:—

Lieutenant-Colonel Charles Cecil Ingersoll MERRITT, The South Saskatchewan Regiment.

For matchless gallantry and inspiring leadership whilst commanding his battalion during the Dieppe raid on the 19th August, 1942.

From the point of landing, his unit's advance had to be made across a bridge in Pourville which was swept by very heavy machine-gun, mortar and artillery fire: the first parties were mostly destroyed and the bridge thickly covered by their bodies. A daring lead was required; waving his helmet, Lieutenant-Colonel Merritt rushed forward shouting "Come on over! There's nothing to worry about here." He thus personally led the survivors of at least four parties in turn across the bridge. Quickly organizing these, he led them forward and when held up by enemy pill-boxes he again headed rushes which succeeded in clearing them. In one case he himself destroyed the occupants of the post by throwing grenades into it. After several of his runners became casualties, he himself kept contact with his different positions.

Although twice wounded Lieutenant-Colonel Merritt continued to direct the unit's operations with great vigour and determination and while organizing the withdrawal he stalked a sniper with a Bren gun and silenced him. He then coolly gave orders for the departure and announced his intention to hold off and "get even with" the enemy. When last seen he was collecting Bren and Tommy guns and preparing a defensive position which successfully covered the withdrawal from the beach.

Lieutenant-Colonel Merritt is now reported to be a Prisoner of War.

To this Commanding Officer's personal daring, the success of his unit's operations and the safe re-embarkation of a large portion of it were chiefly due.   *L.G. 2.10.42*

LIEUT.-COLONEL AUGUSTUS CHARLES NEWMAN
33927, The Essex Regiment (attached Commandos)
Victoria Cross

War Office – 19th June 1945.
The KING has been graciously pleased to approve the award of the of the VICTORIA CROSS to:—
Lieutenant-Colonel Augustus Charles NEWMAN (33927), The Essex Regiment (attached Commandos) (Salford, Bucks.).

On the night of 27th / 28th March, 1942, Lieutenant-Colonel Newman was in command of the military force detailed to land on enemy occupied territory and destroy the dock installations of the German controlled naval base at St. Nazaire.

This important base was known to be heavily defended and bomber support had to be abandoned owing to bad weather. The operation was therefore bound to be exceedingly hazardous, but Lieutenant-Colonel Newman, although empowered to call off the assault at any stage, was determined to carry to a successful conclusion the important task which had been assigned to him.

Coolly and calmly he stood on the bridge of the leading craft, as the small force steamed up the estuary of the River Loire, although the ships had been caught in the enemy searchlights and a murderous crossfire opened from both banks, causing heavy casualties.

Although Lieutenant-Colonel Newman need not have landed himself, he was one of the first ashore and, during the next five hours of bitter fighting, he personally entered several houses and shot up the occupants and supervised the operations in the town, utterly regardless of his own safety, and he never wavered in his resolution to carry through the operation upon which so much depended.

An enemy gun position on the roof of a U-boat pen had been causing heavy casualties to the landing craft and Lieutenant-Colonel Newman directed the fire of a mortar against this position to such effect that the gun was silenced. Still fully exposed, he then brought machine gun fire to bear on an armed trawler in the harbour, compelling it to withdraw and thus preventing many casualties in the main demolition area.

Under the brilliant leadership of this officer the troops fought magnificently and held vastly superior enemy forces at bay, until the demolition parties had successfully completed their work of destruction.

By this time, however, most of the landing craft had been sunk or set on fire and evacuation by sea was no longer possible. Although the main objective had been achieved, Lieutenant-Colonel Newman nevertheless was now determined to try and fight his way out into open country and so give all survivors a chance to escape.

The only way out of the harbour area lay across a narrow iron bridge covered by enemy machine guns and although severely shaken by a German hand grenade, which had burst at his feet, Lieutenant-Colonel Newman personally led the charge which stormed the position and under his inspiring leadership the small force fought its way through the streets to a point near the open country, when, all ammunition expended, he and his men were finally overpowered by the enemy.

The outstanding gallantry and devotion to duty of this fearless officer, his brilliant leadership and initiative, were largely responsible for the success of this perilous operation which resulted in heavy damage to the important naval base at St. Nazaire.

L.G. 15.6.45

MAJOR PATRICK ANTHONY PORTEOUS, R.A.
Captain (Temporary Major), 73033, Royal Artillery

Victoria Cross

War Office – 2nd October 1942.
The KING has been graciously pleased to approve the award of the VICTORIA CROSS to:—
Captain (temporary Major) Patrick Anthony PORTEOUS (73033), Royal Regiment of Artillery (Fleet, Hants.).

At Dieppe on the 19th August, 1942, Major Porteous was detailed to act as Liaison Officer between the two detachments whose task was to assault the heavy coast defence guns.

In the initial assault Major Porteous, working with the smaller of the two detachments, was shot at close range through the hand, the bullet passing through his palm and entering his upper arm. Undaunted, Major Porteous closed with his assailant, succeeded in disarming him and killed him with his own bayonet thereby saving the life of a British Sergeant on whom the German had turned his aim.

In the meantime the larger detachment was held up, and the officer leading this detachment was killed and the Troop Sergeant-Major fell seriously wounded. Almost immediately afterwards the only other officer of the detachment was also killed.

Major Porteous, without hesitation and in the face of a withering fire, dashed across the open ground to take over the command of this detachment. Rallying them, he led them in a charge which carried the German position at the point of the bayonet, and was severely wounded for the second time. Though shot through the thigh he continued to the final objective where he eventually collapsed from loss of blood after the last of the guns had been destroyed.

Major Porteous's most gallant conduct, his brilliant leadership and tenacious devotion to a duty which was supplementary to the role originally assigned to him, was an inspiration to the whole detachment. *L.G. 2.10.42*

Ty. Major William Cranmore Copland
50169, South Lancashire Regt, No. 2 Commando
Distinguished Service Order

On 28th March 1942, during the Commando Raid at St. Nazaire, France. Major Copland was my Second-in-Command and his first duty was, as Commander of the Military personnel on board HMS *Campbeltown*, to supervise the disembarkation and evacuation of wounded. After the *Campbeltown* had rammed the dry dock gate, the ship was on fire forward and under heavy fire from enemy shore batteries and Anti-Aircraft guns.

Under intense fire and very difficult conditions, the disembarkation was completed in very rapid time under his personal direction. Many of the Commando force were wounded, some very seriously, and Major Copland, showing total disregard for his own personal safety effected the evacuation of all wounded on to the light naval craft, by so doing expediting the whole disembarkation.

During the fighting and demolition work on shore, Major Copland was again outstanding in his efforts to overcome the enemy. When the work of destruction was complete and the escape from the port proved to be an impossibility as the Royal Navy had been forced to withdraw, Major Copland played a major part in reorganising the force and breaking out into the town.

He was conspicuous throughout the entire fighting, and his leadership was instrumental in the destruction of many of the enemy and his equipment.

Major Copland throughout this action, proved by his leadership, courage and disregard for danger to be a great example to all.

[L.G. 5.7.45]

TEMPORARY LIEUTENANT-COLONEL BRIAN FORSTER MORTON FRANKS, M.C.
89085, 2 SAS Regt, SAS Bde & 1 Bde
DISTINGUISHED SERVICE ORDER

Lt-Col B. F. M. Franks dropped by parachute behind the enemy lines in the Vosges on 31st August in order to organise SAS operations in that area.

In spite of repeated enemy attacks which forced the SAS parties to move continuously, Lt-Col Franks succeeded in organising successful operations including the reception and employment of armed jeeps.

Owing to his courage and initiative a large party of uniformed troops were able to operate in a strongly held enemy territory and inflict great damage on the enemy with little or no assistance from local partisans.

The parties successfully withdrew through the lines on 11th October, Lt-Col Franks being wounded during the process.

Throughout most of the period the SAS parties were within twenty miles of the front lines in an area constantly patrolled and searched by the enemy. Weather conditions were appalling and prevented regular resupply by air.

By his coolness and cheerfulness throughout a long-drawn out period of danger and hardship, with little food, Lt-Col Franks was an inspiration to all under his command without which the men could not have carried on. *[L.G. 4.3.45]*

ACTING LIEUT.-COLONEL THE LORD LOVAT, M.C.
Major, 44718, The Lovat Scouts (Inverness-shire).
DISTINGUISHED SERVICE ORDER

In recognition of gallant and distinguished services in the combined attack on Dieppe. *L.G. 2.10.42*

TEMPORARY MAJOR PETER YOUNG, M.C.
Captain, 77254, The Bedfordshire and Hertfordshire Regt.
DISTINGUISHED SERVICE ORDER

In recognition of gallant and distinguished services in the combined attack on Dieppe. *L.G. 2.10.42*

North-West Europe before D-Day

Captain Gordon Geoffrey Henry Webb, M.C.
126230, Royal Regiment of Artillery
Bar to Military Cross
In recognition of gallant and distinguished services in the combined attack on Dieppe.
L.G. 2.10.42

Acting Captain H. A. Bray
2nd Dorsets, No. 5 Commando
Military Cross
Captain Bray during the operation has been commanding the Carrier Platoon. On 18th May he held a line under considerable enemy fire, thus permitting the battalion to withdraw. On 28th May he displayed remarkable gallantry in the defence of Festubert when attacked by numerous enemy tanks. His coolness and good leadership under heavy fire has been inspiring to all ranks.
(L.G. 11.7.40)

Temporary Captain Michael Clive Burn
74087, The King's Royal Rifle Corps, No. 2 Commando
Military Cross
On 28th March 1942, during the Commando Raid at St. Nazaire, France.

Captain Burn was in command of an Assault Group. Following a direct hit on the motor launch carrying his Group, the ship was put out of action and most of his Assault Group were killed or wounded. Capt Burn, after being nearly drowned and pulled ashore by one of his men, quickly recovered and proceeded alone to his objective after ascertaining that these gun positions were not in action. Entirely alone he carried out the destruction of these positions, setting them on fire with incendiaries.

He continued causing enemy casualties with hand grenades until all his ammunition was expended, when he was taken prisoner.

This action of Capt Burn's showed his determination to carry out his task although his men were out of action; his courage and initiative being an example deserving the highest praise.
[L.G. 5.7.45]

2nd Lieutenant R. P. Carr, R.A.
52nd Anti Tank Regiment, RA
Military Cross
This Officer was left in command of his battery on the 28th May 1940 when his Battery Commander and Battery Captain became casualties and he showed great qualities of leadership and initiative during that day and during the subsequent withdrawal from the Ypres–Combines Canal.

2/Lieutenant Carr has throughout displayed great powers of leadership, and by his coolness under fire and contempt of danger he has set a high example to all ranks.

Lieutenant Stewart Whitemore Chant
WS/Lieut, 105159, The Gordon Highlanders, No. 5 Cdo.
Military Cross

On 28th March 1942, during the Commando Raid at St. Nazaire, France.
Lieut Chant was in charge of a demolition party whose duty it was to destroy part of the pumping station by the dry dock. Although wounded in the hands, Lieut Chant carried out his task successfully, despite being hampered by his hands being slippery with blood. He remained in the pumping station, helping to carry out the remainder of the demolitions and showing fine leadership to the others carrying out their tasks, until all were completed. Subsequently, in the street fighting he again displayed leadership of the highest order until he was wounded again, this time in the knee, causing him to be taken prisoner.

During the whole of this action, his determination to carry out his task and his dash under fire is worthy of high recognition.

[L.G. 5.7 45]

Ty. Captain John Malcolm Thorpe Churchill
Lieutenant, 2nd Manchester Regiment
Military Cross

On 27th May, this Officer when in command of his Company was continually attacked and eventually surrounded. Nevertheless he fought his two machine-guns until all the ammunition was finished when he destroyed his guns and extricated his command after dark passing through the enemy lines and eventually reported back to Brigade HQ. His action undoubtedly held up the enemy in that area for a considerable time enabling other troops to withdraw across the canal. (L.G. 20.12.40)

Captain Stanley Ambrose Day
70873, Royal Corps of Signals, No. 2 Commando
Military Cross

On 28th March 1942 during the Commando Raid at St. Nazaire, France.
Capt Day was my adjutant. Previous to the raid, his untiring work in the planning and issue of orders was of the greatest assistance.

During the whole of the action on land, his courage and total disregard to his own personal safety were magnificent. Acting as contact with the many small groups, dashing about from one party to another, inspiring confidence and holding them together, he

played a very important part in maintaining unity in the street fighting, and enabling the force to fight far into the town, causing heavy casualties on the enemy and his equipment. His cheerfulness and coolness under intense fire set a fine example to all.
[L.G. 5.7.45]

LIEUTENANT WILLIAM WHITSON ETCHES
W/S Lieut 112866, The Royal Warwickshire Regt, No. 3 Cdo.
MILITARY CROSS

On 28th March, 1942, during the Commando raid at St. Nazaire, France. Lieut Etches was assistant to Capt Montgomery, RE, in supervising the various demolition parties in the dry dock area. Lieut Etches was severely wounded in the legs during the run-in on board HMS *Campbeltown*, but in spite of this and though only just able to walk, he carried on to his objective and supervised the demolitions, only withdrawing to the Old Mole when the whole of the demolition was complete.

Subsequently, although in great pain, Lieut Etches fought with courage and determination in the street fighting in the town of St. Nazaire when the force was trying to break out from the dock area. Although weak from loss of blood and only able to drag himself along, he kept up with the others, scaling walls, breaking into houses and fighting on until finally captured when all ammunition had been expended.

His courage and devotion to duty was an example to all who saw him, and his own personal bravery encouraged other wounded men to follow his indomitable example and continue with the fighting. *[L.G. 5.7.45]*

LIEUTENANT JOHN GOLDING HERON
2nd Dorsets, No. 5 Commando
MILITARY CROSS

On 27th May when the enemy were pressing closely with infantry and the situation was becoming serious, Lieut Heron personally volunteered to take the two carriers available and deliver a counter attack. He led the attack himself under heavy fire, drove back the enemy infantry after inflicting heavy casualties on them.

Lieut Heron by his initiative and leadership completely restored the situation. *(L.G. 20.12.40)*

Acting Major Robert Dyer Houghton, R.M.
Capt RM, Holding Operational Cdo, No. 40 RM Commando
Military Cross

On the 19th August 1942 Major Houghton who was Second-in-Command 40 (RM) Commando during operation 'Jubilee' was ordered to land party from an LCA onto the main beach at Dieppe. On the run in, the LCA in which he was travelling, came under heavy enemy fire, but in spite of this proceeded towards the beach. He eventually grounded about 100 yards out. Major Houghton, with complete disregard for his personal safety, was the first to attempt to land. He found the water too deep to achieve a landing, so under heavy fire he re-embarked and gave orders for the LCA to be beached on another position of its shore. This second attempt was successful and on landing Major Houghton immediately organised his party and engaged the enemy with all weapons at his disposal. In spite of overwhelming enemy fire, he only gave up when all other troops in the vicinity had surrendered. After capture, Major Houghton behaved in a manner which exemplified the highest traditions of the Royal Marine Corps. He maintained a high standard of discipline while acting as a company commander in OKay VIIB and by his personal example, stimulated the morale of all troops with whom he came in contact. He was always ready to give every assistance to potential escapees and it was only as a result of medical advice that he did not himself partake in any attempts to escape. By his devotion to duty, personal example, courage and untiring efforts he rendered to his country and corps a service which can seldom have been surpassed.
Recommended for DSO, awarded MC. (L.G. 14.12.45)

Lieutenant George H. Lane
285687, Buffs, No. 10 (IA) Commando
Military Cross

This officer was the raid commander of military force which landed in the vicinity of Ault, on the north east coast of France, on the night 17th–18th May 1944, to make a detailed reconnaissance of beach obstacles and mines, the nature and potentialities of which were unknown.

The operation was of the highest importance and was of an extremely hazardous nature, involving a two mile approach to a heavily defended enemy coastline.

This operation was attempted on three consecutive nights, the first two attempts having failed due to unsuitable weather, although on one occasion the enemy coast was actually sighted. Despite the physical fatigue resulting from this, Lieut Lane, with superior seamanship, navigated his dory to the selected landing point without error although there were definite indications of the presence of enemy patrols in the beach area.

Having landed, Lieut Lane accompanied and gave material assistance to his sapper officer in obtaining a large part of the required intelligence. Having carried out a preliminary reconnaissance, this officer with the greatest determination set out again on a second reconnaissance with his sapper officer, having first ensured that arrangements had been made for getting the intelligence back to the parent MTB.

Shortly after leaving, these officers were surprised whilst at work by an enemy patrol moving down the beach and, it is thought, were captured.

Although, strictly speaking, it was not part of this officer's duty to go any further than the landing point, he insisted, with the greatest devotion to duty, in taking his share of the hazards of the operation, and by his tenacity of purpose assisted in obtaining vital information. *(L.G. 27.09.45)*

ACTING MAJOR DEREK MILLS-ROBERTS
Temporary Captain, Lieutenant, 69334, Irish Guards
MILITARY CROSS
In recognition of gallant and distinguished services in the combined attack on Dieppe. *L.G. 2.10.42*

TEMPORARY CAPTAIN ANTHONY FANE RUXTON
Lieutenant, 95530, The Royal Ulster Rifles
MILITARY CROSS
In recognition of gallant and distinguished services in the combined attack on Dieppe. *L.G. 2.10.42*

ACTING MAJOR LOGAN SCOTT-BOWDEN, R.E.
Lt., Ty. Capt., 95182, attached to No. 2 S.B.S., SS Bde
MILITARY CROSS
For intrepidity, skill and resource in the execution of a hazardous reconnaissance of an enemy coast in difficult conditions.
The covering letter adds:—
I am sorry that the citations lack detail, but the operation concerned was of so secret a kind that it was necessary for an Officer to give verbal evidence to my Committee.
Note: This award, and the M.M. to Sgt. B. W. Ogden-Smith was for a detailed reconnaissance of the eastern section of Omaha Beach on the night of 18/19 Jan 1944. *[L.G. 2.3.44]*

ACTING CAPTAIN JOHN JASPER SELWYN
Lieutenant, 75243, 13th/18th Royal Hussars (Queen Mary's Own), Royal Armoured Corps
MILITARY CROSS
In recognition of gallant and distinguished services in the combined attack on Dieppe. *L.G. 2.10.42*

LIEUT. KENNETH WILLIAM RIDLEY SMALE, R.M.
Royal Marines.
MILITARY CROSS
For bravery, endurance and inspiring devotion to duty whilst serving in Commando operations in the raid on Dieppe, 19th August, 1942, and later as prisoner of war in Germany, August 1942–May 1945. *L.G. 14.12.45*

TEMPORARY CAPTAIN DOFYDD CARLYLE WILLOUGHBY STYLE
Lieutenant, 71766, The Lancashire Fusiliers
MILITARY CROSS
In recognition of gallant and distinguished services in the combined attack on Dieppe. *L.G. 2.10.42*

SERGEANT FRANCIS ARTHUR CARR, R.E.
1867740, Royal Engineers, No. 5 Commando
DISTINGUISHED CONDUCT MEDAL
On 28th March 1942, during the Commando Raid at St. Nazaire, France. Sgt Carr was NCO i/c the demolition party commanded by Lieut Robert Burtenshaw.

Before reaching the demolition site, Lieut Burtenshaw was killed and immediately Sgt Carr took command and led the party, against heavy enemy opposition, to the dry dock gate.

Sgt Carr then reported to Lieut Brett who commanded another demolition party also detailed to assist in destroying this gate. Lieut Brett had been wounded in the legs and could only move with difficulty. Sgt Carr assisted Lieut Brett in supervising the two parties in their laying of the explosive charges on the dry dock gate. The charges were about to be fired when fighting broke out in the area, forcing the demolition party to take cover. Sgt Carr then went forward alone and fired the charges which completely destroyed this gate.

Sgt Carr then continued to assist Lieut Brett in organising the withdrawal of both parties to the point of re-embarkation. Sgt Carr throughout the entire action showed outstanding courage and devotion to duty. His leadership was magnificent. *[L.G. 5.7.45]*

North-West Europe before D-Day

Sergeant William Albert Challington
3515161, Cameron Highlanders, No. 2 Commando
Distinguished Conduct Medal
On 28th March, 1942, during the Commando raid at St. Nazaire, France.
Sgt Challington was in an assault group covering the dry dock area. Disembarking from the burning bows of HMS *Campbeltown* on to the dock gates, Sgt Challington immediately engaged the enemy gun-crews who were on the roof of the pumping station and whose plunging fire was intense in the immediate area. Under his devastating covering fire, the assault onto the roof of the pumping station and the consequent destruction of the crews and guns was successfully completed. Later, when his assault group formed a covering force in the area in which the demolitions were taking place, this NCO, showing total disregard for his own safety, engaged and knocked out an enemy machine gun position which was bringing heavy fire to bear on the Operational HQ. Continuing to display great courage and initiative, his group later became engaged in the street fighting in the town of St. Nazaire and during the fighting he alone engaged an enemy motor cycle combination which approached at high speed firing an automatic gun from the sidecar.

During this street fighting, this NCO's dash and initiative was outstanding and with a small party he managed to regain the open country through the town in an attempt to escape to Spain. He was captured only after organising other members of his party to set off in pairs to freedom. *[L.G. 5.7.45]*

Driver James Cunningham
T/61556, No. 3 Commando
Distinguished Conduct Medal
18th–19th August 1942, Yellow 2, Dieppe
This man was outstanding throughout the operation. He showed initiative and firmness worthy of a senior NCO and set a fine example in the boat during the trying period of the Naval action. He made a toggle and eye rope to assist his comrades to climb the cliff; he was constantly alert to find the enemy's telephone wires and cut them. He was most forward when the enemy engaged us by surprise and at close range. He was the leader of a group of privates who covered the withdrawals to the beach and to the boats. Hit once on his bandolier, once on his arm, while the LCP lay off shore he coolly continued to shoot at Germans on the cliffs and certainly accounted for some. He helped greatly to make up for the absence of NCOs in this party. *(L.G. 2.10.42)*

Commando Gallantry Awards of World War II

Lance Sergeant Arthur Harry Dockerill
940903, Royal Artillery, No. 1 Commando
Distinguished Conduct Medal

On 28th March 1942, during the Commando Raid at St. Nazaire, France.
L/Sgt Dockerill, as a member of the demolition party under Lieut Chant's command, assisted his officers and other members of the party who had been wounded to climb from the wrecked bows of the destroyer, HMS *Campbeltown*, on to the dock side.

L/Sgt Dockerill, carrying Lieut Chant's equipment, a sixty-pound rucksack, then assisted him to their objective, the pumping station of the dry dock. This was done under enemy fire.

L/Sgt Dockerill again assisted Lieut Chant in descending to the pumping chamber, forty feet below ground.

His work in this pumping station was magnificent.

He stayed with the officer while the latter fired the charges, and although the fuses were only set for a minute and a half, he waited to assist him to climb the stairs to the ground floor, a difficult feat, as the officer could only move slowly and it was completely dark. He got Lieut Chant out with a few seconds to spare before the explosive blew up.

When the force attempted to fight out of the town and docks, heavy opposition was encountered. L/Sgt Dockerill, as a forward scout, armed with only a colt automatic and grenades, assisted in leading the force through the streets in quick time.

When he ran out of ammunition and grenades he used his fighting knife and inflicted many casualties on the enemy.

L/Sgt Dockerill was outstanding in his courage and devotion to duty. Throughout the entire action he showed a total disregard for his own safety. [L.G. 5.7 45]

Troop Sergeant Major George Ernest Haines
6141513, East Surrey, No. 2 Commando
Distinguished Conduct Medal

On 28th March, 1942, during the raid on St. Nazaire, when the Officer-in-Command of the Headquarters' Reserve failed to make a landing, TSM Haines took command of this Group in his place.

When his party arrived at the Operational Headquarters the area was under intense fire from enemy gun positions sited on the roof of a U-boat shelter under 70 yards away.

With complete disregard of his own safety TSM Haines took up a position in the open, engaged and silenced these enemy guns with a 2" mortar.

Shortly after this, the Headquarters Group came under enemy machine gun fire from an armed trawler inside the inner dock.

Again from the open, TSM Haines engaged the new enemy, this time with an LMG. His fire caused the enemy craft to move further up the dock. This reduced the danger in the immediate area and gave the Headquarters freedom to operate.

After the attempt to re-embark had been abandoned, TSM Haines played a splendid part in a running engagement which lasted over half an hour, and in which the force fought its way to the inner dock and across the bridge into the town. The bridge itself was covered by enemy LMG fire but TSM Haines made a determined dash across the bridge and into the direct fire of the enemy weapons. Under his leadership his party managed to silence most of these gun positions, thus enabling the main force to proceed.

During the remainder of the action, in the town of St. Nazaire, TSM Haines set a magnificent example of courage and devotion to duty to all who served with him. *[L.G. 5.7.45]*

Sergeant Bruce Walter Ogden-Smith
6826651, The East Surrey Regiment, COPPs §
Distinguished Conduct Medal

In spite of feeling in bad physical condition, Sergeant Ogden-Smith showed courage, coolness and ability in assisting Major Scott-Bowden to carry out the first experimental beach reconnaissance from 'X Craft,' which entailed amongst other things swimming on to vigilantly defended enemy beaches and moving about there 'under the nose' of sentries on two consecutive nights, the 18th and 19th January 1944. Recommended for the award of the DCM.
(L.G. 15.6.44)

Trooper Frederick Amos Preece
404153, 101 Troop, No. 2 SBS
Distinguished Conduct Medal

On the night of 11th–12th April, 1942, Captain Montanaro, accompanied by Trooper Preece, entered Boulogne harbour in a canoe which had been taken by a Motor Launch to about 1½ miles from the harbour entrance. Successfully avoiding detection by the breakwater forts, and a number of vessels which were active in the harbour, they manoeuvred the canoe alongside an enemy tanker to which eight explosive charges were attached below water. They withdrew still undetected and commenced their return across channel without great expectation of being picked up until daylight some four hours later. Their canoe had suffered some damage during the operation and the sea conditions were deteriorating so that it was fortunate that as planned the motor launch was able to make contact and pick them up an hour after they had left Boulogne harbour by which time they were 2 to 3 miles clear of the enemy coast.

Subsequent air reconnaissance has established that the tanker was damaged and beached.

Trooper Preece contributed his share in the success of the operation by carrying out implicitly the orders of Captain Montanaro and by showing courage and endurance over a long period spent in imminent danger of discovery by the enemy. *(L.G. 16.6.42)*

Sergeant Ronald Charles Randall
2929382, Cameron Highlanders, No. 2 Commando
Distinguished Conduct Medal

On 28th March, 1942, during the Commando Raid at St. Nazaire, France, Sgt Randall was a member of an assault force commanded by Capt Roy. The second in command of this force was wounded in the leg and unable to land, and Sgt Randall, showing great initiative immediately took charge of the section and led it to its objective. On arriving at the objective both his section and the remainder of the force were seriously depleted owing to wounds and it was found impossible to carry out the written orders. Realising this, Capt Roy immediately called for a volunteer to assist him to destroy two gun positions which were on top of the pumping station some 20-feet high at the top of a two-storey building. Sgt Randall immediately volunteered. With Capt Roy, in the face of heavy plunging fire, he reached the top of the building with a scaling ladder and with amazing coolness forced the enemy gun crew to withdraw and placed the charge on the guns and brought about their total destruction.

On completion of this task, Sgt Randall went straight to the bridge where he took up a position without cover with an LMG, and, with total disregard for his own safety, gave covering fire to the remainder of the force which had to cross the bridge.

Throughout the whole action this NCO's individual bravery and total disregard of his own personal danger was an example to all and worthy of the highest traditions of the British Army. His cool courage is worthy of high recognition. *[L.G. 5.7.45]*

Troop Sergt. Major William Richard Stockdale
6910706, RA, No. 4 Commando
Distinguished Conduct Medal

Operation Jubilee, Dieppe Area 19th August 1942

Sgt Mjr Stockdale took command of the troop after all his Officers had been killed or had become casualties. Sgt Stockdale, while leading a bayonet charge, had part of his foot blown away by an enemy stick-bomb. Although in very great pain, Sgt Stockdale continued to engage the enemy. He set a splendid example, and was an inspiration to his men. *(L.G. 2.10.42)*

GUNNER JOHN HERBERT RONALD ABBOTT
927138, *No. 3 Commando*
MILITARY MEDAL

18th–19th August, 1942, Yellow 2, Dieppe.
This young soldier, never in action before, was the only bren gunner to get ashore at Y2 and fortunately proved to be a cool man with no idea of anything but to get a good target without considering his personal safety. In the early stages of the raid on Berneval Battery he helped to turn the tables on the enemy who got in a volley at close range before they were seen. Firing at 60 yards range with hardly any cover he was lucky to escape with nothing worse than a shower of tiles on his head. Doing what literally amounted to the work of three men he became utterly exhausted, and was nearly drowned during the withdrawal. He kept his head and was towed away on the lifelines behind the LCP, until he was finally rescued by Captain Selwyn and others.
(L.G. 2.10.42)

PRIVATE VICTOR ADDERTON
4974035, *No. 3 & 14 Commando*
MILITARY MEDAL

18th–19th August 1942 Yellow 2, Dieppe
Distinguished himself by his skill and fearlessness as a leading scout during the advance to Berneval Church. Although armed with nothing but a pistol he eagerly engaged in the fighting at that point. He was No. 1 on the 3" mortar and after firing all the ammunition, helped to get it out to the LCP under a heavy fire. By his intelligence and courage in assisting one of the sailors with the kedge he helped to get the craft away when it was aground. He was the foremost in assisting Captain Selwyn to rescue Gnr Abbott. *(L.G. 2.10.42)*

Private James Allender
4614105, 1 D.W.R., No. 6 Commando & SBS
Military Medal
May 21st [1940] Pont a Chin Area.
During a bombardment of the Bde area all telephone communication was broken. These men volunteered, went out and mended all lines maintaining them until the end of the action.
   (And Pte William Stead.)   (L.G. 11.7.40)

Serjeant Francois Balloche
4900 F.N. 40, No. 10 (Inter-Allied) Commando, Fighting French Troop (att No. 4 Commando).
Military Medal
Sjt Balloche was attached to No. 4 Commando during the recent operations at Dieppe. He was attached to one of my Troops and played a conspicuous part in the searching and occupation of the village of Le Haut, which lies in close proximity to the German Heavy Battery at Varengeville. He proved of great assistance to the Troop Leader, who could not speak French, and having gained the information required, he subsequently went into action and, with the rest of the troop, inflicted heavy casualties on the enemy.
   I have great pleasure in recommending Sjt Balloche for a Military Medal, or some other suitable award.

Marine George Reginald Bevan
Ch.105010, RM
Military Medal
Operation 'Jubilee' (Dieppe Area 19th August, 1942
When there was no possibility of landing, my Chasseur was ordered to close into the beach to pick up survivors, whilst doing this, the survivors were being machine gunned in the water. Marine Bevan went aft and located one machine gun on the East Cliff which he silenced, with LMG fire. He continued to fire at others until the Chasseur was hit aft and his gun was blown off its mounting. He showed great courage throughout.   (L.G. 2.10.42)

Corporal Charles Harold Blunden
6905806, No. 4 Commando
Military Medal
Operation Jubilee, Dieppe Area, 19th August 1942
Cpl Blunden was the Section Leader in Captain Webb's Troop which played a conspicuous part in the final assault on the battery. Cpl Blunden set a high standard of leadership and showed a great example in house-to-house, and hand-to-hand fighting through

the battery buildings. He was wounded, but refused to receive medical attention and continued to destroy the enemy until there were no Germans left alive.
Recommended for MID, awarded MM. *(L.G. 2.10.42)*

MARINE LESLIE CHARLES BRADSHAW
MILITARY MEDAL
Operation 'Jubilee' (Dieppe Area 19th August, 1943)
Whilst approaching the beach, we were engaged by heavy machine gun and rifle fire, the C.O. ordered the buildings on the beach from where the fire was coming to be engaged by LMG. I passed the order forward and a gun was opened up by Marine Bradshaw. I also ordered the HQ LMG into action which was manned by Marine Singleton. Both guns were kept continuously in action until such time as the targets were obscured by smoke. During this time the MLC was repeatedly hit by bursts of machine-gun fire and very accurate rifle fire from the beach, Owing to the position of this MLC these men had to stand up to engage the targets, and Singleton's gun was in action until all the ammunition at his disposal was used up. Both these men carried out their duties very courageously whilst under heavy fire and without thought to their own personal safety. *(L.G. 2.10.42)*

MARINE TERENCE EDWARD BREEN
Ch.X.105010, No. 40 RM Commando
MILITARY MEDAL
Operation 'Jubilee' (Dieppe Area 19th August, 1943)
During the approach to White Beach in LCA under a continuous and withering fire, Marine Breen took up a position with his bren gun on the port side of his craft. He continued to fire with accuracy and effect at the German positions and succeeded in neutralising the German gun position on the casino. During this time the craft was being continually hit by small arms and mortar fire but Marine Breen continued undaunted until all his ammunition had been expended. *(L.G. 2.10.42)*

COMPANY SERGEANT MAJOR SAMUEL JAMES BRODISON
6977705, R Irish Fus, H.O.C.,No. 12 & 10 Commando
MILITARY MEDAL
This SNCO was a member of a military force which landed to the east of Calais on the north coast of France, on the night 16th–17th May 1944, to carry out a reconnaissance of enemy beach obstacles.

This operation was of the highest importance and was of an extremely hazardous nature, involving as it did, a three mile approach to a heavily defended enemy coastline, by night, in an 18-foot dory.

During the run in and return passage to the parent MTB, the dory was forced to take avoiding action in order to escape detection by enemy vessels which crossed its course.

CSM Brodison, by his cheerfulness and resolution, maintained the morale of the operation, thus allowing his raid commander to concentrate on the conduct of the operation as a whole.

This SNCO has taken part in no less than fourteen operations of a similar nature in the past, and has shown throughout a high sense of duty and great loyalty to his force commander.

(L.G. 3.8.44)

Lance Sergeant Ronald Herbert Butler
5774300, The Royal Norfolk Regt, No. 1 Commando
Military Medal

On 28th March, 1942, during the Commando raid at St. Nazaire, France.
L/Sgt Butler was a member of a demolition party whose task it was to destroy the pumping station. Immediately on landing, some of this NCO's party were wounded. Despite the fact that all the time the party was under intense enemy fire, Sgt Butler disregarded his own personal safety and assisted the wounded members of the party to proceed to their objective. On arriving at the pumping station he managed, in the short time available, not only to complete his task, but also that of another wounded NCO who was unable to work.

In the ensuing street fighting L/Sgt Butler's cool bravery in overcoming by his own personal initiative many of the enemy pockets of resistance inspired many, though wounded, to continue the fight. Throughout the entire action his courage and cheerfulness were a great example to all. His untiring energy and devotion to duty were outstanding, and his own personal action in no small way assisted the eventual success of the whole operation.

[L.G. 5.7.45]

Private Sidney Charles Clarke
5989664, No. 3 Commando
and
Private Alfred James Craft
5950610, No. 3 Commando
Military Medal

Yellow 2 Dieppe—18th–19th August, 1942.
These two soldiers, batman and runner to the senior officer at Y2, reconnoitred the approach to Berneval Village and guided their

party forward from the beach without its being discovered. They set a fine example to the rest of the soldiers by pushing on through the village with great dash, showing a tactical sense, which was most useful in a party not trained to work as a team, and knowing little of infantry work. They exposed themselves most willingly in carrying messages, particularly when the party was sniping the Battery from the cornfields. They were among the last group to leave the beach, covering their officers, whom they guarded most watchfully throughout, as they came down the cliff. They previously did excellent work in the raid on Vaagsö, December 1941, where the former was wounded.
Both recommended for MID, both awarded MM.   *(L.G. 2.10.42)*

PRIVATE ALFRED JAMES CRAFT
(See under Private Sidney Charles Clarke.)

SERGEANT STEWART DEERY
6977293, R Innis Fus, No. 12 Commando
MILITARY MEDAL
On 28th March, 1942, during the commando raid at St. Nazaire, France.
Sgt Deery was in a demolition party commanded by Lieut Brett whose task was to destroy the dry dock installations. Before these were able to be carried out, Lieut Brett was wounded, and Sgt Deery took over command of the party. Under continuous heavy fire he proceeded to carry out the demolitions successfully.

When his task was completed, Sgt Deery assisted his wounded officer under heavy fire back to the point of re-embarkation.

His courage and devotion to duty were a fine example.
[L.G. 5.7.45]

TROOPER WILLIAM FINNEY
7903742, Royal Armoured Corps, No. 4 Commando
MILITARY MEDAL
Operation Jubilee, Dieppe Area 19th August 1942
Trooper Finney showed great courage and a high sense of duty by climbing a telegraph pole and, under heavy fire in broad daylight, cutting lateral communications which were of extreme importance to the enemy. He was fully exposed, but worked coolly with wire-cutters and, although the pole to which he was clinging was hit several times, Finney bore a charmed life and got down again uninjured.   *(L.G. 2.10.42)*

LANCE CORPORAL JOHN FLYNN
3192275, KOSB, Nos 3, 4, & 7 Commando
MILITARY MEDAL
Orange, Dieppe, 19th August 1942.
L/Cpl Flynn was landed on Beach Two, and was stunned by a bomb from a 4″ mortar, which killed the men around him and he himself suffered shock and injury. He recovered consciousness ten minutes afterwards, when the Commando had penetrated a considerable distance inland along the east bank of the River Saane. L/Cpl Flynn knew the plan, and realising that he was of major importance, as 'B' troop had only the one signaller with them, he pulled himself together and under heavy fire made his way forward, covering a distance of nearly two miles in broad daylight before rejoining his troop, which he found despite the fact they had crossed through a large wood and were massing for the final attack in orchards and farm buildings. L/Cpl Flynn got his set working and a situation report was sent back to HQ in time to give the information required for firing the Verey light signal for the final assault. [L.G. 2.10.42]

LANCE CORPORAL JACK LONSDALE HARRINGTON
7014698, Royal Ulster Rifles, No. 2 Commando
MILITARY MEDAL
On 28th March 1942, during the Commando Raid at St. Nazaire, France.
L/Cpl Harrington was given orders to carry a message to start off the withdrawal from the dry dock area, back to the point of re-embarkation. With all means of inter-communication broken down, it became necessary that this important order should be carried by a runner, who would have to cross a bridge which was under intense fire. The cool manner and deliberation with which L/Cpl Harrington proceeded with this message which was safely delivered, and set the withdrawal in motion, is worthy of the highest praise. He returned to Headquarters across a large open space under fire the whole time, and reported his message delivered in a manner which showed a great example to those who saw it. His devotion to duty during the whole of the operation was outstanding.
(L.G. 5.7.45)

PRIVATE R. G. HERBERT
3382401, 5 Northamptons, No. 3 Commando
MILITARY MEDAL
On the night of the 21st May two sections 'A' company were ordered to a forward position to assist 'D' company. Pte Herbert was in one of the sections. On arrival he was told that 2/Lieut

Pemberton was lying out in front of the post near the canal. He went to this officers assistance and found him to be seriously wounded; he attended to the officer and dragged him to the shelter of a nearby house. He then returned and fetched the stretcher bearers from 'A' company and assisted them to get the officer to the battalion regimental aid post. All this time the post was being heavily shelled and machine gunned. *[L.G. 22.10.40]*

PRIVATE PETER HONEY
2930015, Cameron Highlanders, No. 2 Commando
MILITARY MEDAL
On 28th March 1942, during the Commando Raid on St. Nazaire, France.
Pte Honey was in a small protection party whose duty it was to protect demolition parties at work on the destruction of the dry dock installations.

It was due to his personal initiative and bravery that the enemy machine gun post, housed on the roof of a building and sited in such a position that it was a potential danger to the demolition parties, was successfully destroyed. The demolition party were thus allowed to continue their work unhampered and to complete their task.

Throughout the whole five hours of the action, Pte Honey was always to be seen where the fighting was thickest; he was continually dashing from building to building seeking and destroying his enemy. The particular area in which this soldier had to fight was under the heaviest of fire and his individual bravery unflinching devotion to duty and aggressiveness were of the first order. He was a true example to all and his drive and initiative remain imprinted in the minds of all who saw him. 5.7.45

PRIVATE FREDERICK WILLIAM HOPKINS
5948301, No. 3 Commando
MILITARY MEDAL
18th–19th August, 1942, Yellow 2, Dieppe.
This soldier showed himself to be thoroughly alert and resourceful in his job in the intelligence section. He discovered and reported the landing at [......]. He found telephone wires leading to the battery and cut them. He particularly distinguished himself as one of the leading scouts during the advance through Berneval Village, and when the fighting started he was very much to the fore, being fortunately, an excellent rifle shot. By his work with a stripped Lewis gun when the LCP was lying close inshore and completely exposed, he helped to render the Germans' fire erratic and comparatively ineffective. *(L.G. 2.10.42)*

Commando Gallantry Awards of World War II

Corporal James Johnson
2879375, Gordon Highlanders, No. 12 Commando
Military Medal

On 28th March, 1942, during the Commando raid at St. Nazaire, France. Cpl Johnson was a member of a demolition party detailed for tasks in the dry dock installations. This NCO was travelling in the HMS *Campbeltown*, and during the run-in was wounded three times in the leg. Despite the considerable pain which he must have suffered at the time, he carried on gallantly and successfully completed his own personal demolition task. During the street fighting, and although by now suffering from considerable loss of blood, his personal efficiency and bravery were particularly outstanding, and an inspiration to all others.

His example as an NCO in leading his men was in accordance with the highest traditions of the British Army.　　*(L.G. 5.7.45)*

Sergeant Colin Jones
2931662, Cameron Highlanders, No. 2 Commando
Military Medal

On 28th March 1942, during the Commando Raid at St. Nazaire, France. Sgt Jones was a member of an assault group. Despite the fact that he was wounded during the run-in of HMS *Campbeltown*, he refused to be evacuated and after disembarking took part in the attack on enemy gun positions.

His courage and personal bravery in this action were outstanding. Though handicapped by his wounds, his effective fire with an LMG was instrumental in keeping the enemy subjugated round the point of re-embarkation.

Whilst manning the LMG he received further wounds, but without regard for himself continued to engage the enemy. When it had become apparent that re-embarkation was impossible, he continued in the street fighting until, through lack of ammunition and weak through loss of blood, he was taken prisoner.

His high example throughout the whole action was an inspiration to all who had the privilege to see him.　　*(L.G. 5.7.45)*

Corporal Leonard Sydney King
Ex 3058, RM, Special Services Group Signals RM
Military Medal

This NCO was a member of a military force which landed in the vicinity of Ault, on the north east coast of France, on the night 17th–18th May, 1944, to make a reconnaissance of beach obstacles and mines, the nature and potentialities of which were not known.

On the completion of a preliminary reconnaissance, Cpl King was ordered to remain at the landing point with a SNCO, by his officers, who went in search of further information.

Shortly afterwards, these officers were surprised, fired on, and either killed or captured by an enemy patrol moving down the beach.

It also became apparent that a second patrol was searching the beach, and when Cpl King's companion would have engaged the patrol with fire, he exercised a restraining influence and coolly suggested that they both should move forward to the line of beach obstacles and hide amongst them.

This course of action was adopted and allowed the NCOs to remain on the beach for more than one hour awaiting the possible return of the officers.

At the end of this time, Cpl King and his companion were seen and fired upon by a third enemy patrol but by taking avoiding action and wading breast high in the sea both were able to regain the dory.

By his great courage and devotion to duty, Cpl King prevented a situation from developing which might well have resulted in the death or capture of both himself and his companion. His decisive action at a crucial moment was instrumental in ensuring the safe return of vital information. *6.6.44*

PRIVATE PETER PAUL LORAINE
6028870, The Essex Regiment, No. 6 Commando
MILITARY MEDAL

In recognition of distinguished services in the field. *L.G. 12.8.41*

LANCE CORPORAL RICHARD MANN
5344652, No. 4 Commando
MILITARY MEDAL

Operation Jubilee, Dieppe Area, 19th August 1942
L/Cpl Mann was a picked sniper who crawled forward over open ground with a telescopic-sighted rifle and with his hands and face painted green. He worked his way to the edge of the enemy wire, and although fully exposed, succeeded in killing a great number of the enemy gun crews. His sniping was so accurate that it became impossible to service the gun. *(L.G. 2.10.42)*

Commando Gallantry Awards of World War II

Lance Sergeant Peyer Francis McCarthy
3775704, No. 4 Commando
Military Medal
Operation Jubilee, Dieppe Area 19th August 1942
Sjt Macarthy was in charge of the section responsible, under Major Mills Roberts, for engaging the enemy Battery with frontal small arms fire. At a great personal risk Sjt Macarthy worked the bren gunners forward, making skilful use of ground, to almost point blank range of the enemy pillbox defences. All machine-guns were silenced and it was largely due to Sjt Macarthy's intelligent handling of his section, and personal example, that such excellent results were obtained. *(L.G. 2.10.42)*

Gunner Thomas McDonough
2198211, No. 4 Commando
Military Medal
Operation Jubilee, Dieppe Area 19th August 1942
Gunner McDonough fired no less than 60 rounds with the anti-tank rifle at the flak towers (Pincer and Pieface). Each time he fired the anti-tank rifle, heavy fire was immediately brought to bear on the flash from the muzzle of the rifle. McDonough repeatedly changed his position and continued to engage the enemy, each time incurring heavy enemy fire. He scored a great number of hits and his endurance (after ten rounds of an anti-tank rifle the average man becomes giddy) was quite phenomenal.
(L.G. 2.10.42)

Corporal Douglas James Nash
5253563, Worcester Regt, Holding Operational Commando,
No. 12 RM Commando
Military Medal
The above named NCO was a member of a raiding party which landed on the north coast of France near Criel-sur-Mer on the night of 26th December 1943.

Cpl Nash was ordered to carry out a difficult and hazardous climb up a sheer cliff face in order to secure a rope at the top to assist the other members of the force to climb the cliff. In order to accomplish this Cpl Nash was forced to pull himself up by means of a barbed wire obstacle lodged in a gully against the cliff face. After having been joined at the top by L/Cpl Howells, a second member of the force, a light was seen inland which on investigation proved to be a patrol of 15 Germans advancing in extended line.

L/Cpl Howells was anxious to engage the enemy with his TSMG and had taken up position to do so when Cpl Nash, having coolly appreciated the situation with regard to the intention of the operation, gave orders for L/Cpl Howells to descend the rope, he himself descending afterwards.

In making this decision Cpl Nash acted with great coolness and prevented a situation developing which might well have jeopardised the safe withdrawal of the force.

This NCO has participated in ten similar operations and on every occasion has displayed the utmost determination in overcoming the most hazardous obstacles without regard to his own personal safety. By his outstanding example as a NCO he has repeatedly proved an inspiration to the other members of his force.

(L.G. 2.03.44)

SERGEANT BRUCE WALTER OGDEN-SMITH
6826651, East Surrey Regt att. No. 2 SBS, SS Brigade
MILITARY MEDAL

For intrepidity, skill and resource in the execution of a hazardous reconnaissance of an enemy coast in difficult conditions.

The covering letter adds:—
I am sorry that the citations lack detail, but the operation concerned was of so secret a kind that it was necessary for an Officer to give verbal evidence to my Committee.

Note: See the entry under Major L. Scott-Bowden, M.C.

[L.G. 2.3.44]

LANCE SERGEANT I. PORTMAN
1870112, Special Service Brigade, 2nd Canadian Division,
No. 4 Commando
MILITARY MEDAL

Operation Jubilee, Dieppe Area 19th August 1942

Sjt Portman was the last Sjt left in the troop when Troop Sjt Mjr Stockdale and all the Troop Officers had become casualties. He took over command, and rallied the men prior to Capt Porteous's arrival. During the subsequent bayonet charge Sjt Portman was the first British soldier in a German gun pit. Having disposed of the gun crews he proceeded with the demolition task which had been assigned to him. Sjt Portman's good leadership and efficiency made the demolition of the battery a rapid and complete success.

AFW 3121 gives J Portman, RE, L.G. gives I. Portman.

[L.G. 2.10.42]

Commando Gallantry Awards of World War II

LANCE CORPORAL WILLIAM HENRY ALLAN
REGINALD WHITE
5620176, No. 3 Commando
MILITARY MEDAL
18th–19th August, 1942, Yellow 2, Dieppe.
Throughout the early part of the raid this NCO handled his mortar detachment very well as rifleman. Towards the end of the action he was wounded by an anti-personnel mine on the beach and although suffering considerable pain, he got his 3″ mortar into action directly afterwards and fired all the ammunition into the enemy battery before retiring. He succeeded in getting his mortar to the LCP despite small arms fire from the cliffs at about 300 yards. *[L.G. 2.10.42]*

SERGEANT LIONEL CHARLES WICKSON
5950750, Beds & Herts Regt, No. 2 Commando
MILITARY MEDAL
On 28th March, 1942, during the Commando raid at St. Nazaire, Sgt Wickson was in a small party which was the first to land at the Old Mole. Under intense enemy fire this NCO displayed courage and determination of the highest order by immediately proceeding personally to eliminate an enemy blockhouse and kill the occupants.

A little later, when his party was held up by enemy fire in a built-up area, Sgt Wickson, completely disregarding his own personal safety, took up a position in the open with his bren gun, and proceeded purposely to draw all the enemy fire unto himself to make it possible for the remainder of his party to proceed. By this courageous action the advance into the built-up area was able to be continued.

At a later stage, when the officer commanding this party was cut off from the troops, Sgt Wickson immediately took command, and by his personal initiative and leadership brought them safely through the enemy pocket to rejoin the officer. In the subsequent street fighting this NCO's determination and personal gallantry was an inspiration to all, and although wounded, he continued to inflict casualties on the enemy until he had completely run out of ammunition. His great display of valour is worthy of the highest praise. *11.6.46*

CORPORAL ARTHUR FRANK WOODIWISS
5343292, Queen's Royal Regt, No. 2 Commando
MILITARY MEDAL
On 28th March 1942, during the Commando Raid at St. Nazaire.
Cpl Woodiwiss was a member of an assault party whose tasks were the destruction of enemy light coastal defence guns, covering the dry dock.

During the attack on the first gun position, this NCO showed personal bravery of the highest order. He was forever in the thick of the action and after bitter hand to hand fighting with the gun crew, in which he played the most prominent part, he personally was successful in placing the firing charges which resulted in the complete destruction of the gun.

Later in the action, and again showing tireless devotion to duty and outstanding zeal, this NCO took up an extremely exposed position with a bren gun and covered the force away from the bridgehead, personally acting as a rearguard and thus securing the rear of the force from enemy attack.

His personal bravery and tireless devotion to duty were an example to all and his conduct throughout the whole operation is worthy of high recognition. *[L.G. 5.7.45]*

LIEUTENANT-COLONEL JOSEPH CHARLES HAYDON,
O.B.E.
2nd Battalion The Irish Guards
BRONZE STAR
Lt-Col Haydon was in command of a composite Battalion during the operations at the Hook of Holland on May 13th–14th 1940. He was also in command of the 2nd Battalion Irish Guards in Boulogne from May 21st–23rd 1940.

In the unusual and difficult circumstances which arose in both the operations, he was an example in every way to those under him.

His personal bravery, coolness, quick grasp of the situation, and ability to give well thought out orders at a moment's notice were an inspiration to all those around him.

In both operations, his Battalion would have suffered very much more heavily, had it not been for his fine qualities of leadership.

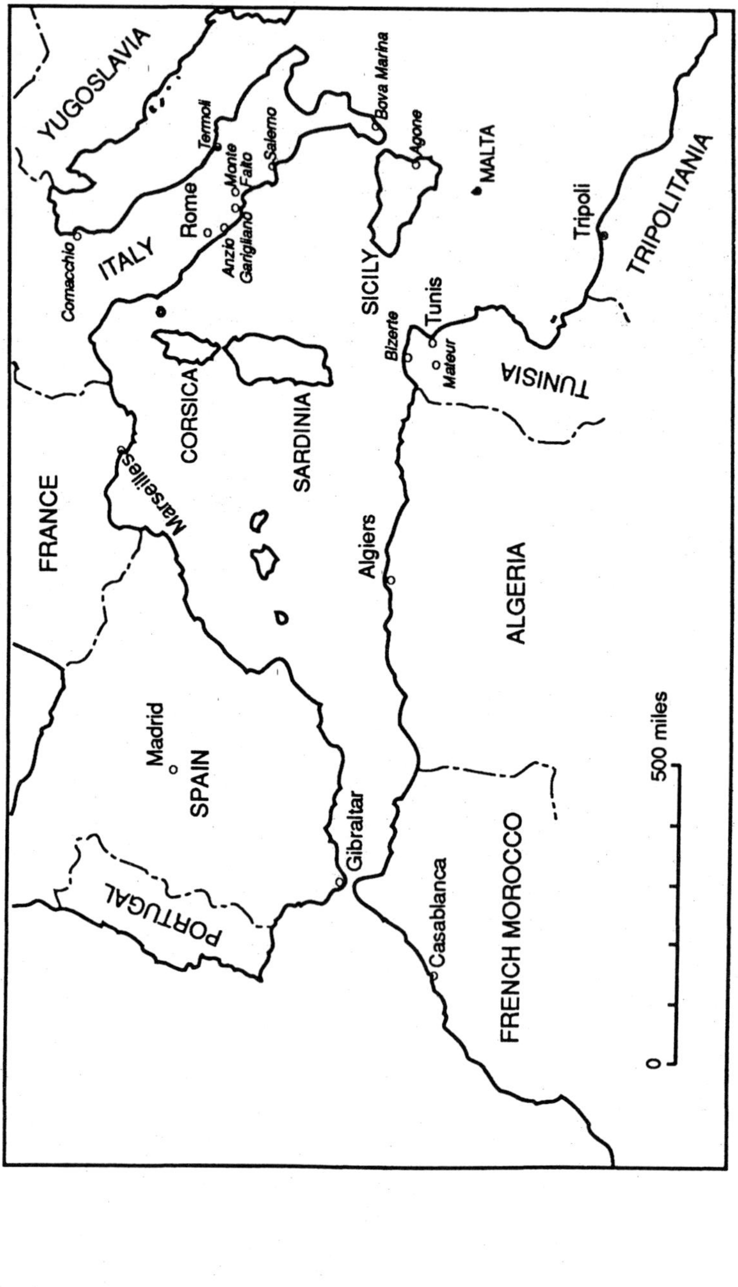
YUGOSLAVIA
Termoli
Monte Falto
Salerno
Bova Marina
Agone
MALTA
Rome
Anzio
Garigliano
Comacchio
ITALY
SICILY
Bizerte
Tunis
Mateur
TUNISIA
Tripoli
TRIPOLITANIA
CORSICA
SARDINIA
FRANCE
Marseilles
Algiers
ALGERIA
Madrid
SPAIN
Gibraltar
PORTUGAL
Casablanca
FRENCH MOROCCO
0
500 miles

North Africa and the Western Mediterranean

TOBRUK – 17/18 JULY 1941

IN the Spring of 1941, despite its earlier successes, the British Army, General Wavell commanding, was now falling back toward Egypt under the Blitzkrieg attacks of General Rommel and his Afrika Korps, supported by their Italian allies.

Tobruk, the strategically vital seaport on the Mediterranean was held by British and Commonwealth units but, unless soon relieved, it could soon succumb to the overwhelming forces confronting it.

Close to Tobruk were two hills set close together and referred to as the Twin Pimples. Taking advantage of the height, the Italians had established a command post on one and were able to observe the movements of Tobruk's defenders and to launch mortar attacks on the cavalry regiment nearest their position.

Having recently returned from Crete, No. 8 Commando were able to deploy 80 men to Tobruk who, with the 18th Indian Cavalry, the regiment under mortar fire, would attack and clear out the Italian position.

Taking with them a few Australian Army Sappers to carry out demolition work, the force, after quietly approaching the position, struck at 0100 hrs. The 18th Cavalry made a diversionary frontal attack while the Commandos, commanded by Capt M. Keely of the Devonshire Regiment, struck from behind. Caught between the two groups, machine-gunned, and with grenades exploding among them, Italian casualties were very high and the few remaining quickly surrendered. The action had been well planned and professionally executed with the result that it was all over in five minutes. One man was killed and five wounded.

In the overall scheme of things the raid appears as a very small operation, but it served a purpose in excess of its dimensions. Tobruk was under siege, morale was difficult to maintain, for defeat appeared imminent, and the success gave the defenders a needed fillip at a critical moment.

The success was a reprieve, for eleven months later, on June 1942 following 580 German and 177 Italian bomber sorties flown against it, accompanied by overwhelming armoured attacks, the exhausted but heroic garrison capitulated and 25,000 men became prisoners.

THE RAID ON ROMMEL'S HEADQUARTERS
– 17/18 NOVEMBER 1941

Heavy casualties in the Commando units operating in the Eastern Mediterranean and North Africa had reduced many of them below their designated strength. No. 11 Scottish Commando, for example, had lost 123 of its members in the Litani River action and had then returned to Cyprus leaving a small detachment at Alexandria.

Rommel's Afrika Korps had recently been reinforced and was proving a difficult adversary for General Wavell's 8th Army and, since Lt-Col Laycock and 59 of his men were now under the command of the 8th Army, the high command decided to employ them in an extremely dangerous attack on what they believed was Rommel's headquarters in a house near Sidi Raafa, 500 miles west of Alexandria and about 100 miles inland.

Lt-Col Keyes volunteered to lead the Commandos in the raid on Rommel's headquarters, while others of Laycock's force would cut telephone and telegraph lines at the Italian Headquarters in Cyrene and Appolonia.

The force embarked in HM Submarines *Torbay* and *Talisman* and, arriving off the coast on 13th November 1941 to await a signal from a British Intelligence Officer, disguised as an Arab, that would guide them ashore. On receiving the signal the group put off in rubber boats, but the wind was strong and the seas very rough. Some of the craft capsized and only half the men reached shore with Laycock and Keyes. The remainder managed to re-board the submarine *Talisman*, awaiting better conditions to try again.

With only half the force, Laycock and Keyes revised the plan. Laycock and three men would remain on the beach to await the men from HMS *Talisman*. Keyes, and Capt Campbell and 17 other ranks would comprise No. 1 Detachment and Capt Cook of No. 2 Detachment with six men would proceed with the wire cutting objectives.

The weather was vile. It was cold and rainy and the small force, guided from time to time by friendly Arabs, slogged forward, sleeping in caves when able. By the 17th, the date planned for the attack, they had reached the HQ area. Cook, with his six men, had earlier left the main party to cut the wires and the remaining men were quickly assigned to their positions around the Headquarters area. Keyes, Campbell and the indomitable Sgt Terry would approach the house. They went up the steps and pushed open the door. A sentry confronted Keyes and while grappling with Keyes he was shot by Campbell. A soldier, attempting to come down stairs was turned back by a burst from Keyes's weapon. He then opened the door to one of the rooms and, seeing soldiers in it, fired into them and quickly slammed the door shut. Reacting quickly, Sgt Terry volunteered to throw in a grenade and Keyes again opened the door. Terry tossed in the grenade but before he could again shut the door one of the Germans fired and Keyes, hit in the chest, fell, mortally wounded. Capt Campbell shut the door seconds before the grenade exploded and no other sound was heard in the room afterwards.

Campbell and Terry carried their leader outside, but by then he had died. Campbell re-entered the house, but unfortunately a Commando guarding the rear entrance mistook him for a German and fired, wounding him severely in the leg. Feeling he would impede the withdrawal to the beach, he refused to be carried and insisted on remaining, subsequently becoming a prisoner of war.

Sgt Terry took the remaining Commandos back to the beach hoping to re-embark on HMS *Torbay* with Laycock and the others but, while waiting for the weather to improve, they were attacked by a mixed force of Arabs, Germans and Italians. Some of the Commandos were killed or captured, but Col Laycock and Sgt Terry evaded capture. After a perilous journey of 41 days covering hundreds of miles, they were found by friendly Arabs and taken to the Eighth Army lines. Lieut Cook and his men successfully cut the telephone and telegraph lines but were subsequently captured and became prisoners.

Lt-Col Keyes was awarded the Victoria Cross posthumously, and Sgt Terry the Distinguished Conduct medal.

The operation was an extremely courageous enterprise, bravely carried out by the participants who paid a heavy price. Ironically however, the building attacked was not Rommel's Headquarters. Indeed it appears he had never occupied it, but may have stopped there for a few hours *en route* to another point. The intelligence that triggered the raid was unfortunately inadequate, but one must remember the difficulties of acquiring such information under the conditions then prevailing. Undoubtedly those who survived and escaped capture gained experience that stood them in good stead as the war continued.

Commando Gallantry Awards of World War II

Temporary Lieutenant-Colonel Geoffrey Charles Tuskor Keyes, M.C.
Major, 71081, The Royal Scots Greys (Dragoons), Royal Armoured Corps

Victoria Cross

The KING has been graciously pleased to approve the posthumous award of the VICTORIA CROSS to the undermentioned officer:—
Major (temporary Lieutenant-Colonel) Geoffrey Charles Tuskor KEYES, M.C. (71081) The Royal Scots Greys (Dragoons), Royal Armoured Corps (Buckingham).

Lieutenant-Colonel Keyes commanded a detachment of a force which landed some 250 miles behind the enemy lines to attack Headquarters, Base Installations and Communications.

From the outset Lieutenant-Colonel Keyes deliberately selected for himself the command of the detachment detailed to attack what was undoubtedly the most hazardous of these objectives—the residence and Headquarters of the General Officer Commanding the German forces in North Africa. This attack, even if initially successful, meant almost certain death for those who took part in it.

He led his detachment without guides, in dangerous and precipitous country and in pitch darkness, and maintained by his stolid determination and powers of leadership the morale of the detachment. He then found himself forced to modify his original plans in the light of fresh information elicited from neighbouring Arabs, and was left with only one officer and an N.C.O. with whom to break into General Rommel's residence and deal with the guards and Headquarters Staff.

At zero hour on the night of 17th–18th November 1941, having despatched the covering party to block the approaches to the house, he himself with the two others crawled forward past the guards, through the surrounding fence and so up to the house itself. Without hesitation, he boldly led his party up to the front door, beat on the door and demanded entrance.

Unfortunately, when the door was opened, it was found impossible to overcome the sentry silently, and it was necessary to shoot him. The noise of the shot naturally aroused the inmates of the house and Lieutenant-Colonel Keyes, appreciating that speed was now of the utmost importance, posted the N.C.O. at the foot of the stairs to prevent interference from the floor above.

Lieutenant-Colonel Keyes, who instinctively took the lead, emptied his revolver with great success into the first room and was followed by the other officer who threw a grenade.

Lieutenant-Colonel Keyes with great daring then entered the second room on the ground floor but was shot almost immediately on flinging open the door and fell back into the passage mortally wounded. On being carried outside by his companions he died within a few minutes.

By his fearless disregard of the great dangers which he ran and of which he was fully aware, and by his magnificent leadership and outstanding gallantry, Lieutenant-Colonel Keyes set an example of supreme self sacrifice and devotion to duty.

L.G. 19.6.42

Temporary Captain Godfrey Basil Courtney
58298, *Royal West Kent Regiment, SBS*
Member of the Order of the British Empire

October 1942—North Africa.
Captain G. B. Courtney was one of three officers of the Special Service Brigade whose duty it was to put Major-General M. W. Clark of the U.S. Army and his mission ashore from the submarine in which they travelled to North Africa for the purpose of interviewing certain French authorities prior to the Allied landing in November 1942. These three officers had also to take General Clark and his party back to the submarine after the negotiations had been completed.

General Clark has said of their services:—

'Without their whole-hearted assistance and skilful use of the fine specialised equipment furnished them, I am sure that we could not have overcome the physical obstacles encountered in getting ashore and re-embarking through a heavy surf. Any consideration that can be given these officers will be well deserved and greatly appreciated by me.'

I consider that Captain Courtney was given a most responsible and difficult duty to perform and that his skill, judgment and steady nerve contributed directly to the successful outcome of this most important preliminary to the main operation.

Recommended for OBE, awarded MBE. *4.6.43*

TEMPORARY CAPTAIN GODFREY BASIL COURTNEY
Lieutenant, 58298, The Queen's Own Royal West Kent Regt..
MEMBER OF THE ORDER OF THE BRITISH EMPIRE
and
LIEUTENANT JAMES PANTON FOOT
189391, The Dorsetshire Regiment.
MEMBER OF THE ORDER OF THE BRITISH EMPIRE
and
TEMPORARY MAJOR RICHARD PERCY LIVINGSTONE
Captain, 149081, The Royal Ulster Rifles.
MEMBER OF THE ORDER OF THE BRITISH EMPIRE

These Officers of the Special Service Brigade put Major General M. W. Clark of the United States Army and his mission ashore from the submarine in which they travelled to North Africa for the purpose of interviewing certain French authorities prior to the Allied landing in November 1942. They also took Major-General Clark and his party back to the submarine after the negotiations had been completed.

Major General Clark said of their services:—

'Without their whole-hearted assistance and skilful use of the fine specialised equipment furnished them the physical obstacles encountered in getting ashore and re-embarking through a heavy surf could not have been overcome.'

The skill, judgment and steady nerve shown by these officers in carrying out a most responsible and difficult duty contributed directly to the successful outcome of this most important preliminary to the main operation.   (L.G. 8.7.43)

LIEUTENANT JAMES PANTON FOOT
(See under Lieutenant Godfrey Basil Courtney.)

TEMPORARY MAJOR RICHARD PERCY LIVINGSTONE
(See under Lieutenant Godfrey Basil Courtney.)

TY. MAJOR PETER CLEASBY-THOMPSON, M.B.E.
15067, 1st Bn Parachute Regiment, Army Air Corps, No. 2 (Para) Commando
MILITARY CROSS (PERIODIC)

On the 17th November, this officer was ordered to take a mobile column and harass enemy lines of communication between S'Nsir–Mateur. On the 18th December Major Cleasby-Thompson by skilful use of the troops under his command was successful in destroying a strong enemy reconnaissance force of three eight-wheeled armoured cars and three reconnaissance cars. The complete enemy force was destroyed and the crews of the car either killed or taken prisoner. None of the enemy were allowed to escape and the vehicles were left unfit for further use with exception of one which was brought back to our own lines. Our casualties were one slightly wounded.

The success of the entire operation was due to the magnificent example of Major Cleasby-Thompson's determination to close with the enemy and his courage and gallantry in face of heavy enemy fire. He had also to overcome opposition by the French at S'Nsir who would give him no assistance and refused to lift the mines from the road to allow his platoon to go through.   *[L.G. 23.9.43]*

ACTING MAJOR GODFREY BASIL COURTNEY
P/58298, Queen's Own West Kents, SBS
MILITARY CROSS

During recent months Major G. B. Courtney has taken part as an officer of the Special Boat Section of the Special Service Brigade in operations concerned with the escape of General Giraud from the South of France, with the landing of agents in enemy territory and in two operations on the east coast of Sardinia designed principally to mislead the enemy.

Admiral of the Fleet Sir Andrew Cunningham, Commander in Chief, Mediterranean, has reported on Major G. B. Courtney's bravery, devotion to duty and leadership in the above operations and I have no hesitation in recommending him for the Military Cross. He has, over a long period, set a magnificent and consistent example to all under his command.   *(L.G. 11.11.43)*

LIEUTENANT DALTON HAYTON COWAP
180592, Royal Artillery (Field), No. 1 Commando
MILITARY CROSS

Throughout the period of 26th February to 4th March 1943, during which time his troop were constantly engaged with the enemy, the above Officer displayed at all times coolness, courage, determination and devotion to duty.

On 2nd March 1943, in area Hill Point 231 at about 1800 hours the enemy were advancing in large numbers trying to cut a road between our positions. Lieut Cowap led an assault with one sub-section of eight men against a force of about 150 Germans. He and his men engaged the enemy at five yards range and during the subsequent hand to hand fighting succeeded in driving the enemy back and thus preventing the road from being cut. During this action his party accounted for at least 50 Germans (of which ten at least fell to Lieut Cowap), took nine prisoners, and a quantity of equipment including four MG 34's. His leadership and courage was such that the attack was carried out with the loss to his party of only one man killed and one man missing.

This Officer's action, powers of leadership, personal courage, and devotion to duty was an example to all.

If this operation had not been successful it would have meant that the line or withdrawal of our forward troops would have been jeopardised.

Recommended for DSO, awarded MC. (L.G. 22.4.43)

Ty. Captain Douglas Malcolm Davidson
Lieutenant, 105288, The South Wales Borderers, attached to Special Service Troops
Military Cross

In recognition of gallant and distinguished services in North Africa.
Since died of wounds. L.G. 22.4.43

Lieutenant George Ian Alistair Duncan, m.c.
132481, The Black Watch (Royal Highland Regiment)
Bar to Military Cross

In support of the vital convoy due at Malta from Gibraltar in Mid-August 1942, a Commando raid was planned to destroy Junkers 88 bombers on Catania aerodrome, Sicily. Three officers and three other ranks landed on the night of August 11th–12th 1942 in poor weather conditions on a defended beach. The party penetrated to the airfield to find armed sentries on every aircraft. After reconnoitring for four hours they were detected but whilst retiring used their explosive to destroy some electric power pylons. During the withdrawal to the beach Sergeant Dunbar was wounded and taken prisoner. The remaining five were unable to find *Una* at the rendezvous and one canoe capsized; they were taken prisoner after daylight some miles out to sea.

Duncan was in command of this raid which was carried out with great determination and courage. Although the object was not achieved due to the enemy's exceptional precautions, the boldness and initiative shown are considered most deserving of recognition.

(L.G. 18.4.46)

North Africa & the Western Mediterranean

TY. CAPTAIN DOUGLAS ARTHUR ROBINSON, R.A.
Lieutenant, 179957, Royal Artillery, Special Service Troops
MILITARY CROSS
In recognition of gallant and distinguished services in North Africa.
L.G. 23.9.43

ACTING CAPTAIN GEORGE HUGH STEPHENSON
TURNBULL
Lt, 72893, The Gordon Highlanders, Special Service Troops
MILITARY CROSS
In recognition of gallant and distinguished services in North Africa.
L.G. 23.9.43

ACTING CAPTAIN HAROLD VERE HOLDEN WHITE
162512, No. 2 SBS
MILITARY CROSS
Oran Landings. Assault on port by HMS WALNEY *and HMS* HARTLAND—*8th November, 1942.*
Was in Command of the Special Boat Section Unit, which was detailed to carry out dangerous and delicate operations in conjunction with assault on the port of Oran. He was in charge of the party operating from HMS *Walney* in folbots and displayed courage and initiative of a high order in attacking with small torpedoes a French destroyer which was leaving the port, and it is believed that one hit on the vessel was obtained. *(L.G. 27.4.44)*

LANCE CORPORAL ALBERT BAKER
2614133, Grenadier Guards, No. 1 Commando
DISTINGUISHED CONDUCT MEDAL
First recommendation (for M.M.)
On 23rd February 1943 in the area of Cemetery Hill the Germans carried out an assault in force on the left flank troop of No. 1 Commando.

The attack was put in with great determination from the rear left. L/Cpl Baker was the No. 1 of a MMG supporting B Sub-Section of Morgan's Troop on the left.

When the attack opened up this NCO immediately brought fire to bear on the enemy. However, as the Germans were advancing from behind they were outside the arc of fire of the MMG. Seeing this L/Cpl Baker with complete disregard for his own safety and with the help of his No. 2 moved the gun into a position from which he could bring fire to bear on the enemy. In order to do this L/Cpl Baker had to change his position in the gun pit and by doing so left himself exposed to the enemy. As a result of the fire, however, he was instrumental in beating off the attack. The gun position was under heavy fire throughout the engagement and the attack was so determined that some enemy were found dead within 20 yds of the gun. The great courage, coolness, and devotion to duty of L/Cpl Baker was instrumental in preventing the position from being over run.

Second recommendation (for D.C.M.)
Throughout the period 26th February 1943 to 4th March 1943 during which time his troop were constantly engaged with the enemy, the above NCO has at all times shown the highest powers of leadership, courage and devotion to duty.

During the attack on Hill Point 231 on 2nd March 1943 he was acting as No. 2 on the bren gun. Altogether, with his No. 1 (Pte Williams 83) he was instrumental in destroying a large number of the enemy and enemy machine-gun positions. When his troop position was being over-run by the enemy his bren gun was responsible for covering the withdrawal of his sub-section. This he carried out to such effect that the section withdrew without loss. After the section had withdrawn successfully this NCO together with his No. 1 advanced under heavy fire and captured two enemy machine-gun positions killing their crews. During this action L/Cpl Baker sustained an injury but he carried on and with his troop succeeded in getting back to the Mine near Sedjenane.

Before the battle of Sedjenane started L/Cpl Baker was sent down to the advance dressing station. He found the battle of Sedjenane had started. He thereupon refused treatment and joined with the 6th Lincolns and was put in charge of a MMG. During the battle of Sedjenane he directed the fire of his team to such good effect that a great many casualties were inflicted on the enemy. Throughout the whole period of operations L/Cpl Baker has at all times shown the highest standard of leadership, courage and devotion to duty.   *(L.G. 22.4.43)*

LANCE CORPORAL ALUN TREVOR BLACKWELL
3655732, South Lancashire Regiment, No. 1 SS Bn & SOE.
DISTINGUISHED CONDUCT MEDAL

L/Cpl Blackwell belonged to the Malta Independent Company under the direct orders of Capt Simpson RN commanding 10th Submarine Flotilla. He was a picked man and had been specially trained in the handling of folbots and their use in night operations. In November 1941 he took part in a special operation for landing two agents and their equipment on the coast of Tunisia from an MTB, but the folbot in which Blackwell landed the party was wrecked and they were all arrested by local police and interned. When the Germans entered Tunisia in November 1942 Blackwell escaped from prison and in company with the same two agents proceeded to form a secret organisation for passing information to the Allied Forces as to German movements and intentions. Blackwell took over the Information side of the group and a total of 585 reports were passed to Allied HQ in the space of four months. The quality of the information was frequently described by the Military Intelligence Branch at AFHQ as most useful.

The group was continually harassed by German counter espionage activities and eventually in March 1943 after six prominent members had been arrested, Blackwell took over leadership and the output of information continued steadily.

Finally Blackwell was himself arrested in April 1943, despite a last desperate attempt to escape by jumping from a second story window, but unfortunately he broke his leg and was eventually deported to Germany. He has recently been repatriated suffering from tuberculosis.

A stout hearted North countryman who displayed courage and resource of a very high order. *(L.G. 2.08.45)*

BOMBARDIER JOHN BRITTLEBANK
930882, RA, No. 3 & 8 Commando & 1 SBS
DISTINGUISHED CONDUCT MEDAL

On the night of the 5th of September 1942, Bombardier Brittlebank accompanied Captain Wilson in a folbot to make an attack with experimental torpedoes on an enemy ship in Crotone harbour.

The craft was so skilfully manœuvred into position by Bombardier Brittlebank that it remained undetected in spite of the dangerously calm water within the harbour.

After the attack had been delivered, the folbot party succeeded in withdrawing from the harbour, although by this time the enemy were actively hunting for them. This enemy activity prevented HM Submarine P.42 from keeping the agreed rendezvous, and so Bombardier Brittlebank and Captain Wilson were forced to spend the night at sea in their craft which gradually became damaged by the sea as the weather deteriorated. This fact obliged them to beach the folbot in order to carry out some necessary repairs before setting a course for Malta, some 250 miles distant. In doing so, both Captain Wilson and Bombardier Brittlebank were detected and captured. Captain Wilson reports that throughout the operation Bombardier Brittlebank's conduct and reactions to the varying circumstances left nothing to be desired, and that during the interrogations subsequent to his capture, he set a fine example of reticence. When told that he was to be shot at dawn, his only request was that he might be granted permission to write to his next-of-kin.

This non-commissioned officer previously had taken an active part in the raid on Field Marshal Rommel's Headquarters and had succeeded in finding his way back to his unit after being 40 days in the desert behind the enemy lines. His selection for this further difficult and dangerous task in Crotone harbour appears to have been thoroughly justified. I consider that his determination and devotion to duty on this occasion were well worth the award for which I now recommend him. *6.11.45*

Sergeant Derek John De Nobriga
6896540, Queen's Westminsters, K.R.R.C.,No. 2 Commando
Distinguished Conduct Medal
(Immediate)

De Nobriga was embarked in HM Submarine *Triumph* for a Commando raid against the main Messina–Palermo railway. *Triumph* first attacked the Italian battle-fleet north of Messina, torpedoing the cruiser *Bolzano*; this was immediately followed by heavy and accurate depth charge counter attack. The submarine withdrew to carry out the Commando raid but, on approaching the shore, encountered a fishing vessel in mist and sank it, having again to withdraw since the gunfire had compromised the position. The next evening, 29th August 1941, *Triumph* approached and launched the raiding party in canoes. At 0320 hrs 30th August, one and a half spans of the bridge were successfully demolished, but the Commando party could not be re-embarked and were taken prisoner.

De Nobriga showed great courage, determination and resource throughout this eventful and disturbing submarine passage and throughout the successful raid.

He was second-in-command of the raid. *(L.G. 11 4.46)*

Squadron Sergeant Major Cyril Feebery
2615284, 1st SAS Regiment, No. 8 Cdo 1 SBS & SAS
Distinguished Conduct Medal

I have known SSM Feebery since 1941 when he was a Corporal in 'B' Battalion, Layforce.

In September 1941 he and I joined the Special Boat Section in the Middle East, and two months later we took part together in the raid led by the late Lt-Col Keyes VC. (November 18th, 1941). Our task was to guide the forces ashore and later to try to get them off again. Both these operations were rendered extremely hazardous by the very heavy seas running. Both times Cpl Feebery showed exceptional courage and coolness, and spent a long time in the water retrieving boats etc. which got washed off the submarine, and saving the men who also went overboard. He and I went ashore to try to get the party off, and were capsized in the surf twice. Our boat was damaged, and I lost my paddle altogether.

Cpl Feebery, when I decided to try to return to the ship, paddled us both back through the heavy surf. I have no hesitation in saying that his strength, presence of mind and courage on this occasion, saved us from a nasty situation.

In the next few months Special Boat Section personnel were sent out on submarine patrols from Alexandria to be put ashore at the Commander's discretion, if opportunity arose. Feebery made eight trips on submarines which included the patrol of HMS *Torbay* for which Lt-Cdr Miers, DSO, RN, was awarded the VC. All the submarines crew received decorations on this occasion. Reports of Submarine Commanders on Feebery's conduct and bearing on these patrols were all excellent.

Early in June 1942 Feebery (then Sergeant) was one of a small party under Major Kealy who landed on Crete. Though no positive results were obtained, Major Kealy's report—which I read—and his story which he told me personally, reflected the greatest credit on Sgt Feebery. Once again his courage and coolness in a difficult situation was excellent. In August 1942 Sgt Feebery took part in the raid on Benghazi led by Lt-Col David Stirling, and again received excellent reports. When the Special Boat Section was reformed in January 1943 under Major The Earl Jellicoe DSO, MC, Feebery was made Sergeant Major of the unit, and I have no hesitation in saying that his enthusiasm and drive played a large share in the success of the unit. *[L.G. 7.7.44]*

SERGEANT J. TERRY
880535, RA, No. 11 Commando & SAS
DISTINGUISHED CONDUCT MEDAL

At Sidi Rafa

After capsizing in his boat during the landing from the submarine and after an exacting march over 18 miles of mountainous country in drenching rain Sgt Terry, in company with two officers, forced an entrance to the German HQ at Sidi Rafa. He covered the two officers while they investigated the ground floor and prevented enemy interference by firing his tommy gun at guards who attempted to descend from the first floor. He afterwards entered a room and; though fired at from the dark interior, he emptied two magazines into it. When the commander of his detachment was killed he conducted his party successfully back to the beach.

On retirement from the beach, after ordering his party to disperse and take to the hills in compliance with instructions, Sgt Terry remained behind under heavy fire and waited for his Commanding Officer, who had hurt his knee. He remained in his company behind the enemy lines for 41 days until they were able to rejoin our own advancing troops. *(L.G. 24.2.42)*

Sergeant James Allender, M.M.
4614105, 1 D.W.R., No. 6 Commando
Bar to Military Medal

February 26th 1943 Fedi et Attia (516128 Sheet 34)
During the action between VI Commando and a Battalion of Herman Goering Jaeger Regiment, Sgt Allander showed exemplary courage and devotion to duty throughout while the section was moving up a hill under heavy machine-gun and mortar fire and without cover. Sgt Allander fired his bren gun resting it on another mans shoulders to get the necessary elevation. During this period he was well exposed and enemy LMG fire was directed at him. He was wounded but carried on. The troop later advanced over the same ground and it was found that a complete German machine-gun team had been killed by Sgt Allander's fire and the gun was captured. *[L.G. 23.9.43]*

Guardsman W. P. Duffy, M.M.
The Grenadier Guards, 1 SBS, SAS & No. 8 Commando
Bar to Military Medal

In support of the vital convoy due at Malta from Gibraltar in mid-August 1942, a Commando raid was planned to destroy Junkers 88 bombers on Catania aerodrome, Sicily. Three officers and three other ranks landed on the night of August 11th–12th, 1942 in poor weather conditions on a defended beach. The party penetrated to the airfield to find armed sentries on every aircraft. After reconnoitring for four hours they were detected but whilst retiring used their explosive to destroy some electric power pylons. During the withdrawal to the beach Sergeant Dunbar was wounded and taken prisoner. The remaining five were unable to find *Una* at the rendezvous and one canoe capsized; they were taken prisoner after daylight some five miles out to sea.

Duffy showed courage and resource of a very high order. The raid was carried out with great determination and although the object was not achieved due to the enemy's exceptional precautions, the boldness and initiative shown are considered most deserving of recognition.

Recommended for MID, awarded Bar to MM *(L.G. 18.4.46)*

Lance Corporal Albert Mailly Andrews
6916421, London Rifle Brigade, No. 3 Commando
Military Medal

Andrews was embarked in HM Submarine *Triumph* for a Commando raid against the main Messina–Palermo railway. *Triumph* first attacked the Italian battle-fleet north of Messina, torpedoing the cruiser *Bolzano*; this was immediately followed by heavy and accurate depth charge counter attack. The submarine withdrew to carry out the Commando raid but, on approaching the shore, encountered a fishing vessel in the mist and sank it, having again to withdraw since the gunfire had compromised the position. The next evening, 29th August 1941, *Triumph* approached and launched the raiding party in canoes. At 0320 hrs 30th August one and a half spans of the bridge were successfully demolished, but the Commando party could not be re-embarked and were taken prisoner.

Andrews showed great courage, determination and resource throughout this eventful and disturbing submarine passage and throughout the successful raid. (L.G. 11.4.46)

Corporal James Simpson Beattie
14241854, Royal Scots, No. 1 Commando
Military Medal

On 4th March 1943 at the battle of the Mine near Sedjenane the above mentioned NCO was instrumental in saving the lives of a great number of his comrades.

At about 1500 hrs he observed a German patrol equipped with MG 34 moving to a position from where they could bring fire to bear on his troop. His troop were unaware of the danger. Seeing this Cpl Beattie took up a fire position with his rifle and accounted for six of the Germans including the machine gun team. During the whole time Cpl Beattie was under heavy mortar fire. By this action Cpl Beattie undoubtedly saved the lives of a great number of his comrades.

During the remainder of the battle this NCO constantly showed great powers of leadership, and throughout his determination and devotion to duty was an example to all who saw him.

(L.G. 22.3.43)

Lance Sergeant Robert Hall Brown
2879761 Lance Corporal, The London Scottish, No. 2 Cdo.
Military Medal

Brown was embarked in HM Submarine *Triumph* for a Commando raid against the main Messina–Palermo railway. *Triumph* first attacked the Italian battle-fleet north of Messina, torpedoing the cruiser *Bolzano*; this was immediately followed by heavy and accurate depth charge counter attack. The submarine withdrew to carry out the Commando raid but, on approaching the shore, encountered a fishing vessel in the mist and sank it, having again to withdraw since the gunfire had compromised the position. The next evening, 29th August, 1941, *Triumph* approached and launched the raiding party in canoes. At 0320 hrs 30th August one and a half spans of the bridge were successfully demolished, but the Commando party could not be re-embarked and were taken prisoner.

Brown showed great courage, determination and resource throughout this eventful and disturbing submarine passage and throughout the successful raid. *(L.G. 11.4.46)*

Corporal Howard Herbert Cosens Butler
South Lancashire Regt, No. 1 SBS & 11 & 9 Commando
Military Medal

In support of the vital convoy due at Malta from Gibraltar in mid-August 1942, a Commando raid was planned to destroy Junkers 88 bombers on Catania aerodrome, Sicily. Three officers and three other ranks landed on the night of August 11th–12th, 1942 in poor weather conditions on a defended beach. The party penetrated to the airfield to find armed sentries on every aircraft. After reconnoitring for four hours they were detected but whilst retiring used their explosive to destroy some electric power pylons. During the withdrawal to the beach Sergeant Dunbar was wounded and taken prisoner. The remaining five were unable to find *Una* at the rendezvous and one canoe capsized; they were taken prisoner after daylight some five miles out to sea.

Butler showed courage and resource of a very high order. The raid was carried out with great determination and although the object was not achieved due to the enemy's exceptional precautions, the boldness and initiative shown are considered most deserving of recognition.

Recommended for MID, awarded Immediate MM. *(L.G. 18.4.46)*

Temporary Sergeant Charles Cooper
4122824 L/Sgt, 2nd Bn The 22nd Cheshire Regiment, No. 40 RM Commando
Military Medal (Immediate)

On 22nd July 1942, L/Sgt Cooper was commanding his MMG section on Taqa plateau during operations.

At about 1700 hours the Germans made an attack on the East Yorkshire front. They attacked with armoured cars containing infantry and troop carriers containing infantry. The attack was supported by artillery and 4" mortar fire.

L/Sgt Cooper's section came under terrific mortar fire, and he himself was wounded in the head. In spite of this he carried on supervising the firing of his guns and definitely assisted in repelling the attack.

The machine-gun platoon of which L/Sgt Cooper's section was a part was very largely the cause of the failure of the German attack, and the courage and devotion to duty of this NCO was an outstanding example to the men under his command.

(L.G. 5.11.42)

LANCE SERGEANT THOMAS DAVIS
4688032, K.O.Y.L.I., No. 6 Commando
MILITARY MEDAL

26th February 1943—Fedi Et Attia (516128 Sheet 34).
In an engagement between VI Commando and three companies of the Hermann Goering Jaeger Regiment, L/Sgt Davis showed entire disregard of enemy fire and led his men in every advance with great courage and skill. When wounded in the stomach he continued to engage the enemy until completely incapacitated by his wound. *[L.G. 23.9.43]*

SERGEANT W. DUNBAR
The Argyll & Sutherland Highlanders, No. 11 Cdo & 1 SBS
MILITARY MEDAL

In support of the vital convoy due at Malta from Gibraltar in Mid-August 1942, a Commando raid was planned to destroy Junkers 88 bombers on Catania aerodrome, Sicily. Three officers and three other ranks landed on the night of August 11th–12th 1942 in poor weather conditions on a defended beach. The party penetrated to the airfield to find armed sentries on every aircraft. After reconnoitring for four hours they were detected but whilst retiring used their explosive to destroy some electric power pylons. During withdrawal to the beach Sergeant Dunbar was wounded and taken prisoner. The remaining five were unable to find *Una* at the rendezvous and one canoe capsized; they were taken prisoner after daylight some five miles out to sea.

Dunbar showed courage and resource of a very high order. The raid was carried out with great determination and although the object was not achieved due to the enemy's exceptional

precautions, the boldness and initiative shown are considered most deserving of recognition.
Recommended for MID, awarded MM.

CORPORAL DEREK CHARLES ELLIS
4032370, No. 2 SBS & No. 6 Commando
MILITARY MEDAL

Oran Landings. Assault on port by HMS WALNEY *and HMS* HARTLAND—*8th November 1942.*
Was Captain Holden-White's partner in the folbot, he displayed coolness and courage in directing his Officer on to the target and later, when by himself, he salvaged and re-floated the damaged folbot, almost under the eyes of a French sentry. *(L.G. 27.4.44)*

LANCE SERGEANT ERIC KHYTOVITCH, R.E.
1876034, Royal Engineers, No. 6 Commando
MILITARY MEDAL

26th February 1943 Fedi et Attia (516128 Sheet 34)
After five hours fierce fighting in an engagement between VI Commando and three companies of the Herman Goring Jaeger Regiment this NCO was ordered with his subsection to cover the withdrawal of two troops. Both troops passed through his position without casualty owing to the effective and well-controlled fire of his subsection. Although under heavy fire and running short of ammunition this NCO conducted such a skilful and offensive rearguard action with his subsection that he successfully neutralised the enemy attack in that locality. *[L.G. 4.5.43]*

LANCE SERGEANT ERNEST THOMAS LILLEY
WS/Cpl, 2660913, 3 Bn Coldstream Guards, No. 3 Cdo.
MILITARY MEDAL (IMMEDIATE)

This NCO was cut off and captured by the enemy when returning from a raid on Berka Aerodrome, in May 1942. Although completely unarmed he subsequently managed to surprise and strangle his guard and to return by himself to the rendezvous.

He has distinguished himself by great coolness and courage in other raids.

It is requested that details of these operations should not be published owing to their secrecy. *[L.G. 26.11.42]*

North Africa & the Western Mediterranean

LANCE CORPORAL FRANK C. MORGAN
6468099, Royal Fusiliers, No. 2 Commando
MILITARY MEDAL

Morgan was embarked in HM Submarine *Triumph* for a Commando raid against the main Messina–Palermo railway. *Triumph* first attacked the Italian battle-fleet north of Messina, torpedoing the cruiser *Bolzano*; this was immediately followed by heavy and accurate depth charge counter attack. The submarine withdrew to carry out the Commando raid but, on approaching the shore, encountered a fishing vessel in the mist and sank it, having again to withdraw since the gunfire had compromised the position. The next evening, 29th August 1941, *Triumph* approached and launched the raiding party in canoes. At 0320 hrs 30th August one and a half spans of the bridge were successfully demolished, but the Commando party could not be re-embarked and were taken prisoner.

Morgan showed great courage, determination and resource throughout this eventful and disturbing submarine passage and throughout the successful raid. *[L.G. 11.4.46]*

LANCE CORPORAL LUKE J. MORRIS
7014390, The London Irish, No. 2 Commando
MILITARY MEDAL

Morris was embarked in HM Submarine *Triumph* for a Commando raid against the main Messina–Palermo railway. *Triumph* first attacked the Italian battle-fleet north of Messina, torpedoing the cruiser *Bolzano*; this was immediately followed by heavy and accurate depth charge counter attack. The submarine withdrew to carry out the Commando raid but, on approaching the shore, encountered a fishing vessel in the mist and sank it, having again to withdraw since the gunfire had compromised the position. The next evening, 29th August 1941, *Triumph* approached and launched the raiding party in canoes. At 0320 hrs 30th August one and a half spans of the bridge were successfully demolished, but the Commando party could not be re-embarked and were take prisoner.

Morris showed great courage, determination and resource throughout this eventful and disturbing submarine passage and throughout the successful raid. *[L.G. 11.4.46]*

Commando Gallantry Awards of World War II

Corporal Mathew Frank Morris
1905889, No. 1 RE Commando
Military Medal

On March 17th 1943 Cpl Morris with a small party were detailed to assist in clearing out an isolated post in a wood in the area of Tamera Mine. At approximately 1730 hrs the area was attacked and the enemy driven out by Cpl Morris and the seven men with him. After the attack one of Cpl Morris's men, Pte Austin, was wounded by a burst of automatic fire that came in from a flank. Austin could not move and so, Cpl Morris went back into the open and succeeded in bringing in the wounded man and carried him until he was able to hand him over to a stretcher party. Cpl Morris did not hesitate to go for Austin in spite of the fact that he realised he was under observation and within very close range of an enemy automatic weapon. This action of Cpl Morris was consistent with the energetic leadership and good example Morris has set while in command of a sub-section.

His courage and devotion to duty was such that, apart from saving the life of one of his section, he was also an example and inspiration to all who saw him. *[L.G. 18.5.43]*

War Substantive Sergeant Gordon Pollard
1480560, 169 Lt AA Bty RA 57 Lt AA Regt RA, No. 3 Cdo.
Military Medal (Periodic)

As a Light Anti-Aircraft detachment commander, W/Sgt Pollard has continually displayed a high standard of courage, devotion to duty and resourcefulness. His conduct has been an example to all his men, and has sustained them in conditions of extreme emergency. One outstanding example of the many occasions on which he has proved his worth was on 27th May [1942], when his troop was protecting the B Echelon of 3 Ind Motor Brigade. When attacked by tanks, Sgt Pollard's gun received a direct hit from a tank shell. So severe was the damage that the Battery Captain ordered the breech to be removed, and the gun abandoned. Under heavy tank and small arms fire, Sgt Pollard personally continued to remove valuable parts of the mechanism. When finally compelled to leave the position he withdrew, but awaiting his chance, returned and recovered the gun, with a fine display of ingenuity and courage. The officer strength of his Bty was soon seriously depleted, and he was given command of a newly formed troop which he commanded with distinction during the next six weeks of fighting. On his own initiative he found and succeeded in salvaging a Bofors gun. Sgt Pollard has shown himself to be possessed of a degree of courage, resourcefulness and devotion, which has been an inspiration to all those serving with him and, under his leadership, his troop steadfastly provided a high standard of protection to the formation they were defending.

[L.G. 18.2.43]

SERGEANT WALTER RAE
2754334, South Staffs, No. 6 Commando
MILITARY MEDAL

26th February 1943 Fedi et Attia (516128 Sheet 34)

Sgt Rae was a member of a troop 46 strong which was ordered to attack and hold a hill held by a company of the Hermann Goering Jaeger Regiment. The fact that this difficult task was so successfully carried out and such heavy losses inflicted on the enemy was largely due to the discipline and inspiration instilled into the men by Sgt Rae's fine leadership and complete personal disregard for danger.

During the whole of the action which lasted six hours he constantly urged his men to greater efforts by his own fine example and never-failing aggressiveness. *[L.G. 4.5.43]*

CORPORAL JOHN SCANTLEBURY
6096409, Middlesex Regt, No. 1 Commando
MILITARY MEDAL

On 23rd February 1943 in the area of Cemetery Hill (—) the Germans carried out an assault in force on the left flank troop of No. 1 Commando. The attack was put in with great determination from the rear left.

Cpl Scantlebury was the No. 2 of a MMG supporting 'B' Sub-Section of Morgan's Troop on the left.

When the attack opened up this NCO immediately brought fire to bear on the enemy. However, as the Germans were advancing from behind they were outside the arc of fire of the MMG. Seeing this, Cpl Scantlebury with complete disregard for his own safety took the belt box and sat on the parapet of the gun pit from which position he fed the gun. This action enabled the gun to be brought to bear on the enemy and the resulting fire was instrumental in beating off the attack. The gun position was under heavy fire throughout the engagement and the attack was so determined that some enemy were found dead within 20 yds of the gun.

The great courage, coolness, and devotion to duty of Cpl Scantlebury was instrumental in preventing the position from being over-run. *(L.G. 22.4.43)*

SERGEANT JAMES BARLOW BROOKS SHERWOOD
[...]6321, RASC, No. 8 Commando & 1 SBS
MILITARY MEDAL

For conspicuous good service and devotion to duty on special operations. Sergeant Sherwood has carried out many patrols in which his work has been of a consistently high order. Also, when detached to work with the Eighty Army on the Cyrenaican coast, Sergeant Sherwood particularly distinguished himself when an attempt was made to capture a party of enemy on an island. Two folbots were used in this attempt, one being manned by Sergeant Sherwood and Captain Grant-Watson, Scots Guards. This boat capsized, and Captain Grant-Watson and Sergeant Sherwood attempted to swim to the mainland. The former, however, collapsed. A search for them was made by the first folbot, and Sergeant Sherwood was eventually found in the surf still supporting Capt Grant-Watson, though in great distress and difficulty himself. After artificial respiration had been applied Sgt Sherwood recovered, but Capt Grant-Wilson unfortunately died. It is clear that Sgt Sherwood made a most gallant and selfless attempt to save him. *[L.G. 5.11.42]*

LANCE SERGEANT JOHN CHARLES HUGHES SOUTHWORTH
4079448, South Wales Borderers, No. 1 Commando
MILITARY MEDAL (PERIODIC)

On the afternoon of 27th February 1943 Davidson's Troop, No. 1 Commando put in an attack on the steep side of a hill north of the Sedjenane valley.

L/Sgt Southworth was i/c Sub-Section of this troop.

The troop attacked under very heavy machine-gun fire and several times were pinned down. Finally the position was taken by assault and L/Sgt Southworth led his section in the forefront of the assault. During this action he was severely wounded in the leg and although in great pain he still led his section forward and urged them on. The assault was successful.

The great powers of leadership, courage and devotion to duty displayed by this NCO was largely responsible for the success of the assault. *[L.G. 23.9 43]*

FUSILIER JAMES C. STEWART
6970882, Royal Welch Fus, No. 1 Commando
MILITARY MEDAL
Operation 'Bizerte' 1st to 5th December 1942.
Fus Stewart was with Lieut Scaramanga throughout the operation and stayed with him to ambush some AFV's which had been engaging his troop. He stayed in an exposed position and let the AFV's come within 50 yards of him before he opened fire with an anti-tank rifle, and obtained at least three direct hits on them. Afterwards when cut off with Lieut Scaramanga and two other men from the remainder of his troop, he showed great cheerfulness and stamina in the subsequent march across most difficult country to rejoin our forces. Throughout the operation he showed the greatest keenness and determination in engaging the enemy.
[L.G. 18.3.43]

SERGEANT NORMAN THOMPSON, R.E.
1896266, Royal Engineers, No. 6 Commando & 2 SBS
MILITARY MEDAL
During recent months No. 1896266 Sgt Thompson, Royal Engineers has taken part, as an NCO in the Special Boat Section of the Special Service Brigade, in operations concerned with the marking of beaches for operation 'Torch,' the landing of agents in enemy territory and in two operations on the east coast of Sardinia designed principally to mislead and deceive the enemy.

He has proved himself utterly reliable in action and he has been reported upon by Admiral of the Fleet Sir Andrew Cunningham, Commander-in-Chief, Mediterranean, as having displayed initiative, devotion to duty and bravery in the operations mentioned above and as having set a fine example to other ranks of the Special Boat Section.

I most strongly recommend that Sergeant Thompson be awarded the Military Medal in recognition of his services and of the extremely high standard he has set over a long period of operational activity. *(L.G. 11.11.43)*

LANCE CORPORAL JAMES WARNOCK
3130993, Army Air Corps
MILITARY MEDAL
In recognition of gallant and distinguished services in the field.
L.G. 5.10.44

Commando Gallantry Awards of World War II

Private John Arthur Williams
4032283, KSLI, No. 1 Commando
Military Medal

(1) Recommendation for M.M.
This soldier is a No. 1 on the bren gun. During the battle on Hill Point 231 on 2nd March 1943 the enemy attacked his troop in large numbers. Displaying great coolness and courage Pte Williams succeeded in silencing two of the enemy's machine gun positions. When the order to withdraw was given Pte Williams stayed behind his bren gun to cover the withdrawal of his sub-section. Having successfully covered this withdrawal he then advanced under heavy fire to silence two more machine gun positions which were harassing our withdrawing troops.

(2) Recommendation for D.C.M.
On 4th March 1943 during the battle of the Mine near Sedjenane his troop was over-run by superior numbers of the enemy and once again Pte Williams covered the withdrawal of his troop. After the troop had withdrawn he remained in position until all his ammunition was exhausted, when he withdrew taking with him his bren gun and magazines.

At all times this man's courage and devotion to duty has been an example to all.
Awarded MM. [L.G. 22.4.1943]

Sergeant Harold Wilmott
4345247, Army Air Corps
Military Medal

In recognition of gallant and distinguished services in the field.
L.G. 5.10.44

The Eastern Mediterranean and the Balkans

Temporary Lieutenant-Colonel John Malcolm
Thorpe Fleming Churchill, D.S.O., M.C.
34657, The Manchester Regt, Att. No. 2 Cdo, No. 2 Cdo.
Bar to Distinguished Service Order
(Immediate)

Island of Solta, Dalmatian Islands, 19th March 1944.
On 19th March 1944 Lt-Col Churchill, who commands No. 2 Commando, led a combined force of Commandos and US Operation Groups in an attack on the German Garrison of Solta Island.

The sea approach was made in darkness and disembarkation was completed by 0200 hrs. Lt-Col Churchill led his heavily laden HQ to its rendezvous overlooking the town of Grohote where the enemy garrison was known to be located. The advance was difficult and slow, over rocky ground intersected by walls and piles of stones, and the guides called many halts because of suspected enemy machine gun posts on the route. Whenever necessary, Lt-Col Churchill went forward alone to investigate and when necessary to pick an alternative route.

Enemy fire was opened at 0530 hrs, by which time the Commandos had surrounded the town. An air bombing attack had been arranged at 0630 hrs and the Commando assault on the town was to follow this bombing. In the hour's interval that intervened, Lt-Col Churchill set up a loud hailer at his HQ and harangued the Germans through an interpreter. The enemy at once directed mortar and machine-gun fire at the instrument, and one shell exploded in the branches of a tree directly above the loud hailer, beside which the Colonel was lying, while machine-gun bursts straddled the locality and one bullet actually hit the instrument.

Col Churchill ordered most of the HQ personnel to move, but with complete disregard of the enemy fire, remained himself beside the instrument and continued to direct the broadcasts, and to control his sub-units by wireless. This persistent broadcasting

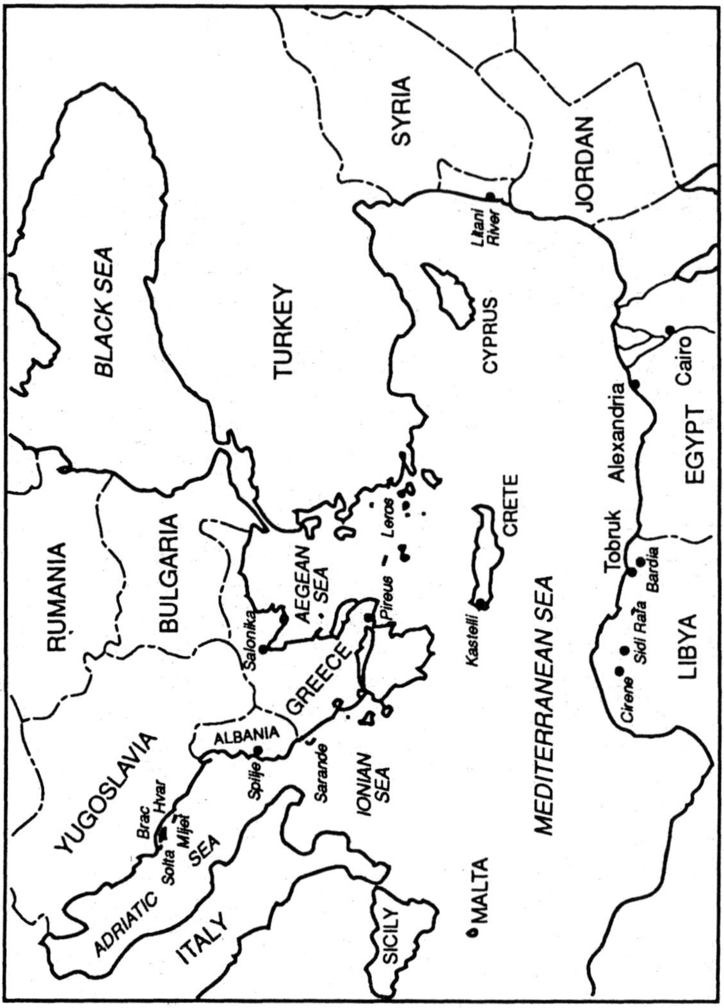
SYRIA
JORDAN
BLACK SEA
TURKEY
Litani River
CYPRUS
Cairo
Alexandria
EGYPT
CRETE
Leros
Tobruk
Bardia
RUMANIA
BULGARIA
AEGEAN SEA
Pireus
Kastelli
Sidi Rafa
Cirene
LIBYA
Salonika
GREECE
ALBANIA
YUGOSLAVIA
Spilje
Sarande
IONIAN SEA
MEDITERRANEAN SEA
Brac
Hvar
Mljet
Solta
SEA
ADRIATIC
ITALY
SICILY
MALTA

The Eastern Mediterranean and the Balkans

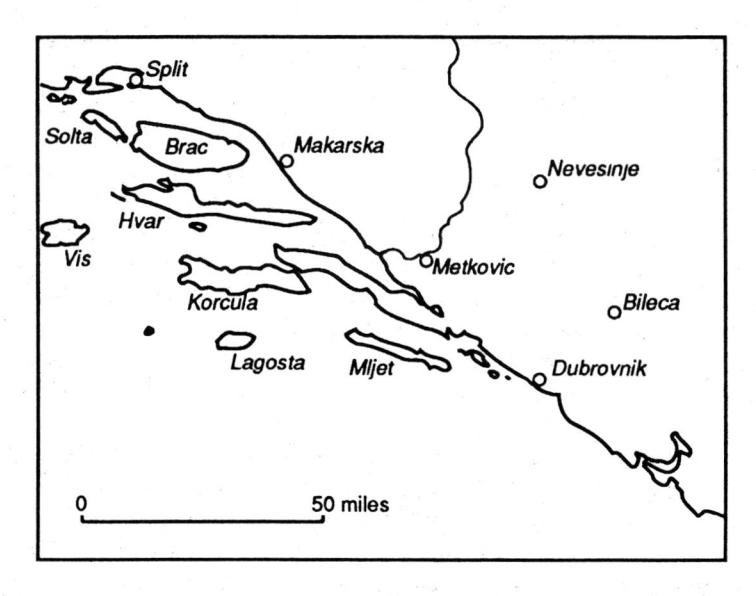

intimidated the enemy, small parties of whom gave themselves up to the nearest British troops on their flanks.

At 0630 hrs the bombing attack by aircraft was carried out, and immediately it was completed the Colonel gave the order to fix bayonets and enter the town. He himself led the advance and directed the house to house searches and street clearance in the face of enemy automatic fire and hand grenades which were thrown from windows and doors. The entire German garrison, consisting of an officer and 108 other ranks, was either killed or captured, the Commando party led by the Colonel himself capturing 34 Germans including the garrison commander.

The complete success of this raid was due to the careful planning and fearless leadership of Lt-Col Churchill, who retained a strict control of the many Commando, American, Naval and Royal Air Force parties that co-operated throughout this bold but complicated operation.

On two previous occasions Lt-Col Churchill has led small raiding patrols to the German occupied Island of Hvar. On 27th January 1944 the Colonel led three troops in an attack on a house which the enemy had converted into a strong point.

On approaching the house in darkness, a sentry challenged and fired from ten yards range. The Colonel, who was in the lead, at once gave orders for the house to be surrounded and directed the fire of a PIAT mortar at the walls of the house. After three of the enemy had been killed and one had surrendered, the Colonel himself ran into the house by a side door and captured a further prisoner single-handed.

On 4th February 1944 the Colonel accompanied another raid on Hvar. In hand to hand fighting that ensued the Troop Leader was killed in the doorway of a house. The Colonel at once took command, and without a moments hesitation rushed into the house, killed the German who was firing from inside a room, and took the eight other occupants prisoner.

In all these actions Lt-Col Churchill has displayed utterly fearless leadership under fire, and has inspired in his Commando soldiers a respect and devotion which has ensured the success of every operation he has undertaken. *[L.G. 20.7.44]*

TEMPORARY CAPTAIN JOHN GORDON COATES
Lieut, 201507, Int Corps att HQ SO(M) No. 10 & 30 Cdo.
DISTINGUISHED SERVICE ORDER

Captain Coates was dropped by parachute into Hungary on September 13th, 1944 in command of a small group with a special mission. Through the arrest of one of his party he was captured and imprisoned. For a period of several months he was subjected to a series of interrogations by Hungarian and German police which included physical torture.

During this period Captain Coates showed unfailing bodily courage and strength of mind. He not only kept the real purpose of his mission secret but succeeded in leading his captors off the scent, thus undoubtedly saving his party from being shot out of hand.

By his sterling example Captain Coates encouraged the other members of his group to stand up to their interrogators and by his unfailing alertness and resourcefulness he was able to animate the resistance shown by his party under the most brutal treatment.

When in prison in Budapest, Captain Coates organised the escape of two other British Officers with great skill and courage and then escaped himself. He hid himself and another officer in spite of continuous searches, and was finally successful in making his way at great personal risk through the Russian lines, bringing with him a great deal of useful information.

During a period of four months Captain Coates showed physical and moral courage of the highest degree. His leadership and sense of responsibility were worthy of the greatest praise, and it is due to his cleverness and resolution that the remainder of his party were saved from death.

Should this award be approved it is requested that no publicity be given to it in the press for security reasons. *(L.G. 4.10.45)*

The Eastern Mediterranean and the Balkans

TY. MAJOR PETER MANT MACINTYRE KEMP
107025, Int. Corps, No. 62 Commando
DISTINGUISHED SERVICE ORDER

Major Kemp was sent on a small clandestine operation to Norway in April, 1940. The infiltration was to have taken place by submarine but on the outward journey the vessel was damaged by torpedoes from a U-Boat and had to return to port and the operation was cancelled. In June, 1940 he was sent on an intelligence mission to Spain and Portugal from which he returned in September, 1940 having completed the work satisfactorily.

In February, 1941 he volunteered for infiltration into Spain from Gibraltar for the purpose of harassing the expected German advance through Spain in order to attack Gibraltar. He returned to this country in August, 1941 and stood by to be parachuted into Northern Spain until March, 1942.

From March, 1942 until May, 1943 he was attached to the Small Scale Raiding Force (No. 62 Commando). This force had been formed to carry out small raids on German installations in Normandy, Brittany and the Channel Islands for the joint purpose of obtaining information and of undermining the morale of the German troops. Major Kemp took part in the raid on the Casquets when the entire garrison of the signal station was carried off as prisoners. He also commanded the detachment in an attack on a strong point on the Point de Plouzec (Brittany) when a number of Germans were killed without loss to the raiding party.

On 10th August, 1943 Major Kemp parachuted into Albania as a member of an Allied Mission to the Partisan Forces. During this period he acted as Liaison Officer with the Partisan Provisional Government. He repeatedly exposed himself to great risk, notably on 21st August, when in conjunction with Albanian guerillas, he attacked and shot up a large troop convoy in spite of heavy machine gun fire from the enemy. On 26th August he showed great gallantry throughout the day with the forward troops of the First Partisan Brigade, encouraging them to offer stubborn defence to the advance of Italian troops which was supported by medium artillery, mortar fire and aircraft. In September, 1943 at the time of the Italian collapse Major Kemp was instructed to provide a clear account of the political situation in Tirana. In spite of the fact that this officer speaks no Albanian he entered Tirana on 22nd September, 1943 in civilian clothes and spent four days in the town. On 25th September whilst making a reconnaissance of Tirana airfield he was stopped by a German patrol and showed great resourcefulness in evading arrest. He returned to his headquarters where he transmitted most valuable intelligence by W/T to his Commanding Officer.

Throughout the winter of 1943–44 until his evacuation in March 1944 Major Kemp continued to show great initiative and personal courage, and he took an active part in the fighting in the Debra area.   *(L.G. 20.12.45)*

ACTING TY. CAPTAIN DAVID CHARLES ANGUS, R.M.
Temporary Lieutenant, No. 40 (RM) Commando
MILITARY CROSS

For gallantry, zeal and skill during the attack on Sarande and the seizure of the Island of Solta.   *L.G. 3.4.45*

TY. LIEUTENANT JEFFREY CHARLES BEADLE, R.M.
Chatham Division, Land Forces Adriatic, No. 40 RM Cdo.
MILITARY CROSS

Lieut Beadle, 40 RM Commando, took part in the night attack on Saturday 3rd June 1944 on Hill 633, Island of Brac, Adriatic, by 40 and 43 RM Commandos. In this attack his troop captured the hill top almost by themselves, but suffered very heavy casualties. The troop leader was killed, then the 2nd in command.

Lieut Beadle, the last remaining officer, took command and pressed forward until the summit was taken. Here he consolidated his position and was violently counter-attacked by the enemy. However he refused to withdraw and finally the hill was retaken by the Germans. Lieut Beadle was wounded and fell into the enemy's hands. There is no doubt that but for this young officer's gallant leadership the hill top would probably never have been taken, and but for his stubborn defence and truculent fighting spirit its recapture by a numerically much superior enemy was greatly delayed.   *23.8.45*

MAJOR ALFRED LAPTHORNE BLAKE
HQ 2 SS Bde (Royal Marines), SB No. 94, No. 45 RM Cdo.
MILITARY CROSS (PERIODIC)
9th November 1943 to 17th October 1944.

During the above-mentioned period Major Blake has served first as Staff Captain 2 SS Brigade and then since 17th January 1944 as Brigade Major.

He took over the latter appointment on the sudden death of his predecessor and only five days before the Brigade landed in the assault wave at Anzio. He has taken part in all Commando operations which the Brigade has carried out since that date, including the attack and capture of Monte Ornito in February 1944,

the operations in the Dalmatian Islands, including the attack on Mljet in May 1944 and the attack on Brac in June 1944, between March and August 1944, and the attack and capture of Sarande in September and October 1944. In all these operations he has displayed the highest standard of staff work, showing himself completely able to take decisions on behalf of his Brigade Commander when occasion warranted it; and he has set an example of conscientiousness method and industry which had had its influence throughout the Brigade HQ staff. His conduct under fire has been exemplary and his careful organisation has ensured the smooth working of the HQ in spite of the fact that, both at Ornito and at Sarande, Brigade HQ was established in close proximity to the enemy, and on the top of mountains nearly 2,000 ft. high. Throughout the eleven months period which this citation covers this officer has gone far beyond the requirements of his appointment in his anxiety and determination to forge an efficient HQ and to render the maximum assistance to the units under his command. He has never spared himself when he considered that he was in a position to help, and he has acquired the goodwill and co-operation of all those with whom he has come into contact.
Recommended for MBE, awarded MC. [*L.G. 21.6.45*]

LIEUTENANT GERALD JACKSON BRYAN, R.E.
Royal Engineers, No. 9 & 11 Commando
MILITARY CROSS

In the action at the Litani River in Syria on June 9th 1941, Lieut Bryan was commanding a section of the force landed north of the river to disorganise enemy resistance from the rear. He led a party containing Sgt Worrall and men against a French 75mm battery, under fire from concentrated machine gun offensive, captured the nearest gun with hand grenades. He directed its fire against the remaining guns, which were quickly silenced. The advance was continued, but Lieut Bryan was very severely wounded through both legs, one being subsequently amputated. As a result he was taken prisoner but has since been liberated. His coolness and courage before and after being wounded was an inspiration to his men, and the capture of the battery greatly facilitated the crossing of the river, which it covered at very short range. *(L.G. 2.12.41)*

Commando Gallantry Awards of World War II

ACTING CAPTAIN ROGER JAMES ALLEN COURTNEY
Queens Westminster Rifles (K.R.R.C.), SBS
MILITARY CROSS (IMMEDIATE)

Captain Courtney carried out a daring recce in enemy territory on night 2nd–3rd April 1941.

He swam ashore from a submarine and carefully recced about half a mile of enemy defences and strong points.

He experienced difficulty in returning to the submarine and exposed himself voluntarily to considerable danger and physical hardship for a period of four hours. *(L.G. 21.10.41)*

TY. CAPTAIN GEORGE IAN ALISTAIR DUNCAN
WS/Lieut, 13248 The Black Watch
MILITARY CROSS

Captain Duncan, with two other British NCOs of the Special Boat Section, carried out an attack on Kastelli aerodrome, Crete, on the night 9th–10th June 1942. They left their hideout on the beach at 1900 hours on 8th June and returned at 0530 on 13th June after a difficult and hazardous march through enemy occupied territory and a successful attack on their objective.

Their bag amounted to seven aircraft, 210–60 gallon drums of petrol, six transport vehicles, three bomb dumps and one large oil fuel dump. Fires and explosions are also believed to have caused 70 casualties to German personnel on the aerodrome. The success of the attack was due to the courage, resourcefulness and good leadership of Captain Duncan. *(L.G. 5.11.42)*

ACTING CAPTAIN BASIL IAN SPENCER GOURLAY
Lieutenant, Royal Marines, No. 43 RM Commando
MILITARY CROSS

For gallantry, zeal and skill during the attack on Sarande and the seizure of the Island of Solta. *L.G. 3.4.45*

ACTING TEMPORARY CAPTAIN JOHN CHARLES DUMOUTIER HUDSPITH
Ty Lieut, No. 43 RM Commando
MILITARY CROSS (IMMEDIATE)

Attack on Jelsa, Hvar Island, Yugoslavia, 22nd–23rd March 1944.
During the night move by 43 RM Commando to surround Jelsa, Captain Hudspith was in command of a troop of 35 men.

This troop met an enemy column, strength 150 approximately, who were attempting to make their escape from the town. At the time, Captain Hudspith was uncertain whether this column was composed of Germans, or of Partisans, who were known to be on the island. Accompanied by another officer, he went forward to identify them. Immediately, heavy machine-gun fire was opened up by the enemy, both from the front and flanks. Despite this fire, Captain Hudspith rejoined his troop, organised them, and led them forward to the attack. The enemy were routed, leaving five dead, four prisoners, and their complete baggage-train of 20 mules.

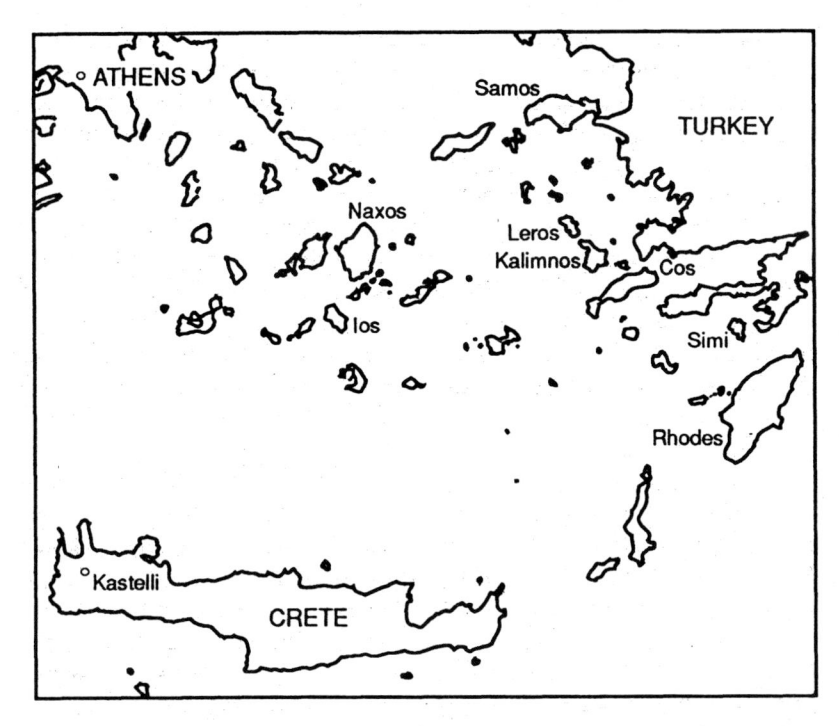

Captain Hudspith, by his disregard for his own safety, personal example, and prompt action, saved a situation which might well have seriously jeopardised the success of the whole operation.

[L.G. 27.6.44]

ACTING MAJOR RAYMOND WALTER KEEP
W/Lieut, 187000, W. Yorks att. No. 2 Commando
MILITARY CROSS

Major Keep landed in Sicily with No. 2 Commando in July 1943. He took part in the Commando raid at Scaletta which led to the capture of Messina. He had since taken part in all the actions of this Commando, including the landing at Salerno in September 1943, the raid on Hvar Island, Dalmatia, in January 1944, the raid on Solta Island in March 1944, the raid on Mljet Island in May 1944 and the raid on Brac Island in June 1944.

During the bitter fighting in the beach head at Salerno from 9th to 20th September 1943 this officer was a section leader who distinguished himself by leading a series of small patrols behind the enemy's lines which brought back nine prisoners in all and much valuable information. His leadership and fearlessness won the admiration of his section and his offensive spirit and anxiety to go forward at a time when most of the troops in the beach-head were on the defensive had an excellent effect on the morale of his unit. On the move of No. 2 Commando to Dalmatia Major Keep was appointed Adjutant, and again distinguished himself as a leader in all the raids in which he took part. In action he has always displayed a keen offensive and truculent spirit and was always the first to volunteer for any duty which involved the penetration of the enemy's lines.

In the raid on Brac in June 1944 the Colonel of No. 2 Commando was taken prisoner by the enemy while leading an assault on the final objective. After its capture the island was evacuated, but Major Keep volunteered to remain behind with one man in order to attempt to release his Colonel. He remained on the island for three days, during which time he personally killed two Germans with his Tommy Gun and reconnoitred the enemy positions which were heavily mined and wired. Not content with keeping these features under close observation he actually penetrated them both, crawling through the minefields and listening to the German conversations in their weapon pits. He did not leave the Island until it seemed beyond doubt that the Colonel had already been evacuated to the mainland of Yugoslavia by sea. This officer was previously recommended for an immediate award after Salerno. His spirit and leadership has consistently been of the highest order, and he had maintained his high standard over twelve months of hard fighting. *[L.G. 22.2.45]*

ACTING CAPTAIN RALPH NICHOLAS PARKINSON-CUMINE, R.M.
Lieutenant
MILITARY CROSS

For gallantry, zeal and skill during the attack on Sarande and the seizure of the Island of Solta. *L.G. 3.4.45*

ACTING TY. MAJOR JAMES DENNIS WAKELING, R.M.
Temporary Captain
MILITARY CROSS

For great courage and exemplary behaviour whilst carrying out commando operations under heavy enemy fire off the Jugoslavian coast. *L.G. 13.3.45*

The Eastern Mediterranean and the Balkans

CORPORAL THOMAS FIELDS SCOTT
2934127 WS Cpl, Queen's Own Cameron Highlanders
GEORGE MEDAL

On 21st September, 1943, Corporal Scott, together with Major Petro and Captain Virkow, were dropped by parachute on Lisee Forest in North-East Serbia within five miles of the enemy occupied village of Elet, but the party was carried by wind far from this zone into deep forest. There was no moon. In trying to disentangle themselves while hanging from trees, Captain Virkow and Corporal Scott fell from heights of about 30–40 feet. Captain Virkow broke a hip bone and both arms, Corporal Scott a leg, and also displaced bones in his spine. Both were found unconscious by Guerillas, they were tended secretly by a Serbian doctor from enemy-occupied territory and in both cases, due to shock and exposure, pneumonia intervened. In about one month Corporal Scott was well enough to hobble about on crutches but Captain Virkow's hip never 'set' and he was immobile. From October, 1943 to April, 1944, Corporal Scott, suffering acutely himself, journeyed with his officer to rejoin British lines. This meant constant sudden moves at the approach of the enemy, and often hiding from the enemy in close vicinity. Corporal Scott was completely out of touch with base so that no medicines, or medical appliances, ever reached them, and always carrying Captain Virkow over difficult mountain tracks. It was only Corporal Scott's selfless devotion and incredible tact in getting help from Guerillas accomplished this amazing feat. The situation was rendered more difficult when in December, 1943, H.M.G. withdrew support from General Mihailovic and gave active assistance to Marshal Tito. By May, 1944, they had joined up with some British officers, and Captain Virkow was left in care of natives for treatment in a nursing camp (he was subsequently captured by the Germans). Corporal Scott, having been officially relieved of his duties of caring for Captain Virkow ultimately got to the coast and then home. *[L.G. 18.10.45]*

CORPORAL JOHN HAMILTON BOOTH
2824715, Seaforth Highlanders, No. 1 SBS
DISTINGUISHED CONDUCT MEDAL

For particularly meritorious service in action against an armed German Naval Auxiliary vessel off Suda Bay on the 21st April, 1942, when his courage and skilful shooting with the bren gun were worthy of the highest praise. The words of the official report were as follows:— 'Some really splendid shooting with the bren gun by Corporal J. Booth of the Seaforth Highlanders had been successful in preventing the enemy from manning their foremost gun and he had just (literally) flattened the crew of the midship gun when our first direct hit completely destroyed this gun, which appeared to be blown over the side. Fire from her machine-gun, which had been ineffective, had now ceased and an attempt to man the after gun was frustrated by Corporal Booth, the gun's crew preferring to jump over the stern rather than face the fire of his bren gun.'

On 13th April as lookout this NCO sighted the masts of an enemy ship at great range in the Ionian Sea and on two patrols his keenness to take his share in all the work of the submarine has been most marked and appreciated. His previous service in the flotilla has included the patrol in HMS *Osiris* in January when a complete failure of the shaft lubrication system occurred and Booth worked in two watches to lubricate the bearings by hand for the entire return passage, and a patrol in HMS *Thunderbolt* in October 1941, when he successfully accomplished his special task and, with Sergeant Sherwood, landed eight agents on the enemy coast. Before this he saw service in the Tenth Submarine Flotilla at Malta, and there is no doubt that Corporal Booth is the best type of NCO to achieve co-operation and good results in combined operations between the services. *(L.G. 5.11.42)*

Lance Sergeant John Murdoch Cooper
2698113, 2 Bn Scots Guards, SAS Bde
Distinguished Conduct Medal
(Immediate)

February 1942.
On returning from the 2nd raid against Buerat aerodrome the raiding party was ambushed by a strong and well-armed enemy force. This force was aligned along the road in an ideal position to throw grenades and to open fire with automatic weapons. The ambush was a complete surprise, but so quick was Sgt Cooper in getting his gun into action and so accurate was his aim in the face of intense fire from the automatic weapons of the enemy that the ambushers were seriously disconcerted. At least five of them were killed at point blank range by his fire. His quickness and courage on this occasion undoubtedly saved his companions. This NCO has taken part in 13 raids and performed many acts of gallantry comparable to the one described. *(L.G. 26.11.42)*

The Eastern Mediterranean and the Balkans

SERGEANT ROY JOSEPH CROOKS
776642, North Somerset Yeomanry, No. 52 Commando
DISTINGUISHED CONDUCT MEDAL

Crete

During operations 18th July–17th August in Crete, Sgt Roy Joseph Crooks after taking part in the rearguard action from Suda, refused to surrender and took to the hills alone.

He later joined Lieut-Cdr F. G. Pool, RNR, and assisted in collecting up troops for evacuation. During actual embarkation, on two successive nights, he volunteered to go ashore from the submarine to help marshal and embark the British troops. His initiative and masterly handling of the men contributed largely to the safe embarkation of so many men in extremely difficult conditions.

His coolness and resource in handling a most difficult situation with the local inhabitants, who were endeavouring to collect boots and clothes, is worthy of recognition. *[L.G. 23.12.41]*

DRIVER FRITZ SIGMUND HAUSMANN
Oal/1344 Driver, P/L/Cpl, RASC, No. 2 Commando
DISTINGUISHED CONDUCT MEDAL (IMMEDIATE)

Island of Brac (Dalmatia) 5th March 1944. Island of Solta (Dalmatia) 19th March 1944.

In the Commando raid on Brac Island on the night of 5th March 1944 Dvr Hausmann was the leading scout of the section which carried out this raid. The section was seen approaching and two sentries opened fire with schmeiser automatics which pinned them to the ground. Dvr Hausmann dashed forward firing his TSMG and killed one sentry, but the other ran into a house. Hausmann followed, kicked open the door and threw in a hand grenade. When it had exploded he dashed in shouting to the Germans to surrender, and having killed one and wounded two more, the remaining five men gave themselves up.

On the morning of 10th March 1944 during the Commando attack on Solta Island the behaviour of this man was exemplary. In the forefront of the final assault on the village, he led a small group of men in house-clearing in an area where the German garrison was holding out, and during this operation severely wounded a German who was holding up the advance with a spandau machine-gun which was mounted in an upper window.

Dvr Hausmann is a Palestinian of German origin serving in the Commando. He has taken part in three Commando raids in these islands during the last six weeks, and in each of these his behaviour has been outstandingly bold and aggressive. He insists on being the leading scout on all approaches by day or night and is not content to await his turn for this duty. He has set a magnificent example and his conduct under fire is in the highest traditions of the Army. *[L.G. 20.7.44]*

Marine Benjamin Vaughan Jones
Ply.X.100514, 23rd Light AA Bty, RM, No. 2 RM AA Regt.
Distinguished Conduct Medal

At his gun position south-west of Canea on 21st May displayed outstanding courage, by shooting down an enemy aircraft by firing a bren gun from the shoulder. Later in the day he made a lone bayonet charge against seven parachutists armed with sub-machine guns who had landed in a glider close to the gun position. He was wounded in this action. This prompt action displayed great bravery and was a fine example to all ranks. *(L.G. 4.11.41)*

Company Sergeant Major Peter Douglas Morland
3655808, South Lancs Regiment, No. 2 Commando
Distinguished Conduct Medal (Immediate)
Spilje Bay, Albania July 28th–29th 1944 Operation 'Healing II'

This Warrant Officer went into action in the role of a Section Officer. Throughout the whole action Morland showed a complete disregard for his own safety, initiative and great powers of leadership. On the first attack, his section came under heavy machine-gun fire and suffered casualties. He rallied his men and led the charge clearing the ridge. On the second attack his section again came under heavy fire causing many casualties, but armed with a pistol, he by his gallantry and leadership, pressed home the attack and cleared his objective. He then immediately gave first aid to the wounded, arranged their evacuations, and made two attempts to get over the crest of a ridge, and rescue two men, after three other attempts had been unsuccessful. In the latter stages, his section was reduced to a mere handful of men. Seeing that the other section was in difficulties, he collected men of different troops and another regiment, put in an attack and enabled the other section to withdraw. In the last stages of the battle, having no men, under heavy mortar and machine-gun fire, he helped evacuate the wounded to the regimental aid post he had formed and thence back to the beachhead. His example, fine and untiring energy throughout were an inspiration to all. This Warrant Officer has consistently shown great courage in previous actions in Norway, Scaletta and Salerno, and on other Commando raids on the Yugo-Slav islands. *(L.G. 5.10.44)*

The Eastern Mediterranean and the Balkans

SERGEANT CHARLES WILLIAM ROBERTS
Ex.1689, RM
DISTINGUISHED CONDUCT MEDAL

At Canea on 19th May whilst in action at his gun position was hit in the abdomen by an explosive bullet. Although knocked to the ground he continued to give orders until he became unconscious and collapsed. His devotion to duty and example to all ranks deserves the highest praise. *(L.G. 4.11.41)*

COMPANY SERGEANT MAJOR GEORGE BARNES, M.M.
Sergeant, (Actg/Warrant Officer Class II), 2617252, SBS
BAR TO MILITARY MEDAL

The above-named, together with another NCO of the Special Boat Section and an officer in charge, carried out an attack on Kastelli aerodrome, Crete, on the night 9th–10th June 1942. they left their hide-out on the beach at 1900 on 6th June and returned at 0530 on 13th June after a difficult and hazardous march through enemy occupied territory and a successful attack on their objective. Their bag amounted to seven aircraft, 210–60 gallon drums of petrol, six transport vehicles, three bomb dumps and one large oil fuel dump. Fires and explosions are also believed to have caused 70 casualties to German personnel on the aerodrome. The success of the attack was due to the good leadership of the Officer in charge, and the courage and skill of CSM Barnes. *[L.G. 5.1142]*

SERGEANT DOUGLAS POMFORD, M.M.
3456406, South Lancs Regt, No. 1 SBS
BAR TO MILITARY MEDAL (IMMEDIATE)

For distinguished conduct during operations on the islands of Ios, Amorgos and Naxos.

This Sgt was the senior NCO of the SBS Patrol which, on the night 26th April 1944, attacked an enemy post in Ios Town. In the close-quarter engagement which ensued, this NCO personally accounted for two of the enemy, whilst the remaining three were captured. The patrol then proceeded to Amorgos and attacked the W/T Station at Katapola Port on the night 1st May 1944. This NCO formed part of the assault party under Capt Clarke, and was able, under cover of very accurate LMG fire, to get within a few yards of the main door of the building in which the W/T Station was situated. From there, this NCO assisted in putting two machine-guns out of action with grenades and SMG fire. The enemy then attempted to escape out of the house, six were immediately killed by the assault party. This NCO then went forward alone in to the house and ascertained that no further enemy remained inside. The whole patrol then entered, destroyed the electric generator and re-embarked together with the W/T set and all the codes and documents. On 22nd May 1944, during the attack on the German garrison in Naxos Town, this NCO conducted himself with coolness and complete disregard for danger, as a result of which 15 casualties were caused to the enemy without loss.

Throughout all these operations the determination, leadership and example set by this NCO was of the highest order.

(L.G. 4.1 45)

Corporal Alec George Aldis
Po.X.1477, RM
Military Medal

Suda Sector, Crete.
This NCO has set the finest example to all ranks during the operation in Crete 20th–31st May. With no regard for his personal safety he worked unceasingly to maintain the Suda Sector communications. He was always ready to volunteer for any special despatch riding however hazardous. His work at all times was of the highest order.
Recommended for DCM, awarded MM. *(L.G. 5.3.42)*

Lance Corporal John Robert Anchor
2616491, Grenadier Guards, No. 2 Commando
Military Medal

Spilje Bay, Albania. July 28th–29th 1944. Operation 'Healing II'
L/Cpl Anchor was in command of a bren gun. At dawn his troop led the assault against enemy positions, strongly fortified and tenaciously defended.

During the early stages of the advance L/Cpl Anchor, coming under vicious enemy machine gun fire, carried his bren gun forward across dangerously open ground. From now onwards, he not only succeeded in giving effective covering fire to the advancing troops and thereby ensuring the steady advance of the leading troops, but continually engaged enemy strong points with deliberate and accurate fire, having complete disregard for his own personal safety.

In the final assault, L/Cpl Anchor, observing several Germans immediately in front of him, displayed great initiative and courage, when, charging forward under intense fire he hurled a grenade in the midst of the enemy, who were making a last desperate attempt to hold the objective. This action contributed largely to their withdrawal from the position.

By now a machine gun in the immediate vicinity was pouring bullets into the captured position. L/Cpl Anchor located this

The Eastern Mediterranean and the Balkans

machine gun and immediately engaged it through the window of his house forcing the enemy to stop firing and withdraw to another position.

Throughout the action this NCO displayed not only courage and determination but great initiative at all times. His efforts contributed greatly to the success of the assault and were largely responsible for dislodging Germans determined to hold out at all costs.

Company Sergeant Major George Barnes
2617252, Grenadier Guards, No. 8 Commando & 1 SBS
Military Medal

On 11th June 1941 this NCO displayed great coolness and courage under fire during a seaborne raid of a dangerous nature into enemy territory, and by great presence of mind ensured not only the success of the operation but also the safe withdrawal of the raiding party. *[L.G. 24.2.42]*

Corporal Edward Barr
3325427, Highland Light Infantry, No. 11 Cdo. & 2 SBS
Military Medal

Corporal E. Barr, together with another NCO of the Special Boat Section and an officer in charge, carried out an attack on Kastelli aerodrome, Crete, on the night 9th–10th June, 1942. They left their hide-out on the beach at 1900 on 6th June and returned at 0530 on 13th June after a difficult and hazardous march through enemy occupied territory and a successful attack on their objective. Their bag amounted to seven aircraft, 210–60 gallon drums of petrol, six transport vehicles, three bomb dumps and one large oil fuel dump. Fires and explosions are also believed to have caused 70 casualties to German personnel on the aerodrome.

The success of the attack was due to the good leadership of the officer in charge, and the courage and skill of Corporal Barr.
(L.G. 5.11.42)

Sergeant Peter J. Berrisford
910524, RA (Field), Att. No. 6 Commando
Military Medal

After the action on Djebel el Azag on 30th November 1942, Sgt Berrisford lay by himself on the plateau for two nights and one day, gaining all possible information about the German machine-gun positions. He came under a good deal of fire, but did not withdraw until he had carried out his task. *[L.G. 23.9.43]*

Commando Gallantry Awards of World War II

Sergeant George C. Bremner
2880295, 1st London Scottish, SBS & No. 8 Commando
Military Medal

From 1st August until December 1941 this NCO has been engaged in three dangerous operations in connection with the rescue of British troops from enemy territory. On all occasions his coolness and courage contributed largely to the success of these hazardous operations. *[L.G. 24.2.42]*

Driver George David Dransfield
T/92276, RASC, No. 2 Commando
Military Medal (Immediate)

Spilje Bay, Albania—28th–29th July 1944—Operation Healing II

This man showed great courage and determination throughout the action. In the early stages he was particularly conspicuous in the bayonet assaults. In the final stage during an attack on a fortified house, Dransfield's section attacked but were held up by withering machine-gun fire across very exposed ground. Dransfield with complete disregard for his own safety, dashed through the fire, across open ground over barbed wire and through a suspected minefield to take up a position behind a wall on the enemy's flank. He immediately brought accurate fire to bear on to the enemy positions in the house. This attracted enemy fire away from his own section onto himself and enabled his section to re-group for a second attack. Under this hail of fire, Dransfield was badly wounded in the leg. Despite this, he continued to return the enemy fire, and when the second attack was launched he immediately joined in the assault, when he was again hit in the other leg. Although in great pain and bleeding profusely he crawled 20 yards and collapsed. This soldier's offensive spirit and magnificent bravery were an outstanding example and inspiration to all.

(L.G. 5.10.44)

Marine John Francis Duggan
Ply.X.2834, Royal Marines
Military Medal

For courage, endurance and determination in a raid on an enemy aerodrome in the Middle East. *L.G. 19.1.43*

The Eastern Mediterranean and the Balkans

TY. SERGEANT MAJOR FREDERICK G. FINDLEY
5041667, RASC, No. 6 Commando
MILITARY MEDAL

During the withdrawal from Djebel el Azag on 6th January 1943, TSM Findley repeatedly showed complete disregard for his own safety by covering his section by advancing under fire and throwing grenades.

I consider that TSM Findley's actions were responsible for numerous men reaching safety. Throughout this action he showed a most excellent example to his men. He is over 40 years of age and put up a remarkable performance. *[L.G. 23.9.43]*

ACTING TEMPORARY SERGEANT RICHARD DOUGLAS FRENCH
Ex 3226, No. 43 RM Commando
MILITARY MEDAL (IMMEDIATE)

Patrol ambush on Hvar Island 12th July 1944.

During this action, a party of enemy ensconced themselves with two machine-guns in an isolated house, with an excellent field of fire in all directions. It was necessary to take immediate steps to liquidate this party. Sgt French first brought his Bren Group up into position, and then alone dashed across the open ground to the house. All this time he was under heavy fire. On reaching the house, single-handed he destroyed one MG, and killed or wounded four of the enemy. His action caused the remaining enemy to surrender, thus contributing largely to the success of the whole operation. Sgt French throughout showed complete disregard for his own safety and a spirited determination to close with the enemy. He set a fine example to all ranks. *(L.G. 29.8.44)*

ACTING TEMPORARY SERGEANT THOMAS CHARLES DENNIS GALLON
Temporary Corporal, Ex.3235, No. 43 RM Commando
MILITARY MEDAL

Operation 'Flounced' Ref Map Yugoslavia 1/100,000 Sheet 109.
Night Attack on Point 622 (0960) 3rd June 1944.

Sgt Gallon was in charge of the leading section whose task it was to blow a gap through the wire and minefield and assault through it. For about a mile his troop was under heavy fire. When the wire was reached he blew a gap through it but was wounded in the leg while doing it. Despite this wound he led his section through the gap and assaulted an enemy position which had been firing at them. When on the objective his Troop Commander was killed and he took charge of the remnants of the troop. He was then ordered to withdraw from the position and he reorganised and led them back still under fire. Hearing that some had been left behind, he went back again although wounded to try to get them back. He was again wounded and could no longer walk. He crawled back and was picked up by a stretcher party who had gone out to search for wounded.

This NCO's courage and devotion to duty, though in great pain, was an example to all ranks. *16.12.44*

LANCE BOMBARDIER JOHN WILLIS GELDER
1606731, RA (Coast), No. 2 Commando
MILITARY MEDAL (IMMEDIATE)

Spilje Bay, Albania. July 28th–29th 1944. Operation 'Healing II.'
This NCO showed outstanding courage, leadership and initiative. The attack in which he took part developed in three phases. In phase 1, the attack was on a ridge studded with machine-gun posts. On the first burst of fire, the Section Sergeant and Corporal were hit, and Gelder immediately took control of the sub-section leading them with dash and no thought of personal danger. He saw that another section had eleven casualties from an machine-gun post, subsequently found to be manned by a German officer, he stalked this post despite the danger, and killed the officer with his Tommy gun. On Phase 2, Gelder collected remnants of the section and put in another attack on an machine-gun post, capturing the post and killing the occupants.

On Phase 3, the objective was a strongly fortified house. The first attack was beaten off and Gelder was wounded. He refused to withdraw, and again went into the attack. He was hit in the face by a grenade, which exploded at his feet seriously wounding him. Despite this fact, he went on firing till his magazine was empty, encouraged the other men, who were now under mortar as well as machine-gun fire, and tried to carry a comrade out of action until finally collapsing. Gelder, who showed courage at Scaletta, Salerno and Hvar, acted as a Sergeant throughout this action, and was a great inspiration to his men. His gallantry in past actions earned him a recommendation at Salerno. *(L.G. 5.10.44)*

LANCE SERGEANT WALTER GOODALL
3593748, Border Regt, Att. No. 6 Commando
MILITARY MEDAL

On the night 12th–13th December 1942 Sgt Goodall proceeded in command of a small recce patrol to gain information about Germans in area Djebel el Keddia.

During the 13th his patrol became involved with the enemy and surrounded by a considerably superior force. Sgt Goodall extricated his patrol with great coolness and skill and brought back information which resulted in a very successful raid during the following night.
Reported missing after the action on Djebel el Azag on 6th January 1943.
[L.G. 23.9.43]

LANCE CORPORAL JOHN DENIS HOWARD
7375194, RAMC, No. 2 Commando
MILITARY MEDAL (IMMEDIATE)

Spilje Bay, Albania. July 28th–29, 1944. Operation 'Healing II'
This NCO displayed untiring zeal, bravery and devotion to duty and was an example to all about him.

Whilst under heavy shell fire he displayed the utmost coolness and disregarding his own safety entirely, he attended to the wounded and endeavoured to move them from the danger area.

Later, during the attack he was constantly up with the assaulting troops in his capacity as medical orderly and he showed complete indifference to enemy fire whilst attending to wounded. He remained out under heavy fire dressing wounds and assisting in evacuating casualties. He went out repeatedly to bring in wounded men although he was continually sniped at and the ground was swept by enemy machine gun fire. He later remained out under heavy shell fire endeavouring to remove wounded to a place of safety. He was untiring in his work and at no time did he show the slightest regard for his own personal safety. His coolness and courage were great examples to those with him.

During previous actions he has shown the same consistent devotion to duty. *(L.G. 5.10.44)*

LANCE SERGEANT WILLIAM LISTER
3595103, Border Regt attached No. 6 Commando
MILITARY MEDAL

During the withdrawal from Djebel el Azag 6th January 1943, Sgt Lister covered the withdrawal of his own troops by advancing and taking on the enemy with a Colt automatic and one grenade. This he did under machine-gun fire, thereby enabling his section to withdraw in safety. Apart from this, he showed great coolness throughout the action. *[L.G. 23.9.43]*

Commando Gallantry Awards of World War II

Lance Bombardier Thomas Joseph Mulcahy
1517069, RA (Coast), No. 2 Commando (RA (Coast))
Military Medal (Immediate)

Spilje Bay, Albania. July 28th–29th 1944. Operation 'Healing II.'
This NCO showed great courage and leadership throughout the action. In the early stages when his section sergeant was missing and his Corporal wounded, Mulcahy immediately took charge. He led his men into the assault showing complete disregard for his personal safety and carried the assault through to destroy two machine-gun posts and several weapon pits. Then when his section were pinned down, he carried out a reconnaissance under fire which enabled him to outflank these posts. In the final stages, his section was driven back in an attack on a strong point, but although wounded he rallied his men, and led a second attack in which he became more seriously wounded. Whilst lying on the ground, he encouraged his men and insisted on being the last to be evacuated. Throughout the action, he displayed great gallantry, determination and devotion to duty which, without question, materially contributed to the success of each assault. This NCO has repeatedly been outstanding in action and was recommended at Salerno.

(L.G. 5.10.44)

Marine Charles Nicholls
Ply.X.2570, RM
Military Medal

For great courage and exemplary behaviour whilst carrying out commando operations under heavy enemy fire off the Jugoslavian coast. *(L.G. 13.3.45)*

Lance Sergeant John Myles O'Reilly
2716586, Irish Guards, No. 8 Commando & SBS
Military Medal (Immediate)

For distinguished conduct during the operation on the island of Santorin. On the night of 23rd April 1944, this NCO together with one Officer and ten ORs entered a house occupied by approximately 30 of the enemy. In the intense close quarter engagement which followed, this NCO conducted himself with coolness and complete disregard for his personal safety. Kicking in the doors of the living quarters, he threw grenades into the rooms in the face of considerable enemy fire, encouraging and directing the return fire of his own men. Throughout the engagement he was master of the situation, and did not finally leave the building until he was certain that all the occupants had been either killed or wounded.

The Eastern Mediterranean and the Balkans

Throughout this operation, the courage and personal example shown by this man was of the highest order. *(L.G. 4.1.45)*

ACTING TY. CORPORAL ERNEST EDWARD PALMER
Marine, Ch.X.103819, No. 40 RM Commando
MILITARY MEDAL

For gallantry, zeal and skill during the attack on Sarande and the seizure of the Island of Solta. *L.G. 3.4.45*

ACTING TEMPORARY SERGEANT KENNETH RICHARD PICKERING
Temporary Corporal, Ex.3877, RM, No. 43 RM Commando
MILITARY MEDAL

For great courage and exemplary behaviour whilst carrying out commando operations under heavy enemy fire off the Jugoslavian coast. *L.G. 13.3.45*

CORPORAL DOUGLAS POMFORD
3456406, The South Lancashire Regiment, The Prince of Wales's Volunteers (Liverpool), No. 1 SBS
MILITARY MEDAL

In recognition of gallant and distinguished services in the field. *L.G. 23.3.44*

LANCE SERGEANT JOSEPH GERARD ANTHONY ROGERS
2933493, Cameron Highlanders, No. 2 Commando
MILITARY MEDAL (IMMEDIATE)

Spilje Bay, Albania. 28th–29th July 1944 Operation 'Healing II'
L/Sgt Rogers personally led his sub-section with conspicuous gallantry. In the face of heavy fire from two spandaus he continued to advance against his objective. Although wounded and in great pain he led his men on to close with the enemy and killed the machine gun teams. By this action, the troops on his left, who had been held up, were enabled to advance again. L/Sgt Rogers throughout showed a complete disregard of danger and continually refused to allow his wound to interfere with his duties until the objective had been captured, and other casualties in his section had been dealt with first. *(L.G. 5.10.44)*

Commando Gallantry Awards of World War II

Lance Corporal Clifford William Smith
7403479, Royal Army Medical Corps, No. 43 RM Cdo.
Military Medal
In recognition of gallant and distinguished services in the field.

L.G. 15.3.45

Lance Corporal Thomas Smith
3655831, South Lancs Regt, No. 2 Commando
Military Medal

This NCO was one of a small party of volunteers who remained behind on Brac after the Allied Forces had left, in an attempt to rescue their Commanding Officer who had been captured. It was thought at the time that there was little chance of them returning. For three days and nights this NCO was outstanding for his coolness and resource when in close proximity to the enemy. (4th–6th June 1944). The party did return to base however and on 8th June 1944, information being received of prisoners this NCO again volunteered to return to Brac. He was again outstanding. He climbed a hill in the German lines to observe enemy movement and was spotted. He was fired at and mortared and with perfect calmness he ignored this fire and continued to observe the enemy and did not retire until the Germans were actually advancing up the hill. He then retreated and made his way back through the German lines to base with very valuable information about the enemy. This NCO has also been conspicuous in several battles during the past year being recommended for the MM at Salerno in September 1943.   *[L.G. 22.2.45]*

Sergeant Robert Arthur Lever Summers
6896822, KRRC attached SBS
Military Medal (Immediate)

This NCO was ordered to carry out a reconnaissance and make an attack on a petrol dump at Dhrasi in the island of Crete. He did a daring and successful reconnaissance in civilian clothes on 6th and 7th July. Having collected his patrol he attacked the dump on the night 22nd–23rd July, cutting his way through considerable wire defences. By cool leadership and courage he directed the laying of all the bombs carried by his patrol and remained in the dump for about an hour. Although discovered and fired upon he kept his patrol together and withdrew them through the wire without casualties. In spite of the fact that he was without an interpreter, and that one of his men was suffering from malaria, he succeeding in leading his patrol from the Kastellion area to the target, and back to the beach over exceptionally difficult country for a period

The Eastern Mediterranean and the Balkans

of eight days. On this and many similar occasions this NCO has shown exceptional qualities as a leader and his courage and devotion to duty have been of a high standard. *[L.G. 4.1.45]*

CORPORAL ALEXANDER VERRI
5337321, R. Berks, No. 2 Commando
MILITARY MEDAL

Cpl Verri, R. Berks and No. 2 Commando, attached HQ No. 2 SS Bde, took part in the night attack on hill 633, Island of Brac, Adriatic on Sat. 3rd June 1944.

He was placed in position on the hill top immediately was taken, and worked his set with great coolness under heavy mortar and machine gun fire. Later he was sent alone to an other position more suitable for signalling. Shortly afterwards the hill was counter-attacked by the enemy and lost. Cpl Verri's wireless set was hit and damaged. The troops in his vicinity withdrew, but Cpl Verri remained attempting to repair his instrument in the moonlight. Just before dawn the hill was heavily bombarded by our guns, the British force being there no longer. Cpl Verri picked up his set and while searching for a more sheltered position bumped into a German post and was captured. This man's bravery in the early part of the attack helped greatly in the taking of the hill. Later his fortitude in remaining where he had been placed was the sole reason of his capture. *23.8.45*

WAR SUBST. SERGEANT FRED GORDON WORRALL
877988, Royal Artillery, C Batt Layforce, No. 11 Commando
MILITARY MEDAL

In the action at the Litani River in Syria on June 9th 1941, this NCO was part of a force landed north of the river to disorganise enemy resistance from the rear. With Lieut Bryan RE, his section Leader, he led a party of [...] men against a French 75-mm Battery, despite considerable opposition from concealed machine-guns. Having captured the nearest gun with hand grenades, Sgt Worral layed the gun with such accuracy that the remaining three guns were rapidly silenced. When ordered to continue the advance, he put this gun out of action before moving on. Shortly afterwards he was severely wounded in the head, and taken prisoner, but has now been liberated. The dash and efficiency of this NCO in silencing the battery, had considerable effect on the successful crossing of the river, as the guns covered the approaches and crossing at very short range.

Recommended for DCM or MM, awarded MM. *[L.G. 2.12.41]*

Squadron Quartermaster Sergeant Jeffrey Evans
2733873 WS SQMS, Welsh Guards att Special Boat Service
British Empire Medal

The above-mentioned NCO was posted to SBS as SQMS on formation of the unit in March 1943 and has served in that capacity since. Owing to the fact that the operations of SBS entail the use of highly varied and diverse equipment and are of their nature extremely dispersed, a far heavier burden of responsibility is imposed upon the QM branch than would be the case in a normal unit. These abnormal responsibilities SQMS Evans has at all times discharged with great zeal and efficiency. In addition SQMS Evans has on two occasions been in a position of exceptional trust and difficulty—in Leros in October and November 1943 and in Castelrosso in May, June and July 1944. In both places he was in charge of advance stores and equipment not only of SBS but also of other Raiding Forces. In Leros during the German attack on the island SQMS Evans not only personally led patrols through enemy held positions to recover valuable stores and MT but also, with skill and courage, performed the duties of a normal patrol commander, in combating enemy parachutists and directing the fire of two sections of MMGs. In Castelrosso SQMS Evans organised, under difficult and trying circumstances, an Advance 'Q' Base for Raiding Forces and when the greater part of the town was accidentally destroyed by fire, he played an invaluable part in salvaging special and much-needed equipment which would otherwise have been lost to the detriment of Raiding Forces' activity in the Aegean.

Note added in the Treasury
The services described in the 4th to 6th sentences seem to fall into the Military Medal, rather than the British Empire Medal, category. Possibly, however, taking the citation as a whole, the Committee may feel able to approve a recommendation for B.E.M.
[L.G. 18.10.45]

Acting Warrant Officer Class II Alexander John Fraser
7908391 WS S/Sgt A/WOII (Q.M.S.), Royal Armoured Corps, attached Raiding Forces
British Empire Medal

QMS Fraser has been Chief Clerk to Raiding Forces (Simi) since 1st January, 1945. Before that he was Chief Clerk (ops) to Force 142 and Raiding Forces. At all times his work and extreme devotion to duty has been most marked. During most of above periods

The Eastern Mediterranean and the Balkans

Raiding Forces have been under-staffed, which threw heavy responsibilities and long hours on QMS Fraser. Since joining up RF (Simi) he has fulfilled his duties in a manner deserving highest praise, during a period of intense operational activity, and by his supreme efficiency has contributed in no mean measure to the successes gained. His resource and initiative is of high order.
[L.G. 18.10.45]

STAFF SERGEANT JAMES HALLEY
7258996 WS S/Sgt, R.A.M.C., B.M.A. Force 281
BRITISH EMPIRE MEDAL

S/Sergeant Halley showed outstanding ability and untiring patience during a period from 30th January to April, 1945 in improvising means to cope with the influx of refugees during a critical period when the weather was at its worst. Had it not been for his resourcefulness a condition of extreme confusion might have arisen. He organised a landing stage, an inspection post, a registration station and organised habitable houses in the village of Panagia, Casos. Cookhouses, dining halls and even a bakery were improvised. The task was an R.E. one to set up a camp for 2,000 refugees but owing to weather conditions these plans were delayed. Refugees, however, were arriving and had to be immediately cared for. This good work was continued throughout the period and there were many times when this NCO literally worked through the 24 hours of the day and night. He was throughout the period doing work which normally would have been the responsibility of a senior officer with a considerable staff. *[L.G. 18.10.45]*

ACTING CORPORAL ALFRED HARRISON
S.2982794, Royal Army Service Corps
BRITISH EMPIRE MEDAL

Corporal Harrison was put in charge of Paromiti refugee camp when first opened on 9th January, 1945 as no officer or senior non-commissioned officer was available. He showed powers of organisation and control of men much above his rank. With the assistance of one interpreter he organised efficiently the arrival, accommodation and rationing of batches of refugees who arrived often without warning and in poor shape owing to overcrowded and hazardous journeys by sea in caiques and other craft. On 16th February, 1945, his duties were taken over by a Friends Ambulance Unit team of five including personnel of officer status. He then worked with equal efficiency and devotion to duty in the Casos and Efialti camps. His normal work is that of a Clerk.
[L.G. 18.10.45]

Commando Gallantry Awards of World War II

SERGEANT REGINALD LUDBROOK MUSK
1866168 W/S Sergeant, Corps of Royal Engineers
BRITISH EMPIRE MEDAL

In October, 1944, Sergeant Musk was sent to Scarpanto to investigate German minefields, booby traps and demolition preparations. He carried out this work with zeal and efficiency and within five days of starting work he had removed all demolition charges in roads and bridges and rendered them safe for all military traffic. His next task was to reconnoitre beaches and agricultural ground for enemy mines. These fields were uncharted and in most cases not marked on the ground. In face of ever present danger from anti-personnel mines he carried out his survey and succeeded in clearly defining the mined areas and marking them for the safety of troops and civilian population. On 4th November, 1944, when in the process of surveying a minefield he trod on an 'S' mine which exploded. However, due to his courage and thorough training he carefully calculated the timing of the explosion and flung himself on to the ground, escaping any injury. His coolness also gave the example to two sappers who accompanied him, and by taking heed of his warning they also escaped injury. In spite of this he carried on with the task of charting and marking the minefields until the whole minefield was marked for the safety of the population.   *[L.G. 18.10.45]*

LANCE SERGEANT NORMAN CHARLES NICKLIN
2362342 WS Corporal, Royal Corps of Signals
BRITISH EMPIRE MEDAL

L/Sergeant Nicklin was dropped by parachute into Greece in January 1944 and returned to the Middle East in December 1944 on completion of his duties. Whilst in Greece he served the whole time as W/T operator. On arrival he was stationed for a few days only in the Thessaly area and moved after that to the South Macedonia H.Q. Station where he carried out, in addition to his W/T operator duties, cipher and station administration duties, as second-in-charge, the Wireless Station. During a German drive in July 1944 Sergeant Nicklin, who had been surprised unawares, was forced to take cover in some bracken within 20 feet of two German mortars. With the Germans walking around him, he scraped a hole in the ground and buried the ciphers and code book which he wanted to save in case of capture. With the enemy so near, he disregarded his own safety and took a considerable risk. In August and September, traffic coming through his station was very heavy, as preparations were being made to harass the retreating Germans. This meant a great strain on the W/T operators and cipher personnel, especially when intercommunications were introduced between the Field Stations, adding greatly to the already considerable traffic with the Middle East. Before going into the field, L/Sergeant Nicklin had worked at Cairo HQs. At all times he proved a reliable and efficient NCO.   *[L.G. 18.10.45]*

ACTING COMPANY QUARTERMASTER SERGEANT
DEREK PARKIN
2580152 WS Sergeant, Royal Corps of Signals
BRITISH EMPIRE MEDAL

CQMS Parkin was dropped by parachute into Greece on 20 February 1943 and was evacuated on 23 December 1944. During the 22 months that he was in Greece, he served as a W/T operator. Parkin was sent into the field to join a small party of British and Greek officers who had been infiltrated in October 1942 and to relieve the W/T operators who were feeling the strain of the hard and difficult conditions under which they were living. As the number of missions in Greece increased, and cipher traffic became very heavy, Parkin, like other personnel, had to work late into every night in order to maintain regular contact with the Middle East. In July 1943 he was transferred to the air landing ground station which was then under construction. Owing to the proximity of the Germans and the complicated arrangements necessary, it was vital to have a first-class W/T operator and Parkin was immediately selected. Subsequently he worked at the Field Commander's static or mobile HQ and was transferred from time to time wherever operations were in progress, or where a reliable and efficient operator was required. CQMS Parkin, during the whole time he was in the field worked with great efficiency as W/T operator. His devotion to duty, and his efficiency never slacked during 22 months' service in Greece.   *[L.G. 18.10.45]*

STAFF SERGEANT CHARLES PHILIP TOMSETT
1869793 WS Staff Sergeant, Royal Engineers
BRITISH EMPIRE MEDAL

Staff Sergeant Tomsett joined Force 281 on 24th October, 1944, and is skipper of 'Z'-craft No. 86 which forms part of the craft operated by 1207 'Z'-Craft Operating Coy, RE. Since joining this Force, Staff Sergeant Tomsett has been continually occupied in all operations in the Dodecanese, performing without a break duties equivalent to the master of a ship. His craft has been to sea in all weathers and has sailed to Simi, Castelrosso, Scarpanto, Casos and Marmaris to offload stores and personnel. Staff Sergeant Tomsett has carried out his duties at all times most conscientiously and efficiently and his drive and initiative are responsible for his craft being kept in continual operation while away from base for over nine months with no repair facilities other than those provided by himself and his crew. On the 12th November, 1944, at Pagadia Bay, Scarpanto, Staff Sergeant received a request for assistance from the Master of the *Empire Patrol*, whose engines had broken down and the ship was in danger of drifting on some rocks. Staff Sergeant Tomsett immediately took his craft out and after considerable difficulty succeeded in towing the ship to a safe anchorage. Again on the 20th February, 1945, at Casos, Staff Sergeant Tomsett saw a large sailing caique named the *Minevoy* being blown on shore during a gale. He again went to the rescue and towed the caique to a safe anchorage in Armatia Bay, where both craft remained until the gale ceased. *[L.G. 18.10.45]*

SERGEANT EDWARD TUCKER
1917029 WS Sergeant, Royal Engineers
BRITISH EMPIRE MEDAL

Sergeant Tucker landed on the island of Casos on February 4th, 1945, with 660 Artisan Works Company. The task of his unit was to erect camp accommodation for refugees who were being driven from enemy occupied islands by starvation. He immediately inspired the rest of the unit to settle down to hard work in difficult circumstances to provide accommodation for these people. Under his direction stores were ferried ashore in small boats and in very heavy seas. They were landed on a small beach and carried over mountainous tracks to places selected for accommodating these people. Within two days derelict houses were made habitable for some 300 people and the work went on with increased energy until 2,000 people had been accommodated. On March 4th, 1945 he moved with the unit to Scarpanto; there was a dearth of officers in the unit due to the scattered locations. On Scarpanto he organised construction works normally done by his Section Officer. His organisation of the small labour force and small stock of materials was so thorough that a piece of barren ground was turned into a camp for 1,000 refugees in seven days and quickly extended to accommodate 5,000 people. Due to the resource and energy of this non commissioned officer what looked like being an acute problem *i.e.* the housing of refugees streaming from enemy islands was alleviated. *[L.G. 18.10.45]*

Norway

FROM the outbreak of war in 1939, Britain was well aware of the strategic importance of the Scandinavian peninsula and the offshore islands. Narvik and Trondheim were the ports through which Sweden shipped iron ore to her customers, among them, Germany. Narvik and Trondheim were coveted by Admiral Raeder who saw them as ideal bases for his Atlantic raiders and put forward these ideas to Hitler.

Lofoten and Vaagsö produced vast quantities of fish and fish oil, some of which was used to produce glycerine, a valuable ingredient in explosives. Two incidents focused Britain's attention on the aforementioned ports and islands; the Russian invasion of Finland and the German prison ship *Aaltmark* which had taken refuge in Josing Fjord. Over the protests of the Norwegians, the Royal Navy's HMS *Cossack* entered the fjord and rescued the allied prisoners who had been captured during the *Graf Spee's* depredations.

Hitler's hope of a coup by Quislings' Norwegian Nazis failed to take place so, on April 9th, 1940, the Germans invaded Denmark and Norway, quickly overcoming the brave but futile attempts to stop them.

LOFOTEN ISLANDS – 4 MARCH 1941

The force assigned for this operation, commanded by Brig J. C. Haydon, totalled 500 men; 250 from No. 3 Commando (Lt-Col J. F. Durnford-Slater), 250 from No. 4 (Lt-Col D. S. Lister), 52 Royal Engineers demolition experts and 52 Norwegian soldiers.

As the islands lie only 100 miles west of Narvik, it had to be assumed that the force would be attacked by the Germans *en route* or when landing on the islands. Accordingly, five RN destroyers escorted the two troopships.

On March 4th 1941 No. 3 Commando landed at Stamsund and Henningsvaer and No. 4 at Svolvaer and Brettesnes. Eleven fish plants, 800,000 gallons of oil, an electric plant, 18,000 tons of shipping including the 10,000 ton fish factory ship *Hamburg*, were destroyed. 225 Germans were taken prisoners and 300 Norwegians—volunteers for services in British forces—were taken to Britain.

Commando Gallantry Awards of World War II

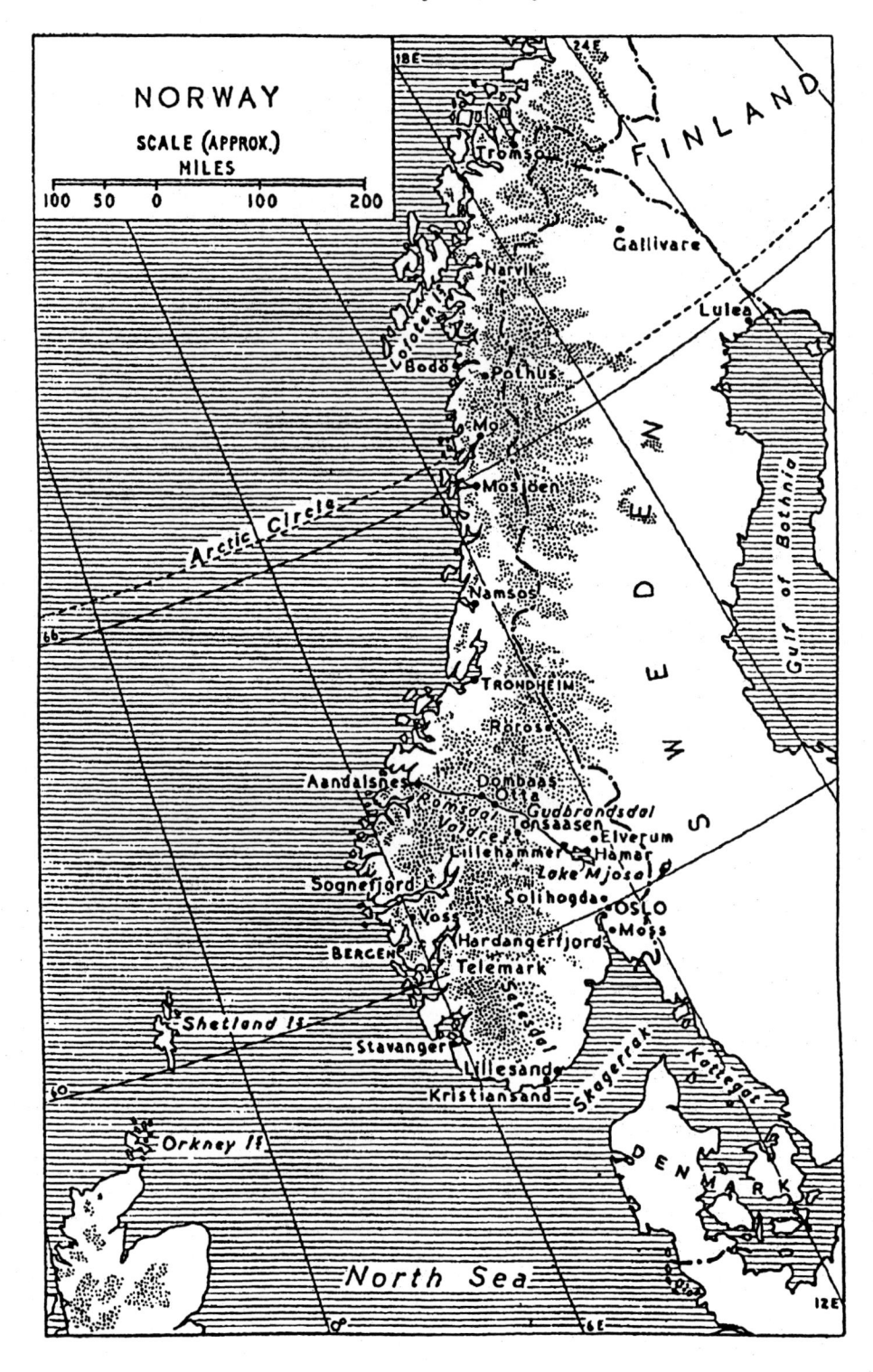

Norway

SECOND RAID ON LOFOTEN – 26 DECEMBER 1941

On Boxing Day, December 26, 1941 a smaller force of 300 under the command of Lt-Col S. S. Harrison was assembled to attack and destroy fish plants or vessels in the villages of Reine and Moskenes on the southernmost island of the Lofoten group.

No. 12 Commando, with 223 men, comprised the bulk of the force and 77 Norwegian volunteers the remainder. Disproportionate to the men engaged the naval force of a landing ship, cruiser, six destroyers plus corvettes and minesweepers appears large. However the Germans had possession of Norway and a spirited resistance was expected.

The Commandos wore white camouflage clothing to be less visible against the snow, but few Germans were present and no opposition was encountered. 29 prisoners were taken, two wireless stations blown up. Along with the prisoners and some 260 Norwegian volunteers, the force returned safely.

VAAGSÖ AND MAALOY – 26 DECEMBER 1941

There were many interesting targets at Vaagsö and Maaloy; coastal defense guns, oil tanks, fish factories, power station and ammunition store, targets worthy of the 600 highly trained members of No. 2 Commando (Major J. M. T. F. Churchill) and No. 3 Commando (Lt-Col J. C. Durnford-Slater) who would carry out a demolition raid on them. They were to be accompanied by detachments of Royal Engineers (No. 6 Commando), Royal Army Medical Corps (No. 4 Commando) and Royal Norwegian Army (Major Linge). A signalling section, War Office intelligence officers and war correspondents completed the force. Ten Royal Air Force bombers and fighter aircraft were to attack nearby airfields and the cruiser HMS *Kenya* with four destroyers would escort the troop carriers, then shell shore installations prior to the landings. The submarine *Tuna* would act as a marker ship.

Sailing on Boxing Day 1941, the force arrived off Maaloy at 7:00 a.m. and the bombardment began. After ten minutes the shelling ceased and Major Churchill, with 105 men from Troops 5 and 6 of No. 3 Commando came ashore to the 'March of the Cameron Men.' Within an hour the German Commanding Officer and 30 men were captured. Maaloy was secured after a bombardment by HMS *Kenya* and all but one of its coastal guns silenced.

As planned, Group 1 had landed on Vaagsö and taken the villages at the south end of the island. Group 2, conversely, in South Vaagsö, were engaged in hand-to-hand fighting for each foot of their

Commando Gallantry Awards of World War II

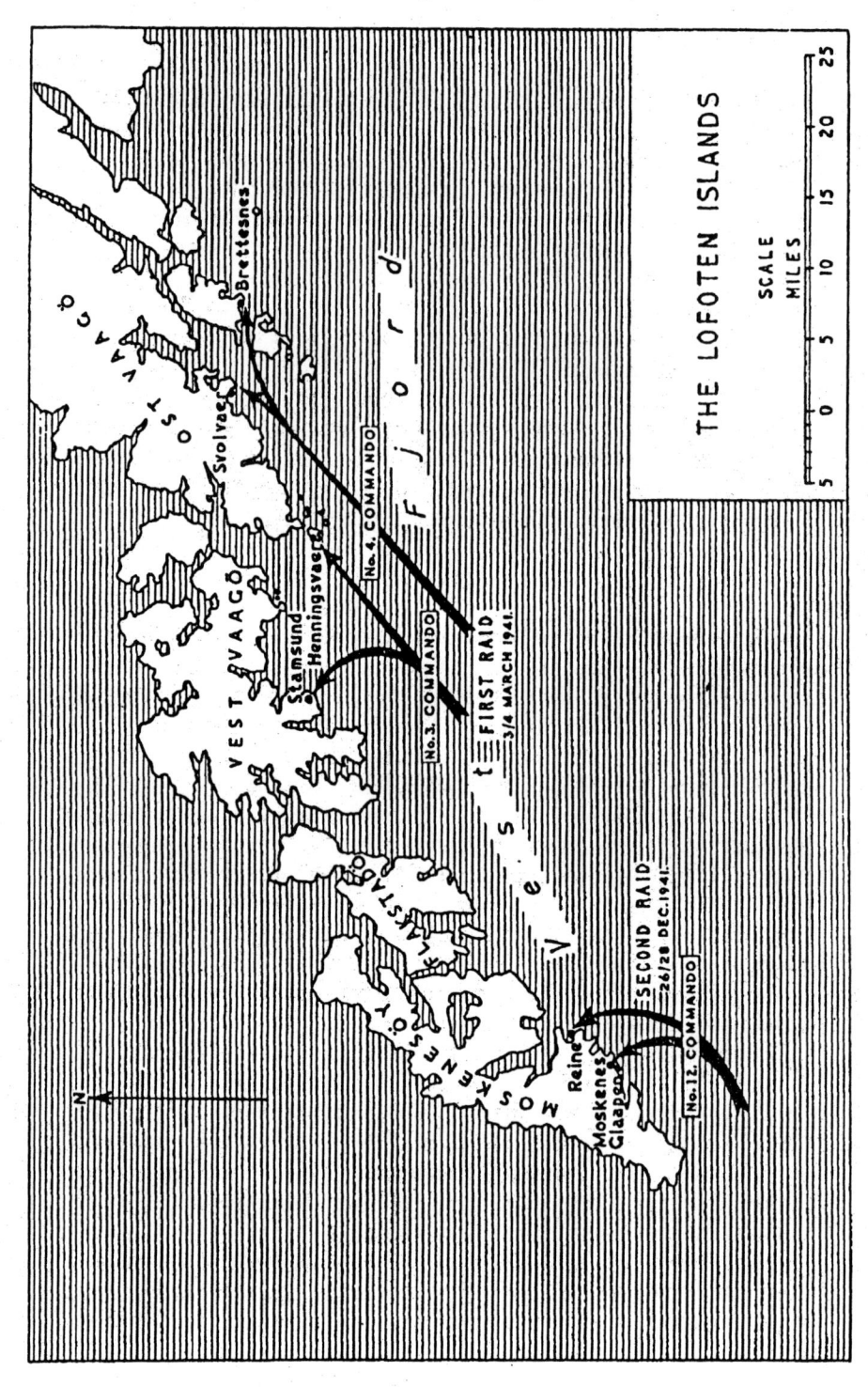

THE LOFOTEN ISLANDS

SCALE MILES
0 5 10 15 20 25

OST VAAGÖ
Brettesnes
Svolvær
VEST VAAGÖ
Henningsvaer
Stamsund
No. 4 COMMANDO
No. 3 COMMANDO
FIRST RAID
3/4 MARCH 1941

FLAKSTAD
MOSKENESÖY
Reine
Moskenes
Glaapsen
SECOND RAID
26/28 DEC. 1941
No. 12 COMMANDO

Vest fjord

N

Norway

objectives. Happily, they were soon reinforced by sections of Group 3 deployed from Maaloy and the reserve unit from Group 4.

Snipers were active and numerous and inflicted several casualties. They were quickly hunted out and killed. Captain Forrester of No. 4 Troop, already wounded, fell on a grenade he was about to throw and was killed. A sniper, refusing to surrender, remained in the house and died as it was set afire.

By early afternoon the battle was over. Many buildings were ablaze, four coastal guns destroyed, all fish-oil factories, barracks and the wireless station were destroyed. Over 100 prisoners were taken and 18,000 tons of shipping sunk.

Probably the most important gain was the capture of the German Naval Code which enabled the navy to 'read' the German mail for many months.

Casualties, considering the ferocity of the defence, were surprisingly low—five killed and 23 wounded. Valuable intelligence was acquired, German morale suffered a severe blow and those who had fought on the day gained valuable experience for their next assignment.

BRIGADIER JOSEPH CHARLES HAYDON, D.S.O., O.B.E.
SS Bde
BAR TO DISTINGUISHED SERVICE ORDER

Brigadier J. C. Haydon was the military force commander for the combined operations against Vaagsö, Norway on 27th December 1941. This operation turned out to be the perfect example of the success that can be achieved by a perfectly planned co-ordinated and executed operation. The credit for the military side must fall entirely to Brigadier Haydon since not only did he plan and execute the operation, but as commander of the Special Service Brigade, was responsible for the training and state of efficiency of the SS Troops, without which this complete success could not have been achieved.

He remained on board the Naval Force Commanders Flagship, under fire, throughout the whole operation and was in the words of the sailors who took part 'an inspiration to all.' *(L.G. 3.4.42)*

Commando Gallantry Awards of World War II

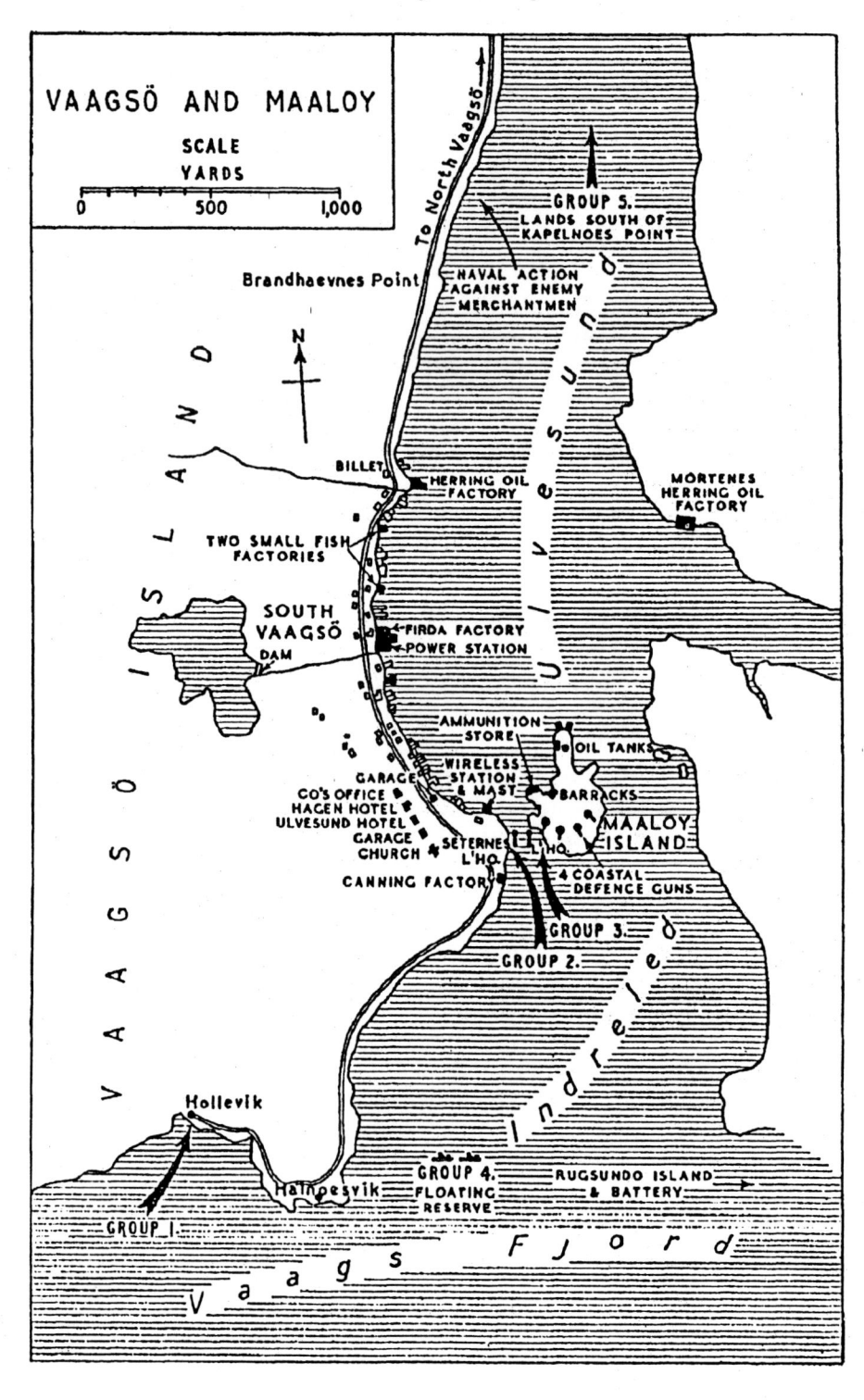

Norway

LIEUTENANT-COLONEL JOHN FREDERICK DURNFORD-SLATER
41090, No. 3 Commando
DISTINGUISHED SERVICE ORDER

Lt-Col J.F. Durnford-Slater was the senior officer ashore during the operations at Vaagsö in Southern Norway on 27th December 1941.

He was in command of the assaults on the Isle of Maaloy at the town of South Vaagsö, and was in immediate charge of the operations ashore following the landing on the latter objective. The task with which he was faced was not easy, the opposition was unexpectedly heavy, and at once developed into house to house fighting. Under such conditions, when it was extremely difficult to maintain effective command over the many independent actions, which were being fought, to gain control of the town in time for the various tasks to be completed.

Lt-Col Durnford-Slater on two occasions went forward to take charge of the situation, only returning to his HQ in order to report progress to the flagship at one period when the street fighting had become very bitter in character, and when the two leading troops had lost five out of six officers and nearly 40% of their effectiveness, he immediately took personal command of the leading troops, reorganised his forces, set the attack in motion again and completed the capture of the town. At this time, any delay or hesitation might have had the most serious results. He was constantly under fire, and both his orderlies were wounded beside him. His personal courage, complete coolness, and quick grasp of the situation were outstanding, throughout the day and rightly inspired complete confidence. As a result all his allotted tasks were completed and the casualties inflicted on the enemy at least doubled those suffered by his own troops from enemy action. He left South Vaagsö in the last craft to put off from any landing place. *(L.G. 3.4.42)*

LIEUTENANT DENIS WILLIAM VENABLES PATRICK O'FLAHERTY, R.A.
106695, Royal Regiment of Artillery
DISTINGUISHED SERVICE ORDER

In recognition of gallant and distinguished services in successful combined operations against the enemy at Vaagsö and Maaloy.
L.G. 3.4.42

Lieutenant Graeme Delamere Black
106240, The South Lancashire Regiment, (The Prince of Wales's Volunteers)
Military Cross
In recognition of gallant and distinguished services in successful combined operations against the enemy at Vaagsö and Maaloy.

L.G. 3.4.42

Temporary Major Francis West Fynn
W/S Capt, 109827, 3rd Bn London Scottish Attached No. 12 Commando & 3 Commando
Military Cross
Operation 'Cartoon.'

Major F. W. Fynn was in command of a force of five Officers and 43 Other Ranks of the Special Service Brigade which landed at Sagvaag Norway on the night of the 23rd–24th January, 1943.

Due to the speed and drive with which the operation was carried out, the main machinery of the pyrite mine at Lillebo and the silo installations at Sagvaag quay were destroyed. In addition, casualties were inflicted on the enemy, three prisoners were taken, four enemy guns destroyed and valuable intelligence material brought back.

The great success of this operation was largely due to the careful planning of Major Fynn, and high qualities of leadership and courage displayed by him during the operation itself.

(L.G. 25.3.43)

Temporary Captain Peter Young
Lieutenant, 77254, Bedfordshire and Hertfordshire Regiment
Military Cross
In recognition of gallant and distinguished services in successful combined operations against the enemy at Vaagsö and Maaloy.

L.G. 3.4.42

Sergeant Roy George Herbert, M.M.
3384201, The Northamptonshire Regt., No. 3 Commando
Distinguished Conduct Medal
During the operations at Vaagsö in South Norway on 27th December 1941, L/Sgt Herbert saw one of the enemy run into a dug-out. He placed his men to cover the entrance and followed the man in alone. He found the German Battery Commander inside with some fifteen of his men whom he captured.

Later he personally bombed the enemy out of the front room of a warehouse, enabling his men to get forward without casualties.

Norway

Throughout the operation he showed great determination, initiative, organising ability and powers if leadership. His personal gallantry and drive set an inspiring example to those under him.

(L.G. 3.4.42)

LANCE SERGEANT RICHARD O'BRIEN
5340890, Royal Berks, att. No. 2 Commando
DISTINGUISHED CONDUCT MEDAL

Sgt O'Brien was one of the detachment of 2 Commando on Operation 'Musketoon.' This highly successful operation resulted in the destruction of the important electric power plant at Glomfjord in Norway on the night of the 20th October, 1942. Sgt O'Brien throughout showed great skill and resolution. He helped reconnoitre the difficult mountain crossing from the landing place to the objective and personally laid the charge which destroyed the pipe-line. He then made his escape, spending, in all, twelve days in enemy-occupied country. When suffering from sickness, privation and exhaustion he showed remarkable endurance and determination. *19.2.43*

CORPORAL ERNEST GERALD WHITE
6941647, No. 3 Commando
DISTINGUISHED CONDUCT MEDAL

Throughout the operations at Vaagsö in South Norway on 27th December 1941, Cpl White displayed leadership of a very high order coupled with a remarkable spirit. When his Troop Commander had been shot, the other officers in his troop put out of action and the Troop Sgt.-Major delayed, Cpl White took command of the remnants of the troop. He carried out a series of assaults and proceeded in destroying a hotel which was manned as a strong point and continued in charge until the end of the operation. He personally accounted for some fourteen of the enemy. His gallantry and leadership were of a high order, and had a direct bearing on the allotted tasks being carried out, within the time limit which had been laid down. *(L.G. 3.4.42)*

LANCE CORPORAL STANLEY BOLDEN
3316568, Camerons (No. 12 Commando), No. 1 Commando
MILITARY MEDAL

Operation 'Cartoon'
L/Cpl Bolden was with the detachment of the Special Service Brigade which landed at Sagvaag, Norway on the night 23rd–24th January, 1943.

Before the actual landing took place, L/Cpl Bolden was wounded in the side, but although in pain, he continued and carried out his duties ably and well. He personally lead a party which cut the communications and was later in charge of a road block party on the Sagvaag–Fitjar Road. Throughout the operation he showed that good leadership and determination upon which a small raid of this nature depends for its success. *(L.G. 25.3.43)*

PRIVATE KENNETH C. DARLINGTON
3605415, Border Regt, No. 12 Commando
MILITARY MEDAL

Operation 'Cartoon.'
Pte Darlington was with a detachment of the Special Service Brigade which landed at Sagvaag, Norway, on the night of the 23rd–24th January, 1943, and was with a party detailed to establish a road block on the road Lervick to Sagvaag.

While maintaining this block, fire was opened on an approaching car which was brought to a halt. Two men escaped from the car, but a third one believed to be an Officer was killed.

Private Darlington under continuous fire from snipers stalked to the car, searched it, and obtained a brief case, a small attaché case and some weapons. His coolness and devotion to duty enabled valuable information to be obtained.

I strongly recommend him for the award of a Military Medal.
[L.G. 25.3.43]

CORPORAL MICHAEL BENEDICT FITZPATRICK
321375, RAC, No. 3 Commando
MILITARY MEDAL

Almost immediately after landing at Vaagsö in South Norway, Cpl Fitzpatrick was acting as leading scout to his section. The advance was held up by a wire obstacle covered by heavy enemy fire. Cpl Fitzpatrick without hesitation moved forward alone and cut a gap through the wire, thus allowing the advance to continue without loss of time.

The moment was somewhat critical as a hold up in the early stages might have had serious delaying affects on the operation as a whole. Cpl Fitzpatrick's coolness and presence of mind quite definitely prevented any such delays occurring. *(L.G. 3.4.42)*

Sicily

PRIMASOLE BRIDGE AND THE PONTE DEI MALATI BRIDGE 10–15 JULY, 1943

In January 1943 the allied leaders had convened the Casablanca conference and there resolved that when the Axis resistance had ended in North Africa, the invasion of Sicily, the stepping stone to Italy, would commence. On July 10th, the invasion began. Allied land, sea and air forces effected the landing, with the Commandos being called upon to carry out the types of unusual tasks at which they had become so proficient.

Those involved in the Sicilian invasion and subsequent actions there were under the command of Brigadier R. E. Laycock and included No. 40 Royal Marine Commando (Lt-Col J. C. Manners), No. 41 Royal Marine Commando (Lt-Col B. J. D. Lumsden) and No. 3 Commando (Major J. F. Durnford-Slater), the latter having been divided into two sections each having three troops, numbered 1–6.

No. 1 ⎫
No. 2 ⎬ Lt-Col P. Young
No. 3 ⎭
No. 4   Lieut B. D. Butler
No. 5   Capt J. B. Pooley
No. 6   Capt Ruxton

The flotilla that was to land No. 40 Commando on the beach at Costellano experienced very heavy seas and landed them 30 minutes late at 03.00 at the wrong beach. That portion of the flotilla carrying No. 41 Commando also erred, taking them into the Canadian 1st Division, and in the ensuing confusion as they sought the correct beach, much valuable equipment was lost. Under fire, they landed and succeeded in overcoming the machine gun posts. Given the strong defences, casualties were slight with nine killed and 37 wounded. Over 100 prisoners were taken.

Troops 4, 5 and 6 of No. 3 Commando (Maj Durnford-Slater) managed a good landing at Scoglio Imbiancato meeting with limited resistance as they landed and began their approach to the heavy batteries they were to destroy. A frontal mortar attack on the batteries, accompanied by blinding parachute flares held the attention of the Italian gun crew who quickly surrendered following

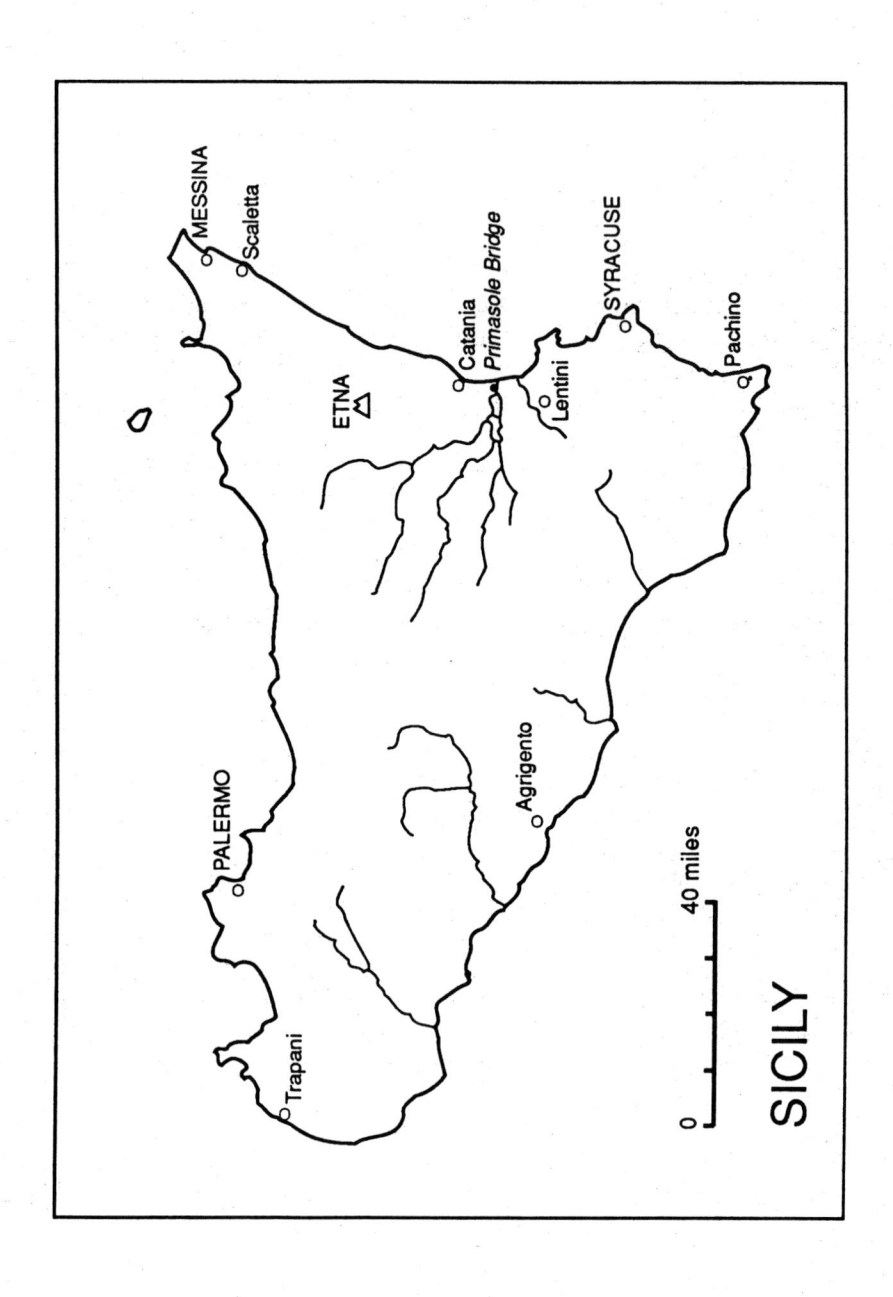

SICILY

Sicily

the Commando's attack with fixed bayonet, and the guns were blown up.

Troops 1, 2 and 3 (Lt-Col Peter Young) had suffered long delays in finding the correct beach, for the flotilla leader confessed he was lost. Ultimately, however, they made their landing and joined up with their colleagues in Troops 4, 5 and 6 who had experienced some heavy fighting during the capture of the gun position.

On July 13th, No. 3 returned to the *Prince Albert,* there to await their next assignment.

Syracuse was essentially now in Allied hands and, although fierce resistance from the Italians and Germans was still ongoing, General Montgomery expected them soon to retreat along a route, Syracuse, Catania then Messina, where they would cross into the 'toe' of Italy at Reggio. On the way they would pass over two bridges; one, two miles north of Lentim was the Ponte Dei Malati which spanned the Leonardo River. Closer to Catania was the second, the Primasole Bridge.

Concerned lest the bridges be destroyed by the retreating enemy, Montgomery decided to drop Paratroops at the Primasole and attempt to block the enemy's escape or their destruction of the bridge. No. 3 Commando, still aboard *Prince Albert,* would effect a landing near the town of Agnone—on the coast about half way between the bridges and ten miles behind the enemy's lines. They then would proceed inland seven miles to the Ponte Dei Malati bridge with similar objectives to those given the Paratroops.

These plans had been hastily conceived at Montgomery's Headquarters in the morning, briefings had taken place and No. 3 Commando were to be landed by 10 p.m. the same day—the Paratroops to be dropped somewhat later near the Primasole Bridge.

At 2130 hrs on July 14th the *Prince Albert* arrived at Agnone with Durnford-Slater and his 160 men, who had escaped disaster when two torpedos narrowly missed the vessel on the way. The group boarded the landing craft and, nearing the shore, came under machine-gun fire from four pill-boxes. Once ashore the defensive wire was cut whilst grenades were being dropped on them from the defenders on the cliff tops. The Commandos returning fire enabled them to move off toward Agnone, with No. 4 Troop (Lieut Butler) in the lead. They found enemy resistance strong in the town but they overcame it and, proceeding toward the bridge, were astonished to have several members of the 1st Paratroop Regiment drop among them. These men had been prematurely dropped, well short of the Primasole Bridge and, wanting to be with their comrades, declined the invitation to remain with 3 Commando and moved on.

No. 3 travelled the three miles to the Ponte Dei Malati Bridge with the object of seizing the pill-boxes at the north end of the bridge, then to take those on the opposite end, holding all until the 8th Army arrived later in the day.

They now were joined by Capt Pooley and his men who had arrived in the second wave at Agnone beach. Casualties were mounting and Parley's group increased the defending force to 350. No. 3 Troop (Capt Nash) was instructed to capture the southern pill-boxes but suffered very severe casualties and his troop was held down by fire directed at their position below the bridge. Expecting a German counter-attack, they had removed the enemy's demolition charges from the bridge.

The Commandos on the north end were now under cannon fire from a Tiger tank which had arrived and wisely remained out of mortar range as it lobbed its 88mm shells at them. In the battle that raged, one young officer, Lieut Cave, fired a PIAT shell at the German ammunition lorry from close range and was killed in its explosion.

Casualties were mounting and there was no sign of the 8th Army's relief force, more 88's and mortars were firing on them and a withdrawal was ordered. Those wounded and too ill to leave were placed in a safer area and individual groups began leaving. Their passage toward Agnone was perilous—many were captured, others killed or wounded, fighting all the way.

The defence of Ponte de Malati bridge had proven very costly; 28 killed, 66 wounded and 60 missing or captured.

Primasole Bridge

Only a third of the Paratroops succeeded in landing at or near the drop zone, for several of the aircraft carrying them were shot down by our own anti-aircraft guns as they approached the coast of Sicily, some became lost and some of the gliders carrying the Paras crashed, other Paras were dropped prematurely, *e.g.* at Agnone. The remaining force was insufficient to hold the Primasole Bridge but they carried out a magnificent defence.

The capture of the north end of the bridge was accomplished rather quickly by Capt Rann and 50 men, and quickly reinforced by about 200 men of the 1st and 3rd Battalions armed with mortars, anti-tank guns and small arms.

Unfortunately, the Germans were reinforcing Catania and some of their paratroops had been dropped near the bridge, thus compounding the problems confronting the defenders. The

Sicily

counter-attack soon began. Anti-tank and mortar fire were no match for cannon-firing Messerschmitts and 88mm guns firing from the Tiger tanks. Although the 8th Army's 4th Armoured Brigade was expected, it had not yet arrived. However, just as night fell a Battalion of the Durham Light Infantry arrived, followed by a Sherman tank, the 4th Armoured Brigade's vanguard. By then the bridge was in German hands and continued so for another day. On July 15th the bridge was retaken and remained thereafter in Allied hands.

The cost to the 1st Parachute Battalion had been high; 27 killed and 78 wounded. The capture and defence of the bridge was an heroic venture and especially so as the Battalion fought with only a third of its force and weapons. Ironically, Montgomery's armies did not reach Catania or Messina over the Ponte Dei Malati bridge or the Primasole bridge but instead fought a longer, more arduous route *via* Etna to reach Messina. He did however, pay an everlasting tribute to No. 3 Commando by renaming the Ponte Dei Malati Bridge Number 3 Commando Bridge, and a plaque citing that fact remains on the bridge to honour the brave defenders.

TEMPORARY LIEUTENANT-COLONEL JOHN FREDERICK DURNFORD SLATER, D.S.O.
WS/Major, 41090, Royal Artillery, O.C. No. 3 Commando
BAR TO DISTINGUISHED SERVICE ORDER
(IMMEDIATE)

Operation Husky (Sicily)
On July 10th and 13th 1943. Lt.-Colonel Durnford Slater carried out two successful operations. The first (10th) which was vital to the safe landing of 5th Division on Beach 44. His task, the destruction of a 5-gun howitzer battery two miles north-east of Cassibile. The second (13th) the capture of a bridge in rear of the enemy lines, vital to the advance of the XIII Corps. In spite of being outclassed in weapons, the Germans employing tanks and heavy mortars, Lt-Col Durnford Slater and his commando having seized the bridge and formed a bridgehead, held on for 18 hours until relief could get through.

Lt-Col Durnford Slater displayed the greatest courage, determination and tenacity. His complete disregard for personal safety proved an inspiration to his men and in the face of heavy casualties he cheered and forced his men to hold on and fight back until relief arrived, thus the bridge being saved from enemy demolition. *[L.G. 21.10.43]*

Commando Gallantry Awards of World War II

TEMPORARY CAPTAIN WILLIAM CUNNINGHAM
Acting Temporary Captain, No. 41 RM Commando
DISTINGUISHED SERVICE ORDER
(IMMEDIATE)

Pachino Peninsula—10th July 1943.
As 'Y' Troop Commander this Officer was responsible for assaulting and capturing the strongpoint 888898.

Owing to weather and mechanical breakdowns only a small portion (eight all ranks) of his troop arrived ashore.

Captain Cunningham lead these men quickly and accurately to the objective and as his bangalore torpedoes were not with him, he succeeded in cutting the surrounding wire and entering the compound from the rear. He was however unable to silence the position from this angle and led an assault round the flank, silencing the position himself with a direct hit through the loophole with a 36 grenade. In doing so he was severely wounded in the arm by a burst of machine gun fire from the position but he remained and mopped up the area killing and capturing many of the enemy. His leadership, especially after a painful wound was an inspiration to all. I consider that less resolute action by this Officer would have resulted in considerable heavier casualties to our troops.

Recommended for MC, awarded Immediate DSO.   (*L.G. 2.11.43*)

ACTING CAPTAIN MICHAEL JARVIS EPHRAUMS, R.M.
Lieutenant
MILITARY CROSS

For gallant and distinguished services in Sicily.   L.G. 2.11.43

TEMPORARY CAPTAIN CHARLES SEARLE HEAD, R.A.
WS/Lieut, 74290, RA, No. 3 Commando
MILITARY CROSS (IMMEDIATE)

On night 13th–14th July 1943, after the landing at Agnone and during the advance to Punta Dei Malati, Captain Head was all the time moving up and down the column exposing himself under fire leading and encouraging the men. At Punta Dei Malati under heavy mortar, machine-gun and shell fire he walked continually in the open from post to post, delivering messages and sighting weapons. He was badly wounded but although unable to walk continued to assist in the withdrawal arrangements. He sent on the men assisting him, so as to avoid having them captured. While lying in the open for the next five or six hours he kept advising and directing parties he saw. After being captured he kept up the spirits of those with him and endeavoured to organise their escape. Later he was recaptured by our troops.

Sicily

Captain Head was also outstanding on the night 9th–10th July during the attack on the Cassibile Battery.
Recommended for DSO, awarded immediate MC.   *[L.G. 21.10.43]*

Temporary Captain Richard Henry Hooper
WS/Lieut, 70956, The Kings Regt, No. 2 Commando
Military Cross
Operation 'Blackcock' Sicily 16th August 1943
Captain R. H. Hooper led his troop, No. 6, with great gallantry and determination in the street fighting in Scaletta village in the early morning of 16th August 1943, which resulted after the commando landing just north of this village. In this action with German troops, he was wounded in the shoulder by a rifle bullet. After his area of the village was cleared, he continued to lead the troop to its correct position, three miles further down the coast. Later, the troop was ordered to march north on the road to Messina, Captain Hooper again leading, until restrained by the medical authorities and removed to the casualty clearing station.

Captain Hooper also took part in the commando raid at Vaagsö and St. Nazaire where he was badly wounded.   *[L.G. 18.11 43]*

Captain Edward Lewis Moore, M.B.
221846, Royal Army Medical Corps, Special Service Troops
Military Cross
In recognition of gallant and distinguished services in Sicily.
L.G. 21.10.43

Ty. Captain John Bertram Vaughan Pooley, R.A.
Lieutenant, 86404, Royal Artillery, Special Service Troops
Military Cross
In recognition of gallant and distinguished services in Sicily.
L.G. 21.10.43

Acting Ty. Captain Henry Ernest Stratford, R.M.
Temporary Lieutenant
Military Cross
For gallant and distinguished services in Sicily.   *L.G. 2.11.43*

Marine/Corporal William Murray
Po.X.106801, No. 41 RM Commando
Distinguished Conduct Medal
Pachino Peninsula 10th July 1943
This NCO was in a leading assault group of 'B' Troop whose duty it was to clear enemy machine gun positions from the cliff edge in

area 8889. Having cleared two posts without much difficulty he encountered considerable opposition from a third post some distance away. As no supporting fire was obtainable because they were on the waters edge, Corporal Murray charged the position with fixed bayonets. Before reaching it he received a hit from a splinter of a hand grenade which penetrated his left eye. He showed an exceptional high sense of duty throughout, continuing to lead the assault, bayoneting two of the enemy himself and then clearing the area capturing four prisoners. Full well knowing that he had lost his eye, his subsequent undaunted courage cheered on his subordinates and is worthy of the highest praise.

[L.G. 7.12.43]

Acting Temporary Corporal Howard Reginald Allen
Marine, Po.X.109393, Provost Coy RMAA & Cdo. Bde
Military Medal (Immediate)

Cpl Allen landed with a reconnaissance party south of Syracuse on the 13th July. At the time of the commencement of the operation he was suffering from an injured eye and knee, but, on being commanded to withdraw from the party, made a special request to be allowed to carry on, which was granted.

During the actual operation he sustained a wound in the upper part of his leg by a bomb splinter, and again, after receiving some medical treatment he proceeded to carry out his duties, although the wound proved very painful. During the whole period this NCO showed the strictest devotion to duty and his courage and endurance was a symbol of encouragement to all ranks.

[L.G. 9.11.43]

Marine Frank Appleyard
Ply.X.106192, 7 Bn RM
Military Medal (Immediate)

Massa Palato, Sicily on 20th July 1943.

This Marine was in 7 Platoon when pinned down in a gully. When the Platoon were evacuating the gully, he remained alone at a turn in the gully and continued firing his rifle every time the snipers fired a burst of machine-gun fire at the troops evacuating wounded. By so doing he diverted attention to himself and undoubtedly greatly increased the chances of the survivors who were carrying the wounded back. Some time after the platoon had been ordered to withdraw, Marine Appleyard returned to the gully to make sure that no wounded on our side had been left behind, and as a result of this further act of bravery was alone for 36 hours without food or water. He had previously gone up the gully to fill the water bottles at a well which was under fire from the enemy, completely disregarding the danger to himself. I consider he showed the greatest courage and gallantry. *[L.G. 16.11.43]*

ACTING TEMPORARY SERGEANT JAMES CROOKS
Po.X.2359 Marine, No. 41 RM Commando
MILITARY MEDAL (IMMEDIATE)

Pachino Peninsula 10th July 1943.
This NCO showed a high standard of courage in leading his section through dug-outs and deep connecting trenches whilst clearing the beach defences. He drove out and destroyed many enemy from the positions whilst being attacked with grenades, and rifle fire from concealed positions dug well underground. His high standard of leadership and courage was responsible for his section completely clearing the area of the enemy personnel who would have otherwise overlooked the beaches from well camouflaged positions and may well have proved very dangerous to follow up troops as their machine guns pointed seawards through apertures in the cliffs. *[L.G. 2.11.43]*

ACTING TEMPORARY SERGEANT RONALD FREWIN DEAN
Ch.X.103144 Ty Cpl, No. 3 RM HAA Regt.
MILITARY MEDAL (IMMEDIATE)

On 21st July 1943, when a 3.7" HAA gun site had a direct hit from a heavy bomb, Sgt Dean was No. 1 of his gun. The bomb landed just clear of the gun pit and completely buried this NCO. When his face had been uncovered he gave orders that he was to be left and that the other buried men were to be cleared first. Whilst still practically buried, he showed coolness and courage in directing the rescue operations and by helping to locate the other members of his crew, although he was suffering from severe eye wounds. When he had been uncovered he refused medical aid until all the remainder had been treated and removed. *[L.G. 9.11.43]*

CORPORAL JOHN DOWLING
4458341, D.L.I., No. 3 Commando
MILITARY MEDAL (IMMEDIATE)

On the night of the 13th–14th July 1943 at Agnone, Cpl Dowling exposed himself fearlessly in the final stages of the invasion of the landing craft while manning a Vickers K Gun. He fired many magazines and accurately directed fire at enemy pill boxes.

On arrival at Punta Dei Malati with his section, he rushed and captured a pill box being wounded during this assault. He continued to operate cheerfully and efficiently showing fine leadership during the disturbance. *(L.G. 21.10.43)*

Marine Joseph Harold Hughes
Po.X.102097, No. 7 Bn, Royal Marines, SBS
Military Medal

Massa Palato, Sicily on 20th July 1943

This Marine wiped out several machine-gun nests and killed several snipers who were holding up the advance by going out alone in the open in daylight with his rifle and grenades, with complete disregard to his own safety. Later he was reported missing, but returned two days later having been behind the enemy lines and captured valuable papers and maps, and made diagrams of enemy dispositions. *[L.G. 16.11 43]*

Corporal Richard Glenville Hughes
5434780, DCLI, No. 3 Commando
Military Medal

At Agnone in Sicily on 13th July 1943, Cpl Hughes showed great courage and determination in the face of vastly superior enemy opposition.

During the Commando withdrawal from the bridgehead, his section was chosen to carry our a rear-guard action to enable the Commando to extricate itself. Casualties had already depleted the section and Cpl Hughes therefore took over the LMG firing it repeatedly with such good effect that the enemy were unable to close.

At last, the enemy succeeded in working round the section's flanks and the Sgt commanding the section gave the order to charge the nearest position in an attempt to disorganise the enemy. Cpl Hughes advanced with the section until it was pinned down by fire from three machine-gun positions. These he engaged one by one with his bren gun and fired so coolly and accurately that he neutralised all three enemy machine-gun positions in turn killing or wounding all of the enemy teams who stayed by their guns. Cpl Hughes continued to fire his gun until all ammunition had been expended, when he was taken prisoner with the remaining survivors of the section. This NCO's skill and cool courage in the face of overwhelming odds was an inspiration to all who saw him and his accurate fire held up the enemy and inflicted heavy casualties. *(L.G. 25.9.47)*

Sicily

Lance Sergeant Edward George King
6911407, No. 3 Commando
Military Medal

On night of 13th–14th July 1943 after the landing at Agnone and during the advance to Punta Dei Malati, Sgt King continually led the HQ Party forward under fire quite regardless of his own safety his only desire being to get forward and engage the enemy. During the fight at Punta Dei Malati and in subsequent withdrawal, Sgt King was continually taking messages and exposing himself under heavy mortar, machine-gun and shell fire. He was of the greatest assistance in organising the withdrawal, always remaining with the rear elements; his steadiness had an inspiring effect on all ranks.

Sgt King was also outstanding in the advance and attack on the Cassibile Battery on night 9th–10th July 1943.   *[L.G. 21.10.43]*

War Subst. Sergeant Albert Edward Myram
Somerset Light Infantry, Indep Coy Gibraltar, No. 2 Cdo.
Military Medal
Operation 'Blackcock' Sicily 16th August 1943.

Pte Myram is serving as a Private in this commando, No. 3 Troop, to which he is attached. He holds the rank of Sgt in the Independent Company of Gibraltar garrison. This man backed up Sgt White, his section sergeant, admirably during the street fighting in Scaletta village on the morning of 16th August 1943. He showed much enterprise and dash in seeking out and killing the German enemy, who were holding buildings in the village, giving no thought to his own safety. Furthermore at all times during the 48 hour operation he showed unbounded energy and enthusiasm and willingness to do all manner of extra duties. He was a fine example to the rest of the rank and file and has been outstanding ever since he became attached to us.   *[L.G. 16.11.43]*

Sergeant Thomas Spears
7266352, RAMC, No. 3 Commando
Military Medal

On the night of 13th–14th July, 1943, during the landing at Agnone and advance on Punta Dei Malati, Sgt Spears remained alone with the Medical Officer for a period of two hours between the arrival of the first and second flights. Some 30 wounded were attended to and Sgt Spears and the MO attacked and silenced an enemy Post. Sgt Spears then joined the second flight and proceeded to Punta Dei Malati. Here he showed outstanding devotion to duty in attending the wounded under intense fire, completely regardless of his own safety. During the withdrawal he again attended to several men under heavy and accurate air-burst high explosive

[L.G. 21.10.43]

Lance Sergeant George Taylor
831819, RA, No. 3 Commando
Military Medal

At Agnone on 13th–14th July, 1943, Sgt Taylor's LCA grounded on a rock 50 yards out. He swam ashore under intense fire and joined his troop. During the advance he was continually in the lead engaging enemy posts. At Punta Dei Malati he was outstanding in an advance under heavy fire. He continually showed a fine offensive spirit and complete disregard of personal safety.

[L.G. 21.10.43]

Lance Sergeant John E. White
2620077, Grenadier Guards, No. 2 Commando
Military Medal

Sgt White was Section Sergeant of No. 1 Section No. 3 Troop 2 Commando. He showed excellent leadership and military ability in the clearing of houses in the village of Scaletta on the morning of 16th August:1943 showing complete disregard of his personal safety, yet making use of cover that was available as opportunity offered. Later in the day, he continued to show much energy and determination in keeping the section together and moving well, in arduous cross-country movement through the hill country northwest of the Catania–Messina road. [L.G. 18.11.43]

Italy

OPERATION 'DEVON,' TERMOLI – 2/3 OCTOBER 1943

As the German forces, retreating before the 8th Army, moved northward through Italy they endeavoured periodically to consolidate their forces and hold firm at various strategically located points in order to delay the advancing 8th. By mid-September they had reached the Bifurno River a few miles south of the town of Termoli on Italy's Adriatic coast and established a defensive position.

It was reasoned that if a successful seaborne landing could be made at Termoli and the port and town held until reinforcements arrived the advancing Germans could be trapped or turned westward. Plans were hurriedly made and orders issued for an attack on Termoli on October 2nd-3rd by the following forces:

22nd Landing Craft Flotilla (Lt-Cdr Lammert, RNVR)
No. 3 Commando (Capt A. G. Komrower)
No. 40 Royal Marine Commando (Lt-Col J. C. Manners)
Special Raiding Squadron (Major P. Mayne)

The flotilla carrying the force sailed at noon October 2nd, covering the 120-mile journey without any enemy contact, landed unopposed and established their bridgehead and headquarters. That morning—October 3rd—Termoli was under the control of the Commandos. No. 40 (RM) Commando and the Special Raiding Squadron advanced to positions outside Termoli in anticipation of German counter-attacks, and in the process the Special Raiding Squadron linked up with elements of the 78th Division and greatly reinforced a defensive perimeter now stood between the town and the roads from which the Germans could be expected.

The attack came on the morning of the 5th when enemy aircraft bombed and strafed the defenders. By noon they were being shelled and German tanks had forced some positions to withdraw. Lt-Col Chavasse succeeded in making wireless contact with an artillery regiment and the air force. The combination of shelling and air attacks kept the tanks at bay. It was only a short reprieve, for by late afternoon enemy tanks and infantry were attacking the positions held by No. 3 Commando. The infantry were machine-gunned but, as night was upon them, the tank commanders stopped for the night just short of Termoli.

AUSTRIA
SWITZERLAND
HUNGARY
Danube
Drava
Sava
Brenner Pass
MILAN
Po
TURIN
TRIESTE
VENICE
Adige
GENOA
BOLOGNA
RAVENNA
FRANCE
YUGOSLAVIA
ADRIATIC SEA
ITALY
ANCONA
LEGHORN
PERUGIA
ELBA
ORVIETO
Corsica
PESCARA
ROME
Tiber
Liri
CASSINO
FOGGIA
ANZIO
GAETA
Garigliano
Volturno
NAPLES
SALERNO
BARI
BRINDISI
TARANTO
Sardinia
TYRRHENIAN SEA
CAGLIARI
MESSINA
TRAPANI
PALERMO
REGGIO
CATANIA
SYRACUSE
PANTELLERIA
ALGERIA
TUNISIA
LINOSA
LAMPEDUSA
MALTA (Br)
0
MILES
200

Italy

At this point Durnford-Slater ordered the outlying units into Termoli.

Meanwhile, offshore, two destroyers of the Royal Navy had supported the landing of another brigade and were shelling the German positions, aided by allied fighter aircraft.

By October 8th German resistance was overcome and they were again in retreat. The valuable port was secured.

Taking, and holding, Termoli was one of the Commandos' most notable actions of the war, but the price paid was 32 killed, 85 wounded and 23 missing.

Temporary Corporal Thomas Peck Hunter
Ch.X.110296 Royal Marines (attached Special Service Troops) (43rd Royal Marine Commando)

Victoria Cross

Admiralty – Whitehall – 12th June 1945.
The KING has been graciously pleased to approve the award of the VICTORIA CROSS for valour to:—
The late Corporal (temporary) Thomas Peck HUNTER, Ch.X. 110296 Royal Marines (attached Special Service Troops) (43rd Royal Marine Commando) (Edinburgh).

In Italy during the advance by the Commando to its final objective, Corporal Hunter of "C" Troop was in charge of a Bren group of the leading sub-section of the Commando. Having advanced to within 400 yards of the canal, he observed the enemy were holding a group of houses south of the canal. Realising that his Troop behind him were in the open, as the country was completely devoid of cover, and that the enemy would cause heavy casualties as soon as they opened fire, Corporal Hunter seized the Bren Gun and charged alone across two hundred yards of open ground. Three Spandaus from the houses, and at least six from the North bank of the canal opened fire and at the same time the enemy mortars started to fire at the Troop.

Corporal Hunter attracted most of the fire, and so determined was his charge and his firing from the hip that the enemy in the houses became demoralised. Showing complete disregard for the intense enemy fire, he ran through the houses, changing magazines as he ran, and alone cleared the houses.

Six Germans surrendered to him and the remainder fled across a footbridge onto the North bank of the canal.

The Troop dashing up behind Corporal Hunter now became the target for all the Spandaus on the North of the canal. Again, offering himself as a target, he lay in full view of the enemy on a heap of rubble and fired at the concrete pillboxes on the other side. He again drew most of the fire, but by now the greater part of the Troop had made for the safety of the houses. During this period he shouted encouragement to the remainder, and called only for more Bren magazines with which he could engage the Spandaus. Firing with great accuracy up to the last, Corporal Hunter was finally hit in the head by a burst of Spandau fire and killed instantly.

There can be no doubt that Corporal Hunter offered himself as a target in order to save his Troop, and only the speed of his movement prevented him being hit earlier. The skill and accuracy with which he used his Bren gun is proved by the way he demoralised the enemy, and later did definitely silence many of the Spandaus firing on his Troop as they crossed open ground, so much so that under his covering fire elements of the Troop made their final objective before he was killed.

Throughout the operation his magnificent courage, leadership and cheerfulness had been an inspiration to his comrades.

[L.G. 12.6.45]

TEMPORARY MAJOR ANDERS FREDERICK EMIL VICTOR SCHAU LASSEN, M.C.
234907, General List.

Victoria Cross

War Office – 7th September 1945.
The KING has been graciously pleased to approve the posthumous award of the VICTORIA CROSS to:—
Major (temporary) Anders Frederick Emil Victor Schau LASSEN, M.C. (234907) General List.

In Italy, on the night of 8th / 9th April, 1945, Major Lassen was ordered to take out a patrol of one officer and seventeen other ranks to raid the north shore of Lake Comacchio.

His tasks were to cause as many casualties and as much confusion as possible, to give the impression of a major landing, and to capture prisoners. No previous reconnaissance was possible, and the party found itself on a narrow road flanked on both sides by water.

Preceded by two scouts, Major Lassen led his men along the road towards the town. They were challenged after approximately 500 yards from a position on the side of the road. An attempt to allay suspicion by answering that they were fishermen returning home failed, for when moving forward again to overpower the

Italy

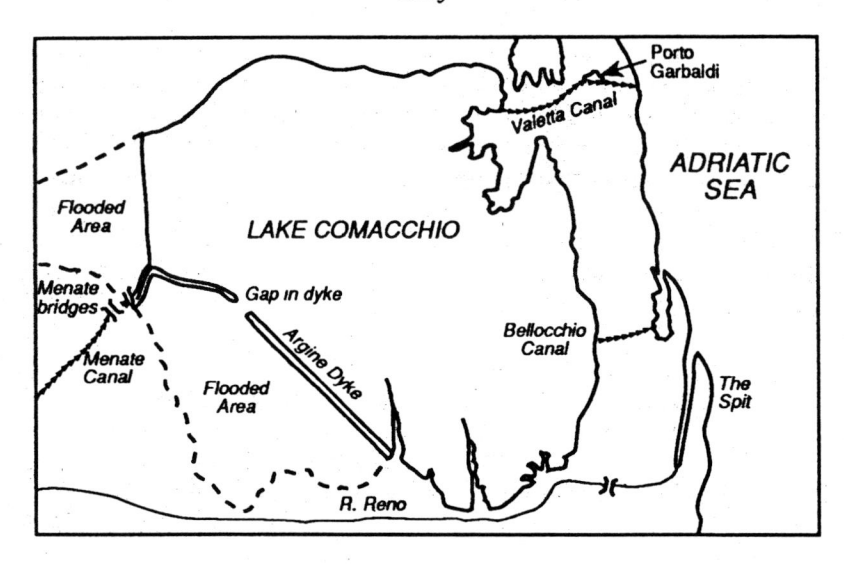

sentry, machine gun fire started from the position, and also from two other blockhouses to the rear.

Major Lassen himself then attacked with grenades, and annihilated the first position containing four Germans and two machine guns. Ignoring the hail of bullets sweeping the road from three enemy positions, an additional one having come into action from 300 yards down the road, he raced forward to engage the second position under covering fire from the remainder of the force. Throwing in more grenades he silenced this position which was then overrun by his patrol. Two enemy were killed, two captured and two more machine guns silenced.

By this time the force had suffered casualties and its fire power was very considerably reduced. Still under a heavy cone of fire Major Lassen rallied and reorganised his force and brought his fire to bear on the third position. Moving forward himself he flung in more grenades, which produced a cry of "Kamerad." He then went forward to within three or four yards of the position to order the enemy outside, and to take their surrender.

Whilst shouting to them to come out he was hit by a burst of spandau fire from the left of the position and he fell mortally wounded, but even whilst falling he flung a grenade, wounding some of the occupants and enabling his patrol to dash in and capture this final position.

Major Lassen refused to be evacuated as he said it would impede the withdrawal and endanger further lives, and as ammunition was nearly exhausted the force had to withdraw.

By his magnificent leadership and complete disregard for his own personal safety, Major Lassen had, in the face of overwhelming superiority, achieved his objects. Three positions were wiped out, accounting for six machine guns, killing eight and wounding others of the enemy, and two prisoners were taken. The high sense of devotion to duty and the esteem in which he was held by the men he led, added to his own magnificent courage, enabled Major Lassen to carry out all the tasks he had been given with complete success. *[L.G. 4.9.45]*

Ty. Captain Bernard James Barton, M.C.
Lieutenant, 134120, Reconnaissance Regiment, Royal Armoured Corps, Special Service Troops
Distinguished Service Order
In recognition of gallant and distinguished services in Italy.
L.G. 20.7.44

Temporary Lieutenant-Colonel John Malcolm Thorpe Churchill, M.C.
WS/Major, 34657, The Manchester Regiment, No. 2 Cdo.
Distinguished Service Order
The Gulf of Salerno September 8th–18th 1943.
Lt-Col Churchill commanded No. 2 Commando during the opposed landing in Marina Bay in the early hours of September 9th and throughout the subsequent actions at Vietri on September 10th, the Molina defile on 12th–13th September and at Piegolette on 15–16th September

In the initial assault Lt-Col Churchill landed with the first flight of the attacking troops. He organised and led personally the attack on a German 4-gun battery.

From 9th–13th September Lt-Col Churchill on several occasions led counter-attacks against enemy infiltration into his positions. By his cool courage and complete disregard of danger he personally inspired his men, exhausted as they were, to hold the position. During this period he found a badly wounded man whom he and his Adjutant carried back under fire on a rucksack to cover behind a ridge some 250 yards away.

On the night of 15th–16th September Lt-Col Churchill organised the advance of his Commando up the Piegolette Valley, personally directing the advance by leading the right hand troop which had only one newly-joined subaltern left.

On reaching the objective he went forward with one man into the village in which the enemy were sniping and throwing hand grenades. Although the bright moonlight made movement in the

Italy

streets dangerous, his disregard of danger resulted in the capture of over 100 prisoners.

Subsequently the captured position was heavily attacked under cover of intense machine-gun and mortar fire. Lt-Col Churchill at once left his headquarters and visited each troop post in turn proceeding alone in order not to endanger the lives of others. Throughout the day Lt-Col Churchill supervised our successful efforts to hold the determined onslaught on the enemy continually visiting our exposed positions.

All through the following night he remained on duty directing artillery and mortar fire onto the enemy patrols which were seeking to turn our position by the wooded valleys.

When dawn broke Lt-Col Churchill had again had no sleep for 36 hours, had personally led two long and heavily opposed attacks and had inspired our troops to beat off all attempts by the enemy to penetrate the positions.

It is beyond any doubt that Lt-Col Churchill's gallantry tilted the scales of battle on more than one occasion.

The magnetic power of his personal leadership frequently rallied his exhausted troops when they could scarcely stagger forward. His powers of endurance and the cool and unflinching manner in which he exposed himself to danger so that he seemed to bear a charmed life were unquestionably a brilliant inspiration ranking with the highest traditions of the British Army.

Recommended for VC, awarded DSO. [L.G. 13.1.44]

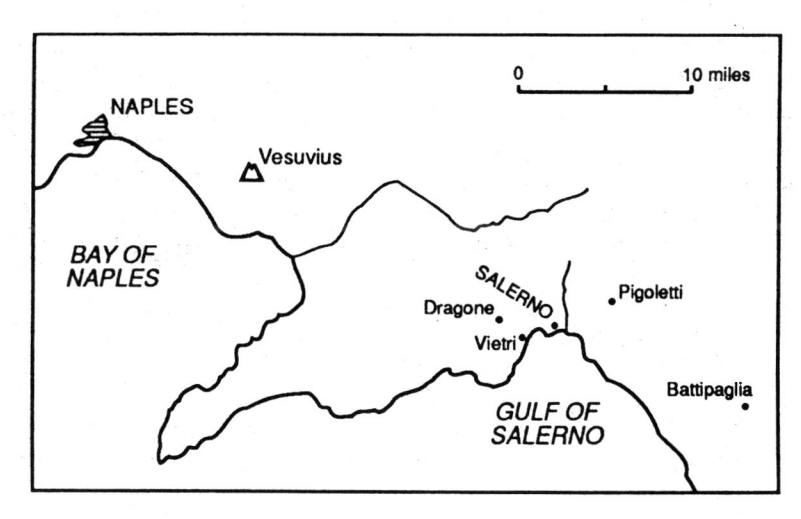

Ty. Captain Arthur Geoffrey Komrower
WS/Lieut, 75236, Lancashire Fusiliers, No. 3 Commando
Distinguished Service Order
(Immediate)

During the period 4th–6th October 1945 this officer was in command of No. 3 Commando who were holding a forward position west of Termoli. During this period the Commando was continually under heavy mortar and machine gun fire. During the early afternoon of 5th October the infantry on the Commando's left flank withdrew, through and to the left of the position, leaving the Commando completely isolated. Later in the afternoon the Commando was strongly attacked on three sides by tanks and infantry, some tanks approaching to within a few hundred yards of the position and concentrating devastating high explosive and machine-gun fire on the area. When darkness fell enemy infantry had also infiltrated to the rear of the position, and on two sides were within two hundred yards. Throughout this period the Commando held firm, with its position intact and its morale unshaken. This was in great part due to Captain A. G. Komrower's great gallantry and devotion to duty: he moved about the forward positions under intense shell and machine-gun fire instilling confidence into the troops by his cheerful manner. His complete disregard for personal safety, and his determination to [hole in paper] the enemy at all costs set a fine example to the troops. Later that night it was discovered that the nearest positions of our own troops were three quarters of a mile to our rear.

Early in the morning of 6th October when ordered to withdraw by the Brigade Commander, he conducted a most orderly withdrawal in face of the enemy without losing a man. Throughout this very difficult period, with a continuous flow of casualties, when all other units had withdrawn, this officer by his leadership inflicted heavy casualties on the enemy, and held with his small force of one hundred and forty men a vital position against strong attacks by the 16 Panzer Division. *[L.G. 27.1.44]*

Acting Lieutenant-Colonel James Calvert Manners, r.m.
Captain
Distinguished Service Order

For gallant and distinguished services in operations leading to the capture of Termoli. *L.G. 8.2.44*

Italy

ACTING LIEUT.-COLONEL IAN HURRY RICHES, R.M.
Captain, Brevet Major
DISTINGUISHED SERVICE ORDER
For outstanding courage, determination and devotion to duty in operations during the campaign in Italy. *L.G. 10.7.45*

CAPTAIN DAVID ARTHUR BLAIR
73177, Seaforth Highlanders §
MEMBER OF THE ORDER OF THE BRITISH EMPIRE
Captured at El Adem on 26th June 1942. Imprisoned in Campo 21 (Chiete). After the Armistice the SBO refused to allow prisoners of war to escape, and the camp was taken over by the Germans who removed the prisoners of war to Germany. Capt Blair had been working on a tunnelling scheme, of which there were several in the camp and hid with five others in the tunnel for 36 hours. They came out after the Germans had left, made their way south, and arrived in British hands on 13th October 1943. *[L.G. 27.4.44]*

TEMPORARY MAJOR PETER YOUNG, D.S.O., M.C.
Captain, 77254, The Bedfordshire and Hertfordshire Regiment, Special Service Troops
SECOND BAR TO MILITARY CROSS
In recognition of gallant and distinguished services in Italy.
L.G. 13.1.44

TEMPORARY CAPTAIN LESLIE STEWART CALLF, M.C.
WS/Lieut, 138421, Royal West Kents, No. 9 Commando
BAR TO MILITARY CROSS (IMMEDIATE)
Captain Callf has served with this unit during the whole period it has operated in Italy since November 1943 and has taken part in all actions which the unit has fought.

Throughout all actions this officer has shown outstanding powers of leadership and fighting ability, and his personal courage and disregard for danger have always been of the highest order. During a landing carried out by the unit behind the enemy lines on the Garigliano (Map Ref. Italy 1/25,000 Sh 171–1 south-west Force Del Garigliano (780932) on 29th–30th December 1943, Captain Callf led his troop through a minefield to reconnoitre advanced positions from which the remainder of the unit could subsequently advance. Although it was night and mines could not be detected or lifted, Captain Callf personally selected an area by means of trial and error, in which the unit could form up.

During an attack by the unit at Monte Faita (Map Ref. Italy 1/50,000 Sh No. 160 II square 8503) on night 2nd–3rd February 1944, Captain Callf commanded the leading troop and although 50% casualties of all ranks was suffered from enemy artillery and mortar fire he continued to lead his troop in the attack until the final objective was captured. During the subsequent withdrawal this officer organised an effective rearguard which prevented the considerably depleted main force from being overwhelmed by a counter-attack. During operations in the Anzio beach-head from 2nd–26th March 1944, Captain Callf at all times led his troop in a succession of actions, the success of which were almost entirely due to his outstanding leadership, courage and determination. Captain Callf's military character is of the highest order, his gallant efficient and courageous conduct in action has at all times been an inspiration and example to men under his command, and he has always displayed the finest qualities of a first class officer.

[L.G. 21.9.44]

Acting Temporary Captain Lionel Guy Bradford Marshall, M.C., R.M.
Temporary Lieutenant
Bar to Military Cross

For courage, leadership and resource in operations which led to the crossing of the Garigliano River in the face of determined opposition from the enemy.   *L.G. 18.4.44*

Ty. Captain Michael Rhys Harvey Allen
W/Lieutenant, 76441, Black Watch attached No. 9 Cdo.
Military Cross (Immediate)

Action at Monte Faito night 2nd–3rd February 1944, Map Ref. 858043, Italy 1:50,000 Sheet 160–II.
During this action Capt Allen was adjutant of No. 9 Commando, when the Commando was caught in a gully and came under very heavy and accurate mortar and artillery fire from which very heavy casualties including both the C.O. and second in command were caused. Capt Allen at once took over command and reorganised all available forces and personally directed operations. Owing to the number of officer and NCO casualties, had it not been for the promptness of Capt Allen in taking the situation in hand, considerable disorganisation might have occurred. Capt Allen then conducted a short withdrawal under fire and organised the Commando in a defensive position. Later again on the evacuation of the C.O. Capt Allen again took over command. Throughout the whole operation Captain Allen showed great powers of

Italy

leadership and set a magnificent example. In the Commando operations on the Garigliano River on night 29th–30th December and during Operation 'Shingle' Capt Allen showed exemplary courage, leadership and determination. *[L.G. 29.6.44]*

ACTING TY. CAPTAIN DAVID SOLOMON BARNETT, R.M.
Temporary Lieutenant
MILITARY CROSS

For outstanding courage, determination and devotion to duty in operations during the campaign in Italy. *L.G. 10.7.45*

LIEUTENANT PAUL BASSETT-WILSON
165718, Royal Inniskilling Fusiliers, Special Service Troops
MILITARY CROSS

In recognition of gallant and distinguished services in Italy.
L.G. 20.7.44

ACTING TY. CAPTAIN JOHN PHILIP BLAKE, R.M.
Temporary Lieutenant
MILITARY CROSS

For leadership, gallantry and devotion to duty while serving with Royal Marine Commandos in Italy. *L.G. 27.6.44*

TY. CAPTAIN JOHN WILLIAM EVANCE BRADLEY
A/Ty Capt (Ty/Lieut.), SS Bde, 13th Corps, No. 40 RM Cdo.
MILITARY CROSS (IMMEDIATE)

Termoli 3rd October 1943

Captain Bradley was commanding Q Troop the leading troop in the advance through Termoli. At the Railway bridge he came under heavy fire from the houses in the vicinity. Very heavy fighting ensued and about 30 Germans were captured including a headquarters. Later he was wounded by a mortar bomb in the arm and chest but carried on in command until ordered to the regimental aid post. Throughout the action Captain Bradley was an inspiration to his troop. He showed great courage. In spite of wounds he fought his troop out of a position surrounded by Germans and withheld some three counter-attacks. *[L.G. 8.2.44]*

ACTING CAPTAIN LESLIE STUART CALLF
138421, R.W.K., No. 9 Commando
MILITARY CROSS (IMMEDIATE)

Ref Map—Italy 1/25,000 Sheet 158 IV SE

On 2nd March 1944 the troop under Command of Capt Callf was ordered to clear a wadi in square 8230 which had been occupied by the Boche, and which threatened the maintenance of the forward positions of the unit which occupied this particular part of the line.

Although the enemy held this wadi in considerable strength, particularly the surrounding high ground which dominated the whole area, Capt Callf led his troop into a most determined assault which finally drove the Boche completely out of his positions, thereby closing a dangerous gap in our own lines. As a result of this action it was officially reported that enemy casualties were 23 prisoners of war and 25 killed, these figures being approximately twice the strength of the whole of Capt Callf's Troop.

It is considered that the success of this action was almost entirely due to this officer's most courageous and determined leadership, as the action was carried out approximately six hours after the unit had disembarked in the Anzio beach-head and before he had any opportunity to carry out a reconnaissance under normal conditions. What reconnaissance Capt Callf was able to do was done under heavy enemy fire, and it was chiefly due to his personal courage and disregard for his own safety whilst doing the reconnaissance, and to his outstanding leadership and determination during the attack, that his troop was able to carry out a difficult task on ground which it had never seen or operated on before. Throughout the action, this officer's gallant and courageous conduct was an example and inspiration to his men, and he displayed the finest qualities of a first class officer. *[L.G. 20.7.44]*

Ty. Captain Ralph Alverne Cyril Cameron
WS/Lieut, 99223, No. 9 Commando
Military Cross (Immediate)
West of Garigliano River on the night of 29th–30th December 1943.
This officer was in command of a force of two troops whose task was to destroy an enemy post near a demolished bridge. He brought his force through a most difficult area of floods and minefields, and led a successful attack on the position. By the time all enemy resistance had been mopped up it was nearly daylight, and Captain Cameron, realising that it would be impossible to withdraw across the river further down, as planned, organised a crossing at the broken bridge. In spite of enemy mortar fire on the bridge, and the absence of any bridging equipment except for one damaged rubber boat, the whole force, including prisoners and wounded, crossed the river with the loss of only one life. This was due to Captain Cameron's excellent organisation and his imperturbable conduct under fire. *[L.G. 4.5.44]*

Italy

CAPTAIN EDWARD JOHN D'ARCY
WS/Captain, 173842, RAMC, No. 9 Commando
MILITARY CROSS (IMMEDIATE)

Action at Monte Faita, night 2nd–3rd February 1944, Map Ref. 858043, Italy, 1/50,000 Sheet 160 II.

During this action, the unit suffered heavy casualties including 50% of all officers and approximately 30% other ranks. After one of the final objectives had been captured the Commando was ordered to withdraw as the position was considered untenable owing to increasing casualties from continuous artillery and mortar fire. This officer, who is the unit's Medical Officer, insisted on remaining behind until he had done everything possible to arrange for the evacuation of our casualties. He remained behind in full view of the enemy and in continuous danger from mortar fire until all casualties who could be carried were evacuated to our own lines. Captain D'Arcy attended to the wounded during their withdrawal under most harassing conditions and through difficult and mountainous country for a distance of several miles until he was physically exhausted. For the next twelve hours he continued to deal with casualties in a position which was continuously being shelled, and showed the utmost courage and determination and exemplary leadership to his medical staff.

Throughout the action he displayed complete disregard for his own safety in order to attend the wounded.   *[L.G. 29.6.44]*

ACTING CAPTAIN MICHAEL ALFRED WILLIAM DAVIES
253496, Northamptons, No. 9 Commando
MILITARY CROSS (IMMEDIATE)

Ref Map—Italy 1/25,000 sheet 158 IV SE.

This officer holds the appointment of Adjutant of this unit which took part in the attack on wadi in square 8230 on 19th March 1944. In this action the unit drove the Boche from his positions in this wadi, and held this position during the day until the final withdrawal the following night. Whilst the position was occupied by the Commando, the Boche delivered a succession of counter-attacks, culminating in a strong attack at last light immediately prior to our withdrawal, which were all repulsed.

Owing to the nature of the ground and the necessity for sending out continual patrols to keep the Boche at a distance, a considerable part of the line of defence had to be held by Commando HQ personnel, who were under command of Capt Davies. Later on in the day the only officer of another troop was killed, and command of this troop was also taken over by Capt Davies. Throughout the day he continuously organised the defences of the sector under his charge which were being steadily depleted by snipers, as well as carrying out in a most efficient manner his other duties as Adjutant.

At last light a very strong Boche counter-attack was delivered into our position, the main force of the attack falling on the sector held by the men under Capt Davies's command. Immediately the attack started, this officer rallied his men in a magnificent manner, and personally led them in an assault which drove the Boche well back from our own positions into his original forming up area. Capt Davies was seen and heard to be personally leading every charge which finally resulted in the Boche attack being completely broken after fierce hand-to-hand engagements. Throughout these engagements Capt Davies was at all times involved where the fighting was fiercest, personally leading his men and taking part in hand-to-hand fighting. His presence, and the gallant and courageous manner in which he continually rallied his men, some of whom had never been in action before, was an inspiration to the whole unit, and his gallant conduct and splendid leadership was entirely responsible for the defeat of the Boche counter-attack.

Throughout the whole action, Capt Davies showed utter disregard for his own safety, as he was always seen to be fighting in those positions where enemy penetration would have caused a critical situation. His personal courage and determined leadership was an inspiration to all ranks, and it is considered that had he not completely dominated the fighting in his sector so that the enemy attack was thoroughly beaten, the whole position might have been over-run by the enemy.

Capt Davies showed the highest possible standard of fearlessness and courage, and his conduct was of the highest order throughout the whole action.
Recommended for DSO, awarded MC. [L.G. 20.7.44]

TY. CAPTAIN PHILIP RUSSELL RENDELL DUNNE
Lt, 30978, Royal Horse Guards, att Special Service Troops
MILITARY CROSS
In recognition of gallant and distinguished services in Italy.
L.G. 13.1.44

ACTING TY. CAPTAIN EDWARD WILLIAM ECREPONT
Temporary Lieutenant, Royal Marines.
MILITARY CROSS
For leadership, gallantry and devotion to duty while serving with Royal Marine Commandos in Italy. *L.G. 27.6.44*

Italy

2ND LIEUTENANT WILLIAM GORDON FIELDING
264688, 1st Bn The Royal Irish Fusiliers, No. 6 Commando
MILITARY CROSS (IMMEDIATE)

At Maletto on 12th August 1943 this officer was in command of a Platoon of 'D' Company which was engaged in clearing the village. After clearing the northern corner, 2/Lieut Fielding moved forward to some rising ground and located a party of eight Germans. Calling for volunteers he quickly formed a small combat group of six men and proceeded to attack. The Germans scattered, one was captured and one shot and the remaining six ran to a culvert under a railway and opened fire with an MG 34. During this attack two of 2/Lieut Fielding's party were killed and the three others became involved in a fire fight with a party of Germans some distance off. On being fired on 2/Lieut Fielding snatched a rifle and replied to the fire, then, crawling forward alone across open ground he reached bombing range of the culvert and threw in his grenades, seriously wounding two Germans including the unteroffizier. Although by now he had run out of ammunition and grenades he dashed forward to the culvert and pointing his empty rifle at the Germans called on them to surrender and after some parleying they emerged reluctantly. By this time another man came up and assisted 2/Lieut Fielding to round up the six Germans. During the whole period 2/Lieut Fielding was under fire from snipers and a machine gunner from a point further to the north.

The dash and fearless leadership shown by 2/Lieut Fielding in accounting for this party of Germans so successfully was beyond all praise. *[L.G. 18.11.43]*

TY. MAJOR BRIAN FORSTER MORTON FRANKS
WS/Capt, 89085, R. Signals (Middx Yeomanry), HQ SS Bde
MILITARY CROSS (IMMEDIATE)
Termoli Italy 3rd–7th October 1943

At Termoli between October 3rd and 7th Major Franks carried out the duties of Brigade Major SS Brigade. Throughout the period this officer showed a fine sense of initiative and complete disregard of personal danger. Early on he saw movement in the station and went forward by himself and captured two German soldiers. Later he was continually visiting the most forward troops making any necessary adjustments and exposing himself fearlessly. During the critical counter-attacks period his personal example and steadiness were an example to all ranks and did much to save the situation, particularly on the extreme right, where he personally organised and placed the troops. He was continually leading and encouraging

the men and his resolute manner and confidence were a most important factor.
Recommended for DSO, awarded MC. [*L.G. 27.1.44*]

LIEUTENANT ROBERT ROY GIBSON
155079, The Cheshire Regiment, Special Service Troops
MILITARY CROSS

In recognition of gallant and distinguished services in Italy.
L.G. 13.1.44

TY. MAJOR PETER WILLIAM CRADOCK HELLINGS
Capt, No. 40 Royal Marine Commando
MILITARY CROSS (IMMEDIATE)

Termoli, Italy, 3rd–7th October 1943

At Termoli from October 3rd to 7th Major Hellings was Second-in-Command No. 40 (RM) Commando. His first task was to capture the port and neighbouring buildings. He showed great skill and initiative during this phase and his party killed and captured a considerable number of enemy. Later, during the critical counter-attack period he showed outstanding leadership and was continually in the advanced positions encouraging and organizing his posts. He moved from post to post completely regardless of danger and by his cheerful and resolute bearing did much to save the situation. [*L.G. 8.2.44*]

TY. MAJOR JOHN PATRICK LEO HENDERSON, R.E.
Captain, 117143, Royal Engineers, Special Service Troops
MILITARY CROSS

In recognition of gallant and distinguished services in Italy.
L.G. 13.1.44

CHAPLAIN ROSS SYDNEY HOOK, R.N.V.R.
No. 43 RM Commando
MILITARY CROSS (PERIODIC)

Before his service with this Commando, the Rev Hook had served some months with 40 (RM) Commando and had been into action with them several times, including one operation on the Island of Brac, where the Commando suffered very heavy casualties.

The Rev Hook has served ten months with 43 (RM) Commando and before the final offensive had been in action with them four times, on the Dalmatian Islands of Hvar, Brac, and Solta, and on the mainland of Jugoslavia, as well as various periods of line holding. Throughout this period the Rev Hook's zeal and efficiency in the presence of the enemy had a fine effect on the spirit of the

Italy

Commando. During the assault on the Comacchio Spit, the Rev Hook's conduct was outstanding. He showed the greatest devotion to duty in carrying out his difficult task under fire and often with the assaulting troops.

This was repeated during the forcing of the Argenta Gap. His selfless interest in all which affect the well-being of the Commando has been most marked. He is highly respected by officers and men who have the utmost confidence in him. He had played a large part in producing the spirit and dash shown by the Commando in action. *(L.G. 22.1.46)*

Temporary Captain Clifford Viztelly James
Lieut, 174099, Royal Corps of Signals, SS Bde, No. 2 Cdo.
Military Cross
Salerno Bay 9th–16th September 1943.
Captain James as Brigade Signal Officer throughout the actions of Marina, Vietri and Piegolette showed an untiring energy, technical skill and a devotion to duty worthy of the highest praise.

No deterrent whether occasioned by the hazards of battle or by physical fatigue, prevented Capt James's efforts to maintain at all costs the best possible communications through the action.

On all occasions he personally conducted the laying of line (with captured material since this equipment is not issued to the SS Brigade) which was often accomplished under fire. He also frequently visited his operators up with with the forward fighting troops.

An example of this tenacity was shown when the Jeep from which he was laying cable during a critical period of the battle broke down on the middle of the Vietri viaduct at that time being mortared by the enemy and under fixed-line machine-gun fire. Instead of temporarily abandoning this mission and returning for another Jeep, Capt James laboriously unloaded the equipment from the disabled vehicle and continued to lay the line on foot.

I consider that such success as may be credited to the SS Brigade would not have been possible without the excellent communications which were maintained at all times, an achievement for which Capt James, through his disregard of danger, endurances, enterprise and skill was primarily responsible.
[L.G. 13.1.44]

Commando Gallantry Awards of World War II

TY. LIEUTENANT WILLIAM GLYN JENKINS, R.M.
No. 43 RM Commando
MILITARY CROSS

For gallant and distinguished service displayed in the Italian campaign when taking part in the operations in April, 1945, north of the Reno and west of Argenta.   *L.G. 14.8.45*

LIEUTENANT DONALD BAYLEY LONG
WS Lieut, 284561, L.F., No. 9 Commando
MILITARY CROSS (IMMEDIATE)

In operation Roast which took place from 1st–4th April 1945 the task of this unit was to carry out an opposed landing on the western side of the spit of land between Lake Comacchio and the Adriatic and destroy or capture all enemy troops and material in this area. This task was completed, resulting in the capture of 1,000 prisoners of war by the Commando Brigade and elimination of the entire enemy force in this area. The early part of this operation consisted of a most exhausting journey over Lake Comacchio in stormboats which had to be pushed or paddled most of the way due to engine breakdowns or shallowness of water. All craft had to be pushed approximately 2,000 yards before shore could be reached and everyone almost without exception was physically exhausted before the actual battle began.

This operation was the first one in which this very young officer experienced being under fire, but he displayed neither of the usual reactions of cautiousness or recklessness. Lieut Long commanded the first assault section during the landing and led his section into the attack on the forward enemy positions which were opposing the landing of the rest of the unit.

He was wounded early on in the action and subsequently evacuated,—but not before he had led his section in a charge in the face of point-blank fire from enemy dug-outs which resulted in hand-to-hand fighting and the complete annihilation of the enemy position. The first bound of the advance was made in mist and smoke, and it was only due to Long's fearless personal reconnaissance of the correct lines of approach under continual and intense fire from all directions that the final attack was launched on the correct objective. Long personally led the final charge on the enemy dug-outs after satisfying himself of their exact dispositions and was the first man to get among the enemy. His courage and fearlessness during the previous reconnaissances and standard of leadership during the final attack were almost entirely responsible for the success of his section's attack. Even after being wounded he directed his men onto attacking individual enemy

Italy

dug-outs and pillboxes and maintained complete control of his section by passing messages to individual sub-sections as the battle progressed. At all times his men had complete faith and confidence in his leadership before he was wounded and also in his ability to control the battle after he was wounded. His splendid example of fighting ability, courage and determination both before and after being wounded undoubtedly was the major factor responsible for the success of his sections battle.

After his section's task was completed he crawled back to his troops headquarters and assisted his Troop Leader to launch attacks on other objectives which he had seen when making his previous recces. It was not until all these objectives had been dealt with would he allow himself to be evacuated to the regimental aid post.

This officer's devotion to duty, personal courage and standard of leadership were of the highest order to be expected from an officer. *[L.G. 5.7.45]*

TEMPORARY CAPTAIN MICHAEL LONG
WS/Lieut, 97967, No. 9 Commando
MILITARY CROSS (IMMEDIATE)
West of Garigliano River on the night of 29th–30th December 1943.
This officer was in command of one of the troops under Captain Cameron. He led his troop in the attack, and then swam across a strong current under mortar fire to a pile of the demolished bridge, taking a rope, after efforts to cross in a rubber board had failed. He organised a bridgehead on the far bank, which was still in enemy occupation, and held it until the whole force was safely over.
[L.G. 4.5.44]

ACTING TEMPORARY CAPTAIN LIONEL GUY
BRADFORD MARSHALL, R.M.
Temporary Lieutenant
MILITARY CROSS
For gallant and distinguished services in operations leading to the capture of Termoli. *L.G. 8.2.44*

TEMPORARY CAPTAIN JOSEPH EDWARD
CHANCELLOR NICHOLL, R.A.
179442, Royal Regiment of Artillery, Special Service Troops
MILITARY CROSS
In recognition of gallant and distinguished services in Italy.
L.G. 5.7.45

Acting Ty. Captain John Patrick O'Brien, R.M.
Temporary Lieutenant
Military Cross

For courage, leadership and resource in operations which led to the crossing of the Garigliano River in the face of determined opposition from the enemy. *L.G. 18.4.44*

Lieutenant George Alexander Parsons
162020, The Somerset Light Infantry (Prince Albert's),
Special Service Troops
Military Cross

In recognition of gallant and distinguished services in Italy.
L.G. 13.1.44

2nd Lieutenant George Pollard, M.M.
No. 3 Commando
Military Cross (Immediate)

During operations around Bova Marina between 27th August 1943 and 5th September 1943, this officer led a patrol of six other ranks who were to send back on a 21 set, information about the enemy in the Bagaladi area. He entered the village of Ghorio with one man on the morning of 28th August to capture four Italians whom he had seen there. They took one and returned to the rest of the party which was then attacked by four Italian riflemen, two of whom they wounded. The wireless set failed and while they were loading it on to a mule, they were attacked on both flanks by about 50 Italians. Lieut Pollard fought a delaying action while the signallers withdrew. At the last ridge he had only one man with him who was shot, and the Italians were firing on him from a range of 200 to 300 yards. Despite this he got his party away and concealed them. About 1700 hours he heard more firing and going alone to see what it was, he was cut off. On the night of 29th–30th August he went alone to the beach near Bova Marina and flashed a lamp out to sea between 0200 and 0300 hours. This was a pre-arranged signal in case a follow-up force should be sent: none came. On the night of 30th–31st August he repeated the process.

He fell sick from eating bad food and did not rejoin the British Forces until 5th September. This officer behaved with great determination throughout a most trying period. *[L.G. 13.1.44]*

Italy

Temporary Captain Martin Luther Preston
South African Union Defence Force, Seconded to Royal Marines.
Military Cross
For outstanding courage, determination and devotion to duty in operations during the campaign in Italy.   *L.G. 10.7 45*

Temporary Captain Robert Gibson Waldie
Lieutenant, 126151, The King's Own Scottish Borderers, Special Service Troops
Military Cross
In recognition of gallant and distinguished services in Italy.
L.G. 27.1.44

Temporary Captain Guy Faulkner Whitfield
143475, Reconnaissance Corps, R.A.C., Special Service Troops
Military Cross
In recognition of gallant and distinguished services in Italy.
L.G. 5.7.45

Acting Temporary Captain Anthony Douglas Wilkinson, R.M.
Temporary Lieutenant
Military Cross
For leadership, gallantry and devotion to duty while serving with Royal Marine Commandos in Italy.   *L.G. 27.6.44*

Private Harry Watt Calder
14421247, RAMC, No. 40 RM Commando & HOC
Distinguished Conduct Medal (Immediate)
(Operation 'Impact' 11th–12th April 1945)
At daybreak, two troops of the Commando, plus Tactical HQ, to which Pte Calder was attached in the capacity of medical orderly, found themselves on the tip of a narrow dyke with impassable mud and water on either side. From one flank they were subjected to intense and accurate artillery and mortar fire; and from the other they were under close and accurate small arms and snipers' fire. Within a few minutes eight officers and men were killed or seriously wounded, and one of the troop medical orderlies who had tried to reach them was forced to take cover in some swampy grass.

At this stage Pte Calder crawled forward, and when all cover gave out he tied some white bandage round one arm in lieu of his Geneva Cross which he had lost and advanced in the open. He was followed by Sgt Bostock RAMC, who witnessed the next incident. Calder was now so close to the enemy position that a

German NCO, thinking he wished to surrender, came out and signaled to him to come in; Calder somehow managed to make him understand that he intended to look after the casualties; the German politely agreed and returned to his strongpoint.

Calder and Sgt Bostock evacuated the only surviving casualty successfully. Throughout the next three hours Calder left his slit-trench repeatedly to deal with other casualties as they occurred: during which time he had repeated narrow escapes. As soon as the enemy strongpoint in the pumping-station was captured Pte Calder advanced entirely on his own initiative to help with the casualties there. It now became known that the troop that had advanced to the canal bridge (our main objective) had been attacked from both sides by the enemy, supported by two self-propelled guns, and had been wiped out.

Without a word to anyone Pte Calder set off alone down another dyke which was completely devoid of cover and subjected to heavy fire of all kinds. He swam a gap through which flood water was pouring, which had been deemed impassable to troops, and near the bridge found the bodies of the medical orderly and other members of the missing troop.

Although he was now half a mile in advance of the Commando's most forward position he pushed on beyond the bridge. Here he found two seriously wounded men of the Commando, one of them lying in the water. He did what he could for them and then pushed on half a mile further through still uncaptured territory until he found a stretcher party of the 2/5 Queens in Menate village. He led these back to rescue the two wounded men, and then returned alone to our positions. Throughout the whole day he continued to display a complete indifference to danger and a cheerful stoicism that was most remarkable.

His behaviour was an outstanding display of the most exceptional initiative and courage with which he is endowed, and which he has shown on several previous operations.

[L.G. 18.10.45]

ACTING SERGEANT JOHN JAMES CONVERY
Ply.X.1394, Marine, No. 40 RM Commando
DISTINGUISHED CONDUCT MEDAL (IMMEDIATE)
Termoli 3rd October 1943

Sgt Convery in Q Troop became the only SNCO in the troop remaining unwounded after all three officers had become casualties. He took command of the troop and carried on holding the left flank where severe fighting was taking place. Later when ordered over to the right flank he himself killed 15 Germans with

Italy

a bren gun. Throughout the action Sgt Convery displayed courage and leadership of the very highest order and he was responsible for organising the troop in its defensive position during two counter-attacks. *[L.G. 8.2.44]*

LANCE SERGEANT W. CYRIL ELLWOOD
6019994 WS/Cpl, Essex Regt, No. 2 Commando
DISTINGUISHED CONDUCT MEDAL (IMMEDIATE)
Gulf of Salerno 13th September 1943
During the fighting on the 13th September 1943 on Dragone Hill the enemy attempted to come through our positions. They threw stick grenades and brought automatic fire to bear, killing one man and wounding another. Lieut Peters went forward and was also wounded. Sgt Ellwood with complete disregard for enemy fire and grenades ran forward in the open and fired magazine after magazine into the enemy from his TSMG at point-blank range. Seven enemy dead were found in this area after the action. Throughout the operations he has set a fine standard of leadership, and although hit twice by shell splinters, has continued to command his sub-section with dash and determination. *[L.G. 13.1.44]*

LANCE SERGEANT LESLIE WILLIAM HOPKINS
6213259 WS/Cpl, U/L/Sgt, Middlesex Regt, No. 9 Cdo.
DISTINGUISHED CONDUCT MEDAL (IMMEDIATE)
Ref Map Italy 1:25,000, Sheet 88.1. NE, Fossa Marina
During Operation Impact Royal on 13th April 1945, this unit landed from fantails on the south-west shore of Lake Commachio approximately three miles from Fossa Marina with the intention of advancing to the canal and capturing the bridges before demolition by the enemy.

On night 15th–16th April 1945 an unsuccessful attempt was made to cross the canal by means of assault boats. It was unsuccessful on account of mud, strong tide, heavy casualties among personnel, and damage to all the craft except one by shell fire. The first anxious moment occurred when this NCO's section Sgt became a casualty during the approach to the canal. L/Sgt Hopkins immediately protected this wounded Sgt with his own body, replying to the spandau fire whilst the casualties managed to crawl to safety. This was the first instance of this NCO's courageous actions. Later on during this action L/Sgt Hopkins was in charge of the leading assault boat which was to cross the canal. In spite of heavy mortar fire which almost prevented the carriage of the craft to the canal bank, L/Sgt Hopkins encouraged his men with his determination to complete the task in such a manner that his craft was successfully launched. Once they were in the water, however, enemy fire increased, inflicting casualties among his crew and also on the boat itself. Added difficulties consisted of a strong tide, waist high mud and an enemy spandau position firing at point-blank range from the opposite bank. Once his craft had been damaged, however, Sgt Hopkins immediately returned to the craft assembly area to organize further craft being brought forward and it was only due to his splendid leadership and control of the situation that this task was completed. Once again when in the water launching the craft, Sgt Hopkins was wounded in the wrist by mortar shrapnel but he remained in the water and refused to return to the bank until he had ensured that the following craft had been successfully launched and were put on the right route. He refused to be helped out to the bank until all the craft had been launched, and although he was slowly sinking in the mud and could not guarantee any assistance to help him out he remained their until ordered to be evacuated. Even at this stage, although in considerable pain, he returned to his Troop HQ and asked for another task which he would be capable of carrying out with only one arm in action. He was in such pain, however, that his Troop Leader ordered him to return to the regimental aid post.

Throughout this entire operation this NCO displayed courage over and above that which could normally be expected, both before and after being wounded. He maintained complete control of the general situation and the men under his command under appalling conditions in the canal when he himself was in grave danger of being drowned and under continual enemy fire. His coolness, fearlessness and devotion to duty were factors which contributed greatly to avert disaster when the remaining boats started to sink, and his example throughout was one of utter fearlessness and determination to complete the task assigned to him.

Recommended for MM, awarded DCM. (L.G. 23.8.45)

SIGNALMAN WILLIAM ADAMSON FORBES KIRKHOPE
7662003, R. Signals, S.S. Bde Signal Troop, No. 2 Cdo Bde.
DISTINGUISHED CONDUCT MEDAL
Gulf of Salerno 13th September 1943
On the 13th September at SS Brigade HQ on the Vietri–Salerno Road Sgmn Kirkhope volunteered to repair a vital line to one of the forward units which had been cut by shell fire.

After proceeding along the line the break was found, and as the enemy was mortaring the area heavily Sgmn Kirkhope had to perform the repairs under conditions of extreme danger.

Italy

On the return journey Sgmn Kirkhope visited a relaying station where he found the operator exhausted from long hours on duty under fire. He at once relieved the operator and himself continued to operate the station though he had had no rest since the assault landing five days earlier. He continued on duty all day.

A few hours later the line was again cut by enemy fire during the ensuing battle on Dragone Hill. In spite of very heavy mortar fire and his great fatigue Sgmn Kirkhope continued to man the relaying station which now served as the only link forward.

Throughout the operation this man showed the greatest willingness to undertake all tasks however dangerous and his unflurried efficiency and technical skill under fire ensured the maintenance of communications during a critical period of 24 hours.

[L.G. 13.1.44]

WARRANT OFFICER CLASS II GEORGE ARTHUR REACE
2881169 W/CSM (WO.II), Att. No. 9 Commando
DISTINGUISHED CONDUCT MEDAL (IMMEDIATE)
Ref: Maps Italy Sheets 13 and 19, Sqs (w) M55, 56, 65 & 66

In Operation Roast which took place from 1st–4th April 1945 the task of this unit was to carry out an opposed landing on the western side of the spit of land between Lake Comacchio and the Adriatic and destroy or capture all enemy troops and material in this area. This task was completed, resulting in the capture of 100 prisoners of war by the Commando Brigade and elimination of the entire enemy force in this area. The early part of this operation consisted of a most exhausting journey over Lake Comacchio in stormboats which had to be pushed or paddled most of the way due to engine breakdowns or shallowness of water. All craft had to be pushed approximately 2,000 yds before shore could be reached and everyone almost without exception was physically exhausted before the actual battle began.

Not only in this operation but in all previous actions in which this unit has taken part this WO has carried out his duties as a CSM most efficiently, conscientiously and courageously. During this particular operation his Troop HQ was, at many times, left in a very isolated position in completely open country and in enemy-held territory whilst sections were detached mopping up enemy strong points. At one stage when he and three men of his HQ were guarding approximately 80 prisoners of war the HQ was counter-attacked and stonked by a battery of enemy mortars. Not only did he retain his control over the prisoners of war but he also drove off the counter-attack with only two other men under his command. Had the counter-attack penetrated his position it would have resulted in his troop being split. His general coolness, skill and devotion to duty whilst advancing to the final objective resulted in a total bag for his troop of 100 prisoners of war which would have had to have been abandoned during the advance had he not kept his head at all times. Earlier in the operation the Troop HQ was heavily mortared and he was seriously wounded in the groin, but he continued to advance with his troop and did not report his injuries to his Troop Commander until the operation was completed as it would have entailed reorganization within the troop and possible failure in capturing the final enemy positions had the enemy been given time to reorganize. When he was finally ordered to be evacuated he refused to do so as there was no other NCO available to take over his duties and in great pain he continued throughout the operation for the next eight hours to assist his Troop Leader and to control another section when its officer became a casualty.

CSM Reace has at all times shown outstanding ability, bravery and courage. His utter disregard for safety and determination to complete all his duties has always been of the highest order.
[L.G. 5.7.45]

SERGEANT WILLIAM F. RUDGE
3654948, South Lancs Regt, No. 2 Commando
DISTINGUISHED CONDUCT MEDAL (IMMEDIATE)
Gulf of Salerno 13th September 1943
On the 13th September 1943 on the Dragone Hill, Sgt Rudge, one of the six survivors of the forward section of 22, showed outstanding bravery whilst in close contact with the enemy. After being mortared and shelled for two and a half hours and during a period of close confused fighting he twice rallied the men near him and repeatedly drove off the enemy. He also organised a party to go forward, under enemy machine gun fire, to retrieve a Vickers gun (whose crew were all casualties). The gun was used afterwards and inflicted casualties. Sgt Rudge carried back on three separate occasions badly wounded men, always returning immediately to the firing line, and his behaviour under a most severe concentration of mortar and machine-gun fire for a period of about three hours was an inspiration to the section. *[L.G. 13.1.44]*

Italy

LANCE SERGEANT CLIFFORD F. SEARLE
14241831, No. 9 Commando
DISTINGUISHED CONDUCT MEDAL

Operation 'Roast'—Lake Comacchio 'Spit'—2nd April 1945

This NCO came abroad as a private. He has twice been promoted in the battlefield. During extremely heavy and accurate sniping which had pinned the troop to cover, his Section NCO was hit. L/Sgt Searle made a 30-yd dash, under full view of enemy snipers, and, ascertaining that his superior NCO was killed, he calmly knelt and took map and compass and other necessary articles from the body, receiving a bullet through his steel helmet in the middle of his operations. He then took over the section and led his men through a thick smoke screen which obliterated both own troops and enemy. This smoke was subjected to heavy 3" mortaring but Searle kept the men going by voice control although he suffered a further three casualties. He led the final charge and overran two spandau positions capturing two 75-mm howitzers. Immediately following this the area was covered by defensive fire task and the troop suffered a further 15 casualties. L/Sgt Searle now infiltrated with two men on the troop right flank, and silenced a spandau which was firing on and holding up the advance of the troop on the flank. Under a further accurate defensive fire mortaring of the troop, bringing the total casualties to 29, L/Sgt Searle rallied three men and started to lead them over an open space to the next objective. All the party were wounded by shrapnel or automatic fire and Searle, although badly wounded in the chest assisted in dragging one other to safety. He then reported to his Troop Leader and would not be helped back to the regimental aid post until he had furnished a full report. Under continuous mortaring, shelling and small arms fire which inflicted 35 casualties out of 58, L/Sgt Searle's behaviour was outstanding in his complete disregard for his own personal safety, and his coolness and excellent leadership in controlling his men under the hardest possible conditions.

Recommended for periodic MM, awarded DCM. (L.G. 13.12.45)

LANCE SERGEANT JOHN THOMSON
3190591, KOSB, No. 9 Commando
DISTINGUISHED CONDUCT MEDAL (IMMEDIATE)

Ref Map—Italy 1/25,000 Sheet 158 IV SE

During the operation carried out by this unit in wadis in square 8230 on 19th March 1944, this NCO commanded two bren LMGs. which were sited well forward of this troop main position. At one stage his post was attacked by a party of ten Boche, who attacked from a dominating position and under cover of strong support from

LMGs and rifle grenades. L/Cpl Thomson was wounded in this attack, and one of his LM Gunners killed, but he took over this bren himself and his small force of four men succeeded in driving off the Boche attack, killing two and wounding several more.

Later in the day, although still wounded, he and his other LMG covered the movement of his troop by holding off a strong Boche counter-attack, which, had it been successful, would have turned the flank of the whole unit position.

Throughout the entire action, Thomson was unable to move from his position owing to accurate enemy sniping which inflicted heavy casualties on the rest of his troop and after he was wounded he refused to allow attempts to be made to evacuate him owing to the danger to the stretcher-bearers. In spite of his wound and although being under continuous rifle, LMG and grenade fire, he maintained his two LMGs in position in a most determined manner, and it was entirely due to his complete control of the situation while giving covering fire to his troop that it was able to take up new positions, which in turn covered the successful withdrawal of the whole force.

Throughout the action this NCO displayed a remarkably high standard of leadership, and his personal courage, determination and disregard for his wound set a magnificent example to all ranks.

[L.G. 20.7.44]

Ty. Sergeant Richard Douglas French, M.M.
Ex.3226, Royal Marines, No. 43 RM Commando
Bar to Military Medal

For outstanding courage, determination and devotion to duty in operations during the campaign in Italy.   L.G. 10.7 45

Lance Sergeant V Peachey, M.M.
3654154, WS/Cpl (A/L/Sgt), S Lanc R, No. 2 Commando
Bar to Military Medal (Immediate)

On 17th April 1945, L/Sgt Peachey was acting Section Sgt in a troop ordered to attack the bridges across the River Reno and neighbouring canals west of Argenta. Owing to an earlier casualty he had no Section Officer.

Peachey lead the assault section into the attack on the bridge himself and was then ordered to proceed forward to attack positions beyond the bridge. At this stage, the enemy reinforced his positions and counter-attacked strongly. His Troop Commander was wounded and more than half his section had become casualties when the German counter-attack carried the enemy onto our forward positions in this sector. Peachey with superb coolness and

Italy

disregard for himself rallied the remnants of his section and led an attack with bayonets and grenades on the advancing enemy with such ferocity and determination that the enemy were driven back, he personally killing or wounding at least three Germans. During this assault, Peachey was badly wounded in the chest, but he continued from a prone position to encourage his men and engage the enemy.

Peachey's bravery and high standard of leadership materially contributed to the smashing of the enemy counter-attack and the securing of our defensive position. *[L.G. 23.8.45]*

TROOPER ALFRED EDMUND AMESBURY
4536995, 44th Reconnaissance Regiment, No. 2 Commando
MILITARY MEDAL (IMMEDIATE)

On 16th September 1943, Trooper Amesbury was one of the crew of an anti-tank gun in a position south-west of Battipaglia.

During the morning a strong enemy attack preceded by mortar and artillery concentrations, was made on this position. The gun position was heavily fired on by enemy machine guns and mortars at close range, but Trooper Amesbury displayed great coolness and succeeded in knocking out two enemy mortar posts by sniping with his rifle and subsequently helped to carry ammunition to forward section posts under heavy enemy fire.

During the whole of this engagement Trooper Amesbury showed conspicuous courage and coolness. *[L.G. 27.1.44]*

ACTING SERGEANT BASIL MCGONIGLE AYLETT
Temp/Corporal, Ch.X.1409, No. 40 (RM) Commando
MILITARY MEDAL (IMMEDIATE)

Termoli 3rd October 1943
Sgt Aylett was acting as TSM to A Troop whose objective was the port and eastern end of Termoli. An LMG post was located in a house which was holding up the advance of the troop. His Troop Commander had just been shot in the head from the position. In spite of a bullet wound through his arm causing great pain Sgt Aylett proceeded clear of the house with a small party and killed two Germans in the position. Later he collapsed and was taken to the regimental aid post. Sgt Aylett displayed great courage and disregard for his own personal safety throughout this action.
Recommended for DCM, awarded MM. *[L.G. 8.2.44]*

Commando Gallantry Awards of World War II

LANCE SERGEANT HAROLD BARTON
Corporal, 3533801, Manchester, No. 9 Commando
MILITARY MEDAL (IMMEDIATE)

Ref Map—Italy 1/25,000 Sheet 158 IV SE.
During a Commando operation on 19th March 1944, Cpl Barton led a section in the initial attack during the hours of darkness. A spandau position manned by three enemy opened fire on them at point-blank range. Cpl Barton coolly ordered 'left flanking' and led two men round to the attack, leaving his LMG to cover him. He was observed and the two men with him were wounded, but without hesitation Cpl Barton hurled a grenade and charged the post single-handed, capturing the only uninjured occupant. Later in the day, although his remaining men had all been killed and wounded, Cpl Barton continued to man his LMG single-handed, accounting for another five certain enemy casualties. His leadership and courage were of the highest standard throughout the entire operation. *(L.G. 20.7.44)*

LANCE CORPORAL THOMAS BOSTOCK
3659812 Pte (A/Cpl.), S Lancs, No. 9 Commando
MILITARY MEDAL (IMMEDIATE)

Action at Monte Faita, night 2nd–3rd February 1944, Map Ref. 858043, Italy 1/50,000, Sheet 160 II
During this action this NCO showed a standard of initiative determination and leadership far above that expected of an NCO of his rank. During a period of heavy enemy artillery and mortar fire on the unit, in which severe casualties, including 50% of the officers were incurred, he showed exemplary courage, discipline and determination to continue on to the final objective.

Although the unit was under by opposition from enemy mortar and small arms fire, he led his section on to his objective, which was captured and all the enemy in the particular Company HQ were either killed or captured. Although the position was still being heavily mortared, L/Cpl Bostock reorganised his section and started to lead them forward onto a secondary objective until ordered to withdraw.

L/Cpl Bostock showed similar determination and courage in two previous operations. During operation 'Partridge' (Garigliano River operation night 29th–30th December) he unhesitatingly led his section through a minefield where several casualties occurred, and drove the enemy from a defended position which would otherwise have held up the advance of the main force. During operation 'Shingle' (Anzio landing), L/Cpl Bostock led a fighting

Italy

patrol far into enemy territory, and after he had been separated from his section he captured eight prisoners single-handed.

In all actions this NCO had shown exemplary courage, leadership and determination. *[L.G. 29.6.44]*

TY. CORPORAL DONALD CHARLES BULLOCK
Ch.X.3346, Mne (A/Ty/Sergeant), No. 41 RM Commando
MILITARY MEDAL
Gulf of Salerno—9th–10th September 1943
On 10th September 1943 in the Vietri Sul Mare defile. During attacks on his position he was a continual inspiration to his machine-gun sub-section. When enemy broke through a troop position on his flank he moved his machine-gun to a position further forward from where he could bring better fire to bear on the enemy. While the gun was being moved the enemy appeared about 50 yards away and he himself went forward with a Tommy Gun to cover the gun and was badly wounded.
Wounded in action 10th September 1943; missing (presumed killed) 10th September 1943.
Recommended for DCM, awarded MM. *[L.G. 27.6.44]*

PRIVATE KENNETH HAROLD CHAPMAN
5958297, Beds & Herts Regt, No. 3 Commando
MILITARY MEDAL (IMMEDIATE)
During the operations at Termoli between 3rd and 6th October 1943 in the second attack on D+2 a trooper of this unit was badly wounded in the leg. Pte Chapman in the next weapon pit immediately went to his assistance although he was exposed to fierce enfilade MG.

He applied a tourniquet which involved kneeling in the open for a considerable time. He then reported the casualty and went to find a stretcher. Owing to the disorganisation he was unable to do this, but he returned with two medical orderlies. The wounded man was then carried back on a blanket, Chapman assisted. All this coming and going was done under intense machine-gun and shell fire and Chapman showed a disregard of danger in the highest tradition of the Commando. *(L.G. 27.1.44)*

TEMPORARY CORPORAL ROLAND WILLIAM COLE
Ex.4373, Sergeant (A/Ty), No. 41 RM Commando
MILITARY MEDAL (IMMEDIATE)
On September 13th 1943, at Vietri Sul Mare, this NCO during an attack on his troop position showed great gallantry when he frequently fetched ammunition which had been left in an exposed

position and carried it under heavy fire to LMG Groups who were themselves being engaged by the enemy. At all other times throughout the operation he showed the highest standard of courage and devotion to duty, organising his troop which was left without officers, encouraging and inspiring his men.
Recommended for DCM, awarded MM.   *[L.G. 27.6.44]*

FUSILIER DUDLEY EDWARD COOPER
14241655, L.F., No. 2 Commando
MILITARY MEDAL (IMMEDIATE)

Fus Cooper was No. 1 of a PIAT in a troop ordered to cross 1,500 yds of open ground to attack enemy positions defending a bridge during Operation 'Roast' on 2nd April 1945.

When 300 yds from the objective, the troop came under withering spandau fire. Cooper, with great coolness, gave accurate support to his troop which succeeded in capturing the bridge. Before he could rejoin the troop, a strong counter-attack was launched during which his No. 2 was killed. Cooper, in the face of intense fire, moved his PIAT to a fire position on the flank and being without a No. 2 had to make two separate journeys across open ground to bring up bombs.

There, although under automatic fire, he engaged the advancing enemy, firing at low angle and succeeded in halting them. When his bombs were exhausted he continued to engage the enemy with his Colt automatic.

When the counter-attack was finally beaten off he returned with his weapon under cover of smoke from a burning haystack to rejoin his Troop HQ.

Throughout the operation he showed great initiative and personal courage.   *[L.G. 5.7.45]*

LANCE CORPORAL JOHN CRAMER
P/L/Cpl 2568791, RAMC, No. 9 Commando
MILITARY MEDAL

Ref Map Italy 1:25,000, Sheet 88.1.NE, Fossa Marina.
During Operation Impact Royal on 13th April 1945 this unit landed from fantails on the south-west shore of Lake Commachio approximately three miles from Fossa Marina with the intention of advancing to the canal and capturing the bridges before demolition by the enemy.

This NCO landed with Commando HQ M.I. Section and set up an regimental aid post in the vicinity of the beach. At 1300 hrs the regimental aid post came under heavy and intense shell and mortar fire for over an hour and a half. During this time casualties

Italy

were sustained both in Commando HQ and in troops in the forward FDLs. During the shell fire, however, Cpl Cramer repeatedly led stretcher parties to bring in these casualties from the forward positions over ground continuously swept by fire. When the regimental aid post itself came under particularly accurate fire this NCO organised its removal to what was considered a safer location. By his imperturbability and command of the situation under most difficult conditions and continuous shell fire this NCO was largely responsible for excessive casualties being avoided and the competent assistance given to casualties evacuated from forward positions.

During the whole time his technical skill remained unimpaired by the difficulties and danger of the moment and he displayed complete disregard for his own safety, and coolness under fire whilst dealing with all the casualties evacuated to the regimental aid post.

On 15th April Cpl Cramer led a stretcher bearing party 300 yards forward of our forward defended lines through an anti-personnel minefield to search for our own dead and wounded and to evacuate a German who had been wounded two days previously. The whole area of his search was under direct observation by the enemy, covered by known enemy machine-gun fixed lines, and under continuous mortar fire. In spite of these hazards Cpl Cramer treated and evacuated all the wounded that he could find and did not complete his search until he was satisfied there were no more of our own casualties to be evacuated. Not only did this NCO display most efficient medical skill when dealing with casualties but also fearlessness, devotion to duty and courage which was an example to all ranks with whom he worked and a great source of confidence and assistance to the casualties which he attended.

[L.G. 23.8.45]

LANCE BOMBARDIER SAMUEL DANIELS
14322499 P/L/Bdr, RA (Fd), No. 9 Commando
MILITARY MEDAL (IMMEDIATE)
Ref Map Italy 1:25,000, Sheet 88.1.NE. Fossa Marina.
During Operation Impact Royal on 13th April 1945 this unit landed from fantails on the south-west shore of Lake Commachio approximately three miles from Fossa Marina with the intention of advancing to the canal and capturing the bridges before demolition by the enemy.

On 15th April this NCO's troop was forming up on the start line for the final attack on the canal bridge when a spandau opened fire on the troop from approximately 20 yds distance. Without the slightest hesitation L/Bdr Daniels immediately charged this position, killed two of the occupants with a hand grenade picked up by the LMG and hurled it at another weapon pit occupied by Boche, and then returned to his troop with the information that immediate opposition had been destroyed. In this action it was only due to this NCO's immediate and fearless action in dealing with the enemy opposition that casualties were not inflicted on the troop on the start line before the attack was launched.

Later, during the attack, this NCO led the forward sub-section through a maze of houses, all of which were occupied by German LMG schmeisser positions. It was only on account of this NCO's dash and determination in dealing with one position after another that the troop was able to advance through these houses on to its ultimate objective. At one period, as the troop was advancing round the back of a house, an enemy self-propelled gun behind a wall opened fire on it at point-blank range. L/Bdr Daniels, without the slightest hesitation and consideration for his own safety jumped on the gun, fired a burst of his tommy gun into the turret and killed or captured the crew single-handed. Had this gun remained intact the success of the whole operation of the entire Commando would have been jeopardised.

During the whole battle this NCO was invariably the first to enter any enemy occupied building or attack any enemy position. He led his section with determination, skill and courage. In spite of his personal courage he always concentrated on his responsibilities to his section which carried out some splendid fighting under his competent, skilful and courageous command.

[L.G. 23.8.45]

CORPORAL JOHN CYRIL DAVISON
14241659, RAC, No. 3 Commando
MILITARY MEDAL (IMMEDIATE)

During the operations around Bova Marina between 28th August 1943 and 5th September 1943, this NCO was in charge of one of four parties which had to abandon ship when LCI 107 ran aground. He led his three men on fighting patrols on the nights of 1st and 2nd November having kept them safely concealed up to that time as one of them was sick. On the night of the 2nd September he ambushed an enemy lorry causing casualties with his LMG. On the morning of the 3rd September hearing an Italian patrol in the woods he surprised it, taking five prisoners. Encouraged by this success he determined to capture the bridge west of Bova Marina, which he did taking three more prisoners. Deciding to patrol the town he and one man went through it on bicycles and took eight more prisoners. On the 4th September he attempted to contact a destroyer which was two miles out to sea, by swimming. On the 5th September, he safely contacted British troops leading a party now of five soldiers and seven sailors.

Throughout these operations he showed the same offensive spirit and cool-headedness by which he had distinguished himself during the previous operation at Agnone on the 14th–15th July 1943. His conduct has been an outstanding example on both occasions to the soldiers under his command.

Recommended for DCM, awarded MM. [*L.G. 13.1.44*]

LANCE SERGEANT JOAB SELWYN DENHAM
14241763, W/S Cpl, Sherwood Foresters, No. 3 Commando
MILITARY MEDAL (IMMEDIATE)

Cape Spartivento Italy 27th August–5th September

This NCO was part of a patrol of one officer and six other ranks detailed to report by wireless on enemy activities around Cape Spartivento, between 27th August and 5th September 1943. On 28th August the wireless having become useless the patrol was ordered by their officer to fend for themselves as the party was too large to subsist. On 1st September Cpl J. Denham, together with L/Cpl J. McClelland, was concealed in some scrub on the side of a mountain. Three Italian soldiers came towards them searching the ground and firing into the bushes. These NCOs shot them dead. On 3rd September they saw an Italian Cpl come out of a farm and followed him for five miles, when he entered a valley full of Italian soldiers.

Soon after they captured a Sgt, three Privates and an officer who could speak English. The Italian Sgt was sent to inform his Colonel of this and returned asking them to go to him. The NCOs said the Colonel was to come to them alone, which he did. He surrendered to them six officers and approximately 400 men of the 143 Infantry Regiment. The NCOs took it in turns to guard the prisoners until they handed them over to the Canadians 48 hrs later on 5th September. In the meanwhile they were able to keep them quiet by giving them a short talk on British Policy. Throughout these operations this NCO behaved with coolness and boldness. [*L.G. 27.1.44*]

PRIVATE JOHN KEIL FARQUHAR
1821551, Seaforth Highlanders, No. 9 Commando
MILITARY MEDAL (IMMEDIATE)

West of Garigliano River on the night of 29th–30th December 1943.

This man was wounded in the leg during the assault on the demolished bridge position. In spite of this he carried on, attacking the enemy with grenades, and when the enemy ran away he chased them and captured two single-handed. He crossed the river unaided and did not disclose the fact that he was wounded until the crossing had been completed. *[L.G. 4.5.44]*

ACTING TEMPORARY CORPORAL JAMES JOHN THOMAS GORMAN
Marine, Ch.X.100536, No. 40 RM Commando
MILITARY MEDAL (IMMEDIATE)

22nd January 1944. Crossing of the Garigliano.
This NCO was in command of a platoon which were the only troops on the forward slopes of the Damiano feature. His position was being heavily mortared and covered by intense enemy small-arms fire. As it was impossible to move his platoon without sustaining many casualties he himself took two men round to a flank under heavy fire from the enemy, where, with bren gun and two TSMG's he forced the enemy to withdraw from their position, causing some casualties. Through his extreme courage and decisive action, he no doubt saved his platoon from further casualties.
[L.G. 18.4.44]

GUNNER JAMES GORNALL
3856286, Royal Artillery, Commandos, No. 11 Cdo.
MILITARY MEDAL
In recognition of gallant and distinguished services in the field.
L.G. 13.9.45

FUSILIER ANDREW GRAY
3185419, Royal Fusiliers, No. 2 Commando
MILITARY MEDAL (IMMEDIATE)

Gulf of Salerno 13th September 1943.
On 13th September 1943 on the Dragone Hill Fusilier Gray was with the forward section, and when the position had been outflanked attacked the enemy together with Pte Hamble, and dislodged the enemy from the top of the forward ridge with hand grenades. Throughout the heavy enemy attack on the hill Fus Gray showed great coolness and slowed down the enemy's progress for several hours. Fus Gray was later severely wounded on the hill. *[L.G. 13.1.44]*

Italy

ACTING LANCE CORPORAL ERIC RICHARD CLIFFORD GROVES
Dvr, T/83555, RASC, No. 2 Commando
MILITARY MEDAL

On 17th April 1945, L/Cpl Groves's Troop attacked along the dykes west of Argenta to capture the bridges across the River Reno and neighbouring canals.

Shortly after the objectives were captured, the enemy counter-attacked in strength down all three dykes. The bren group defending the western dyke was knocked out by a mortar bomb, leaving the left flank badly exposed.

L/Cpl Groves saw enemy troops with panzerfaust and spandau infiltrating down the western dyke. Realising the danger, he immediately, and on his own initiative, led his bren group across the demolished bridge over the canal which was under heavy small-arms and mortar fire. He reached the dyke when the enemy had advanced to within less than 100 yards of the bridge and ordered his bren to open fire, but the bren jammed. Groves drew his revolver and rushed towards the enemy over completely bare ground, which was subjected to heavy enemy small-arms fire. He fired rapidly into the enemy, driving them back, and enabled his bren team to get their gun working again.

His prompt and courageous action undoubtedly saved a critical situation and prevented the enemy over-running the left flank.
23.8.45

MARINE JOHN WILLIAM HADFIELD
Ply.X.104358, No. 41 RM Commando
MILITARY MEDAL (IMMEDIATE)

On September 13th, 1943, at Vietri Sul Mare this NCO by his outstanding coolness and disregard for danger when his officer was killed leading a counter-attack, rallied his men and succeeded in driving home the attack. When later having only a few men left he was forced to withdraw he succeeded in extricating his men from a very dangerous position. Subsequently he lead numerous patrols wisely and well and was at all times and inspiration to his men. *[L.G. 27.6.44]*

Commando Gallantry Awards of World War II

ACTING TEMPORARY COMPANY SERGEANT MAJOR KENNETH SCOTT HAWKINS
Corporal, Ch.X.1120, No. 40 RM Commando
MILITARY MEDAL (IMMEDIATE)
22nd January 1944 Crossing of the Garigliano River

On 22nd January 1944, north of the River Garigliano, CSM Hawkins led a small patrol consisting of himself and six men. On encountering a German patrol of greatly superior strength he outwitted, by skilful leadership, and succeeded in capturing twelve prisoners.

Later he led out a second patrol and this time returned with a further 18 prisoners. During the whole operation his courage, initiative and coolness were of the highest order and were a fine example and inspiration to the men under his command.

[L.G. 27.6.44]

LANCE SERGEANT JOHN HODKINSON
Corporal, 3446114, Lancs Fus, No. 9 Commando
MILITARY MEDAL
Ref Map—Italy 1/25,000 Sheet IV SE

During a Commando operation on 19th March 1944, Cpl Hodkinson commanded a bren team sited in a forward position subjected to heavy machine-gun fire and enemy sniping. With his bren gunner killed, he took over the gun, and, in the space of less than an hour, inflicted a minimum of twelve certain casualties on enemy groups infiltrating forward. At one period he was knocked unconscious by the blast of a shell, but on recovering consciousness he immediately re-manned his gun and continued to inflict casualties on the enemy. For the space of ten hours, in an extremely cramped and dangerous position, he continued coolly to fire his gun, breaking up three enemy attempts to dig in a machine gun on the high ground before him and with five of his own men lying dead around him.

His coolness and complete disregard for his own safety was an inspiration to all ranks. *[L.G. 20.7.44]*

SERGEANT WILLIAM MORGAN HOPE
Ply.X.110136, No. 40 RM Commando
MILITARY MEDAL
(Operation 'Impact' 11th–12th April 1945)

During the early stages of the attack the patrol attached to 'P' Troop found themselves in exposed positions on the left of the main dyke.

Italy

Heavy and sustained small-arms fire was brought to bear on their positions from enemy positions on their left.

Self-propelled and mortar fire was also brought to bear, the position being well and truly straddled.

The O.C. patrol ordered his men to the sheltered side of the dyke, as many casualties had been received.

The above-mentioned NCO with total disregard for his own safety made three separate trips over the dyke under accurate and withering cross small-arms and mortar fire to try and pull out the wounded who were still lying on the exposed bank of the dyke.

Heavy shell fire was also in progress.

In the new position the patrol were under accurate sniping from 50 yards and spandau fire from 150 yards. The patrol were ordered to withdraw to a better and less exposed position. Sgt Hope remained with the wounded men; he continued moving amongst them, cheering them on and tending their wounds. During this time the sniper continued to fire, two of the wounded men being hit again. Finally Sgt Hope jumped on to the bank, completely exposing himself to the enemy in an endeavour to stop them firing on the already wounded.

The enemy continued to fire and shelling commenced once again. Sgt Hope remained with the wounded giving what assistance he was able. When eventually medical aid arrived only one wounded man remained alive, the remainder having been either killed by sniper fire or shelling.

Throughout the entire action this SNCO displayed the utmost bravery and complete disregard for his own life. His devotion to duty and encouragement to his section on the death of his section officer was an inspiration to all around him.   *23.8.45*

LANCE CORPORAL GEORGE WILLIAM STANLEY HUGHES
7360074 Private, P/L/Cpl, R.A.M.C., No. 9 Commando
MILITARY MEDAL

This NCO has served in the RAMC Section of this Commando in all the actions in which the unit has fought in Italy since November 1943. At all times he has displayed the greatest efficiency, devotion to duty and disregard for his own safety whilst dealing with casualties in the field. The Medical Officer of this unit, Captain E. J. D'Arcy, MC, states that L/Cpl Hughes's individual actions on all occasions whilst treating and evacuating casualties have been responsible for saving a very considerable number of men's lives.

On night 29th–30th December 1943, the unit carried out operation 'Partridge' which consisted of an assault landing behind enemy lines near the Garigliano (Map Ref. Italy 1/25,000 Sh. 171-1 south-west Force Del Garigliano, (780932)). L/Cpl Hughes landed in the first flight and dealt with casualties under continuous enemy fire whilst the unit was operating behind enemy front line positions.

In Operation Ornito on night 2nd–3rd February 1944 (Map Ref. Italy, 1/50,000 Sheets No. 160 II square 8503) the unit advanced several miles into enemy territory, but was compelled to withdraw after suffering 50% casualties of all ranks. Not only did L/Cpl Hughes accompany the leading troops in the attack, dealing with casualties on the way, but after the withdrawal he led forward several stretcher-bearer parties to collect casualties left behind in enemy territory, and in the process captured a party of Boche with the assistance of one unarmed walking wounded case, who he organised as stretcher bearers and brought back to our lines.

During an attack carried out by the Commando whilst serving at Anzio on 19th March 1944, the unit was surrounded and pinned down in a wadi for 20 hours, and suffered very heavy casualties from continuous enemy artillery and mortar fire. Throughout this period L/Cpl Hughes displayed exemplary courage while evacuating casualties from exposed positions under direct fire from the enemy, and rendered indispensable assistance to the MO in organising a regimental aid post only 100 yds from enemy positions.

During the period that L/Cpl Hughes has served in this unit, from March 1941 he has rendered most conscientious service as a medical orderly. Casualties in the field were never in a too dangerous or exposed position for him to deal with. His disregard for personal danger whilst carrying out his duties has at all times been outstanding, and his efficiency, zeal and devotion to duty have at all times been of the highest order.

Recommended for DCM, awarded MM. [L.G. 21.9.44]

LANCE CORPORAL WILLIAM MCCLEAN HUMBLE
2940188, Queens Own Cameron Highlanders, No. 2 Cdo.
MILITARY MEDAL (IMMEDIATE)
Gulf of Salerno 13th September 1943.

On September 9th on the Salerno Road Pte Humble engaged at 100 yards an advancing Mk. III Special enemy tank, which was shelling the house from which Pte Humble was sniping.

On 13th September 1943 on the Dragone Hill when the section had been outflanked, Pte Humble together with another soldier went forward under heavy machine-gun fire with all the hand grenades he could collect, and drove the enemy off the forward

Italy

ridge. Pte Humble was also seen to kill a machine-gun crew of three single-handed in close hand-to-hand fighting.

Throughout the operations 9th to 18th September Pte Humble was an inspiration to all he came in contact with, always showing coolness and determination to get to close grips with the enemy.
[L.G. 13.1.44]

ACTING SERGEANT HARRY CHARLES JACKSON
4919445, South Staffs, No. 9 Commando
MILITARY MEDAL (IMMEDIATE)

Ref Map—Italy 1/25,000 Sheet IV SE
During a Commando operation on 19th March 1944, L/Sgt Jackson was in command of six men protecting the right flank of his troop.

Throughout the entire operation, although exposed to extremely heavy mortar and machine gun fire, he continued to crawl between his slit trenches and the high ground where three of his men lay wounded, completely exposing himself in order to direct the fire of his men and to observe the enemy. Later in the day, although his party had suffered 50% casualties, he led his remaining three men in a counter-attack against a group of enemy infiltrating between his position and Commando HQ, killing four and wounding and driving off the remainder. His magnificent coolness and determination enabled him to lead a party through an enemy position in order to bring in one of his severely wounded men. He was at all times an example and inspiration to the men who fought under his Command. *[L.G. 20.7.44]*

ACTING TEMPORARY CORPORAL GEORGE ALBERT THOMAS WILLIAM JOHNSON
Marine, Po.X.3191, No. 40 RM Commando
MILITARY MEDAL (IMMEDIATE)

22nd January 1944 Crossing of the Garigliano River.
Whilst holding a position north of the river Garigliano on 22nd January 1944 one man of Corporal Johnson's section was hit by machine gun fire and lay, in the open, badly wounded. Any attempt to reach the injured man was met with intense fire but Cpl Johnson, completely disregarding his personal safety, went forward. Before he had completed the journey he fell severely wounded in the hip. Undeterred he continued to crawl forward until he reached the wounded man. He then remained with him until it was possible under cover of darkness for them both to be brought in.

His action undoubtedly saved the life of his comrade. His personal courage and devotion to duty was a great inspiration to all who saw him. *[L.G. 27.6.44]*

LANCE CORPORAL ROBERT KING
Private, 7357784, RAMC, No. 9 Commando
MILITARY MEDAL (IMMEDIATE)
Ref: Maps Italy Sheets 13 and 19, Sqs (w) M 55, 56, 65 & 66.

In Operation Roast which took place from 1st–4th April 1945 the task of this unit was to carry out an opposed landing on the western side of the spit of land between Lake Comacchio and the Adriatic and destroy or capture all enemy troops and material in this area. This task was completed, resulting in the capture of 1,000 prisoners of war by the Commando Brigade and elimination of the entire enemy force in this area. The early part of this operation consisted of a most exhausting journey over Lake Comacchio in stormboats which had to be pushed or paddled most of the way due to engine breakdowns or shallowness of water. All craft had to be pushed approximately 2,000 yds before shore could be reached and everyone almost without exception was physically exhausted before the actual battle began.

This medical orderly was wounded in the mouth very early on in this operation. At the same time, seven men became casualties from grenades and small arms fire. With complete disregard for his own wound L/Cpl King attended to each man in turn and was still engaged in this task when three more stonks fell in his position inflicting a further 15 casualties. The entire area in which he was operating was covered by enemy defensive fire tasks and he carried out his duties under continual and intense enemy fire. Although wounded and in a most exposed position he dealt with one casualty after another with complete disregard for his own safety or his wound. After dressing all the badly wounded men of his troop he returned to the regimental aid post with the first batch of casualties where he had his own wound dressed. Afterwards he immediately returned to the final positions again and proceeded to deal with further casualties. On one occasion he made his way over open ground covered by enemy fixed lines of fire to deal with a casualties who had been lying out in the open. During this journey he captured four prisoners of war and with their assistance he evacuated the casualties back to his troop aid post and again went forward single-handed to deal with further wounded men. All together, this orderly dealt with 30 casualties single-handed before they were evacuated to the regimental aid post and it was only due to his utter disregard for his own safety and own wound, and his determination to evacuate or attend to every casualty that occurred that many of these men were not either killed or captured in later stages of the battle. Throughout the operation L/Cpl King

Italy

displayed exemplary courage and efficiency, and devotion to duty whilst dealing with casualties was of the highest order.

[L.G. 5.7.45]

Ty. Sergeant Ernest Arthur Kinnear
Po.X.105560, No. 40 RM Commando
Military Medal

(Ref. Map Italy 1/200,000. Sheet 12)

Sgt Kinnear was acting in the capacity of Troop Sergeant Major during Operation 'Impact' 10th–13th April 1945, and became at once an outstanding figure on the battlefield. In the area of Menate the Commando met stiff enemy opposition on a narrow front, with the additional hazards of deeply sown minefields. Heavy toll was taken of unit personnel. During this critical period, with morale badly shaken and the success of the operation in the balance, Sgt Kinnear emerged as a leader of the highest qualities. Tirelessly applying himself to the welfare of his men he moved freely through his section positions, succouring the wounded and exhorting tired men to renewed effort. In so doing he was repeatedly exposed to enemy small-arms fire, but by demonstrating complete disregard for his own safety he so stimulated the troop that it was able to resume the attack and capture the objective.

During the many operations carried out by 40 (RM) Commando from Sicily to Argenta, Sgt Kinnear has been conspicuous by his gallantry.

During an operation on the Dalmatian Island of Brac in June 1944, he was again acting as Troop Sergeant Major. When heavy casualties had been sustained he went out alone over open ground to evacuate many of them under fire. Again in the same action he evacuated two casualties from the middle of a Schu minefield, and later returned to the summit of a hill within easy range of the enemy positions to evacuate wounded left behind in the withdrawal, although he was forced to retire by accurate sniping.

Within his troop and within the unit, Sgt Kinnear has been a tower of strength. With always a helping hand for the weak, a word of encouragement to the faint hearted and above all, by his own shining example he has upheld the highest traditions of his Corps and of the British SNCO. *(L.G. 22.1.46)*

Commando Gallantry Awards of World War II

Private John Ernest Leech
5948937, Bedfordshire & Hertfordshire, No. 3 Commando
Military Medal (Immediate)

During the operations in Calabria between the 28th August and 5th September 1943, Pte Leach took a prominent part in ambushing an Italian army lorry on the night of 30th–31st August and in capturing an Italian post on the 31st August This was despite his having malaria at the time, which fact he concealed. While escorting three Italian prisoners on the 31st August he fainted and was lost until the next day, when, his party being pursued by a company of Italian parachutists, rather than risk the safety of his companions he left them and concealed himself on a farm. On 2nd September 1943, being somewhat recovered, he and a sailor joined themselves to a party under Cpl Davison and the same day he, alone, captured six Italians in Bova Marina.

This soldier though sick, did more than many a man in perfect health and was a great asset to both patrols he found himself with.
[L.G. 13.1.44]

Lance Sergeant Hugh Howell Lewis
2585875, WS/Corporal, Royal Corps Signals, No. 3 Cdo.
Military Medal

Owing to the fact that the Signal Officer had been wounded in a previous action L/Sgt Lewis was in charge of the section during the action at Termoli, 3rd to 6th October 1943. Throughout the 4th, 5th and 6th October, during which the unit maintained its position, he constantly visited all troops. With complete contempt for danger he personally laid a line to the two flank troops in order to conserve the wireless batteries. In order to do this he had to cover one mile of ground which was being constantly machine gunned, mortared and shelled. The Signal communication was excellent throughout and the morale of the signallers was of the highest order. This was very largely due to the example set by L/Sgt Lewis. *[L.G. 27.1.44]*

Lance Sergeant Samuel Joseph Leyland
1434937, The Welch, No. 3 Commando
Military Medal (Immediate)

During operations around Agnone, Sicily, on 13th–14th July 1943, when he was a Lance Corporal he distinguished himself by leading back to the British lines a party of four other ranks who were cut off.

Italy

Meeting a German patrol of equal strength he out-manœuvred it. Two Germans were killed and his own party came through without loss.

During operations around Bova Marina, Italy between 25th August 1943 and 4th September 1943, L/Sgt Leyland was to begin with i/c of one of the small parties which had to take to the hills when LCI 107 went aground and was abandoned. He succeeded in rejoining his O.C. after two days and took a prominent part in an ambush on the 31st August 1943. Later on the same day he was one of a party which pursued some Italians. At the end of a long chase he was the only man who had been able to keep up with his officer. They captured an Italian post with a garrison of nine. On 1st September 1943 when the party was attacked by a company of parachutists he exposed himself with a complete contempt for their fire and succeeded firstly in observing the enemies dispositions, which could only be done from a skyline, secondly, in bringing in rifles which had been left in full view of the enemy when they first opened fire. This NCO was a splendid example to his men and an invaluable assistant to his officer throughout a period which many found trying.

Calm consistent and cheerful he proved himself in every way an exceptional soldier. *[L.G. 13.1.44]*

ACTING TEMPORARY COMPANY SERGEANT MAJOR GEORGE MALCOLM
Sergeant, Ply.X.639, No. 40 RM Commando
MILITARY MEDAL (IMMEDIATE)
22nd January 1944. Crossing of the Garigliano.
During the patrol to Rotondo the party was held up by an enemy machine-gun post. CSM Malcolm made his way forward under heavy small-arms fire from the enemy and reached a flank of the position. He threw grenades into the emplacement killing two of the occupants and wounding one. Due to this action the machine-gun post was silenced and the main body was able to advance without loss through casualties. CSM Malcolm showed extreme courage and coolness and was an inspiration to the men under his command. *[L.G. 18.4.44]*

Commando Gallantry Awards of World War II

LANCE SERGEANT GEORGE MCGREGOR FRASER MCPHERSON
2761028, Black Watch, No. 9 Commando
MILITARY MEDAL

Ref Map—Italy 1/25,000 Sheet 158 IV SE

During a Commando operation on March 1944, the above NCO was in charge of a bren LMG covering the left flank of the forward positions. Although subjected to continual heavy sniping and machine gun fire, he coolly and determinedly broke up group after group of enemy attempting to form up counter-attacks, and to infiltrate forward from the high ground.

Later in the day he was withdrawn from this forward position but made repeated journeys back to it, across 50 yds of open and bullet swept country, in order to break up enemy recce parties and direct the fire of our own 2" mortar. Before last light he again took up this forward position, although under heavy and continuous fire, despite the fact he was completely isolated from the remainder of his troop.

Shortly before dusk his position was attacked by a party of 20 enemy led by an officer with a map. L/Cpl McPherson held his fire until they were at point-blank range and then opened up with his bren LMG, killing the officer and seven of the enemy and wounding and driving off the remainder.

Throughout the day his personal courage and devotion to duty was an inspiration to all his comrades. *[L.G. 20.7.44]*

ACTING TY. COLOUR SERJEANT THOMAS MORGAN
Po.X.4905, No. 41 RM Commando
MILITARY MEDAL

At Vietri Sul Mare on 13th September, 1943 the troop of which this NCO was Serjeant Major carried out a counter-attack in which the two remaining officers were killed. Colour/Serjeant Morgan immediately took command of the troop. The enemy continued to attack fiercely and during the close fighting which ensued Colour/Serjeant Morgan noticed that two bren guns had stopped firing owing to stoppages. He immediately went forward and remedied the guns under heavy fire. By his disregard for his own safety and the skill with which he remedied the guns he did much to assist the successful repulse of the enemy. At all times this NCO showed a high standard of devotion to duty and was an inspiration to his men. *[L.G. 29.6.44]*

Italy

ACTING SERGEANT RICHARD O'BRIEN, D.C.M.
5340890, Royal Berks Regt, No. 2 Commando
MILITARY MEDAL (IMMEDIATE)
Gulf of Salerno 9th–19th September 1943.
At the battle of Salerno on 10th–11th September 1943 and Dragone Hill 13th September and Piegolette 15th–18th September 1943 this NCO showed complete disregard for personal safety.

On the morning of 10th September 1943 he went forward to contact a missing section under heavy fire and lead them to safety. Later, in the battle at Piegolette after his troop leader had been killed he led a patrol in daylight through the enemy lines and brought back valuable information and a prisoner. He then took charge of the troop after all four of his officers had become casualties. *[L.G. 13.1.44]*

BOMBARDIER RICHARD WILLIAM PANTALL
14241750 WS Bdr, RA (Fd), No. 3 Commando
MILITARY MEDAL
During operations around Bova Marina between 24th August and 5th September, 1943, this NCO took part in two landings. The object of the first was to capture a prisoner and the second to report by wireless the activities of the enemy around Bagaladi. During the morning of the 28th, this patrol of one officer and six other ranks became heavily engaged with between 50 and 60 of the enemy which they kept at bay for over an hour, during which the signallers were able to pack up and take away their wireless, while at least eight of the enemy were seen to fall. During the action Cpl Pantall played a prominent part. Later in the day his officer left him in charge while he went on a reconnaissance from which he did not return. Cpl Pantall took charge and kept his men concealed throughout the afternoon, although the valley was full of enemy troops and civilians armed with shotguns, some of whom came within three yards of his position. He counted 168 enemy in all. During the 29th August he successfully evaded an Italian patrol of one officer and 20 men although handicapped by the fact that one of his men had malaria, and the two RA signallers were exhausted. On 2nd September his party cut the telephone lines between Melito and Bova Marina. On the 5th September he brought his party into the British lines.

Through the operations he kept his men cheerful although he had not the least idea of when the invasion of Italy was to take place, and although their diet consisted mostly of figs. He succeeded in extricating this party, of which throughout only one man was capable of rendering him complete support. He has shown himself to be an excellent NCO. [L.G 13.1 44]

Acting Sergeant Cecil Douglas Parsons
WS/Cpl, 5952876, Bedfordshire & Hertfordshire, No. 2 Cdo.
Military Medal

On 17th April 1945 Sgt Parsons was Section Sgt of 3 Troop, No. 2 Commando when his section was ordered to attack the bridges over the canals west of Argenta.

Owing to the formation of the four dykes and the flooded area to the west of the canals, a frontal assault was essential. Shortly after the attack commenced Sgt Parsons's Section Officer became a casualty and Parsons took over command of the section. He led his section with great ability against heavy enemy opposition, to capture the bridge over his area, silencing at least one spandau position himself in the process. The enemy shortly afterwards counter-attacked in some strength and though out-numbered, Sgt Parsons's section, sustained by his magnificent coolness and inspiring example, succeeded in repulsing the counter-attack. Sgt Parsons maintained his position against three further counter-attacks during the morning, inflicting considerable loss on the enemy. Throughout the remainder of the operation Sgt Parsons displayed outstanding leadership, and his fine example inspired great confidence in the remainder of his section. [L.G. 23.8.45]

Acting Temporary Corporal Neil Patrick
Ply.X.103894, No. 40 RM Commando
Military Medal (Immediate)

22nd January 1944. Crossing of the Garigliano.

This Corporal accompanied the patrol to Rotondo. The force was pinned to the ground by enemy small arms fire and was also being engaged by tanks. Despite this, Cpl Patrick worked his way forward to the road and threw a 77 grenade under an armoured car which was set on fire. He then withdrew his section into a gully under cover. Later, whilst on a night patrol 'S' mines were encountered and seven men were wounded including the officer in command. Cpl Patrick, being the only NCO left, was entirely responsible for organising the evacuation of the wounded despite a German patrol passing within ten yards of him. He himself carried many of the wounded back to safety. Throughout the operation, Cpl Patrick showed extreme courage and was responsible for the saving of many lives.

Recommended for immediate DCM, awarded MM. [L.G. 18.4.44]

Italy

Lance Sergeant Frederick Peachey
3654154, South Lancs. Regt, No. 2 Commando
Military Medal (Immediate)

Gulf of Salerno 17th September 1943.
At Piegolette on the 17th September 1943 this NCO performed his duties fearlessly and with extreme keenness. On more than one occasion in darkness and in daylight he went out with another man to locate enemy machine-guns which were firing at his section position, as a result of which effective fire was brought to bear on the enemy. Throughout the operation from the initial landing he was always in the forefront of the sections activities and served as a very fine example to all the troop. He was wounded at a later stage in the Piegolette operation.

This NCO had previously taken part in the Commando raids of Vaagsö and St. Nazaire where he distinguished himself for his coolness and steadiness under fire. On the later raid he was seriously wounded but continued his LMG fire from the deck of his ML. *[L.G. 13.1.44]*

Acting Ty. Corporal Frederick William Pryor
Ch.X.104490, No. 41 RM Commando
Military Medal (Immediate)

On September 13th, 1943, at Vietri Sul Mare, this NCO (his section officer having previously been wounded) commanded his section with great foresight and initiative, maintaining complete control under trying conditions and using his fire power to the maximum advantage. When his position was attacked he repeatedly led small counter-attacks which drove the enemy back and inflicted many casualties upon them. His courage and coolness were an inspiration to his section on this day and at all other times. *[L.G. 27.6.44]*

Private Edward Ralphs
3656776, South Lancs Regt, Special Raiding Sqn. & No. 7 Cdo.
Military Medal

In the fighting south of Termoli during the morning of 3rd October 1943 Pte Ralphs served his bren gun to very good effect while engaging superior enemy forces.

When the Intelligence Officer was wounded he moved his gun forward across exposed ground to cover his evacuation and by daring of his action surprised and killed four of the enemy, wounding several more.

In subsequent fighting west of Termoli while employed as a runner he made repeated journeys with important messages across the open ground between two sectors under very heavy enemy fire.

At the height of a barrage of artillery, mortar and machine gun fire he learned that the crew of an anti-tank gun had been knocked out. He immediately went forward and evacuated one of the wounded men and, on hearing that there was still another, went back and dragged him to safety. When ten minutes later a machine gun was hit by mortar fire he again went forward to evacuate the wounded although the position was swept by fire.

He stayed on the forward position carrying messages till an enemy flanking movement threatened to cut him off. He then made his way back to our main positions, where during the whole ...... *[remainder missing].* *[L.G. 27.1.44]*

ACTING TY. COLOUR SERGEANT WILLIAM REID
Po.X.100232, No. 41 RM Commando
MILITARY MEDAL (IMMEDIATE)

At Vietri Sul Mare on 23rd September 1943 Sgt Reid was a section serjeant with the forward troop on the left hand slope of the defile. During the heavy mortaring which preceded an attack his Section Officer was killed and other casualties were sustained. Serjeant Reid then took over the section and during the subsequent attack he showed great gallantry and initiative. Although under heavy small arms fire he twice lead small sorties to deal with enemy who were infiltrating through our lines and inflicted heavy casualties on the enemy. This NCO showed a very high standard of leadership and devotion to duty and was an inspiration to his men.

[L.G. 27.6.44]

PRIVATE PEARSON RIGG
7402326, Royal Army Medical Corps, No. 3 Commando
MILITARY MEDAL (IMMEDIATE)

All the casualties caused in 4 Troop during the operations at Termoli between 3rd October and 6th October, 1943 occurred in the positions in the forward defended line which were enfiladed by enemy tanks on the left. By the [...] machine gun fire had ploughed a track through the [...] in rear of our forward weapon pits and any movement along this fixed line brought a burst of fire, yet Trooper Rigg never hesitated to go forward immediately any casualty occurred. He dealt with five of our casualties in these conditions, often exposing himself for considerable periods while dressing them.

His conduct throughout the operation was in accordance with the highest traditions of the RAMC. *[L.G. 27.1.44]*

Italy

Lance Corporal B. J. Rozen
20221 A/P, No. 10 Commando att 2/6th Queen's Royal Regt.
Military Medal (Immediate)

This English-speaking Polish NCO was attached to 'A' Company, 2/6th Queen's Royal Regiment for the crossing of the River Garigliano on the night of 17th January, 1944. Immediately after crossing the river, the company ran into mines, and one of the two leading platoon commanders and a dozen men were wounded, when three mines went up. This NCO immediately got in front and encouraged the remainder forward, showing a fine disregard for his personal safety. On reaching the enemy wire, he halted the men,cut it himself, and then led them through. He then stayed with the officer-less platoon and led it forward to the road, and up to its objective.

L/Cpl Rozen showed exceptional powers of leadership for his rank and a complete disregard for his personal safety, and was instrumental in getting the leading platoons on to their objective. *Polish Forces, therefore not in London Gazette. Award approved 23.3.44.*

Lance Corporal Edward Charles Saberton
Marine, Ch.X.101281, No. 43 RM Commando
Military Medal

For outstanding courage, determination and devotion to duty in operations during the campaign in Italy.   L.G. 10.7.45

Private Andrew Scott
2938003, Camerons, No. 9 Commando
Military Medal (Immediate)

Action at Monte Faita, night 2nd–3rd February 1944, Map Ref. 858043, Italy 1/50,000, Sheet 160 II.

During this action in which Pte Scott's Troop captured an enemy Company HQ, Pte Scott was rendered unconscious by the blast of a shell. When he recovered consciousness the Commando had withdrawn after heavy casualties and the position had been reoccupied by the enemy. In full view of the enemy position, however, he immediately started to attend to wounded men who it had been impossible to evacuate during the withdrawal. When he saw that the position had been reoccupied by the enemy, Scott unhesitatingly advanced to the position to obtain assistance for the injured, and although unarmed, took seven of the enemy occupants of the position prisoner. He persuaded the prisoners to carry five wounded men into a house where he compelled the prisoners to dress their wounds. Scott remained in the enemy lines with the wounded and prisoners until our own stretcher parties came forward and with their assistance he organised the prisoners into stretcher-bearer parties to carry the casualties back to our lines. By approaching the enemy position unarmed and single-handed and taking seven prisoners, Scott showed outstanding courage and his actions were responsible for saving the lives of at least five of our casualties. *[L.G. 29.6.44]*

Corporal Charles Arnold Simister
7363858 WS/Cpl., RAMC, No. 2 Commando
Military Medal (Immediate)

Gulf of Salerno 9th–18th September 1943.
The above NCO acted as troop medical orderly to No. 3 Troop during the actions at Liberatore, Dragone and Piegolette on 10th, 13th, 16th and 18th September 1943 respectively, performing his duties with complete disregard for his own personal safety. He was responsible for saving the lives of at least six badly wounded men. At Dragone he attended to wounded under direct mortar and machine-gun fire from close range and by his actions and coolness of bearing encouraged the members of the troop to remain steady in their positions under heavy fire. *[L.G. 13.1.44]*

Temporary Sergeant Harold Smith
Po.X.105414, No. 40 RM Commando
Military Medal (Periodic)

This NCO has served with the unit from Garigliano to Argenta and has made a lasting impression on all ranks. Although out of the line he is of a quiet unassuming nature he performs his administrative duties with the utmost efficiency. Once on the battlefield, however, he undergoes a complete mental and physical change and conducts himself with great gallantry and coolness. His acts of bravery are too numerous to cite individually although the following have contributed to his legendary fame within the unit. At Anzio his Section Commander was wounded at an early stage in the battle. The section was in an isolated position and although wounded himself in the arm and legs Sgt Smith refused to recognize defeat and held his section to its position until relieved the following day.

On the Dalmatian Island of Brac his Section Commander was killed at a critical stage in the battle. Left alone to conduct his defence, Sgt Smith found that his men had expended their ammunition and that the enemy, vastly superior in numbers, had encircled the position. Emerging once more indefatigable in adversity, Sgt Smith gave the order to fix bayonets and fought his section back to a beach-head in the face of heavy fire and strongly

Italy

pressing enemy. Later that night he went back with a patrol to recover the dead left behind in the withdrawal, although he was forced to retire by accurate small-arms fire.

At Sarande, Lake Commachio and Menate Sgt Smith displayed the same sterling qualities of leadership and bravery which the unit had come to expect of him. In Operation 'Impact' (Menate) the unit suffered its most serious reverse and casualties were heavy. Throughout a critical period, with unit morale at its lowest ebb, Sgt Smith with his customary brilliance, encouraged, exhorted and inspired his section to such good effect that it was able with the remainder of the unit to win through to the final objective.

Twice previously recommended for decorations, this NCO has given little thought to personal recognition, and has never allowed personal consideration to influence his selfless devotion to duty. It is strongly recommended that Sgt Smith's outstanding service with the unit over a long operational period, be given the recognition it deserves. *(L.G. 21.1.46)*

ACTING SERGEANT WILLIAM THOMAS SMITH
WS/Corporal, T/6288218, RASC, No. 3 Commando
MILITARY MEDAL

For devotion to duty and great powers of leadership under fire.

During the action at Termoli on 5th October 1943 this NCO commanded a section of ten men exposed on the forward slopes of a hill covering [hole] and dead ground in front. The section [hole] under heavy shell fire. Sgt Smith inspired confidence in his section by his own example of coolness. They remained in this exposed position for six hours though casualties were being inflicted.

When given the order to withdraw 400 yards to a new position he brought his men back without loss, finding the only covered line available. This manœuvre was carried out under heavy mortar fire. He placed his section and gave the order to dig in. They were then shelled and machine-gunned by four Mark IV tanks for six hours. It was through Sgt Smith's fine and courageous example that his section stood their ground with confidence and cheerfulness. He was alive to every changing situation and had complete disregard for his own personal safety. *[L.G. 27.1.44]*

Commando Gallantry Awards of World War II

ACTING TEMPORARY CORPORAL ERIC STRINGER
Ch.X.104430, No. 41 RM Commando
MILITARY MEDAL (IMMEDIATE)

On September 10th, 1943, at Vietri Sul Mare this NCO showed great gallantry when he took out a small patrol to mop up an enemy machine gun post, which was being particularly troublesome. Although his route was occupied by the enemy he succeeded in his attack destroying the gun and bringing back two prisoners. At all other times throughout the operation he was an inspiration to his men leading them bravely and wisely.   *[L.G. 27.6.44]*

ACTING TY. SERGEANT WALTER ERNEST TILNEY
Po.X.108009, No. 41 RM Commando
MILITARY MEDAL (IMMEDIATE)

During the darkness on the morning of the 17th September, 1943, in the attack on White Cross Hill (Salerno Sector) this NCO was ordered to destroy an machine-gun post which was impeding the advance of the section. With five men he began to work his way to a position from which he could assault. During this approach four out of the five men were wounded but he pressed on and with the one remaining man and the additional grenades from the wounded men he silenced the gun.   *[L.G. 27.6.44]*

ACTING WARRANT OFFICER CLASS II RICHARD TOMLINSON
W/Sergeant, 840175, RA (Field Branch), No. 2 Commando
MILITARY MEDAL (IMMEDIATE)

Owing to navigational difficulties on Operation 'Roast' on the morning of 2nd April 1945, 3 Troop HQ became separated from its Rifle Sections and was ordered to form part of an *ad hoc* force to storm the beaches and form the Commando bridge head.

By setting a peerless example, CSM Tomlinson led his HQ weapons to attack and subdue at least six enemy weapon pits and pill-boxes, and secure the right flank as far as the Canale de Bellocchio.

Later during the same day after re-organisation further inland, the Commando was running short of 3" mortar ammunition owing to a counter-attack on the right flank. Tomlinson volunteered and personally and successfully led a patrol to a cache on the beach to collect more bombs, knowing that this involved running the gauntlet over ground covered by enemy fire. On the following day during the advance up the Spit, Tomlinson's Troop was pinned by intense shellfire. His coolness and disregard for his own safety were

Italy

a great inspiration to a body of men already severely strained by fatigue. *[L.G. 5.7.45]*

MARINE FREDERICK PHILIP TYMAN
Ch.X.113132, No. 40 RM Commando
MILITARY MEDAL (IMMEDIATE)

Davido [?] Valentia ... 1943
Mne Tyman was sent forward by himself to try and locate a German LMG position which causing trouble to the main position. He worked his way forward about three-quarters of a mile in front of our forward position and located a mortar position by the cemetery above Pizzo, which was firing. He threw a grenade into the battery and withdrew. Later one German was found dead. This action of Mne Tyman caused the mortar to discontinue firing. The LMG had moved and could not be located. On his way back he saw an Italian section moving forward and he shot two with his snipers rifle. Throughout this patrol he displayed great initiative besides skill and determination, gathering valuable information.
(L.G. 8.2.44)

ACTING CORPORAL FREDERICK GEORGE USHER
Marine, Ch.X.104066, No. 40 RM Commando
MILITARY MEDAL (IMMEDIATE)

Cpl Usher was in command of a patrol ordered to the railway bridge two miles north of Termoli. He was informed by some Italians that the bridge was held by Germans. He decided to attack it. The sentry was surprised and shot by the bren gunner and several Germans retreating over the bridge were wounded. He found the bridge prepared for demolition and although knowing little about it he cut all the wires he could see. Two days later he took out another patrol and succeeded in accurately finding out the enemy positions to our front. His initiative and leadership throughout the action were of a very high standard. *[L.G. 8.2.44]*

ACTING SERGEANT FRANK WALSH
2986730, A & SH, No. 9 Commando
MILITARY MEDAL (IMMEDIATE)

Ref: Map Italy 1/50,000 No. 158 IV.
On 5th March 1944 No. 2986730 Sgt Walsh F. was commander of a section of a Fighting Patrol operating in Area Square 8230. Throughout the Patrol Sgt Walsh showed outstanding courage and leadership whilst under heavy small arms and mortar fire, both in locating enemy positions and in the final assault on these positions. During a period in which the patrol was pinned down by enemy

fire and suffered 40% casualties, Sgt Walsh organised and led small parties to outflank the enemy position in a most determined and courageous manner. Whenever his party was held up, he pushed on himself in order to outflank the enemy and cause their fire to be lifted from his section's position. During the final assault on the enemy position, he displayed an outstanding example of leadership to all the men and although he was wounded during this assault he carried on until he had bayoneted and killed the Boche who had wounded him. After being wounded he refused to return to the regimental aid post until he had re-organised his section and was ordered to return by his patrol leader.

[L.G. 20.7.44]

ACTING CORPORAL WILLIAM WAUGH
2991737, A & SH, No. 9 Commando
MILITARY MEDAL (IMMEDIATE)

Ref Map—Italy 1/25,000 Sheet 158 IV SE

This NCO was a team leader during the Commando attack on wadi in square 8230 on 19th March 1944. Although painfully injured from barbed wire gashes incurred in the original advance to the objective, L/Cpl Waugh displayed a standard of leadership far in excess of that normally expected from an NCO of this junior rank.

During the initial stages of the attack L/Cpl Waugh's Troop became completely cut off from the rest of the unit, and there existed no means of communication other than by a runner, who had to cross ground that was completely dominated by enemy fire.

L/Cpl Waugh twice volunteered to cross this open ground to contact other troops, which he did with the utmost coolness and determination while under heavy LMG and mortar fire. His self-control and coolness which he displayed the whole day while under heavy mortar fire was a magnificent example to all ranks, and particularly to the team under his command, which drove off several determined enemy counter-attacks which were delivered under strong support from enemy mortars.

When the Commando broke up the final enemy counter-attack, L/Cpl Waugh most gallantly led his assault team forward with determined dash and courage inflicting heavy casualties on the Boche.

Throughout the operation, this NCO set a splendid example of fearlessness and leadership and handled his team in a most determined and successful manner. *[L.G. 20.7.44]*

Italy

Lance Corporal John Webb
Private, 7377410, RAMC, No. 2 Commando
Military Medal (Immediate)
Gulf of Salerno September 9th–18th 1943

During the period 9th–18th September 1943 this NCO carried out his duties as medical orderly tending the wounded whilst under fire with complete disregard for personal safety. He searched a hill after our own troops had withdrawn owing to heavy enemy fire and casualties, and brought in two severely wounded men.

[L.G. 13.1.44]

Acting Corporal John Howie Wham
3065655, R. Scots, No. 3 Commando
Military Medal (Immediate)
Ref Map—Italy, 1/25,000 Sheet IV SE

This man was a member of an assault team that took part in the Commando attack on wadi in square 8230 on 19th March 1944.

At last light the Commando position was heavily counter-attacked, and the whole unit became involved in fierce hand-to-hand fighting. During a critical period on one flank, Wham seized a bren LMG from a wounded member of his troop and advanced onto the crest of a ridge from which the Boche was grenading our positions. This single-handed attack was largely responsible for the repulse of the first enemy wave of attack.

During the final withdrawal of the Commando, all bren LMGs were left to cover the evacuation of casualties and the first phase of the withdrawal. During this period heavy enemy fire was directed into our positions, and a burst of LMG fire smashed Wham's bren and wounded him in the arm. He immediately manned another bren LMG whose gunner had been killed and continued holding his rearguard position despite his wound, until ordered to withdraw.

Throughout the whole operation, Pte Wham set a splendid example of determination and coolness while under heavy fire, and his complete disregard for his wound and devotion to duty was of the highest order.

[L.G. 20.7.44]

Lance Sergeant George R. Wilkins
2881259, P/Lance Sergeant, London Scottish, No. 9 Cdo.
Military Medal (Immediate)
Action at Monte Faita, night 2nd–3rd February 1944, Map Ref. 858043, Italy 1/50,000, Sheet 160 II

During this action, No. 4 Troop of which L/Sgt Wilkins was a Section Commander, acted as advance guard of the attack and was under continuous enemy artillery and mortar fire during the advance.

Throughout heavy opposition, L/Sgt Wilkins controlled and directed his section with the utmost determination and coolness, and led them forward to the attack with efficiency and disregard for his personal safety.

Although under heavy artillery and mortar fire, L/Sgt Wilkins succeeded in capturing a strongly defended enemy position with the assistance of only two men, the remainder of his section having become casualties. All the members of the enemy position were either killed or captured.

After the attack the Commando was ordered to withdraw, and although L/Sgt Wilkins was cut off from his section he remained behind to arrange for the evacuation of casualties, which he did under continuous mortar fire. His courage and determination were an example to all the men who remained to assist the wounded, and his leadership was responsible for the lives of several of the casualties as well as preventing the enemy force from reoccupying the position while he was organising the evacuation of casualties.

[L.G. 29.6.44]

Lance Sergeant James William Wilkinson
5957086, Bedfs & Herts, No. 3 Commando
Military Medal (Immediate)

L/Sgt Wilkinson was Second-in-Command of a patrol of one officer and six other ranks which was landed near Bova Marina on night of 27th–28th August 1943 with the object of going to Reggio and reporting enemy activities with a wireless set. His officer left him in a defensive position and with one L/Cpl went to do a reconnaissance. While he was away the Sgt's party came under rifle fire, so he moved to join his officer but coming again under small arms fire had to extricate his party. The officer never reappeared. While making towards Melito on the 29th August they came under fire. Seeing only four Italians they returned it driving them off and capturing their food, water and kit. This helped the party to carry on. On the third day the wireless failed and on the fourth day, the Sgt was warned by a peasant that Caribineiri were

Italy

searching the farms so he moved to Sanpantaleone. During the afternoon he was able to observe and avoid two parties of German infantry. The next six days he kept his patrol concealed in a farm as one of them was sick and on the 6th September succeeded in joining our own Army.

It was entirely due to the efforts of this NCO that this party of two Commando signallers and two RA signallers were able to survive a week with little water and food and no exact knowledge of when the British Invasion was intended to take place.

[L.G. 13.1.44]

LIEUTENANT-COLONEL FRANCIS W. FYNN, M.C.
109801, London Scottish Infantry, 8 Commando
BRONZE STAR

Francis W. Finn, M.C., 109801, Lieutenant-Colonel, London Scottish Infantry, 8 Commando, British Army, for heroic achievement in connection with military operations in Italy on 1st April 1945.

By superb leadership and complete devotion to duty in the face of every possible difficulty attached to a water-borne operation, Lieutenant-Colonel Fynn led the 2nd Commando in an attack, with only one third of his force, against well-entrenched enemy positions near Lake Commachio, Italy. His inspiring influence materially affected the outcome of a hazardous and daring operation behind the enemy lines, as did his encouraging of his weary troops in successive assaults on a vital bridge and an enemy force of of

Commando Gallantry Awards of World War II

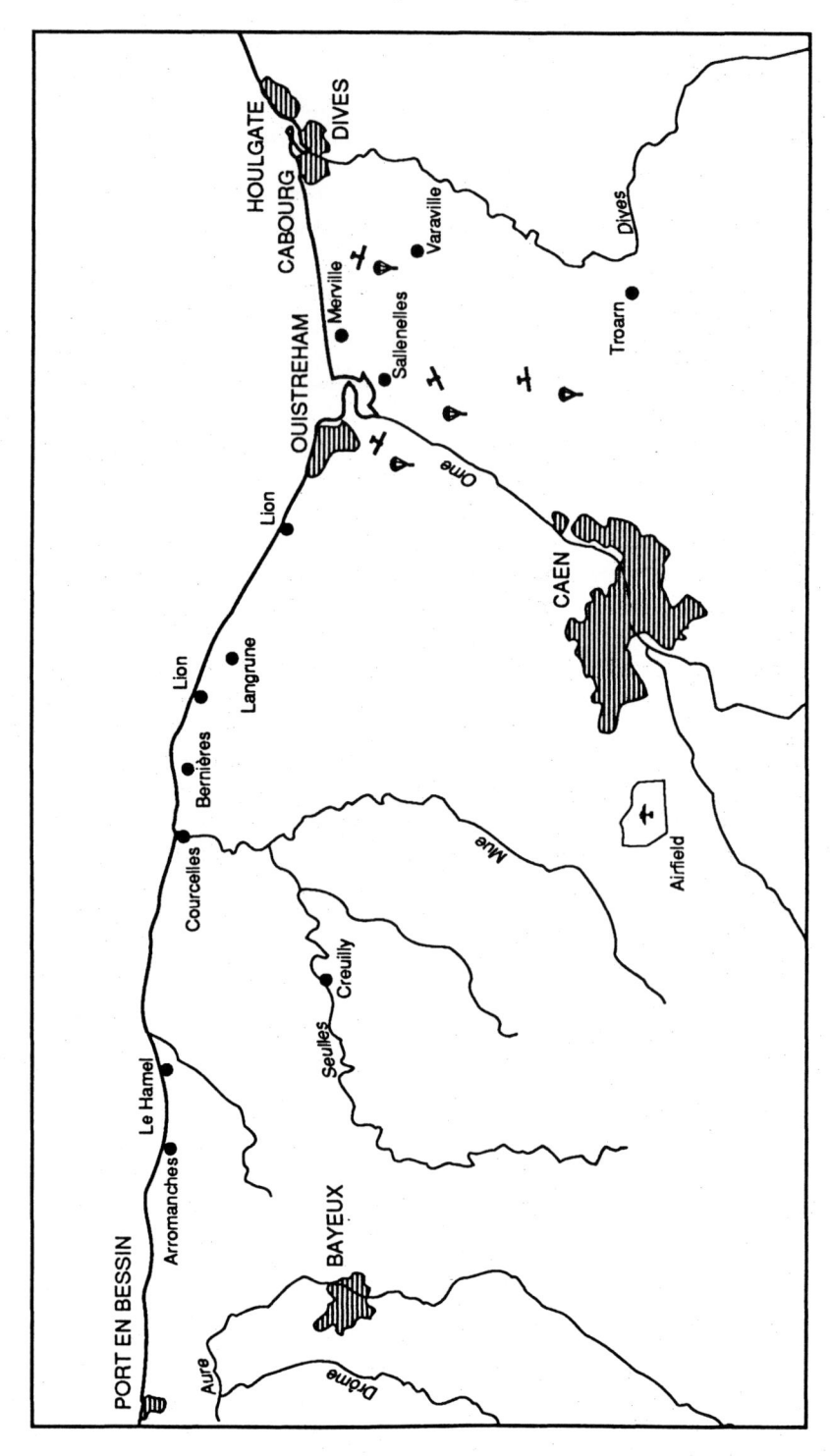

D-Day and the Normandy Break-Out

ACTING LIEUTENANT-COLONEL CAMPBELL
RICHARD HARDY, D.S.O., R.M.
Capt (Brevet Maj), No. 46 RM Commando
BAR TO DISTINGUISHED SERVICE ORDER
(PERIODIC)

Lt-Col Hardy has commanded his Commando with outstanding success from 6th June to 8th October 1944. During this period, the Commando has distinguished itself on many occasions. Lt-Col Hardy has consistently shown a complete disregard for his own personal safety when under fire and has on all occasions set a magnificent personal example. Two occasions are cited, typical of several, when his personal courage and leadership have been the decisive factor in winning the battle.

On 20th August, at Putot en Auge, the Commando was ordered at very short notice to attack by night a strong enemy position in close country which has repulsed a battalion attack during the day.

Little daylight was left for recce. While the recce parties were assembling, a mortar bomb wounded two troop leaders, the Adjutant, the Signals Officer and the Forward Observation Officer. Lt-Col Hardy, in order to overcome the setback, personally placed every officer and NCO in his correct position on the start line. Since it was too dark to point out objectives he led the assault himself from the centre of the leading wave and was the first man into the enemy position.

The complete success of this attack was due entirely to his courage, determination and leadership.

On 25th August at Quetteville, he again displayed the greatest resolution and devotion to duty when his commando was held up by sustained opposition after suffering considerable casualties.

Although wounded at the beginning of the action, his determination to find a way into the enemy position never faltered.

It was at his suggestion that the final and successful attack was made. It was entirely due to his inspiration and personal disregard of danger that the objective was finally won. *[L.G. 29.3.45]*

TEMPORARY LIEUTENANT-COLONEL ROBERT WILLIAM PALLISER DAWSON
130068, Loyals, No. 4 Commando
DISTINGUISHED SERVICE ORDER

Col Dawson fought his way to the Commando objective and captured the Ouistreham Battery despite heavy casualties suffered in street fighting on the way. No artillery support was available as both the Commando Forward Observation Officer and FOB became early casualties.

Col Dawson was himself twice wounded during the course of the battle, but refused to relinquish his command. It was due to his leadership and direction that the attack was successfully pressed home. *[L.G. 31.8.44]*

MAJOR WILLIAM NICHOL GRAY
No. 45 RM Commando
DISTINGUISHED SERVICE ORDER

Since his Commanding Officer was wounded on D Day Major Gray had commanded No. 45 RM Commando and has shown himself to be outstanding on numerous occasions both as a Commanding Officer and as a daring and fearless leader.

On 7th June 1944 the Commando was ordered to attack and hold the area Merville and Franceville Plage. Major Gray with a skeleton HQ personally directed the fierce fighting that took place in both villages. On one occasion the Support Troop was unable to move forward being pinned down by accurate MG 34 fire from a well protected position at the top of the main street.

Major Gray gathered a few men together and led a bayonet attack against the enemy, shot the gunner with his revolver and put the rest to flight.

He continued to fight his unit for the next 36 hours until almost out of ammunition when he received the order to withdraw. This he achieved successfully and under difficult circumstances brought his unit back to our lines intact.

Major Gray's tireless energy, devotion to duty and unfailing cheerfulness throughout all difficulties has been an example to all, and it is largely through his fine leadership that his unit has inflicted such heavy casualties upon the enemy.

Recommended for MC, awarded DSO. *[L.G. 20.2.45]*

D-Day and the Normandy Break-Out

ACTING LIEUTENANT-COLONEL JAMES LOUIS MOULTON, R.M.
Captain
DISTINGUISHED SERVICE ORDER

For gallant and distinguished services while operating with the Army during the successful landing in Normandy. *L.G. 29.8.44*

ACTING LIEUTENANT-COLONEL CECIL FARNDALE PHILLIPS, R.M.
Captain
DISTINGUISHED SERVICE ORDER

For gallant and distinguished services while operating with the Army in Normandy. *L.G. 12.9.44*

TEMPORARY LIEUTENANT JOHN ANTHONY CRAWFORD HUGILL, R.N.V.R.
No. 30 Commando
DISTINGUISHED SERVICE CROSS

For gallantry, skill, determination and undaunted devotion to duty during the landing of Allied Forces on the coast of Normandy.
L.G. 26.12.44

LIEUTENANT GORDON POLLARD, M.C., M.M., R.A.
288876, Royal Artillery, No. 3 Commando
BAR TO MILITARY CROSS

On the evening 11th June 1944 at the Château d'Amfreville the position of the troop which this officer was in was heavily shelled and the Troop Commander was killed at once. Lieut Pollard immediately ran to his assistance and finding there was nothing he could do he went from slit trench to slit trench dealing with casualties and heartening the soldiers, many of whom had never been under such fire before.

There is no doubt that he was instrumental in saving several lives.

On the night of 12th June 1944 a Para Battalion which was forming up 100 yards forward of his position for the assault on Breville, suffered some fifty casualties through shell fire. Accompanied by one Medical Orderly Lieut Pollard immediately went forward and dealt with between 15 and 20 casualties most of whom lives would otherwise have been lost. He did not cease his efforts until he came to the village of Breville, a distance of some 800 yards ahead of his position. During this time he was continually under fire and it is little short of a miracle that he himself did not lose his life.

At Termoli, Italy, on 5th October 1943 he distinguished himself by directing an artillery shoot from a position on a forward slope in close range of the enemies's infantry.

His reputation for coolness and gallantry had become a byword in the unit and is an inspiration to the soldiers under his command.
Recommended for DSO, awarded Bar to MC.   *[L.G. 31.8.44]*

TEMPORARY CAPTAIN JOHN ALDERSON
Lieutenant, 113655, The Seaforth Highlanders (Ross-shire Buffs, The Duke of Albany's), Special Service Troops
MILITARY CROSS

In recognition of gallant and distinguished services in Normandy.
L.G. 31.8.44

ACTING TY. MAJOR IAN NIGEL NEVILLE BEADLE
Temp Captain, No. 45 RM Commando
MILITARY CROSS

At Merville on 8th June 1944, Capt Beadles Troop was surrounded and were heavily and repeatedly attacked by the enemy. He selected the enemy position that was causing the most casualties and personally led a counter-attack. Due to his quick appreciation and to the great dash and gallantry with which the assault was led, the counter-attack was completely successful, destroying the enemy's positions and inflicting heavy casualties. This action restored a critical situation, and its success was primarily due to Captain Beadle's sound judgement, intrepid gallantry and great devotion to duty, which was an inspiration to all ranks. He has shown these fine qualities consistently during the campaign.
Recommended for DSO, awarded MC.   *[L.G. 20.2.45]*

TEMPORARY LIEUTENANT CECIL ARTHUR
DOUGLAS BIRCHER
S.A.U.D.F.
MILITARY CROSS

For gallant and distinguished services while operating with the Army during the successful landing in Normandy.   *L.G. 29.8.44*

TEMPORARY CAPTAIN HUTCHISON BURT
Lieutenant, 231543, The Royal Norfolk Regiment, Special Service Troops, No. 4 Commando
MILITARY CROSS

Date of action : 6th June 1944.
Captain Burt displayed outstanding leadership and courage in assaulting the Battery at Ouistreham and pressing home the assault

in the face of very heavy defensive fire. Capt Burt's Troop sustained heavy casualties in this attack, but he rallied them and carried them through. In subsequent operations, Capt Burt has shown great skill and resource. *[L.G. 31.8.44]*

TY. LIEUTENANT DAVID JOHN COGGER, R.M.
MILITARY CROSS

For gallant and distinguished services while operating with the Army in Normandy. *L.G. 12.9.44*

CAPTAIN JAMES CYRIL FRASER CREGAN
RAMC, No. 41 RM Commando
MILITARY CROSS

La Brech–Lion Sur Mer 6th–7th June 1944.
This officer showed great personal bravery, coolness and devotion to duty in dealing with a very large number of casualties, both on the beach under heavy fire, and when Commando HQ was heavily bombed. His example and perseverance resulted in the successful evacuation of the majority of wounded in the unit. His conduct has been of the very highest order. *[L.G. 31.8.44]*

TEMPORARY LIEUTENANT ISAAC GOLDSTEIN
S. A. U. D. F.
MILITARY CROSS

For gallant and distinguished services while operating with the Army in Normandy. *L.G. 12.9.44*

ACTING LIEUTENANT-COLONEL THOMAS MALCOLM GRAY
Capt, No. 41 RM Commando
MILITARY CROSS

At Lion sur Mer on the 6th of June, from the moment of landing under heavy and accurate mortar and shell fire, Lt-Col Gray showed a complete and utter disregard for his own safety. His coolness, cheerfulness and personal bravery were an inspiration to all. On the first morning he was slightly wounded on two occasions and insisted on continuing. His example contributed enormously to the success of the Commando task.
Recommended for DSO, awarded MC. *[L.G. 29.5.44]*

Ty. Captain Ronald Graham Kennell Hardey
WS Lieut, 121641, H.L.I., No. 6 Commando
Military Cross

6th June 1944.

Capt Hardey was in command of the leading troop in the approach march from the Brigade forming up point off the beach to the Caen Canal. It was essential that he should push ahead and brush aside all opposition.

His troop neutralised no less than seven enemy emplacements and took the surrender of a four gun battery.

Capt Hardey's judgement and leadership were faultless, and his fearless example was beyond praise. *[L.G. 31.8.44]*

Temporary Major Donald Charles Hopson
87593, RAC, No. 3 Commando
Military Cross

Since the time of the landing in Normandy on 6th June 1944 this officer had shown the same determination gallantry and coolness under fire which he had already shown in Agnone, Sicily and in Termoli, Italy, on 14th July 1943 and 5th October 1943.

On the 6th June 1944 when the 2nd i/c was wounded bringing the unit forward, Major Hopson took charge and led the troops across the bridges Benouville with great speed and skill, and with slight casualties.

Subsequently, although wounded in the head when the self-propelled gun in which he was operating struck a mine, he insisted on proceeding out with another self-propelled gun and completing his task.

On the occasion of the attack on Breville he performed invaluable service by leading tanks up to forward positions which the Commanders had not had time to recce.

Several times during the heavy shelling of the Unit's forward defended lines he again showed great courage and coolness in directing the bringing to shelter of the wounded although he himself was again slightly wounded.

His service with this unit had always been an example of courage, coolness and efficiency and an inspiration to his fellow officers and men.

Recommended for DSO, awarded MC. *[L.G. 1.3.45]*

D-Day and the Normandy Break-Out

LIEUTENANT WILLIAM THOMAS BRINLEY JAMES
WS/Lieut, 186188, Welsh Regt, No. 4 Cdo. & 47 RM Cdo.
MILITARY CROSS

For courage and leadership displayed during enemy attack at Hauger on the evening of 8th June 1944. The enemy had broken through the position covering the Commando left flank and were advancing up a valley straight towards Commando HQ which was being held by only a few men. Lieut James realised the danger of the situation and immediately called a few men and started a counter-attack. Although the enemy strength was estimated at one platoon he advanced with his small force and held the enemy's thrust. He personally accounted for many of the enemy by first firing a bren gun until the ammunition for that gun was expended. He then continued to fire with a rifle until all the ammunition for that weapon was gone and finally he picked up a Garrand rifle continued to fire and succeeded in holding the enemy until a force arrived to assist his small party to drive the enemy back. By his prompt and brave action he undoubtedly prevented the enemy overrunning the position and by containing them formed the base for the counter-attack which restored the position. *[L.G. 31.5.44]*

CAPTAIN PHILLIPE KIEFFER
Capt (13 Fn 40) 1 A.Cdo, Comd French Det 10 (IA) Cdo.with No. 4 Commando
MILITARY CROSS

Commandant Kieffer was responsible for the mopping up of the town of Ouistreham in conjunction with 4 Commando's assault on the battery. His unit suffered severely, nine out of his eleven officers becoming casualties, while Commandant Kieffer was himself wounded. The dash and resolute action of this officer led to the final liquidation of a series of enemy strong points in the coastal built-up area, and of an enemy company in the town itself.

ACTING TEMPORARY MAJOR JOHN LEE, R.M.
Temporary Captain
MILITARY CROSS

For gallant and distinguished services while operating with the Army during the successful landing in Normandy.   *L.G. 29.8.44*

Commando Gallantry Awards of World War II

LIEUTENANT ROSS ROBERTSON LITTLEJOHN
197229, The Black Watch (Royal Highland Regiment),
Special Service Troops
MILITARY CROSS
In recognition of gallant and distinguished services in Normandy.
L.G. 31.8.44

ACTING TEMPORARY CAPTAIN RODERICK GIMSON
MACKENZIE, R.M.
Temporary Lieutenant
MILITARY CROSS
For gallant and distinguished services while operating with the Army during the successful landing in Normandy.   L.G. 29.8.44

TEMPORARY CAPTAIN LYLE LOUWRENS
ARCHIBALD MCKAY
S.A.U.D.F.
MILITARY CROSS
For gallant and distinguished services while operating with the Army during the successful landing in Normandy.   L.G. 29.8.44

ACTING TEMPORARY CAPTAIN KENNETH
REGINALD MAURICE PERROTT, R.M.
Temporary Lieutenant
MILITARY CROSS
For gallant and distinguished services while operating with the Army during the successful landing in Normandy.   L.G. 29.8.44

ACTING TY. MAJOR JOHN NICHOLSON RUSHFORTH, R.M.
Temporary Captain
MILITARY CROSS
For gallant and distinguished services while operating with the Army during the successful landing in Normandy.   L.G. 29.8.44

ACTING CAPTAIN TERENCE MORTON PATRICK
STEVENS, R.M.
Lieutenant
MILITARY CROSS
For gallant and distinguished services while operating with the Army during the successful landing in Normandy.   L.G. 29.8.44

D-Day and the Normandy Break-Out

CAPTAIN PETER HUGH TASKER
231980, Royal Army Medical Corps, Special Service Troops.
MILITARY CROSS
In recognition of gallant and distinguished services in Normandy.
L.G. 31.8.44

CAPTAIN JOHN EDWIN THOMPSON
138288, The South Wales Borderers, Special Service Troops
MILITARY CROSS
In recognition of gallant and distinguished services in Normandy.
L.G. 31.8.44

ACTING TY. MAJOR DENNIS HARDING WALTON, R.M.
Temporary Lieutenant
MILITARY CROSS
For gallant and distinguished services while operating with the Army in Normandy. *L.G. 12.9.44*

LANCE SERGEANT JOHN D. COUTTS, M.M.
4746052, Hallamshire Bn Y & L Regt, No. 52 ME Cdo.
BAR TO MILITARY MEDAL

On 16th July 1944 Sjt Coutts was commanding a platoon of a company ordered to reinforce Barbee Farm. His platoon HQ was twice attacked with grenades, and on both occasions he beat off the attack with his own grenades. Almost immediately afterwards he killed four of the enemy with a bren gun as they attempted to infiltrate into his platoon positions.

Later, during the action when the members of his posts were killed or wounded and the post was occupied by the enemy, who were able to infiltrate another platoon in the position, he personally dealt with them with a 2-inch mortar. During the day, the position was under direct fire from enemy riflemen and LMGs, and was frequently mortared. Quite regardless of his own personal safety Sjt Coutts moved to and fro in his platoon position, organising its defence and the evacuation of wounded, and encouraging his men. When the company was ordered to evacuate Barbee Farm Sjt Coutts platoon was given the task of protecting the left flank.

The Bren Group detailed by him to cover his own flank was under fire from three directions. He remained with this gun and was wounded. He refused to leave his position until his platoon was clear of Barbee Farm.

Throughout the day Sjt Coutts displayed complete disregard for his personal safety and set an example of leadership and fighting spirit of the highest order.
Recommended for DCM, awarded Bar to MM.   *[L.G. 21.12.44]*

War Substantive Sergeant John Ernest Leech, M.M.
5948937, Bedfordshire & Hertfordshire, No. 3 Commando
Bar to Military Medal

On Queen Red beach on 6th June 1944 Sgt Leech's Section Officer was wounded and he immediately took command and re-organized. Casualties had occurred in the boat.

During the counter-attack on Le Plein woods on the morning of 8th June 1944, he led the section with great distinction, and he himself killed several of the enemy, and his section took numerous prisoners. Although wounded he continued to lead the section until the operation was successfully completed.

He displayed powers of leadership, military knowledge and courage of the highest order.   *[L.G. 31.8.44]*

Sergeant Albert Brown
Po.X.4113, Corporal, No. 45 RM Commando
Military Medal

After fighting at Merville, 45 Commando was ordered to withdraw to Le Plein at 1900 hrs 8th June 1944. During the return journey, the leading troop was heavily engaged by three enemy positions at a range of 50 yards in close [hole in paper]. Sgt Brown was ordered to take charge of the party detailed to engage the enemy positions. He destroyed the first position by accurately aimed 68 grenade from an EY rifle, but was unable to deal with the remaining two positions owing to the position of a thick hedge between him and them. With complete disregard to personal safety, he left all cover and standing in the open, fired all his remaining bombs with such good effect that the two remaining positions were neutralised.

His cool courage was an inspiration to all, and enable the remaining troops to continue their withdrawal unimpeded.
        [L.G. 29.5.44]

Corporal Cyril Kenneth Bryce
Ch.X.101818 Temporary Corporal, No. 47 RM Commando
Military Medal (Immediate)

During a large scale raid on an enemy position east of Sallenelles on the evening of 18th June, Cpl Bryce was in command of No. 1

MMG detachment which, advancing to take up a fire position, walked into an unlocated minefield.

An explosion wounded Cpl Bryce and two marines. Despite serious injuries to his foot, including a compound fracture of his leg, and in great pain, Cpl Bryce took charge of his detachment and the situation, got his gun into action against three located enemy machine-gun positions which had meantime opened fire on the detachment.

It was due to Cpl Bryce's determination to accomplish his task, disregarding his own serious injuries, that a serious dislocation of the fire plan did not occur and that fire support was forthcoming when it was required. *[L.G. 19.12.44]*

Marine Sidney Charles Burgess
Ply.X.120533, No. 48 RM Commando
Military Medal (Periodic)

Troarn. August 1944

During five days of very close contact with the enemy at Troarn in August 1944 Mne Burgess was acting as troop cook. He showed conspicuous gallantry and devotion to duty in getting hot food forward to the troop during the hours of daylight. It was impossible to cook in the troop area as any noise attracted enemy fire, and cooking was done about 200 yards behind the troop.

Mne Burgess, with containers strapped to his back, made this trip two and often three times a day, frequently through mortar fire. On three separate occasions he was blown into ditches and brambles, and once was slightly wounded. In spite of occasional mortar fire continually on his cooking area, he never failed to arrive at the correct time. He always issued the food himself, crawling to the foremost fire to do so. His steadiness and disregard of personal danger were an example to the entire troop. *20.1.45*

Temporary Corporal Rutter Thomas Clark
Po.X.100345 TSM, No. 48 RM Commando
Military Medal

June 6th 1944 St. Aubin.

Assisted Lieut MacKenzie to rally A Troop on the beach under fire in very trying circumstances, when he showed high qualities of leadership, calmness and determination. He was always well forward in the street fighting in Langrune in the last stages of which he handled the 2-in mortar team under fire with disregard for his own safety. He gave the troop a fine example throughout the action.
[L.G. 29.8.44]

Commando Gallantry Awards of World War II

Sergeant Samuel Cooper
Po.X.105978, No. 46 RM Commando
Military Medal

After the bulk of the officers and SNCOs in his troop had been killed during the initial assault this Sgt took a leading part in directing street fighting operations within his troop. Later on he led a courageous assault on to a strong enemy machine-gun position in the open fields on the south west side of the town.

[L.G. 29.8.44]

Lance Sergeant William E. Ellis
Ex.4013 (T) Corporal, No. 47 RM Commando
Military Medal (Immediate)

On the evening of 8th June on the outskirts of Port-en-Bessin, Sgt Ellis was sent out in a carrier to collect two wounded men who were known to be lying by the side of the Pont Fatu road.

Sgt Ellis came under fire from close range from two directions. When he reached the wounded men he leapt out of the carrier and still under fire, lifted them up, put them in the carrier and returned with them to our position. Throughout these actions Sgt Ellis's conduct and devotion to duty were an example to all.

[L.G. 12.9.44]

Marine Roy Emsley
Po.X.105331, No. 47 RM Commando
Military Medal (Immediate)

During the attack on Port-en-Bessin on 7th June, Mne Emsley was seriously wounded by a German mortar bomb. Despite his injuries, he continued to give supporting fire with his bren and throughout showed an excellent offensive spirit.

By this fine act and devotion to duty Marine Emsley very materially assisted the advance and final success of his comrades.

[L.G. 12.9.44]

Lance Sergeant Arthur W. Evans
2045969, Royal Fusiliers, No. 3 Commando
Military Medal

On 8th June 1944, the enemy attacked in force and the troop position was threatened. L/Sgt Evans seeing that his officer had become a casualty, took over control of the whole section of 30 men and counter-attacked with such determination that 15 of the enemy were killed and forty prisoners were taken. Later on in the day, his troop being in an exposed position came under very heavy shelling. Some of the trenches were blown in and became unusable.

L/Sgt Evans with complete disregard for personal safety left his slit trench to go round his section encouraging the men.

By this fine example and devotion to duty he maintained the fighting spirit of his men at a very high level and has demonstrated time and again throughout the campaign his resourcefulness and bravery. *[L.G. 1.3.45]*

MARINE DEREK ROY GADSDEN
Po.X.115030, No. 47 RM Commando
MILITARY MEDAL

On 7th June, during the attack on Port-en-Bessin, Commando Headquarters and one weakened troop on Point 72 feature were over-run by an enemy counter-attack which was supported by mortar and machine-gun fire.

Mne Gadsden, showing a complete disregard for his own safety, moved about bringing fire to bear from different positions for a long time deceiving the enemy as to our actual strength on the position.

His gallant conduct and cool bearing were a great encouragement and inspiration to his comrades and materially assisted in frustrating the enemy's attempts to overcome the position. *[L.G. 12.9.44]*

ACTING TEMPORARY SERGEANT DONALD HUGH GODFREY GARDNER
Ch.X.105333, No. 47 RM Commando
MILITARY MEDAL

At about 1730 hrs on 7th June, during the attack on Port en Bessin, Sgt Gardner's section came under heavy machine-gun fire which caused four casualties. Immediately afterwards, a German mortar inflicted further casualties including Sgt Gardner. Despite his wound, Sgt Gardner pressed forward and occupied the position ordered. Throughout, Sgt Gardner was very cheerful and later showed an excellent spirit whilst waiting to be evacuated from the Regimental Aid Post. *[L.G. 12.9.44]*

LANCE CORPORAL PATRICK EDWARD GRAY
3783344, The King's Regiment (Liverpool), Special Service Troops, No. 6 Commando
MILITARY MEDAL

On 10th June 1944 during an attack on Breville, the section of which L/Cpl Gray was a member became pinned in open ground by fire from a 20-mm gun and also a LMG.

L/Cpl Grey, using his own initiative and shewing extreme coolness and disregard for danger, called for fire support from the remainder of the section, while he himself worked forward with a bren gun until he flanked the 20-mm gun whose crew he then killed. He then closed on to the LMG and again silenced the crew. The whole of this action was carried out single-handed and under heavy fire and by knocking out the crews of these two guns he enabled the section to continue its advance. *[L.G. 31.8.44]*

MARINE NORMAN GREEN
Ply.X.106617, No. 45 RM Commando
MILITARY MEDAL

On the 8th June 1944 during the withdrawal from Merville to Le Plein, 'E' Troop No. 45 RM Commando came under heavy fire. Mne Green being in charge of an LMG was ordered to take up a position on the right hand side of a hedge and to engage the enemy. This he found he was unable to do owing to low branches and long grass. Mne Green therefore abandoned all cover and running into the open under intensive and accurate fire during which time a bullet lodged in the magazine of his gun, open fired with such effect into the enemy position that it was silenced. This man's calm and coolness under intense fire was an inspiration to all, and enabled the withdrawal to continue successfully. *[L.G. 29.8.44]*

MARINE JAMES ALFRED GRIFFIN
Po.X.106712, No. 47 RM Commando
MILITARY MEDAL

During the assault on Port en Bessin on 7th June, Mne Griffin's section came under fire from an enemy MG. The remainder of the section went to ground but Mne Griffin immediately went forward alone and captured the occupants of the post. Throughout the assault, Mne Griffin was always in the thick of the fray, always cheerful. *[L.G. 12.9.44]*

LANCE SERJEANT CHARLES HATTON
3390354, 1st Battalion, The East Lancashire Regt.
MILITARY MEDAL

On the 12th August 1944, during the advance on, and attack on the village of Bois Halbout, this NCO displayed great coolness and courage throughout, despite very heavy fire from mortars and small arms throughout the battle from 1130 a.m. to 5 p.m. After the assault on the village a counter-attack by four tanks was started by the enemy. Sjt Hatton engaged the counter-attack with a few men and a PIAT in the narrow street of Bois Halbout.

He hit two tanks and brought them to a standstill, stopping their counter-attack, which, had it come through, would have taken the

whole company in the flank and must have resulted in heavy casualties.
Recommended for DCM, awarded MM.   *[L.G. 21.12.44]*

LANCE CORPORAL GEORGE HODGSON
2764113, Black Watch, No. 3 Commando
MILITARY MEDAL

On 6th June 1944 on the landing beach at La Breche when his section commander was wounded and unable to continue in advance from the beach, this man showed great coolness when under heavy mortar fire in rallying the section. During the attack on Le Plein on 8th June 1944 he again showed great courage when on recce patrol by exposing himself to enemy fire in order to find their position. During the attack he showed great courage and killed several of the enemy.   *[L.G. 31.8.44]*

ACTING TY. SERGEANT HARRY HORSEFIELD
Marine, Po.X.115384, No. 47 RM Commando
MILITARY MEDAL

Sjt Horsefield was a volunteer for a raid on the enemy forward defended lines, east of Sallenelles, during the early morning of 23rd July.

The enemy had been in position for at least six weeks and his defences were well prepared and covered with wire and mines.

Sjt Horsefield was the senior NCO of a small party, led by Lieut Collett, who had been ordered to sweep to the left on reaching the enemy forward defended line.

When about 50 yards from the enemy forward defended line, Lieut Collett trod on a mine and became a casualty. Surprise was lost and the enemy opened heavy automatic fire aided by flares.

Sjt Horsefield immediately took command of the unwounded numbers of his party, who were considerably shaken, led them forward and by his fearless example restored their confidence.

In the darkness the finding and searching of enemy weapon slits was very difficult but, not content to return empty handed, Sjt Horsefield persevered, the whole time under heavy automatic and mortar fire. His party captured and returned with an officer prisoner.

He later returned with Lieut O'Brien and assisted in carrying his own seriously wounded, clear of the enemy minefield to safety.
19.2.44

Private Thomas A. Jennings
5958758, Bedfordshire & Hertfordshire, No. 3 Commando (and 2, 6, 14, Commando)
Military Medal

On 6th July 1944 an attack of troop strength was launched by No. 3. Commando against enemy holding out in Le Plein. This troop came under heavy and accurate fire from a well concealed enemy strong point whilst advancing up the main street as a result of which the Troop Commander was wounded and the troop pinned down. An attempt to dislodge the enemy resulted in further casualties. Pte Jennings summed up the situation and called out that he would give covering fire. With supreme contempt for his own safety he advanced down the main street firing a Bren Gun from the hip. Almost immediately his water-bottle was shot away by a burst of machine-gun fire. Undismayed, he continued to advance firing from the hip and neutralised the enemy fire so effectively that his troop was able to bypass the enemy strong point and liquidate it.

Pte Jennings's complete disregard for his own safety combined with the skill and accuracy he displayed under intensive fire from close range was largely responsible for the rapid capture of the objective. His courage from the date of landing and throughout the campaign has been in the highest traditions of his service.

[L.G. 1.3.45]

Sergeant George Jones
Ply.X.109237, No. 5 (I) RM Bty.
Military Medal

Serjeant Jones displayed coolness and great devotion to duty and complete disregard of his personal safety when during the disembarkation at Ouistreham on 6th June 1944 he exposed himself outside the turret of his tank under heavy and accurate enemy fire. The tank of which he was in command had become jammed on the ramp leading from the tank deck of the LCT and this NCO climbed halfway out of the turret in order to receive verbal orders from his Troop Commander. The tank was successfully disembarked. Although wounded in the head while still on the craft Sjt Jones continued to command his tank throughout the disembarkation and subsequently during the action on shore until sent away to have his wound attended to.

[L.G. 29.8.44]

D-Day and the Normandy Break-Out

ACTING TY. COLOUR SERGEANT JEFFREY NOEL KAY
Marine, Ply.X.109571, No. 2 RM Armd Sp Regt.
MILITARY MEDAL

Displayed great courage and initiative in carrying out a street-fighting task in support of 48 RM Commando at Berniers-sur-Mer at approximately 2000 hrs 6th June 1944. In three hours the Centaur Tank which he was commanding, although not provided with AP shot, successfully neutralized an enemy strong point from a range of 200 yds and thus greatly assisted the capture of the town. None of the training given to him and his unit had been designed to fit him to carry out an independent task of this kind. *(L.G. 29.8.44)*

LANCE CORPORAL PERCY GEORGE KENDRICK
5336379, RAMC, No. 47 RM Commando
MILITARY MEDAL

On 7th June, during the assault on Port-en-Bessin, X Troop came under accurate close range machine-gun fire. Without hesitation or orders, and with complete disregard of danger, L/Cpl Kendrick went to, and attended, the wounded, although casualties were still being inflicted. The devotion to duty and the prompt courageous conduct of L/Cpl Kendrick was a grand and inspiring example to all his comrades. *[L.G. 19.10.44]*

MARINE WILLIAM MACDONALD
Ch.X.109660, No. 47 RM Commando
MILITARY MEDAL

Throughout the assault on Port-en-Bessin on 7th June Mne MacDonald was absolutely fearless. As the Troop Commander's runner, he time and time again crossed open ground under close range enemy automatic fire, carrying messages and orders of vital importance. By his gallant and courageous conduct he played a major part during the closing stages of the successful assault on the port. His devotion to duty was quite exceptional and a most inspiring example to his comrades. *[L.G. 12.9.44]*

LANCE CORPORAL RICHARD MCCARTHY
7407321, Royal Army Medical Corps, Special Service Troops
MILITARY MEDAL

In recognition of gallant and distinguished services in Normandy.
L.G. 31.8.44

SIGNALMAN ANGUS MCKENZIE MCGREGOR
2598341, SS Bde Sig Tp (RC of S).
MILITARY MEDAL

During the landing of Advanced HQ of the Brigade, all signallers were wounded by mortar and machine-gun fire, 50% being incapacitated. Signalman McGregor received two shrapnel wounds in the head, three bullet wounds in the arm, and a shrapnel wound in the leg. In spite of his wounds he continued to operate his set, and enabled essential information to be passed to the main body of Brigade which was still afloat. He refused all assistance, denying that he was seriously hurt, and continued to operated his set during the initial stages of the advance until he was unable to rise after taking cover from mortar fire. It was only then that the seriousness of his wounds became apparent. His devotion to duty was largely responsible for communications being maintained at an extremely critical period of the operation.

Date of action: 6th June 1944. *[L.G. 31.8.44]*

LANCE CORPORAL VINCENT ARTHUR OSBORNE
3974535, Welch Regt, No. 3 Commando
MILITARY MEDAL

On 6th June 1944 in the attack on Le Plein, this man showed exceptional courage and devotion to duty when he continued to engage the enemy in the open to enable the wounded, including his Troop Commander, to be evacuated. He immediately killed the German who had wounded his Troop Commander. He later showed great bravery and initiative in the second and successful attack.

Recommended for DCM, awarded MM. *[L.G. 31.8.44]*

LANCE CORPORAL GEORGE SCANLON
7386392, RAMC, No. 4 Commando
MILITARY MEDAL

On 6th June 1944 during the landing near Ouistreham Corporal Scanlon tended numerous casualties under heavy mortar and shell fire bringing them to safety and saving some from drowning. During the subsequent assault on the Battery at Ouistreham when the area came under shell fire Corporal Scanlon moved about without regard for his own safety bringing in six wounded men to a shelter where he tended them for two hours until he was able to take them out. He brought them to the regimental aid post and then to the beach although heavily sniped on the way and continued to look after wounded in the beach area until the morning of 7th June 1944 when he rejoined his unit at Hauger. Corporal Scanlon

behaved according to the highest traditions of his service and his complete disregard of self provoked the admiration of all officers and men. This high standard has been maintained throughout the campaign.
Recommended for DCM, awarded MM. [*L.G. 1.3.45*]

SERGEANT JOHN CLIVE STRINGER
Po.X.112235, No. 48 RM Commando
MILITARY MEDAL

June 6th 1944. Staubun.
Rallied his sub-section on the beach under fire after landing through deep water. He showed great calmness and resolution under these trying circumstances and was unmoved by enemy fire. During the street fighting in Langrune he repeatedly volunteered for and carried out tasks of extra risk, leading and inspiring his sub-section by his personal example. [*L.G. 29.5.44*]

LANCE CORPORAL JOHN WILLIAM THWAYTES
7367051, Royal Army Medical Corps, Special Service Troops
MILITARY MEDAL

In recognition of gallant and distinguished services in Normandy.
L.G. 31.8.44

LANCE CORPORAL FREDERICK BARNARD TICKLE
735941, Royal Army Medical Corps, Special Service Troops
MILITARY MEDAL

In recognition of gallant and distinguished services in Normandy.
L.G. 31.8.44

LANCE SERGEANT EDWARD WALSH
2716717, Irish Guards, Special Service Troops
MILITARY MEDAL

In recognition of gallant and distinguished services in Normandy.
L.G. 31.8.44

TEMPORARY SERGEANT RUSSELL JOHN WITHER
Ch.X.2244, No. 41 RM Commando
MILITARY MEDAL

[...] sur Mer 6th–7th June 1944
This NCO assumed the duties of Signal Officer on the beach where his officer was wounded. Throughout the two days action he has displayed great determination and efficiency in maintaining communications. Often under fire he visited his out stations repeatedly and on one occasion successfully laid a line in spite of

being sniped at. His personal example resulted in a high standard of communications. [L.G. 29.8.44]

ACTING TEMPORARY LIEUTENANT-COLONEL PATRICK MARSHALL DONNELL
Ty Maj, No. 47 RM Commando
CROIX DE GUERRE WITH VERMILION STAR

When 47 (RM) Commando landed near Le Hamel in Normandy on the morning of 6th June the Commanding Officer became separated from his unit. Major Donnell the second-in-command collected the very disorganised unit together, under fire, and brought it forward to a pre-arranged rendezvous just east of Buhot.

During the assault on Port-en-Bessin the following day, B Troop came under devastating fire from two flak ships lying alongside the wall of the outer basin. Hearing the sound of heavy sustained firing, Major Donnell went forward and quickly sizing up the situation, assembled as many of B Troop as he could find taking cover in the houses, and with complete disregard for his own safety personally led the attack on these ships.

Major Donnell, by his determination, his unflinching courage and his personal inspiration was largely responsible for the success of this attack which was so vital to the whole operation. During the attack by the whole Commando on the enemy position at Sallenelles, east of River Orne on the evening of 17th June, a MMG section, advancing to take up a fire position, walked into an unlocated minefield. Casualties were inflicted on both gun detachments. As soon as the first mine exploded an enemy machine-gun opened fire at a range of 200 yards inflicting further casualties.

Major Donnell, with complete disregard of the danger of further mine explosions and under accurate close range machine-gun fire, went back, picked up the gun, carried it forward and personally acting as No. 1, got it into action. The fire support provided by the MMG section contributed largely to the success of the raid. During the whole period 6th June–31st August 1944, as second-in-command of the unit, he has been a tower of strength. His coolness under fire, his cheerfulness, his anticipation and his sound common sense have been of inestimable value.

Walcheren

WALCHEREN ISLAND, HOLLAND – 1/8 NOVEMBER 1944

The island of Walcheren, approximately 150 square miles in area, lies at the mouth of the Scheldt River and, as of October 1944 was still held by the Germans. It formed a strategic block to the Allies reaching the great port of Antwerp which the Allies had captured two months earlier and from which the rapidly advancing armies could be supplied. Unless Walcheren could quickly be taken the advances would be dangerously slowed.

It would not be an easy victory, for the island, roughly circular, was surrounded by sea walls some 30 feet high, surmounted by coastal batteries and anti-aircraft guns. The German defenders were determined, and well supplied with ammunition and food sufficient for a long siege. Parts of the sea-walls had been breached by allied bombings and consequently much of the interior, well below sea level was flooded. Recognizing the nature of the objective those selected for the assault were of a calibre that ensured ultimate success.

The attack began on November 1st, 1944 at 9:45 a.m. preceded by a bombardment by RAF Mosquito aircraft then later, as it progressed, by Spitfires and Typhoons. Offshore, HM Ships *Warspite*, *Erebus* and *Roberts* shelled shore installations.

The landings took place at four points: No. 4 Commando landed on the south coast at the town of Flushing, attacking gun emplacements, barracks and, as they progressed through the town, being engaged in house-to-house fighting. 155 Brigade with the Royal Scots and the Kings Own Scottish Borderers soon joined them and after some severe fighting the town was secured.

On the west coast Nos. 41, 47, and 48 Royal Marine Commandos had landed on three fronts: Tare Red (Lighthouse), Tare White (The Town of Westkapelle), and Tare Green (Radar Station). The distance from the Lighthouse to the Radar Station was approximately two miles.

Defensive fire was heavy and accurate, with the result that several tank and infantry landing craft were sunk or disabled. Supported by HMS *Warspite's* bombardment and RAF Spitfires, 41 Commando (Palmer) and elements of the Belgians and Norwegians of 10 Inter-allied Commando, with 30 Armoured

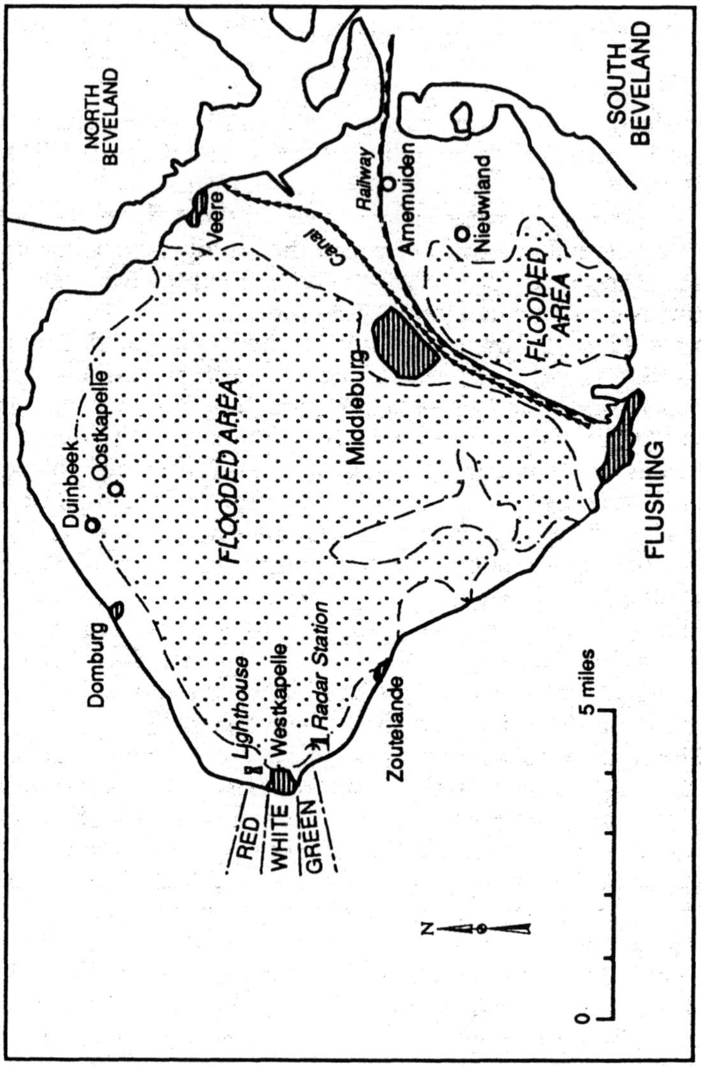
NORTH BEVELAND
SOUTH BEVELAND
Veere
Canal
Railway
Amemuiden
Nieuwland
FLOODED AREA
FLOODED AREA
Middleburg
Duinbeek
Oostkapelle
Domburg
Lighthouse
Westkapelle
Radar Station
Zoutelande
FLUSHING
RED
WHITE
GREEN
N
0
5 miles

Walcheren

Brigade, Royal Engineers Sappers, Medical and Signal units fought their way ashore, quickly overcame the German defences and were within the village outskirts in six minutes. By 11:15 it was in the possession of the Commandos.

Following at H+5, the second wave of 41 Commando (Lt-Col J. L. Moulton) landed along with 48 Commando and headed toward the Radar station. Finding it vacated they set up a defensive position on the south sea wall to await the arrival of the other elements of 41 and 48 Commando with their machine guns. Unfortunately the vessels carrying them had been destroyed by shellfire and those troops coming ashore were at a serious disadvantage in respect to armament. By D+1 the Commando forces had possession of the villages of Domburg, Zouteland and critical areas of the sea-wall. On November 4th (D+4), Nos. 41, 47, 48 Commandos had linked up with No. 4 Commando, but German resistance continued until the 8th when they surrendered near the village of Veere.

The price paid for Walcheren was high. In eight days, casualties—killed, wounded and missing—totalled 8,000. It was truly a Combined Operation in every sense of the word for the Navy, Army, Air Force had each played a vital role interdependent on the other for the achievement of the objective.

The way to Antwerp was open.

TEMPORARY BRIGADIER BERNARD WILLIAM
LEICESTER, D.S.O.
Major, Brevet Lieutenant-Colonel, Acting Colonel Commandant, Royal Marines.
BAR TO DISTINGUISHED SERVICE ORDER
For gallantry, leadership and undaunted devotion to duty during the assault on the Island of Walcheren.   *L.G. 20.2.45*

ACTING LIEUTENANT-COLONEL ERIC CHARLES
ERNEST PALMER, R.M.
Captain
DISTINGUISHED SERVICE ORDER
For gallantry, leadership and undaunted devotion to duty during the assault on the Island of Walcheren.   *L.G. 20.2.45*

Acting Temporary Captain Paul Spencer, R.M.
Temporary Lieutenant
Distinguished Service Order
For gallantry, leadership and undaunted devotion to duty during the assault on the Island of Walcheren.   *L.G. 20.2.45*

Captain Edward Lionel Knivet Augustus Carr, R.A.
No. 4 Commando
Military Cross
At Flushing on 1st November 1944 the LCA in which Captain Carr and the Mortar Section were landing, struck an anti-landing mine and was sunk. Despite heavy fire from both flanks, Captain Carr extricated himself and his men and then returned with a small party to the wreck and salvaged the mortars. This he accomplished with complete disregard of enemy fire and after setting up the mortars went forward to make contact with his machine-gun section. This was in a very exposed position in the heart of the town, and closely engaged by a considerable force of the enemy. The machine-gun section officer having become a casualty, Captain Carr himself took command and maintained the section position through the next 24 hours, during which contact with other troops was cut by an enemy counter-attack, and the machine-gun section position heavily pressed. By his outstanding courage and devotion in holding this vital point, the forming up and further operations of the follow up troops were made possible.   *[L.G. 22.3.45]*

Acting Temporary Captain Edwin Dunn, R.M.
Temporary Lieutenant
Military Cross
For gallantry, leadership and undaunted devotion to duty during the assault on the Island of Walcheren.   *L.G. 20.2.45*

Ty. Captain Richard Talbot Flower, R.M.
Military Cross
For gallantry, leadership and undaunted devotion to duty during the assault on the Island of Walcheren.   *L.G. 20.2.45*

Acting Ty. Captain Daniel John Flunder
Ty Lieut, Po 515, No. 48 RM Commando
Military Cross
On 1st November, during the invasion of Walcheren by 4 SS Bde, Capt Flunder displayed great and sustained gallantry throughout the first 72 hours.

His troop (A Troop) landed in the second wave and suffered some casualties and disorganisation from the shelling on the beaches. Capt Flunder lead the troop forward to reach the remainder of the commando just before the first attack on Battery W.13. He was ordered to act as fire troop. During the difficult period after the failure of the first attack, his troop by good tactics and determination, succeeded in winning the fire fight against an enemy superior in numbers and weapons and in prepared positions. This greatly contributed to the success of the second assault. At first light on 2nd November, Capt Flunder was ordered to move forward with his troop as a fighting patrol. Although reduced in numbers his troop gained over 1,000 yards, mopped up two enemy posts and eventually forced the surrender of the Zouteland garrison after a brisk fire fight and assault. At 0600 hrs on 3rd November, A Troop was detached to 47 Commando and during the operations of that unit again acted as fire troop with considerable success, winning fire initiative against a superior enemy, who made every effort to silence A Troop's fire. Finally the troop advanced and mopped up enemy parties in the close country on the flank of 47 Commando.

Through three days fighting, Capt Flunder showed great determination, tactical skill, and courage. He was always on top of the enemy, aggressive and never allowed himself to be impressed by difficulties and dangers which might have deterred a less able leader. *[L.G. 20.2.45]*

CAPTAIN JOHN OLDROYD FORFAR
WS Capt 227049 RAMC, No. 47 RM Commando
MILITARY CROSS (IMMEDIATE)

At Walcheren, on the afternoon of 2nd November, during the advance along the dunes south-east of Zouteland, the leading troop of 47 (RM) Commando came under extremely heavy and sustained enemy mortar fire which killed 15 and wounded 21, including three officers.

Amidst the bursting mortar bombs and whilst casualties were still being inflicted on those around him, Captain Forfar went forward to attend the wounded.

The troop commander could not be found and Captain Forfar went on another 50 yards in incessant mortar fire, where he found him lying grievously wounded.

Whilst he was dressing his wounds, five Germans appeared over a sand dune 250 yards away and opened fire with a MG 34, killing one and wounding another of the stretcher party who had meanwhile crawled forward and joined him.

Captain Forfar with complete disregard for his personal safety coolly went on giving the wounded first aid and he, together with the wounded, were later withdrawn under cover of smoke.

Throughout the whole course of the first three days of the battle for Walcheren, when 82 ranks were wounded, many of whom were recovered by this officer personally with the greatest heroism, the courage and devotion to duty of this officer were above praise.

[L.G. 22.3.45]

LIEUTENANT JOHN SIMON HUNTER-GRAY, R.A.
271536, RA, No. 4 Commando
MILITARY CROSS

At Flushing on 1st November 1944 this officer led a section of his troops against strong enemy opposition on the flank of the point of landing, himself clearing two pillboxes which were engaging the landing craft and beach, and taking some 20 prisoners, When his section was stopped by fire coming across a wide stretch of open ground, Lieut Hunter-Gray promptly manned an enemy anti-tank gun mounted on the roof of a pillbox, and without regard for his exposed position engaged and disposed of the enemy positions consisting of several pillboxes and two guns in casemates, whose occupants finally came out and surrendered. By this action Lieut Hunter-Gray ensured the safety of subsequent flights of landing craft, two of which had previously been sunk by the guns of this strongpoint. *[L.G. 22.3.45]*

ACTING TY. MAJOR NORMAN PETER WOOD, R.M.
Temporary Captain
MILITARY CROSS

For gallantry, leadership and undaunted devotion to duty during the assault on the Island of Walcheren.   *L.G. 20.2.45*

ACTING TEMPORARY COMPANY SERGEANT MAJOR JAMES PATERSON ENGLAND
Po.x 1372 Sgt, Nos 43, 46, & 47 RM Commando
DISTINGUISHED CONDUCT MEDAL (IMMEDIATE)

On 2nd November, TSM England was TSM of one of the troops of 47 (RM) Commando detailed to attack one of the strongly defended battery positions south-east of Zouteland which commanded the Scheldt estuary.

The defences included concreted casemates and pillboxes and unusually thick belts of wire covered by machine guns. The advance was over 1,500 yards of deep soft sand.

Walcheren

By the time the attacking troops had reached assaulting distance they had become very depleted and disorganised and it seemed as if there would be insufficient weight in the attack to storm the enemy defences.

At this critical time TSM England came under heavy fire at close range from an enemy machine gun. Seizing a bren gun lying on top of a dead marine, and firing from the hip as went, this brave NCO plodded up the soft sandy slope and charged this heavily bunkered position alone. He shot and killed two of the occupants and, running out of bren ammunition, he turned the German machine gun with good effect on three more Germans who had fled. Still alone, he worked forward to a second position 30 yards further on where he killed three more Germans, two others surrendering. Here he was later joined by men from another troop.

In a situation where the odds were strongly against him, and knowing that he was unsupported, the courage and determination of this NCO was above praise.

Later, in the growing darkness when it was impossible to give our forward troops any close support, the enemy counter-attacked and our men were driven off the enemy position on which they had gained a foothold.

The next morning another attack was put in on this enemy battery and TSM England's troop was given the task of mopping up behind the assaulting troops.

The enemy was putting up the most desperate resistance and soon attacking and mopping-up troops became intermingled. The enemy opened concentrated and sustained cross fire from the position which TSM England had rushed the previous evening and from a concrete fire control position known as the 'umbrella' on the seaward side of the dunes. On his own initiative and with total disregard for his safety he threw a smoke grenade to screen himself from the view of the 'umbrella' and rushed the machine-gun post in front of him. Killing or capturing the occupants, he continued to work through the network of trenches and tunnels.

Throughout the course of the battle for Walcheren, especially in the fluctuating and bitter fighting, his immense courage and total disregard for his safety had a decisive influence.

[L.G. 20.2.45]

LANCE SERGEANT PETER MCVEIGH
3853876, Loyals, No. 4 Commando
DISTINGUISHED CONDUCT MEDAL

At Flushing on 1st November 1944, this NCO in command of a sub-section, went to the assault of the Naval Barracks, defended by approximately 60 enemy. With great skill and pertinacity L/Sgt McVeigh harassed the enemy while searching for a means of breaking in. When engaged from the houses surrounding the barracks he detached himself and disposed of a least two enemy pockets of three to six men with machine-guns, thus paving the way for the break-in to be made. He then led the assault on the barracks which he cleared, accounting for 25 enemy killed and wounded and taking between 30 and 40 prisoners. L/Sgt McVeigh showed personal bravery to an outstanding degree, and by his cunning leadership attained his objective at the cost of only one man killed, though fighting throughout against great odds.

[L.G. 22.3.45]

ACTING TY. CORPORAL FRANK LEWIS NIGHTINGALE
Ch.x.101330 Marine, No. 41 RM Commando
DISTINGUISHED CONDUCT MEDAL

At 1545 hrs. on 5th November 1944, Y Troop 41 (RM) Commando as part of a Commando attack, assaulted Battery W.18 at Domburg on Walcheren which contained some 200 Germans.

During the fighting in the battery, Cpl Nightingale was forward with his section officer and one other marine. They were heavily engaged by enemy machine-gun and rifle fire from the surrounding woods, and the marine was killed and the officer seriously wounded. Cpl Nightingale attempted to carry on the fire-fight with his bren gun but this fired only a few rounds and stopped. Cpl Nightingale seized a captured German MG 34 and continued to fire this until the enemy was forced to withdraw. After a while the enemy counter-attacked in a determined manner but Cpl Nightingale once again drove them to ground and alone held on to this flank until the remnants of his section were able to advance and join him. Through this NCO's personal disregard for safety, and his determination to kill the enemy, the troop was able to hold on to the position. *[L.G. 20.2.45]*

LANCE CORPORAL HARRY CUNNINGHAM
7357055, RAMC, No. 4 Commando
MILITARY MEDAL

At Flushing on 1st November 1944 this NCO medical orderly accompanying the leading troops, displayed gallantry of the highest order during prolonged and bitter street fighting in the town. He showed complete disregard for his personal safety, and on one occasion when a street was under enemy machine-gun fire, he left cover to attend a wounded man who was lying in the open and who required immediate attention, and remained with him under enemy sniper and machine-gun fire. His conduct throughout the action was beyond praise and an inspiration to all those with whom he served. *[L.G. 22.3.45]*

ACTING TEMPORARY SERGEANT RAYMOND WILLIAM WADE ESTHER
Ch X.114336 Marine, No. 47 & 42 RM Commando
MILITARY MEDAL (PERIODIC)

During the assault on Walcheren Island by 47 RM Commando on 1st November 1944, the LCT in which Sgt Esther was travelling was hit twice by shells and unable to beach, all LVTs had to swim off and owing to strong tidal conditions in the Westkapelle gap and heavy enemy shell fire, the LVT became disorganised and sub-units were landed at widely separated points.

Sgt Esther immediately rallied his men and went in search of other scattered bodies of the Commando. By his energy, a large part of the unit was reorganised, officers were contacted and a most difficult situation cleared up.

Later, on November 2nd, when the Commando were attacking enemy positions beyond Zouteland, Sgt Esther's troop came under very heavy and concentrated mortar fire while crossing a large enemy anti-tank ditch in the sand dunes. Two of the three officers were severely wounded and it seemed doubtful if a footing could be gained on the far side. Sgt Esther collected a bunch of scattered and shaken men and at a most critical moment led a charge through the mortar and machine-gun fire to gain a footing on a high dune overlooking the ditch. Although severely wounded, he remained on the position encouraging his men to hold on until further troops arrived and the situation was reorganised. Only then did Sgt Esther allow himself to be evacuated.

As an example of the great spirit of this NCO when in hospital, although he knew that the Naval authorities were evacuating all Royal Marine personnel to the United Kingdom, Sgt Esther insisted that the location of his unit should be found and on leaving hospital he immediately rejoined the Commando by getting lifts from passing vehicles.

Since the landings on 6th June 1944, Sgt Esther's name has become famous in the Commando for his continued keenness to get at the enemy, for his coolness under fire and for his consistent cheerfulness. *(L.G. 5.6.45)*

Commando Gallantry Awards of World War II

Marine Harold Jones
Ch X.104562, No. 4 Commando Bde Sig Tp.
Military Medal

During the assault on Flushing on 1st November 1944, Mne Jones was attached to 4 Commando in charge of rear link communications. His equipment was an extremely heavy and bulky wireless set in a handcart. On the landing Jones led his detachment with great gallantry under heavy direct fire, across a mined palisade and the open beach to HQ. In position his detachment was under interrupted long range fire from MMG and constant mortaring for two days, the wireless set being hit several times. Throughout the whole of the operation Jones displayed the greatest calm and never lost communication with his rear unit. His courage throughout was an inspiration to the rest of his detachment.   *(L.G. 5.6.45)*

Temporary Sergeant George Lamb Kemp
Po.X.102383, No. 48 (RM) Commando
Military Medal

At Westkapelle, throughout the day of 1st November, this NCO was conspicuous for his fearlessness and his desire to come to close grips with the enemy. When his subsection landed in the first wave, he immediately gained control of it and led it forward under heavy shellfire to its first objective. Later, when his troop was called upon at short notice to assault battery W.13, he was conspicuous for the way in which he led his subsection directly at the core of the enemy resistance, and silenced, with bursts from his tommy gun and grenades, an LMG which was firing at the attacking troop. His example, leadership and dash contributed greatly to the success of the initial break-in to the fortified battery position.
(L.G. 20.2.45)

Marine Frederick Woodman Laynon
Ply.X.103196, No. 47 RM Commando
Military Medal (Immediate)

Closing the beach near Westkapelle during the assault on Walcheren on 1st November, the LCT carrying Mne Lanyon's troop, 47 (RM) Commando, was hit by a shell. Three amphibians in the LCT caught fire and there were large and loud explosions. A number of Mne Lanyon's troop were killed, wounded or burnt and among these was a marine who had been literally blown into the sea and had had his leg broken.

There was a general 'sauve qui peut.'

Mne Lanyon, who is not a strong swimmer, without hesitation jumped into the sea and assisted this marine, who was quite helpless and in great pain, to reach the beach, some 200 yards distance. By his time Mne Lanyon was in a state of complete exhaustion and had swallowed so much salt water that he had to be given medical attention in the beach dressing station.

Here his clothes were taken away, but as soon as he recovered his faculties this marine, wrapped only in a blanket, rejoined his troop. He was subsequently fitted out in the unit's regimental aid post with casualty clothing.

The next day Mne Lanyon's troop was ordered to attack the battery south-east of Zouteland. They came under heavy fire at close range from several enemy riflemen, killing his section NCO and wounding three others in the section. The men scattered and took cover.

At this critical junction, Mne Lanyon, calling upon the others to follow him, without hesitation, rushed the enemy post, killed three of them and wounded the fourth.

But for his fearless example and leadership on this occasion there is little doubt that the attack would have been held up and possibly never put in that evening. *20.2.45*

LANCE CORPORAL CHARLES LEGRAND
No. 1299, No. 10 (IA) Commando (Belgian Troop)
MILITARY MEDAL

This NCO was in charge of the Mortar Section of 'A' Section of the Belgian Troop.

On D–day, 1st November 1944, his Section was given the task of clearing part of the north of the town of Westkapelle. L/Cpl LeGrand was wounded in the back by shrapnel from a mortar bomb. He did not disclose this fact until the task given to his Section was completed and the fighting in the town of Westkapelle had ceased that evening. He was treated by the medical officer and returned to duty with his troop.

On 5th November 1944, the Belgian Troop of No.10 (IA) Commando was given the task of clearing the enemy from a Sector of the wooded country to the east of the town of Domburg. L/Cpl LeGrand was put in charge of a Sub-Section of 'A' Section. 'A' Section came under heavy fire from enemy machine guns and were pinned down. The officer commanding the Section was killed and the Section Sergeant badly wounded, whilst other casualties were suffered. L/Cpl LeGrand rallied his Sub-Section, and on the orders of his Troop Commander personally gave the fire orders to his Sub-Section to cover the attack on the enemy machine gun positions which was put in by 'B' Section on his right flank. During this action L/Cpl LeGrand was again wounded by a machine gun bullet in the shoulder. He nevertheless refused to leave his Sub-Section, and subsequently continued in charge of them until the task given to the Belgian Troop had been satisfactorily concluded at 1800 hrs that evening. L/Cpl LeGrand was wounded at 1530 hrs.

L/Cpl LeGrand set a very fine example of leadership and courage to the men under his command. Although severely wounded, his devotion to his duty was such that he refused to leave his post and continued to lead his men in the final assault.

Not Gazetted. Submission dated 29.1.45

SERGEANT STANLEY JOHN MULLARD
14241800, Cameron Highlanders, No. 4 Commando
MILITARY MEDAL

At Flushing on 1st November 1944, this NCO, after the initial assault on the beach, assisted his Section Officer in manning a captured anti-tank gun, mounted on the roof of a pillbox, and engaged several enemy pillboxes which were interfering with the approach of subsequent flights of landing craft. To enable more effective fire to be brought to bear, Sgt Mullard unhesitatingly went forward and took up a desperately exposed position from which he controlled the fire by signals. His coolness and courage in the accomplishment of this task were instrumental in the silencing of the series of pillboxes and two strong gun positions in casements which were surrendered by enemy. *[L.G. 22.3.45]*

TEMPORARY SERGEANT LESLIE MUSGROVE
Ply.X.101123, No. 41 RM Commando
MILITARY MEDAL

At Westkapelle at 1010 hrs on 1st November 1944 the section officer of Sgt Musgrove's section was knocked out before landing, together with almost half the section. The section's primary task was to capture a large pill-box which enfiladed the beach. Although he was very seasick Sgt Musgrove dashed forward on landing towards the pill-box firing his TSMG and throwing grenades. He assaulted and captured the pill-box single-handed, killing or capturing the ten occupants. He then rallied the remnants of his section and by his magnificent example restored their spirits and led them forward to their next task, which they completed successfully. *[L.G. 20.2.45]*

Walcheren

Marine Donald Nicholson
Ch.X.106544, No. 48 RM Commando
Military Medal

Half mile offshore, near Westkapelle, Walcheren Island, 1st November
LVT (Birmingham) aboard LCT 1133 was hit in the engine room by shell fire from a coastal battery and so was unable to leave the craft. This shell caused an outbreak of fire, the flames from which caused a second fire in the hold of the LVT which contained 57,000 rounds of .303 Mk.VIIIZ, five RE explosive packs and ammunition for LVT's Brownings.

While the Browning ammunition was exploding Mne Nicholson remained alone in the hold of the LVT, throwing out inflammable material and ammunition and so eliminated the danger to the lives of three wounded men in the cabin of the wheelhouse of the LCT, one of whom could not be moved to a safer place. Later LCT 1133 hit a mine which threw several men into the sea. Mne Nicholson, disregarding the enemy fire, alone rescued two of these men, one of whom had two broken ankles. *20.2.45*

Acting Ty. Sergeant Mark Charles Packer
Ch.X.105314 Temporary Corporal, RM
Military Medal

For gallantry, leadership and undaunted devotion to duty during the assault on the Island of Walcheren. *L.G. 20.2.45*

Marine Kenneth John Ryalls
Po.X.109903, No. 48 RM Commando
Military Medal (Immediate)

At Westkapelle, on 1st November this marine drove his amphibious vehicle ashore in an early flight. Owing to the nature of the ground, all vehicles were forced to remain on the restricted beach which was an obvious and important target for enemy shellfire. Casualties were numerous and vehicles were continuously being hit and catching fire. Marine Ryalls, with a fine disregard of his own safety, worked continuously, salvaging vehicles and ammunition and helping with the wounded. After his own vehicle had been hit, he helped to remove two others from the side of a burning LVT which was loaded with ammunition and threatened to blow up at any minute. In all, this marine was working for over 24 hours under accurate shellfire, which included spells of intensive fire. He showed outstanding courage, never stopped a job to take cover, and set a fine example. *11.12.44*

Commando Gallantry Awards of World War II

TY. SERGEANT CHARLES LESLIE STOKELL
Ch.X.2754 Corporal, RM
MILITARY MEDAL

For gallantry, leadership and undaunted devotion to duty during the assault on the Island of Walcheren. *L.G. 20.2.45*

North West Europe after D-Day

LANCE CORPORAL HENRY ERIC HARDEN
11006144, Royal Army Medical Corps
𝔙𝔦𝔠𝔱𝔬𝔯𝔦𝔞 𝔘𝔯𝔬𝔰𝔰

War Office – 8th March 1945.
The KING has been graciously pleased to approve the posthumous award of the VICTORIA CROSS to:—
No. 11006144 Lance-Corporal Henry Eric HARDEN, Royal Army Medical Corps (Northfleet, Kent).

In North-West Europe on the 23rd January 1945, the leading section of a Royal Marine Commando troop was pinned to the ground by intense enemy machine gun fire from well concealed positions. As it was impossible to engage the enemy from the open owing to lack of cover, the section was ordered to make for some near-by houses. This move was accomplished, but one officer and three other rank casualties were left lying in the open.

The whole troop position was under continuous heavy and accurate shell and mortar fire. Lance-Corporal Harden, the RAMC orderly attached to the troop, at once went forward, a distance of 120 yards, into the open under a hail of enemy machine gun and rifle fire directed from four positions, all within 300 yards, and with the greatest coolness and bravery remained in the open while he attended to the four casualties.

After dressing the wounds of three of them, he carried one of them back to cover. Lance-Corporal Harden was then ordered not to go forward again and an attempt was made to bring in the other casualties with the aid of tanks, but this proved unsuccessful owing to the heavy and accurate fire of enemy anti-tank guns. A further attempt was then made to recover the casualties under a smoke screen, but this only increased the enemy fire in the vicinity of the casualties.

Lance-Corporal Harden then insisted on going forward again, with a volunteer stretcher party, and succeeded in bringing back another badly wounded man.

Lance-Corporal Harden went out a third time, again with a stretcher party, and after starting on the return journey with the wounded officer, under very heavy enemy small arms and mortar fire, he was killed.

Throughout this long period, Lance-Corporal Harden displayed superb devotion to duty and personal courage of the very highest order, and there is no doubt that it had a most steadying effect upon the other troops in the area at a most critical time. His action was directly responsible for saving the lives of the wounded brought in. His complete contempt for all personal danger, and the magnificent example he set of cool courage and determination to continue with his work, whatever the odds, was an inspiration to his comrades, and will never be forgotten by those who saw it.

L.G. 8.3.45

Lieut.-Colonel William Nichol Gray, D.S.O.
No. 45 RM Commando
Bar to Distinguished Service Order

Lt-Col Gray commanded No. 45 RM Commando during the assault across the Rhine and the capture of Wesel on the night 23rd–24th March 1945. Lt-Col Gray's task was to force his way to the Northern sector of the town and seize a factory which was vital in order to achieve a successful consolidation. Following up rapidly behind the leading unit who had broken into the city, he passed through and debouched into the streets. While leading his troops at speed and clearing all opposition in his path with great determination he was wounded by a panzerfaust fired at close range. In spite of his wound he refused to be evacuated and completed his important task. Having captured the factory he disposed his troops so skilfully that during the next thirty-six hours they were able to beat off three major counter-attacks by infantry and self-propelled guns with enormous casualties to the enemy. Throughout this time although he was suffering considerably from the pain of his wound he was constantly encouraging his men, who were inspired by their Commander's example. Not until the last counter-attack had been broken, forty-eight hours after he had been wounded did this gallant officer allow himself to be evacuated.

Recommended for MC, awarded Bar to DSO.   *[L.G. 19.6.45]*

NorthWest Europe After D Day

ACTING LIEUTENANT-COLONEL PETER IAN BARTHOLOMEW
Temp/Major, 73118, Somerset Light Infantry, No. 3 Cdo.
DISTINGUISHED SERVICE ORDER

Lt-Col Bartholomew was in command of 3 Commando during the crossing of the River Weser and the attack on Leese. He was ordered to probe to the northward to capture an important factory. He had in support one squadron of tanks. His leading infantry were approaching a group of houses when they came under intense and accurate small arms fire. One officer was severely wounded and the remainder of the troop were pinned by fire in open ground. Lt-Col Bartholomew saw that quick and decisive action was necessary, and immediately climbed onto the commanders tank and brought the leading troop of tanks within close range of the houses. Here under close range sniper and automatic fire he personally directed the fire of the tanks onto individual targets. His runner, who was riding beside him on the tank was severely wounded, but Lt-Col Bartholomew continued to direct the tanks fire until the enemy was completely destroyed. This officers prompt and gallant action was an inspiration to all under his command, and led to the complete rout of the enemy in this sector.
Recommended for MC, awarded Bar to DSO. [L.G. 21.6.45]

ACTING TY. MAJOR PATRICK MARSHALL DONNELL, R.M.
Ty Capt, No. 47 RM Commando
DISTINGUISHED SERVICE ORDER (PERIODIC)

Lieutenant-Colonel Donnell fought through the majority of this campaign as second in command 47 RM Commando, the unit he now commands. He has throughout shown outstanding qualities of gallantry and leadership. In the assault landings on 6th January 1944 he organised the unit under fire when his Commanding Officer was temporarily separated from it. Later he commanded a detached force in the successful attack on Port en Bessin, which he greatly assisted by his quick reaction in an unexpected emergency. Throughout the summer he was always well to the fore in raids and patrols and performed several acts of gallantry.

In the assault on Walcheren he took command of a troop when its officers had become casualties, and later, during the night after an enemy counter-attack, continually moved around the forward posts encouraging the men and bringing forward ammunition and rations.

In the words of his late Commanding Officer he was a tower of strength as second in command, his coolness under fire, his imperturbability and his sound common sense have been of inestimable value.

Later, as Commanding Officer, it has not fallen his lot to take part in any major actions, but he has commanded and administered his unit and, by his skilful planning and direction of patrols and raids, inflicted casualties on the enemy and gained information at minimum cost. *[L.G. 24.1.46]*

ACTING TEMPORARY LIEUTENANT-COLONEL THOMAS MALCOLM GRAY, M.C.
Captain, T/Maj, 717, No. 46 (Royal Marine) Commando
DISTINGUISHED SERVICE ORDER
(IMMEDIATE)

Date 23rd–24th March 1945.
On 23rd–24th March 1945 Lieut-Colonel Gray was in command of 46 (Royal Marine) Commando which captured the original bridgehead over the River Rhine. He attacked across the river in Buffaloes and fought his way inland with unparalleled determination and skill. His men captured two large groups of houses killing over thirty enemy and capturing eighty three enemy in the first ten minutes of the operation. This was only made possible by the speed and dash of this fearless advance where a number of key personnel were lost. Lt-Col Gray never allowed the impetus to slacken despite every enemy opposition, and his dauntless courage and sure progress made the brigade task possible. He was in every way an inspiration and example to the men under his command.

He was continually under fire from small arms fire from the Rhine to Wesel, and in Wesel was under fire from enemy armed with panzerfausts which wounded many of the men around him. His cool judgement and his complete contempt for danger inspired his men and influenced the battle at a most critical stage.
[L.G. 20.2.45]

ACTING LIEUTENANT-COLONEL CAMPBELL RICHARD HARDY
S/Capt, Bt/Maj, No. 46 RM Commando
DISTINGUISHED SERVICE ORDER

On 11th June 1944, while serving under command of this brigade, Lt-Col Hardy led his troops during the difficult and trying operation of clearing the woods on both banks of the river from Barbiere to Rots.

Lt-Col Hardy displayed great coolness, good judgement and personal bravery in the capture of Le Hamel and Rots which were only cleared out after the stiffest fighting in the hours of darkness after a long day's fighting. Although he would have been justified in recommending that the capture of Rots should be left until the following morning after proper artillery preparation, this officer insisted on carrying out his task even though darkness was falling, adding to his difficulties. The operation was a complete success, and evidence of the fierceness of the fighting is that 122 German dead were buried on the following day. As a result of the action taken by Lt-Col Hardy and his Commandos, this brigade was able to occupy Rots on the following day with only two casualties and thereby considerably improving the position.

In my opinion the success of the operation was to a great extent due to the leadership of the C.O. and I recommend he be awarded the DSO. *[L.G. 12.9.44]*

Major Donald Charles Hopson, M.C.
WS/Major, 87593, RAC, H.Q. 1 Commando Bde & 3 Bde
Distinguished Service Order

Since January 1945 Major Hopson had been Brigade Major of the First Commando Brigade, and has taken an active part in all operations since that time. He crossed in the first wave both in the battle of the Rhine and the Weser Crossing. In the battle of Esseller Forest he particularly distinguished himself. The brigade encountered a strong Kreig Marine Fusilier force of three battalions, two companies of SS troops and a detachment of self-propelled guns. The brigade consolidation area was in the form of a tight bridgehead over the River Aller, which was of the greatest importance to 11 Armoured Division.

At about 1130 hours on 11th April 1945 the brigade was heavily counter-attacked from three sides. Brigade H.Q. was under mortar and small arms fire and several officers and men were killed by sniping. Physical contact with units was impossible. Major Hopson was in a slit trench with a No. 22 Wireless Set and was very much exposed from one flank to enemy fire. Nevertheless during the whole battle when vital messages were being sent, Major Hopson continually exposed himself to fire in order to ensure that there should be no fault or delay in the passing of the orders. The whole battle was a great success and the bridgehead consolidated, allowing 11 Armd Div to pass complete over the River Aller. Major Hopson's complete disregard for his own safety, and his wholehearted devotion to duty materially contributed to the success of the operation. Both before and since that date Major Hopson has distinguished himself on every occasion the brigade has been in action, and has been an inspiration and an example to all members of the First Commando Brigade. *[L.G. 11.10.45]*

ACTING LIEUT.-COLONEL ANTHONY DAVID LEWIS
W/Capt (T/Maj.), 95626, Dorset, No. 6 Commando
DISTINGUISHED SERVICE ORDER

Lt-Col Lewis was in command of No. 6 Commando on 23rd March 1945 when this unit led the First Commando Brigade from the banks of the Rhine into the City of Wessel.

Speed was the vital factor in this operation, as it was necessary to enter the city as soon as possible after the bombing. This was achieved largely by the skill and daring displayed by Lt-Col Lewis who led his troops with such dash that three separate platoon localities were quickly over-run on his way to the city. His entry into the city itself in spite of considerable opposition from small arms and panzerfausts was effected so quickly that the remainder of the brigade was enabled to consolidate before the enemy became aware of the situation. Lt-Col Lewis was at all times at the head of his troops, and his trust and courage contributed largely to the success of the whole operation.

Recommended for MC, awarded DSO. [L.G. 21.6.45]

ACTING LIEUTENANT-COLONEL NORMAN HASTINGS TAILYOUR, R.M.
Captain
DISTINGUISHED SERVICE ORDER

For gallant and distinguished services in North West Europe.

L.G. 12.2.46

TEMPORARY CHAPLAIN THE REVD. REGINALD HAW, B.A., R.N.V.R.
No. 47 & 45 Commando
DISTINGUISHED SERVICE CROSS

For gallantry, steadfastness and inspiring devotion to duty whilst serving with the 45th Royal Marine Commando during the liberation of Holland. L.G. 26.6.45

CHAPLAIN THE REVEREND HARRY KENNEN
Probationary Ty. Chaplain, RNVR, No. 45 & 46 RM Cdo.
DISTINGUISHED SERVICE CROSS

For great bravery in bringing in the wounded under fire during operations in France. L.G. 23.1.45

NorthWest Europe After D Day

Temporary Major Logan Scott-Bowden, D.S.O., M.C., R.E.
95182, Corps of Royal Engineers.
Bar to Military Cross
In recognition of gallant and distinguished services in North West Europe.   L.G. 24.1.46

Temporary Captain Raymond Thomas Casamajor Addington, R.A.
Lieutenant, 85533, 13th (HAC) Regt RHA, No. 5 Cdo.
Military Cross
This officer is the Battery Captain of H Battery HAC RHA. Throughout the last three months he has set the very highest example to all by his quiet and unostentatious hard work. Whatever job he has done he has done extremely well, usually in charge of the Gun line and the echelons, at times as a Forward Observation Officer in support of the armoured regiments or in some well-registered farmhouse a few hundred yards from the enemy. His personal bravery is beyond praise, but above all it is his quiet competent handling of difficult and dangerous situations and his complete disregard of personal safety that has been of the highest order. His work in the organisation of the echelon and the care and supply of all vital necessities to his battery has been excellent, and throughout, his cheerfulness and good humour has been a never failing tonic to all his men.   *[L.G. 21.6.45]*

Ty. Lieutenant Athole Jack Allen, R.M.
Military Cross
For gallant and distinguished services in North West Europe.   L.G. 12.2.46

Temporary Major David Arthur Blair
WS/Capt, 73177, 5th Bn The Seaforth Hldrs, No. 11 Cdo.
Military Cross
This officer was commanding B Company on the 4th November 1944 when the battalion made its first assault crossing over the Aft–Waterings Canal. Prior to the crossing he displayed complete disregard for the enemy's fire which was spraying the canal bank in answer to our tank shooting, by walking about in the open under fire encouraging the men and giving last minute instructions. When H hr came he was the first to cross the bank and as a result of his leadership his whole Company were up and across as one man. The speed of their advance after crossing was remarkable and they had the enemy completely on the run. On pausing at the first bound

Major Blair quickly appreciated that he could cut off an enemy strong-point by a rapid out flanking movement. His action was completely successful and a great many enemy were trapped and killed. This manœuvre enabled the next battalion of another brigade on the right to push on to their objective at a critical time when delay might have seriously affected the whole plan. This successful move was carried out after last light without any casualties to the company. After reorganising quickly Major Blair again got his company driving on and as a result the retreating enemy had no chance of reorganising or stopping the fight. The company were therefore able to overrun their final objective with little opposition, all remaining enemy being easily disposed of.

This success was entirely due to the fine leadership displayed by the commander of the company who moved at the head of his men throughout, encouraging them on and moving under fire at all times with complete disregard of his own safety. His calm bearing was an inspiration to all around him and his keen perception at the most critical moments of the battle saved many lives. His courage was of the highest order and his conduct worthy of recognition.   *[L.G. 5.4.45]*

LIEUTENANT THOMAS JOHN CHRISTIE
337687, Royal Signals, No. 1 Commando Bde Signal Troop
MILITARY CROSS (PERIODIC)

Lieut Christie is the lines officer in the 1st Commando, Brigade Signal Troop. He was in charge of the line party detailed to produce line communication across the Rhine after the brigade had made good the bridgehead at Wesel. It was considered vital that this line should be laid at the earliest possible moment. This task was extremely hazardous. All bridges across the Rhine had been demolished and there was considerable shelling and sniping of all bridge exits.

As soon as a message had been received that the objective had been captured, Lieut Christie took a small picked line party down to the demolished railway bridge. At this point the town of Wesel had not been completely cleared of the enemy and the line party had to work in full view of the enemy machine gun post sited upstream on the east bank of the River.

Ordering his small party to pay out the line, Lieut Christie commenced climbing across the twisted bridge spans carrying the line with him. At times he had to climb over girders 100 feet above the river while at other times he picked his path along spans which were partly submerged in the water.

The pull on the quadruple cable whenever it touched the water was tremendous, nevertheless by sheer courage and determination, Lieut Christie crossed the full 1,500-ft. length of the demolished bridge under heavy shell fire and spasmodic sniping and machine gun fire, and thus enabled vital communication to be established before the first pontoon bridge had been commenced. This officer's devotion to duty and complete disregard for his own safety was an inspiration to all who witnessed it.

Throughout the campaign he has continuously shown a high standard of efficiency, and his work in line laying during the difficult operations over the Rhine, Weser, Aller and Elbe has, at all times been beyond praise. *[L.G. 11.10.45]*

LIEUTENANT JOHN FRANCIS CLAPTON
W/Lieutenant, 258657, Cameronians, No. 6 Commando
MILITARY CROSS (IMMEDIATE)

Near Linne on the 28th January 1945, Lieut Clapton was in command of a recce patrol consisting of himself and four men, whose job was to search a wood. On arriving 30 yds from the forward edge of the wood he got down with his patrol, in dead ground, to give final orders. On looking up he saw six German parachutists with a spandau positioned in a long trench on the forward edge of the wood.

Acting immediately, he dashed forward on his own and so dismayed the two Germans who were behind the gun, by his determined and immediate action that they deserted their post and fled. The other four, when they grasped the situation, immediately made a grab for the gun but Lieut Clapton reached it first and took them prisoner.

By his determined initiative and complete disregard for personal danger, Lieut Clapton saved what might have been an ugly situation and might have resulted in casualties to our side. As it was four prisoners of a true Nazi type were taken without a shot being fired. *[L.G. 12.4.48]*

TEMPORARY MAJOR LEONARD NICKSON COULSON
W/Capt, 155037, D.L.I., No. 4 Commando
MILITARY CROSS (PERIODIC)

Maj Coulson landed with his commando in the assault on Ouistreham on D-Day, in support of the airborne assault by 6 Airborne Division. He was in command of a troop position vital to the defence of the important Orne bridges, which at that time were under continual heavy fire from enemy mortars and self-propelled guns.

During this period Major Coulson exposed himself to fire to keep his positions organised and to his unflagging energy and determination and disregard for his own safety can be attributed the relatively low casualties his troop suffered. His own example was an inspiration to his men under extremely difficult and trying conditions.

One instance of Major Coulson's outstanding courage and example was on 10th June 1944, when he had been without sleep for five days, with very little food, and under almost continuous fire. After a particularly heavy bombardment, an enemy unit formed up to attack his positions. Regardless of his own safety, Major Coulson rallied his men with the result that the enemy attack was completely smashed.

Throughout the whole campaign in North-West Europe, this officer has shown the highest qualities of leadership, courage and devotion to duty in the face of the enemy. *[L.G. 24.1.46]*

ACTING TEMPORARY CAPTAIN JOHN DEXTER, R.M.
Temporary Lieutenant
MILITARY CROSS

For gallant and distinguished services in North-West Europe.

L.G. 12.2.46

TEMPORARY CAPTAIN NORMAN KIDSTON EASTON
P/277394, W/Lieut, No. 46 RM Commando
MILITARY CROSS (IMMEDIATE)

On 29th April, in the initial assault over the River Elbe at Lauenberg, Capt Easton was commanding the leading troop of this unit. As the craft approached the far bank, the enemy opened up fierce fire with light anti-aircraft guns, mortars and grenades on the landing point. Capt Easton immediately led his men off the craft through the fire and started to climb the 100-ft cliff feature down which the enemy were hurling grenades. The grenade throwing was becoming accurate and casualties were occurring both on the beach and among the troops climbing the cliff whom the enemy could obviously see and hear. Despite this fire Capt Easton made his way up and standing up in full view he personally silenced with grenades the strongly held enemy post at the top. He then immediately led the way forward himself, despite enemy artillery and mortar and infiltrated through enemy posts at great speed. He led the advance for two miles to the objective and over-ran the enemy company on it.

NorthWest Europe After D Day

Capt Easton showed complete disregard for his personal safety and his action in silencing the enemy post saved many lives and greatly contributed to the success of the whole operation.

[L.G. 2.8.45]

ACTING TY. MAJOR NORMAN ARTHUR ESSEX, R.M.
Temporary Captain
MILITARY CROSS

For gallant and distinguished services in North West Europe.

L.G. 12.2.46

TEMPORARY CAPTAIN JOHN DOUGLAS GIBBON
67147, Border Regt, No. 46 RM Commando
MILITARY CROSS (IMMEDIATE)

On the night of 23rd March, 1945 during the assault across the Rhine near Wesel, Captain Gibbon commanded the leading troop of his Commando in the first wave of LVTs. Immediately before touching down, one of his LVTs was hit and burst into flames, thus reducing his strength by a quarter. Captain Gibbon however, led his troops inland at such a pace and with such determination that the enemy on the river bank were unable to check his advance. His objective was a farmhouse 500 yards inland, and he pressed his advance so relentlessly behind the barrage put down by our guns that his own Sergeant Major and another soldier fell by his side casualties to our own shellfire. Without hesitation and with complete disregard for his safety he led his men on to his objective where he killed three officers and took sixty prisoners. The capture of the vital first objective was entirely due to the dash and dauntless devotion to duty displayed by this officer. *[L.G. 12.7.45]*

ACTING TY. CAPTAIN ARTHUR HAMBLETON, R.M.
Temporary Lieutenant
MILITARY CROSS

For gallant and distinguished services in North West Europe.

L.G. 8.2.46

LIEUTENANT EVAN CHARLES BEVERLY SCOTT KEAT
328922, RAMC, No. 6 Commando
MILITARY CROSS (IMMEDIATE)

Near Essel on 11th April 1945, the enemy put in a strong counter-attack of two companies on the unit position in a wood, just before the unit had had time to consolidate its recently won position.

Lieut Keat had his regimental aid post situated in the rear of the unit but the flatness of the ground was such that during the counter-attack those in the rear were just as exposed to the enemy small arms fire as those in the front. Realising that there was no alternative but to cope with the casualties in the open Lieut Keat calmly stood in the open throughout the 75 minutes of the counter-attack attending the casualties, completely undaunted by the heavy small arms fire, even though one of his medical orderlies was shot whilst assisting him. Never once did he make any attempt to take cover but used what pits had been dug to shelter his casualties until there was an opportunity of evacuation.

By sheer personal example, force of character, complete disregard for his own danger he not only inspired his medical section with the same spirit but also by immediate and skilful attention saved the lives of badly wounded men. *[L.G. 12.7.45]*

LIEUTENANT PETER F. KING
WS/Lieut 328163, DCLI, No. 4 Commando
MILITARY CROSS

Since 6th June 1944 this officer has continually been conspicuous both in action and on patrol, and displays the highest qualities of leadership and courage. He had fought in all the actions in which the commando has been involved.

For example, on the night 9th–10th April 1945, Lieut King with a party of two crossed the Volkerak into the enemy held island of Overflakee. During the night he made and extensive reconnaissance of enemy dispositions, Lying up the next day to observe the habits of the enemy. He determined to remain longer and penetrate deeper, and during the following two days directed a large number of harassing artillery shoots against the enemy, frequently from positions within the danger zone. Lieut King withdrew on the night 12th–13th April 1945 with very complete information on the enemy dispositions in the south eastern half of the island.
[L.G. 11.10.45]

ACTING TEMPORARY CAPTAIN PETER WALTER JAMES NEALE, R.M.
Temporary Lieutenant
MILITARY CROSS

For bravery and great devotion to duty whilst operating with the Allied Armies in North-West Europe. *L.G. 12.6.45*

NorthWest Europe After D Day

Temporary Lieutenant Thomas Frederick Rowbottom, R.M.
Military Cross
For gallant and distinguished services in North West Europe.
L.G. 12.2.46

Acting Major Patrick Henry Bligh Wall, R.M.
Captain
Military Cross
For bravery and great devotion to duty whilst operating with the Allied Armies in North-West Europe. *L.G. 12.6.45*

Acting Temporary Captain Thomas Ernest Williams, R.M.
Temporary Lieutenant
Military Cross
For gallant and distinguished services in North West Europe.
L.G. 12.2.46

Company Sergeant Major Sydney Hubbard
5255533 Sergeant, Worcester Regt, No. 3 Commando
Distinguished Conduct Medal (Periodic)
CSM Hubbard has been in 3 Commando for three years and has consistently distinguished himself in action throughout his career. In Normandy on D+1 during the fierce fighting east of the River Orne he showed magnificent gallantry by lying on a Teller mine thus preventing it exploding and wounding many of his comrades. Miraculously he escaped with his life, although badly wounded. He rejoined the unit and fought with them throughout Holland and Germany, where his conduct has been continually of the highest order. In the woods, during the fierce fighting subsequent to the crossing of the River Aller, CSM Hubbard at great personal risk so handled a section of twenty five men of his troop that they were largely instrumental in holding and driving back a German attack that threatened to overrun Commando and Brigade HQ. Again during the River Elbe crossing CSM Hubbard's troop was the first to reach the dominating ground overlooking Lauenburg and thus secure, without casualties, this vital feature. A more gallant, unselfish WO it would be difficult to find anywhere.
[L.G. 24.1.46]

Commando Gallantry Awards of World War II

Lance Corporal Eric E. Wadge
No. 3 Commando
Distinguished Conduct Medal

L/Cpl Wadge is medical orderly in No. 3 Commando. At Amfreville on 12th June 1944 although wounded by shellfire he refused to have his wounds attended to until he had dressed and evacuated five of his wounded comrades. Throughout the campaign in Holland and Germany his conduct has been consistently excellent. At Linne in January 1945 he re-entered the town after a fighting patrol had withdrawn and with the assistance of a comrade managed to evacuate one of four wounded men left behind. At Leese after the crossing of the River Weser he walked out with the medical officer over completely open ground on two separate occasions and helped carry back a wounded officer and OR, during this time being under continual rifle fire from enemy troops some four hundred yards away. After the crossing of the River Aller and whilst the the initial fighting was still in progress he voluntarily went out through woods infested by the enemy to attempt an evacuation of two wounded men of his troop. Subsequently on hearing at 0200 hrs 13th April that a wounded Sgt of the Commando was in an enemy regimental aid post in a village some three miles away, he immediately went out, through the enemy lines to look for the Sgt, but was unsuccessful. He returned at first light, despite the fact that SS troops were holding the village, found the wounded Sgt, carried him back through the German lines, and saw him evacuated. By this action L/Cpl Wadge was largely instrumental in saving the amputation of one of the Sgt's legs. Again on the crossing of the River Elbe L/Cpl Wadge distinguished himself by walking out, under fire from the cliffs above, and across ground which was being mortared and shelled, and successfully brought to cover, and then evacuated two wounded men from his troop who had been hit on disembarking from their Buffalo, and who were lying in the open.

L/Cpl Wadge's bearing, devotion to duty and complete disregard for his personal safety have been an inspiration to all throughout the entire campaign.

Recommended for periodic MM, awarded DCM.   [L.G. 24.1.46]

Acting Company Sergeant Major Arthur Edward Anscombe
Sergeant, Po.X.675, 30 Bn RM
Military Medal (Periodic)

During the assault crossing of the River Maas in the area of Alem Island by 30 RM on the night 23rd–24th April 1945, CSM

Anscombe showed resource and qualities of leadership unsurpassed by any NCO in the battalion.

By his far-sighted and thorough arrangements, he was mainly responsible for the successful organisation and operation of his company's boats for the river crossing which was accomplished under heavy small arms and mortar fire. Later he moved forward, close behind the leading platoons and ably assisted in the reorganisation on the objective. On the 25th April in the same area at about 2300 hrs, while his Company Commander was with an out-lying platoon, Company Headquarters was fired upon at close range by an enemy patrol. A certain amount of confusion arose in the dark and one man was wounded. CSM Anscombe who was the senior rank at HQ took charge immediately. He rallied the Headquarters personnel, located the enemy patrol and organised immediate return fire, himself firing with a captured enemy LMG. The enemy ceased fire. CSM Anscombe then passed through orders to the neighbouring platoons which enabled one of our own patrols to locate and drive off the enemy patrol who left two dead and one wounded prisoner behind.

By his steadiness and courage under fire, by his initiative and resourcefulness he set a very fine example. By his willingness to shoulder responsibility, he proved of the utmost assistance to his officers.

During the whole time he has served as CSM he has shown unflagging energy and devotion to duty and has done far more than could normally be expected of him. In actual operations he has always shown outstanding ability and courage. *[L.G. 24.1.46]*

TEMPORARY SERGEANT HENRY AVERY
Ex 1317, 27 Bn RM
MILITARY MEDAL (PERIODIC)

Sgt Avery is the mortar platoon sergeant of 27 RM. In the Engellen area on 20th March 1945 and in the Heusden area the following night, when under heavy enemy counter-mortar fire, this NCO remained in an exposed position, coolly directing the fire of the mortars until the enemy mortars were silenced. On 22nd and 23rd March he accompanied fighting patrols which crossed the River Maas in the Heusden area and was able to engage opportunity targets with devastating effect. On the first occasion, when the patrol came under heavy close range automatic fire he put down a very effective smoke screen which enabled the patrol to withdraw from an exposed position.

On the 28th April, his mortars were supporting a fighting patrol operating across the Kusten Canal and Sgt Avery was wounded in the shoulder. Despite his wound and the intense enemy mortar and small arms fire, Sgt Avery moved his observation post to a more exposed position because it afforded better observation. If the patrol had lacked the fire support provided by his mortars, it would have had very serious consequences.

By his enthusiasm, courage and resource, Sgt Avery has consistently set a remarkably fine example. During periods of intense activity his devotion to duty has been most praiseworthy. By his complete disregard for his own safety and his determination, whatever the circumstances, to achieve good results, Sgt Avery has contributed in no small way to the successful efforts of 27 RM.

[L.G. 24.1.46]

ACTING COMPANY SERGEANT MAJOR HARWOOD FREDERICK GEORGE BEAVEN
Ply.X.458, Sergeant, RM, No. 40 & 45 RM Commando
MILITARY MEDAL

For bravery and great devotion to duty whilst operating with the Allied Armies in North-West Europe. *L.G. 12.6.45*

ACTING TROOP SERGEANT MAJOR HENRY BENNETT
Ch.X.512 Corporal, No. 40 & 45 RM Commando
MILITARY MEDAL (PERIODIC)

North West European Campaign—6th June [1944] to 7th May 1945.
TSM Bennett rejoined his unit in Normandy after being badly wounded. He insisted on rejoining in spite of having a permanently damaged elbow. Since rejoining, TSM Bennett's troop has been in hard fighting and has suffered many casualties. On two separate occasions, all the officers of the troop were killed or wounded and TSM Bennett had to command under difficult circumstances. He fully justified his unit's faith in him on each occasion.

He has in addition personally distinguished himself in action on several occasions, the outstanding example being the time when he went out to bring in the body of L/Cpl Harden, VC, at Maasbracht, during the action for which Harden's decoration was awarded. TSM Bennett had proved himself in many severe tests to be not only a very brave man but also a determined, aggressive and skilful leader. When out of action he has done sterling work in re-forming his troop and keeping morale high and aggressive spirit to the fore. Successes which the troop has had are to a very considerable degree due to TSM Bennett's leadership and magnificent performance right through the campaign.

(L.G. 12.2.46)

TROOP SERGEANT MAJOR JAMES WILLIAM BLACK
Ty Sjt (A/Ty CSM), Ply.X.102166, No. 48 (RM) Commando
MILITARY MEDAL

Throughout the North-West European campaign, Troop Sergeant Major Black has behaved outstandingly well. His cheerful and determined manner and his coolness and offensive spirit under fire have, in all circumstances, in major actions, patrols and routine duties, been an example to all ranks.

During raids on Schouwen in February and March 1945 TSM Black by his vigorous and efficient handling of his party contributed more than any other factor to the success of the actions.

For example, during a raid near Bruinisse, TSM Black engaged five enemy machine-guns with two Brens to such effect that he drew all the fire on to himself, thus enabling the rest of the patrol to withdraw unmolested. This is typical of many incidents in the past. *(L.G. 23.10.45)*

COMPANY SERGEANT MAJOR WILLIAM MAURICE JOHN BROOKING
Ply.X.120078, Sergeant, 30 Bn RM
MILITARY MEDAL (PERIODIC)

During the time 30 RM Battalion has been formed, CSM Brooking had consistently shown devotion to duty of a very high order. In actual operations against the enemy, he has always displayed outstanding courage and ability to get things done, especially when a lead is required at critical times.

In particular, on 23rd April, 'X' Company, 30 RM was one of the two leading companies of the battalion during the crossing of the River Maas and the capture of Alem on the north bank. During the later stages of the attack, when the leading platoons had suffered casualties among the officers and senior NCOs and were making little progress CSM Brooking went forward to one of these platoons and by his own personal example and efforts got them on the move again, despite incessant and at times heavy enemy mortar and aimed small arms fire.

Subsequently, during the capture of the Heerewaarden isthmus between the River Maas and the River Waal, this NCO collected a small party of men from a rather disorganised platoon and led them in an assault on an enemy position which had been holding up our attack for over two hours.

Inspired by his example and encouraged by his exceptional powers of leadership, this small party killed or captured the eleven occupants of the enemy position, which was later completely over-run. The regaining of the initiative and the success of this attack was almost entirely due to the personal efforts of this NCO.

CSM Brooking had consistently shown initiative and resource far above the average. In various small actions he has always been to the fore, exercising a steadying influence and inspiring confidence. *(L.G. 23.10.45)*

ACTING TY. SERGEANT JOHN EDWARD BROWNFIELD
Ch.X.907 Cpl, No. 48 RM Commando
MILITARY MEDAL

Throughout the winter, Sgt Brownfield has shown outstanding leadership both in static conditions at Goes and in action. During the three raids on Schouwen in which he took part in recent months. His imperturbable demeanour was a source of inspiration to the less experienced members of the raiding parties. In particular during his last raid near Bruinisse. Sgt Brownfield was second in command of a fighting patrol. When his officer was severely wounded Sgt Brownfield personally charged an enemy strong-point and, having killed or wounded the occupants, rallied and withdrew the patrol under the instructions of the wounded officer; all this in spite of being wounded himself. *(L.G. 23.10.45)*

LANCE CORPORAL FRANCIS G. BURTON
Ply X.105925, Marine, No. 45 RM Commando
MILITARY MEDAL (IMMEDIATE)

23rd January 1945—Vloot Beek.

On 23rd January 1945 during the initial battle for the bridgehead at Vloot Beek from which the final attack on Linne was launched, Mne Burton was carrying the Commando Rover Set. Mne Burton followed his Commanding Officer from Commando HQ to visit the forward troops, who were hotly engaged. On the way Mne Burton encountered heavy mortar fire and also came under accurate rifle fire. After some 300 yards had been covered Mne Burton was badly hit in his right arm. Although obviously in great pain and with a useless right arm Mne Burton continued to follow his Commanding Officer, maintaining vital communications and passing orders for supporting fire to aid the forward troops. This he continued to do, refusing to return to the regimental aid post until another signaller was obtained to take over the set.

Mne Burton's conduct was a shining example of a signaller's devotion to duty and loyalty to his unit. *(L.G. 24.4.45)*

Sergeant Patrick Joseph Byrne
2719257 Cpl (A/Sjt.), 3rd Bn Irish Guards, No. 4 Cdo.
Military Medal (Immediate)

On 9th April 1945 Sjt Byrne's platoon was the Right leading platoon during the attack on Furstenau. They came under very heavy spandau and bazooka fire and were pinned to the ground. The company commander coming up to visit them was killed.

Sjt Byrne ordered his platoon into a sheltered position while he himself remained to cover their movement with an LMG. When a plan had been made to continue the advance with close tank support, Sjt Byrne led his platoon with the greatest dash and vigour, and dealt with a number of enemy posts, until finally their objectives were gained. Throughout the action this NCO's courage and personal example were of the highest order. His complete disregard of his personal safety and coolness did much to encourage the whole company during a difficult period, and were of the greatest assistance to the successful outcome of the attack.

[L.G. 12.7.45]

Marine Harry Charlwood
Ch X.105642, No. 46 (RM) Commando
Military Medal (Immediate)

During the attack on Rots 9571 on 11th June, Mne Charlwood was wounded in the neck. Shortly afterwards fire was opened on the section from an unexpected direction at short range and he was wounded in the arm. This Marine then picked up a grenade and rushed at the enemy post shouting that he would deal with it, thereby drawing all the fire to himself and enabling the remainder of the section to disengage and rejoin their troop.

Mne Charlwood is missing.

This recommendation has been delayed in order to obtain evidence of wounded men. *[L.G. 19.12.44]*

Marine Frederick George Cretney
Po.X.109930, 30 Bn Royal Marines, No. 30 RM Commando
Military Medal (Immediate)

At Alem on the north bank of the River Maas during the afternoon of 23rd April 1945, 'B' Company 30th Battalion RM was carrying out an attack on an enemy position in a fort. This fort overlooked a backwater of the river which it was necessary for 'B' Company to cross in order to reach the fort. Initially the company started to approach the fort with its forward troops in assault boats moving up the backwater. Fire from the fort was, however, considerable and accurate. It became necessary to land the company on the shore furthest from the fort with a view to working up overland to a position on the river bank opposite and close to the fort. In order to put the company over the river it was necessary to bring boats up the backwater to where the company could embark and cross quickly to the fort. The boats were paddled and pulled by a small party of men working close along the river bank.

Marine Cretney played a leading part in the work of bringing up the boats. He took charge of the leading boat and though under considerable close range fire, got it forward to the embarkation point. For much of the time he was wading up to his waist in the river, knowing that he was in full view of the enemy. By his action he undoubtedly encouraged the men manning the other boats and was chiefly instrumental in ensuring that the boats were got forward. Had the boats not been got forward to the company it would have been necessary to abandon the operation, which, as it was, turned out to be highly successful. *[L.G. 2.8.45]*

TY. SERGEANT WILLIAM GEORGE DEACON
Ch.X.106276, Royal Marines
MILITARY MEDAL

For bravery and great devotion to duty whilst operating with the Allied Armies in North-West Europe. *L.G. 12.6.45*

ACTING SERGEANT CYRIL DOBBS
4914036 W/Cpl, South Staffs, No. 6 Commando
MILITARY MEDAL

On the night 24th–25th February 1945 at Well, Sgt Dobbs was a member of a fighting patrol sent out to cross the River Maas and bring back a prisoner. Having crossed the river the assault party was advancing towards an enemy post when heavy accurate fire was opened from three different positions, pinning them to the ground. Sgt Dobbs, who was in command of the covering party acted immediately. Exposing himself without hesitation to heavy machine-gun fire he brought his party across the open ground at speed, and opened fire on the nearest enemy post. His fire was so effective that the machine-gun was knocked out, and he was able to dash in and take prisoner the two soldiers manning the gun. He then engaged the other enemy posts with fire from an exposed position, thus drawing all enemy fire on to himself and allowing the assault party to withdraw. Meanwhile an enemy NCO came running up to retrieve the situation, and Sgt Dobbs shot him dead at close range. He then withdrew his party to the river bank without suffering a single casualty.

From this successful patrol important enemy identifications were obtained. Its success was in great part due to the tremendous dash and initiative displayed by Sgt Dobbs. [L.G. 3.5.45]

COLOUR SERGEANT JAMES LINDSAY FENWICK
Po.X.105797, No. 45 RM Commando
MILITARY MEDAL

Reconnaissance across River Maas 27th–28th February 1945.

On the night 27th–28th February 1945, D Troop 45 RM Commando crossed the River Maas near Roermond to carry out a raid on enemy positions. Fanatical enemy paratroops were encountered and bitter close quarter fighting ensued. The Troop Officers, Troop Sergeant Major and senior sergeant were all killed or wounded. Colour Sergeant Fenwick rose to the occasion and commanded the troop during the difficult withdrawal back across the river. He was himself taken prisoner by the enemy whilst looking for wounded men of his troop. He shewed great initiative and escaped very quickly during a moment's confusion. Returning to the river bank he contacted a patrol of the Commando which was looking for survivors and was brought back across the Maas. He gave detailed information of enemy positions and numbers together with maps, got from a German Artillery officer which shewed the enemy gun areas in that locality. On return C/Sgt Fenwick continued to command his troop, which had suffered 50% casualties, for some days until an officer was available. Throughout the whole action C/Sgt Fenwick shewed great coolness, determination and leadership. Unfortunately the full story of his exploits was not available until one of the wounded officers was later able to give it, and it was therefore not possible to recommend C/Sgt Fenwick for an award at the time.

Bridgehead across River Weser—6th April 1945

Again on 6th April 1945 this Senior NCO shewed outstanding courage and leadership. On this occasion he was a sub-section Commander of D Troop, 45 RM Commando during that unit's attack along the bank of the River Weser on the outer defences of Leese. Heavy opposition was met from well dug in and concealed enemy positions at close range. D Troop was the leading troop as the Commando advanced out of the existing bridgehead and at once was met by heavy fire, but C/Sgt Fenwick with great determination and leadership led his men forward unflinchingly and personally cleared several enemy slit trenches with phosphor and HE grenades. Later he took a bren gun forward and from an exposed position on the top of the river bank pinned the enemy down in their trenches under 100 yards away to the left flank thereby enabling the rest of the Commando to continue its advance. He undoubtedly inflicted many casualties on the enemy.

Apart from these two instances, C/Sgt Fenwick has on many occasions shewn coolness and determination in many actions. His disregard for his own safety and his unflinching determination and leadership have gained for him the complete confidence of those under his command and the respect and admiration of the whole unit. *[L.G. 23.10.45]*

CORPORAL IAN HARRIS
6387036, No. 45 RM Commando
MILITARY MEDAL

Crossing of River Weser—6th April 1945

This NCO was the official interpreter with HQ 45 RM Commando during the attack launched by that Commando on the outer defences of Leese across the River Weser on the afternoon of 6th April 1945. Immediately it left the existing bridgehead the Commando came up against extremely heavy and accurate small arms fire from dug-in enemy positions to the front and left flank. Owing to the flat nature of the ground the only line of advance was along the river bank but every inch of ground was bitterly contested. Throughout Cpl Harris was always to the fore seeking for every opportunity to engage the enemy at close range with his Thompson Machine Carbine. On one occasion the HQ found itself only five yards from three occupied enemy slit trenches up the river bank and on the other side of a hedge, and it was obvious that spontaneous action was necessary to save an awkward situation. Immediately Cpl Harris climbed the bank and in full view of other enemy to his left flank fired his weapon at the enemy then at his feet, killing two and taking one prisoner. Before he could return to the cover of the bank again he was wounded by a burst of spandau fire from his left. The courage of this NCO has seldom been surpassed and he undoubtedly saved the lives of several of his comrades by his spontaneous action. His unceasing determination to get at the enemy will always be an inspiration to all.

LANCE SERGEANT ARTHUR HERBERT HARRISON, R.E.
1877319, No. 6 Commando
MILITARY MEDAL

At Osnabruck on 4th April 1945 L/Sgt Harrison and his sub-section were ordered to enter a large factory and clear it of enemy snipers.

L/Sgt Harrison entered one doorway of a large machine workshop, and as he did so a group of five enemy fired a panzerfaust at him from the other end of the workshop. This wounded L/Sgt Harrison in the leg. However, completely undaunted, L/Sgt Harrison went on, best his wound would allow, firing his carbine at the enemy, killing one and driving the remainder of the party, which included a spandau team out of the building where he killed another. Leading his sub-section on to where the enemy had taken cover, he drove them out once again and was responsible for wounding yet another before the other two enemy surrendered. Up to this moment the unit had been held up as the factory overlooked the route which the unit had to take and several casualties had been caused by the spandau.

L/Sgt Harrison by his gallant and dashing action, in which he showed complete disregard for his own personal safety, enabled the advance of the unit to continue without further casualties.

(L.G. 12.7.45)

TEMPORARY SERGEANT THOMAS HARRISON
Ex.3466, No. 45 RM Commando
MILITARY MEDAL
Establishing the River Aller bridgehead 10th–12th April 1945.
On 12th April 1945, 45 RM Commando was advancing through the woods in order to extend the Aller bridgehead.

C Troop was the right hand troop on the axis of advance. Very strong opposition was encountered from the German Marine Division. After approximately an hour of close confused fighting Sgt Harrison's section was cut off from the remainder of his troop and his Troop Commander was killed. Harrison with great coolness continued to fight his section against impossible odds. It became obvious to Harrison that in order to stabilise the attack and save lives he must regain contact with the main body of the unit. With complete disregard for his own personal safety, although under heavy fire, he dashed forward with a bren gun and engaged the enemy at close range. This action enabled the remainder of the section to withdraw. During the 20 minutes in which time his comrades were rejoining the unit, Harrison displayed amazing courage. When his bren gun ammunition was expended he finally engaged the enemy with grenades and TSMG taken from the body of his dead officer. Immediately on rejoining his troop Harrison rallied his men in their new positions and finally beat off the enemy. His fine aggressive spirit was undoubtedly responsible for preventing the enemy from outflanking his troop.

In this and previous actions fought by the unit Sgt Harrison has displayed outstanding leadership, courage and devotion to duty whatever the odds. His conduct in battle has inspired great confidence in the men of his section. *(L.G. 19.6.45)*

Marine James Henry Hazell
Po.X.108682, No. 46 RM Commando
Military Medal

During the establishment of the initial bridgehead over the Rhine near Wesel on 23rd March, 1945 a section had advanced too quickly and was in danger from our own artillery barrage. Marine Hazell was ordered to bring them back. He ran forward, and at that moment the barrage, fired by six Field Regiments, came down in the vicinity. Shewing complete disregard for his own safety he dashed forward and ordered the section to withdraw. When on his return it was discovered that two men from the section were missing, Marine Hazell acting on his own initiative immediately went forward again without orders, and in spite of the barrage, which was still falling, brought back the two men. The cool initiative and high courage shewn by this Marine was a magnificent example to his comrades. *[L.G. 19.6.45]*

Sergeant Samuel Moses Hurwitz
D26248, 22 Cdn Armd Regt (CGG)
Military Medal (Immediate)

On 8th August 1944 during the fighting around Cintheau (Map Ref. 0754) Sgt Hurwitz was ordered to cover by fire his troop leader's assault on an enemy position. On arriving at the position it was found necessary to dismount and attack on foot. During the fight a burning enemy self-propelled gun blew up and killed and wounded a number of men of the troop. Sgt Hurwitz was pinned under a tree by the explosion, but managed to extricate himself and although burned from the blast and slightly wounded he picked up a bren gun and with his officer led the assault on the German position. The position, which was a strong one and had been holding up the entire squadron, was taken, 31 prisoners were captured and a number of the enemy killed.

Sgt Hurwitz displayed a fine degree of leadership and offensive spirit and by this action was largely responsible for the subsequent capture of the town of Cintheau itself. *(L.G. 21.12.44)*

Sergeant Harold Robert Francis Kendall
5412410, D.W.R., No. 6 Commando
Military Medal

Near Lauenburg on the night 28th–29th April shortly after crossing the Elbe, Sjt Kendall was put in charge of nine men ordered to patrol to a bridge over the Elbe–Trave Canal and if possible to take it intact.

Approaching the bridge cautiously Sjt Kendall saw a party of four German engineers preparing to fuse the charges that had already been placed on the bridge. The engineer party was covered by two machine-gun teams. Making his plan quickly Sjt Kendall led his patrol as near as possible without being seen, then placing his bren on the ground to cover his attack he led his patrol forward in a dash for the bridge. The Germans were completely surprised and only had time to fire a few bursts of wild and inaccurate fire before they were overpowered, three being killed and the remainder taken prisoner.

Sjt Kendall immediately disconnected the demolitions and rendered them useless, thus capturing the bridge intact, which was of supreme importance to the 6th Airborne Division in their widening of the bridgehead. *[L.G. 2.8.45]*

SERGEANT GEORGE DOUGLAS LANDER
Po.X.1757, No. 27 Bn RM
MILITARY MEDAL (PERIODIC)

Since the conversion of 27 RM to the War Establishment of a normal infantry battalion in January 1945, Sgt Lander has been the Signals Sgt. In the organisation, preparation and training of the signals platoon he has shown great keenness and has proved himself to be very efficient. Owing to the late arrival in the unit of a signal officer, the smooth working of communications within the battalion is to a very great extent the result of his efforts, and just credit is due to him for the way in which he has overcome difficulties in the very short time available.

In particular, in April, when 27 RM was placed under command of 4 Canadian Armoured Division, the battalion was constantly on the move, re-adjusting its positions and in contact with the enemy. Communications were maintained at all times, frequently under extreme difficulties and in spite of enemy action. The signal platoon was put to a very severe test, operating under such mobile conditions at such an early stage in the battalion's life.

Whenever it was possible to run line to forward companies Sgt Lander personally supervised the laying of the cable. The maintenance of these cables, under shell and small arms fire, was due largely to his untiring efforts and personal leadership in charge of the line party. *[L.G. 23.10.45]*

Commando Gallantry Awards of World War II

ACTING TEMPORARY COMPANY SERGEANT MAJOR JAMES SYKES LEES
Sergeant, Po.X.1707, No. 41 RM Commando
MILITARY MEDAL

TSM Lees has served throughout the campaign in Europe and has always shewn himself to be a most outstanding and fearless SNCO.

By his leadership and forceful character he has controlled his troop under the most difficult conditions when officers were either killed or wounded.

On a great number of occasions and especially in recent months the personal actions of this SNCO has been directly responsible for the success of the troop battle and his fine and cheerful leadership has been an example to all.   *[L.G. 23.10.45]*

ACTING TY. CORPORAL HARRY LITHERLAND
Marine, Po.X.119150, No. 47 RM Commando
MILITARY MEDAL

Throughout the campaign in North-West Europe, Cpl Litherland's cheerfulness and devotion to duty, no matter what have been the circumstances, have been beyond praise. In action, at Port en Bessin as a marine, he took charge of a section when his section commander was wounded and by his personal example was largely responsible for the successful completion of the task allotted to his section.

Throughout the period of the bridgehead, he volunteered for and took part in several patrols of a hazardous nature. Later at Walcheren, he again cheerfully took over the responsibilities of commanding his section on his NCO becoming a casualty.

At Kapelsche Veer on the river Maas, on the night of 16th–17th January 1945, he was in the leading group of a strong fighting patrol which was sent to secure a firm base from which the Commando could make an attack. Before the firm base was reached two enemy patrols were met and wiped out due almost entirely to his initiative. Later, when the main Commando attack was held, and heavy casualties had been incurred, he volunteered to take his Bren Group to help the leading troop. On arrival there his cool direction of the bren gun, and his personal bravery in attacking (in company with only one other marine) an enemy slit trench from which an enemy machine gun was dominating our own positions, were largely instrumental in beating off the counter-attack.

Situations as cited above are but a few examples of this NCO's magnificent personal example on all occasions.   *(L.G. 12.2.46)*

ACTING TEMPORARY COMPANY SERGEANT MAJOR HERBERT MALLORIE
Temporary Sergeant, Po X.106665, No. 46 RM Commando
MILITARY MEDAL

This Warrant Officer has served with 46 (RM) Commando with great distinction throughout the campaigns in Normandy, Holland and Germany. In Normandy he proved himself an outstanding and fearless patrol leader. He took over duties of Troop Sergeant Major shortly before the battle of the River Rhine, and in every battle since then has shown such fearless determination and high qualities of leadership that his men would literally follow him anywhere.

During the severe fighting in the River Aller bridgehead, when another troop had had all its officers and TSM killed or wounded and was in a precarious position, he personally led a party to their assistance and acted with such daring and initiative that he completely restored the situation and completed the destruction of the enemy, thus enabling his Commando to capture the important village of Hademstorf.

During the storming of the River Elbe his troop led the brigade into Lauenburg, and it was largely due to his dash and relentless determination that the brigade were able to break into the city with such speed. *(L.G. 12.2.46)*

ACTING TEMPORARY COMPANY SERGEANT MAJOR THOMAS MEAKIN
Temporary Colour Sergeant, Po.X.22498, No. 28 Bn RM
MILITARY MEDAL

CSM Meakin of 'B' Company 28 RM has shown devotion to duty and gallantry of the highest order over the whole period his company has been in action in Holland.

On the night 5th–6th April, at Doeveren, one of our patrols was engaged by the enemy whilst it was crossing the River Maas and their rubber boat was holed and sunk. CSM Meakin, under heavy enemy machine-gun and rifle fire, organised and led a small patrol down the forward slope of the dyke and by his personal efforts, brought in an officer and two OR whom they had rescued from the river.

On the night 12th–13th April, near Herpt on the River Maas an enemy patrol infiltrated through our forward posts and attacked 'B' Company HQ with panzerfaust, stick grenades and rifles. Although much shaken by the explosion of the panzerfaust bombs, CSM Meakin, with commendable coolness led the small reserve immediately available in a counter-attack on the enemy patrol and caused it to withdraw leaving behind two dead and three wounded. Had it not been for his personal example and determined leadership, this raid might have had serious consequences. Although neither strong nor robust physically, his unflinching courage and unsparing efforts have been an example to all during a time when exhaustion and strain might have had a very adverse affect on the alertness of the men. At night he could often be found in the forward posts, encouraging the men by his steadiness under fire. He was tireless in his efforts to ensure their well-being.

(L.G. 12.2.46)

Temporary Sergeant William James Noakes
Ex.977, No. 45 RM Commando
Military Medal

North West European Campaign—6th June 1944 to 7th May 1945.
Sgt Noakes landed with his unit on D Day near Ouistreham. During this landing he distinguished himself by getting out gangways on the LCI(s) after the seamen had become casualties. On D+1 he again showed himself to be a cool and aggressive leader, on this occasion during street fighting at Sallenelles. His subaltern was killed and Sgt Noakes rose to the occasion and commanded his section with skill and courage. After those early days he went out on many difficult patrols at night. For his patrol work he gained the respect of his officers and the complete confidence of his men. Since then Sgt Noakes has been in hard fighting, a lot of which was at very close quarters, at Angerville (20th August 1944), Linne (January 1945), in addition to being in an assault troop in the forcing of the rivers Maas, Rhine, Weser, Aller and Elbe. In all these actions his unit was involved in stiff fighting. Sgt Noakes was on each occasion absolutely reliable, cool and aggressive. He has never missed a chance of inflicting casualties on the enemy. His loyalty to his unit and his devotion to duty are quite outstanding and his personal courage and disregard of danger beyond question.

(L.G.12.2.46)

Marine Charles W. Paton
Po.X.108528, No. 4 RM Eng Commando
Military Medal

Marine Paton, of the Royal Marine Engineer Commando Detachment attached to 4 Commando Brigade, landed in Normandy on 26th June 1944.

From that date, until the end of the War in Europe, he has borne himself in a manner that has been a source of inspiration to his comrades both in and out of battle. He has continually been to the fore when there were, as happened not infrequently, mines to be lifted, and booby traps to be disarmed. In spite of the fact that casualties were suffered in his detachment he did not once fail to volunteer for any job, however hazardous. His powers of endurance, his courage, fortitude and ability to be cheerful in depressing circumstances, have often been sorely tried but have never been found wanting. Indeed, in the words of the Staff Officer Royal Engineers attached to 4 Commando Brigade, 'his conduct has always encouraged his companions to further efforts.' These qualities were particularly noticeable and effective during the severe winter of 1944 on the island of Walcheren. There, Paton's detachment was, for some considerable time, daily engaged on the most arduous task of clearing amphibian tracks along flooded roads which had been mined with large calibre shells. Working under almost impossible conditions, his spirits never flagged, and his example was an inspiration to his comrades.

On two occasions, both in De Haan in October 1944, when casualties occurred in mine-clearing parties, Mne Paton had not the slightest hesitation in immediately re-entering the mined area. His prompt action encouraged others to follow and on both occasions the casualties were successfully evacuated.

(L.G. 12.2.46)

ACTING TY. CORPORAL ARTHUR LESLIE PYMM
Ch.X.103623, No. 47 RM Commando
MILITARY MEDAL (PERIODIC)

During the landings on D-Day on the Normandy Beaches, Cpl, then Marine, Pymm's boat struck some underwater object, causing him and many others to be thrown into the sea; he saved one man who was wounded, from drowning and not content with this, he went back into the water and saved two more of his comrades.

Throughout the campaign in Normandy and in the chase across France, Cpl Pymm set an example of courage and fortitude which was a source of inspiration to many a younger man. Later in November, having landed at Westkapelle on Walcheren Island, the Commando found its forward troops pinned down by accurate and heavy machine gun and mortar fire. Cpl Pymm in his capacity as a stretcher bearer worked coolly and efficiently at his job of evacuating wounded, many of whom owe their lives to his calmness and complete disregard of his personal safety.

These are but two instances of this NCO's exemplary behaviour throughout this campaign, which are rendered the more exceptional when his 39 years of age are taken into consideration.

(L.G. 12.2.46)

Marine Frederick Raynor
Ply.x.111322, 30 Bn RM
Military Medal (Immediate)

At Kerkdriel on the north bank of the River Maas during the afternoon of 23rd April 1945, a patrol of one section from 'A' Company 30 Battalion RM was cut off from the main body of the battalion by strong parties of the enemy. Mne Raynor was a member of this section. The return route to the boats, by which the section was to re-cross the river ran along a low bank and ditch which were commanded from two sides by higher banks from which the enemy kept up considerable automatic and rifle fire directed at the section. The section succeeded in reaching an area of rough wooded ground near the river where they were pinned by enemy fire for nearly one hour. Most of the section's ammunition was exhausted and, with some hours of daylight still left, its position seemed very bad. One severely wounded man was being carried back by the section, it did not appear that he would live unless quickly attended to by a doctor.

Mne Raynor on his own initiative volunteered to make his way back to one of our own forward companies in order to fetch help. This he succeeded in doing, crossing ground under enemy observation and fire. He was able to bring help to the section and medical aid to the wounded man. His action was undoubtedly a major factor in helping his whole section to return to our own lines and resulted in saving the life of the wounded man.

(L.G. 7.8.45)

Marine William Rennie
Po X.105943, No. 46 RM Commando
Military Medal (Immediate)

In the initial assault over the River Elbe on 29th April, Mne Rennie was a member of the leading group whose duty was to mark the route to the objective with white tape.

As the craft approached the far bank, the enemy opened fire with light anti-aircraft guns, mortars and grenades on the landing point and craft. Immediately off the beach was a steep cliff, 100-ft high, down which the enemy, who were strongly entrenched at the top, were throwing grenades.

Although the NCO in charge of the taping party and the other Marine who was sharing an awkward 'two man' load of tape with Mne Rennie were both wounded, Mne Rennie, without further orders, carried on on his own. Despite the fierce enemy fire, he managed to find and mark a passable route to the top of the cliff carrying the 'two man' load himself. This was a considerable feat of endurance even had he not been under fire and had it been daylight. Having reached the top he then continued to lay the tape for some two miles to the final objective in Lauenburg with great speed and coolness despite concentrations of enemy mortar and gun fire.

Mne Rennie's gallant action in finding and taping a passable route up the cliff, whilst carrying his companions load was beyond all praise. But for his courage and perseverance a considerable delay would have occurred and many casualties inflicted on the succeeding flights of troops on the beach. His action materially assisted in the success of the operation. *(L.G. 7.8.45)*

TEMPORARY CORPORAL JAMES PATRICK SCULLION
Ch.X.104842, RM
MILITARY MEDAL

For bravery and great devotion to duty whilst operating with the Allied Armies in North-West Europe. *L.G. 12.6.45*

ACTING TY. SERGEANT DEREK JAMES SHARPLES
Temporary Corporal, No. 27 Bn RM
MILITARY MEDAL (PERIODIC)

Sgt Sharples is the senior NCO in the Assault Pioneer Platoon of 27 RM He has invariably performed his duties in a more than exemplary manner. He has directed a large number of difficult mine clearances, with marked skill. By his leadership and unsurpassed example he has encouraged men working under him to complete seemingly impossible tasks in exposed positions, under fire.

On the night 9th–10th March 1945, in the Hedikhuizen area, it was necessary to extend the flank of the right company. To do this an area had to be cleared of anti-personnel mines which was covered by enemy spandau fire. Showing great coolness and unperturbed by the enemy fire he was responsible for the successful completion of his task.

Such is Sgt Sharples's reputation in the unit that he was in constant demand to accompany patrols. On 15th March 1945, he was sent out with a small escort to clear a footbridge and its approaches of mines and booby traps. It was a difficult and dangerous task for the bridge was under spasmodic automatic and rifle fire throughout the night. But by dawn the task was completed and the next night he led a fighting patrol over this bridge. Under fire he has at all times set a fine example of coolness, initiative, resource and quiet determination to finish the job. On several occasions the successful completion of tasks without loss has been entirely due to the personal efforts of this NCO.   *(L.G. 12.2.46)*

Temporary Corporal Ronald Stuart
Po.X.106959, No. 45 RM Commando
Military Medal

During an attack on the school at Franceville [...] Major J. N. Rushforth who was leading the assault was wounded when the party came under heavy fire from concealed positions ten yards from the building. Cpl Ronald Stuart immediately rallied three men and drove out the enemy with grenades and bayonets and pressed on until the enemy, who were in superior numbers, had been forced to withdraw from the buildings. Cpl Stuart held his ground in spite of several counter-attacks. He showed a high example of leadership, courage and complete indifference to his personal safety. His prompt action was directly responsible for restoring an awkward situation. His example and personal courage has shown itself again and again throughout the campaign.

[L.G. 20.2.45]

Lance Corporal John Sykes
Po.X.106961, No. 45 RM Commando
Military Medal (Immediate)

Capture of Wesel—23rd–24th March 1945

On 24th March B Troop 45 RM Commando were in position at the north eastern end of the Wesel wire factory. During the period of airborne landing no artillery was available to the unit for 3½ hours. Two 88mm self-propelled guns approached to approximately 500 yds and engaged the troop position L/Cpl Sykes was in charge of the forward Bren Group sighted outside the north-east corner of the building.

A shell burst four feet above his position on the wall seriously wounded his No. 2 of the bren. He immediately assisted the Medical Orderly to remove the casualty and organised a relief and then engaged an enemy machine-gun position 250 yds his right front. Five minutes later another shell burst immediately in front of his trench blowing his bren gun out of the position. Sykes again left his cover and under machine-gun fire recovered the gun, which was still serviceable, returned to his trench, and again engaged the enemy.

A third shell hit the wall to the left of his position, this time breaching the barrel of the gun, Sykes jumped from his trench with the damaged gun ran to Troop HQ for the spare bren and returned to his post and returned the enemy's fire. His aggressive spirit and determination to fight back was a shining example of courage during a most trying period and was an inspiration to all ranks. *[L.G. 19.6.45]*

ACTING TEMPORARY COMPANY SERGEANT MAJOR JOHN WILLIAM TANSWELL
Marine, Ply.x 3849, No. 41 RM Commando
MILITARY MEDAL

This NCO landed in Normandy On D Day, and since then he has led his sub-section continuously during the campaign in North-West Europe with outstanding bravery and devotion to duty. He has several times been called upon to perform the duties of Section Officer when his officers became casualties, and his leadership has always been of the highest quality.

As one instance of Sergeant Major Tanswell's fine example, in the assault on Walcheren on 1st November, 1944 he led his sub-section in the attack on W.19 battery. Although he knew the enemy positions to be manned, without thought for his own safety he went forward in broad daylight to cut the wire obstacles, through which he successfully led the assault.

In the capacities of Section Officer and sub-section commander TSM Tanswell's personal example of coolness and courage under fire has throughout been an inspiration to the men under him.
(L.G. 12.2.46)

PRIVATE ROY FRANK THOMAS
5180266, Glosters, No. 3 Commando
MILITARY MEDAL (IMMEDIATE)

During the battle for the Essel bridgehead on April 11th 1945, No. 3 Commando was heavily counter-attacked.

Tpr Thomas was in a forward exposed position and fifteen enemy were within fifty yards of his slit trench. He was wounded in the shoulder and a NCO beside him in the slit trench, was killed at the beginning of the action. In spite of these handicaps he continued to fire his bren gun over a period of one and a half hours with such effect that the attack was held up and then beaten off. Tpr Thomas accounted for four enemy killed and six more wounded. His complete coolness in the face of heavy enemy opposition was an inspiration to all. *[L.G. 12.7.45]*

Private Harry Tibbles
3860540, Border Regt, No. 6 & 12 Commando
Military Medal (Immediate)

Near Lauenburg on the night 28th–29th April, Pte Tibbles's Troop was responsible for the left flank of the bridgehead over the River Elbe.

As the troop advanced along the line of the river to its objective it was suddenly fired on by an machine-gun from the top of the high bank on the inland side. The troop had no other alternative but to take cover in the angle of the bank as the beach was completely open. Pte Tibbles was in the rear of the troop with his bren gun and immediately appreciating what was happening in the front he dashed up the slope calling to his No. 2 to follow him. The slope was 200 feet high and at a gradient of 1 in 2.

Pte Tibbles when he reached the top worked his way along on the shadow side of a line of trees until he was immediately on top of the machine-gun post which was still in the act of firing down on his troop.

From here he killed all three of the machine-gun team and enabled his troop to continue its advance.

By his own immediate initiative, determination and personal courage Pte Tibbles enabled the advance of his troop to continue and on his own liquidated a strong-point that might have proved expensive. *[L.G. 2.8.45]*

Marine Douglas Towler
Ex.4188, No. 45 RM Commando
Military Medal (Immediate)

Crossing of the River Elbe and capture of Lauenberg 29th April 1945.
On the night of the Elbe crossing Mne Towler was a Bren Gunner in D Troop 45 RM Commando. His troop became involved in confused street fighting in the dark on its way to its objective. Mne Towler was ordered to take up a position to cover a flank whilst his troop pushed on. He selected a position in a house and engaged the enemy immediately. A section attack was put in against his house by the enemy. This was beaten off by steady and accurate shooting. As his ammunition was getting low, Mne Towler sent his No. 2 of the gun to get more. During his absence another attempt was made by the enemy to dislodge Mne Towler. Again this was beaten off. When his No. 2 returned together with a sub-section to assist, there was only one magazine left containing a few rounds. Two dead Germans were within ten yards of the gun and eleven other dead or wounded in the immediate vicinity. Although Mne Towler was not actually wounded he was consid-

erably grazed by brick splinters and stones raised by the 2-cm flak guns which were used against his position.

Mne Towler's tenacity and determination was largely responsible for this troop being able to push on, without undue interference, to their objective. *[L.G. 2.8.45]*

MARINE THOMAS VARDY
Ply.X.103900, No. 46 RM Commando
MILITARY MEDAL

This Marine was signal operator attached to Y troop during the attack on Le Hamel and Rots on 11th June He was carrying a 38 set. Despite this load he pushed himself to the front and took a leading part in three assaults on enemy positions his dash and determination when under heavy fire had an inspiring effect on the men of the troop. *[L.G. 29.8.44]*

MARINE JAMES HERBERT WOOD
Ply.X.3377, No. 48 RM Commando
MILITARY MEDAL (PERIODIC)

Marine Wood landed in the assault on the Normandy beaches on D-day and has throughout maintained a high standard of zeal and cheerfulness both in and out of the line. He has always been an example of willingness to undertake any task or accept any risk that came along. One outstanding example of his gallantry occurred at Kapelsche Veer during an attack across the River Maas on the night of the 10th–11th April 1945. Marine Wood was posted on top of the river dyke with his bren gun to cover a wiring party going forward. The wiring party inadvertently set off a trip flare and the enemy immediately opened fire with two machine-guns from their positions 500 yards away on the other side of the Maas. Marine Wood at once engaged these two machine-guns and drew the fire of three more to himself. In spite of the fact that five machine-guns were firing at him and were hitting the dyke all round him and in spite of the fact that his own position was completely exposed, Marine Wood continued to fire for about ten minutes until all the working party were safely back across the dyke. He fired 14 magazines in all, and not only were his great determination and personal courage the means of saving the wiring party a large percentage of casualties, but he succeeded by his vigorous and accurate fire in silencing two of the enemy's machine guns. *[L.G. 24.1.46]*

SERGEANT FREDERICK ARTHUR WORTHINGTON
6398404, R Sussex Regt, No. 6 Commando
MILITARY MEDAL (IMMEDIATE)

At Wesel on the 24th March 1945, Sgt Worthington was in charge of a small defensive position on the outskirts of the city when he saw an enemy bicycle patrol coming towards him at a range of about 1,000 yards. The patrol suddenly turned off down a side street and disappeared from view. Realising that they were heading for a part of the town which had not yet been consolidated, Sgt Worthington acted immediately and sent a runner to tell his Troop Commander of his action. He then left a skeleton force in the defensive position and taking the remaining eight of his men he set off to ambush the patrol. He struck the side road just in time to meet the patrol head-on and fired on them from houses by the side of the road. Eight of the enemy were killed or wounded, five taken prisoner and the remainder fled. Sgt Worthington himself was wounded at the start but refused to hand over or even have his wound dressed until the action was over and the patrol brought back.

By this successful action and by his own initiative, gallantry and immediate action Sgt Worthington liquidated the enemy patrol and prevented them from running into another unit who were just then at that awkward stage prior to consolidation. *[L.G. 21.6.45]*

LANCE SERGEANT WILLIAM WRAITH
4698570, K.O.Y.L.I., No. 6 Commando
MILITARY MEDAL (PERIODIC)

This NCO has served with No. 6 Commando throughout the North African and North-West European campaigns and has at all times shown the highest standard of devotion to duty and exemplary courage. During the recent advance towards the River Elbe, Sgt Wraith was in charge of a patrol sent forward to gain information about the enemy. On his return a mortar bomb fell close to his patrol seriously wounding one man and inflicting blast injuries on himself which affected his sight. With his sight failing he nevertheless returned and carried back the wounded man to our own lines under mortar fire. He then reported to the Intelligence Officer, and in spite of his grave condition, insisted on giving detailed reports of his patrol before being evacuated.

During the period 12th January to 15th April, Sgt Wraith has been on 23 patrols many of which he commanded, and on all of them he has shown the greatest example and devotion to duty. On three separate occasions he has been wounded but in spite of this he has always continued to show complete fearlessness and a splendid example to his men in action. *[L.G. 11.10.45]*

ACTING LIEUT.-COLONEL ANTHONY D. LEWIS
Temporary Maj, 95626, Dorsets, 6 Commando
CROIX DE GUERRE WITH PALM

This officer assumed command of his unit when his Commanding Officer was called upon to take over command of the brigade, the Brigade Commander having been wounded. The take over was made at a critical stage of a heavy and prolonged enemy counter-attack, and the successful repulsion of the enemy in 6 Commando's section with heavy loss to the enemy was largely due to the courageous leadership and exemplary conduct of LieutCol. Lewis under heavy and accurate harassing fire.

He continued in command of 6 Commando very ably and throughout the campaign displayed the greatest gallantry and devotion to duty.

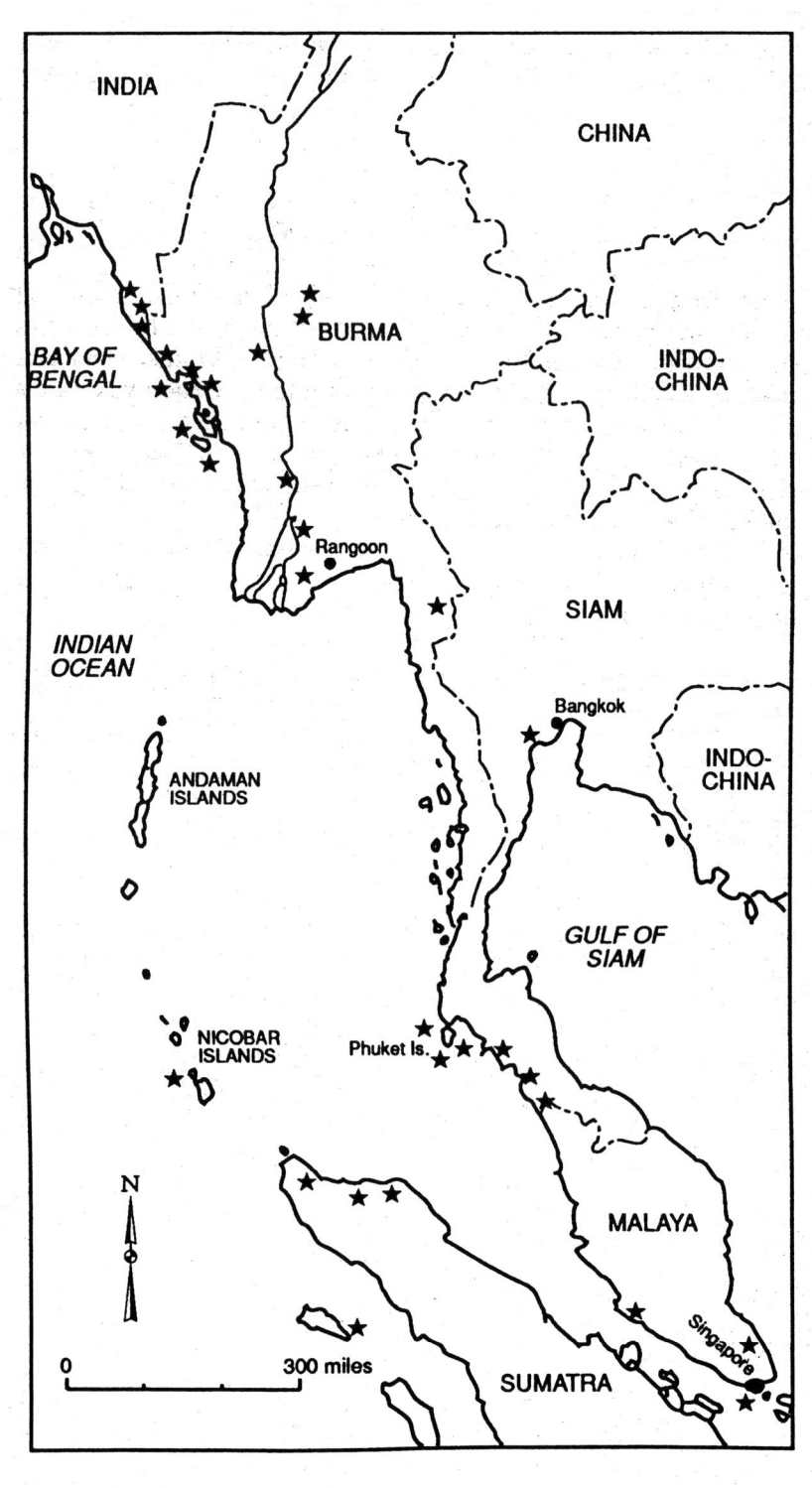

Commando Gallantry Awards of World War II

The Far East

FEW PERSONS would argue the fact that jungle fighting is unique and, while no commando raids could be considered a 'piece of cake,' those who fought against the Japanese experienced extreme conditions of climate, terrain, disease and a ferocious enemy.

From the first Commando patrol on the Irawaddy River in early 1942, by Burma Commando 11, until the Japanese surrender, the campaign in the Arakan, Burma, Sumatra, Malaya, the Nicobar Islands, and Siam was highly fragmented. Divisions in command in the early stages, lack of equipment and difficulties in the coordination of training imposed unusual stresses on commanders and soldiers alike.

The appointment in late 1943 of Lord Louis Mountbatten as Supreme Commander of South East Asia was the turning point, assisted in large part by increasing pressures from the American forces in the Pacific on the Japanese.

The map indicates approximately thirty points where the Commandos struck. There were many more, and to enumerate them or select 'typical' raids is beyond the scope of this book. The many citations in the awards section speak for themselves.

LIEUTENANT GEORGE ARTHUR KNOWLAND
323566 The Royal Norfolk Regiment (attached Commandos)
Victoria Cross

War Office – 12th April 1945.
The KING has been graciously pleased to approve the posthumous award of the VICTORIA CROSS to:—
Lieutenant George Arthur KNOWLAND (323566), The Royal Norfolk Regiment (attached Commandos) (London S.E.1).

In Burma on 31st January, 1945 near Kangaw, Lieutenant Knowland was commanding the forward platoon of a troop positioned on the extreme north of a hill which was subjected to very heavy and repeated enemy attacks throughout the whole day. Before the first attack started, Lieutenant Knowland's platoon was heavily mortared and machine gunned, yet he moved about among

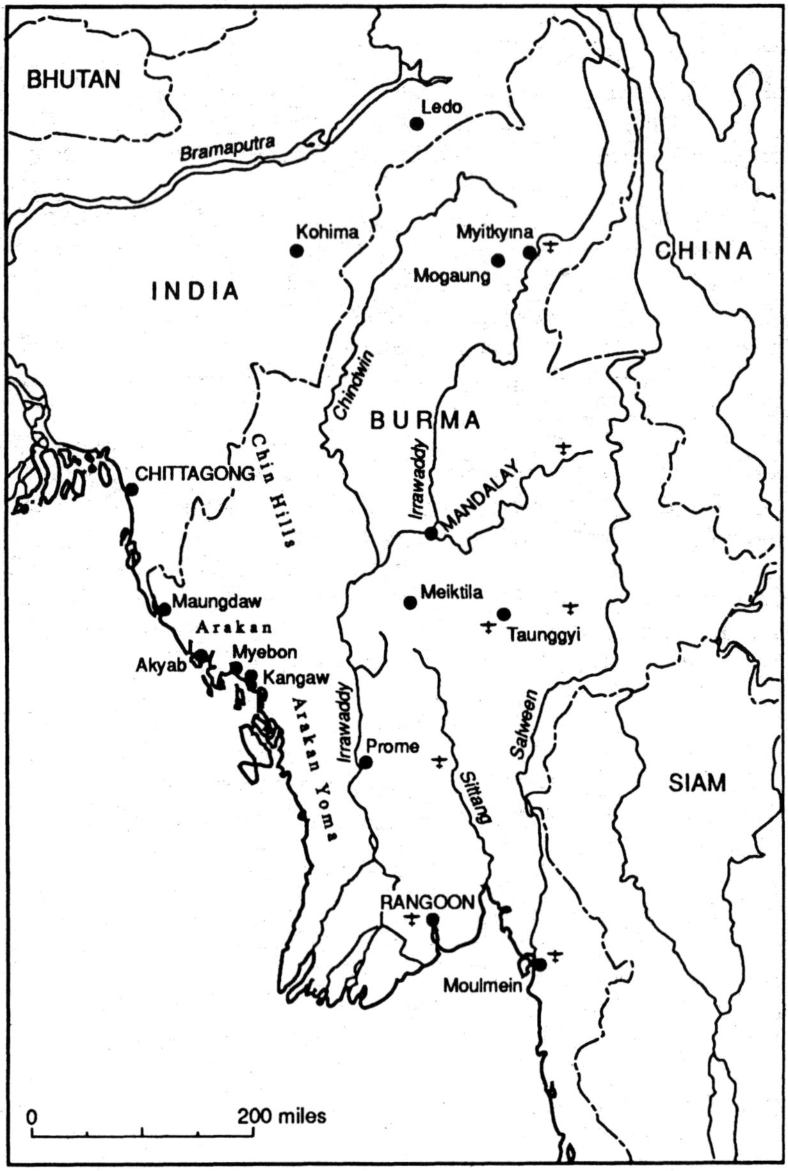
BHUTAN
Ledo
Bramaputra
Kohima
Myitkyina
Mogaung
CHINA
INDIA
Chindwin
BURMA
Chin Hills
Irrawaddy
MANDALAY
CHITTAGONG
Meiktila
Taunggyi
Maungdaw
Arakan
Akyab
Myebon
Kangaw
Arakan Yoma
Irrawaddy
Salween
Prome
Sittang
SIAM
RANGOON
Moulmein
0
200 miles

The Far East

his men keeping them alert and encouraging them, though under fire himself at the time.

When the enemy, some 300 strong in all, made their first assault they concentrated all their efforts on his platoon of 24 men, but, in spite of the ferocity of the attack, he moved about from trench to trench distributing ammunition, and firing his rifle and throwing grenades at the enemy, often from completely exposed positions.

Later, when the crew of one of his forward Bren Guns had all been wounded, he sent back to Troop Headquarters for another crew and ran forward to man the gun himself until they arrived. The enemy was then less than ten yards from him in dead ground down the hill, so, in order to get a better field of fire, he stood on top of the trench, firing the light machine gun from his hip, and successfully keeping them at a distance until a Medical Orderly had dressed and evacuated the wounded men behind him. The new Bren team also became casualties on the way up, and Lieutenant Knowland continued to fire the gun until another team took over.

Later, when a fresh attack came in, he took over a 2 in. Mortar and in spite of heavy fire and the closeness of the enemy, he stood up in the open to face them, firing the mortar from his hip and killing six of them with his first bomb. When all bombs were expended he went back through heavy grenade, mortar and machine gun fire to get more, which he fired in the same way from the open in front of his platoon positions. When those bombs were finished, he went back to his own trench, and still standing up fired his rifle at them. Being hard pressed and with enemy closing in on him from only ten yards away, he had no time to re-charge his magazine. Snatching up the Tommy gun of a casualty, he sprayed the enemy and was mortally wounded stemming this assault, though not before he had killed and wounded many of the enemy.

Such was the inspiration of his magnificent heroism, that, though fourteen out of twenty four of his platoon became casualties at an early stage, and six of his positions were over-run by the enemy, his men held on through twelve hours of continuous and fierce fighting until reinforcements arrived. If this Northern end of the hill had fallen, the rest of the hill would have been endangered, the beach-head dominated by the enemy, and other units further inland cut off from their source of supplies. As it was, the final successful counter-attack was later launched from the vital ground which Lieutenant Knowland had taken such a gallant part in holding.

L.G. 12.4.45

Commando Gallantry Awards of World War II

Ty. Brigadier Campbell Richard Hardy, D.S.O.
S/Major (Actg Col Comdt.), Royal Marines, Comd No. 3 Commando Bde
2nd Bar to Distinguished Service Order
(Immediate)

In Burma in January 1945, this officer personally planned the assault phase of the two combined operations against Myebon and Kangaw during a period of a fortnight under conditions of great haste and difficulty. He led his brigade in both assaults and during the continued heavy fighting was involved in the subsequent deep advances inland. Throughout the whole of the operation he was in control in the area where fighting was most stubborn, where his calm and cheerful bearing was an inspiration. His brigade was the spear-head in both operations and their success was very largely due to Brig Hardy's able planning and confident leadership.
[L.G. 15.5.45]

Ty. Brigadier Alfred Rimbault Aslett
W/S Lieutenant-Colonel, 15528, Late King's Own, Comd. 72 Inf Bde, SS Bde HQ
Distinguished Service Order

North Burma Campaign 1944.
During the recent operations in which this Division has been involved, Brigadier Aslett has commanded the 72 Inf Brigade with the greatest skill and determination.

After his brigade had been flown into Myitkyina from Ledo and had marched the 45 miles to Pahok, they were concentrated at the 12th mile-stone from Mogaung by 3rd August The brigade had been ordered to capture Hill 60 on 5th August; this gave the Brigadier only two days to reconnoitre the position and make his plan. He achieved this only by flying very low over the enemy positions and by crawling forward on the ground in full view of enemy bunkers. Although fired on several times, he was able to see enough to formulate his plan; the success of which was proved on 5th August when his brigade captured Hill 60, inflicting heavy casualties to the enemy and causing them to start a retreat which has continued ever since.

During the battle the Brigadier was at all times well forward, encouraging his men and setting them an excellent example by his steady determination and complete disregard for enemy snipers and shelling. By 7th August the brigade had captured Nampadaung and established a road block on the Sahmaw road. By that date more than 100 Japs had been killed. Taungni was taken on 9th August, Mingon on 12th August and Thaikwagon on 17th August.

During all these operations some 250 Japs were killed after putting up a stiff fight in each successive village. The weather conditions were appalling, roads almost non-existent and rivers in full flood.

Practically all movement was on foot and the Brigadier had to do all his reconnaissances either from the air, at about 300–500 ft, owing to low cloud, or by literally wading all over the country. The whole of these operations were carried out in the most difficult conditions and with an ever decreasing fighting strength owing to casualties and sickness. Communications could hardly have been worse, but despite all this, the brigade more than achieved its objective. Brigadier Aslett, by his personal bravery and unsparing energy during these 14 days, kept the morale of his troops at a very high standard. His plans were carried out with the greatest determination, and he very quickly established a complete superiority over the enemy. He allowed no obstacle to prevent him from attaining his objective, and after the capture of Thaikwagon on 17th August, 72 Brigade, although somewhat depleted, was still in fine fighting spirit, in spite of hard fighting, and no dry clothes for nearly three weeks. Too high praise cannot be given to Brigadier Aslett for this most successful advance, which started the rout of the Jap forces in the Railway Corridor.

(L.G. 22.3.45)

ACTING LIEUTENANT-COLONEL HALFORD DAVID FELLOWES, R.M.
Capt, Bt Maj, att. No. 42 RM Commando
DISTINGUISHED SERVICE ORDER
(IMMEDIATE)

Arakan 1945

At Myebon on 12th January 1945, the unit of which Lt-Col Fellowes was in command was the first to land.

The landing was effected under the most extraordinary difficulties due to beach obstacles, mines, and knee-deep mud, which caused an operation which is normally a matter of seconds to take an abnormal length of time.

Nevertheless the unit, which was under fire for the first time, cleared the beach defences and pushed on inland to their second objective.

Lt-Col Fellowes then led them in a successful attack on a hill inland, in which he was wounded, refusing to be evacuated until the position was consolidated.

The magnificent steadiness and efficiency of this unit is entirely due to this officer's strong character and determination. He has been throughout an inspiration to his men.   *(L.G. 15.5.45)*

Temporary Lieutenant-Colonel Kenneth Rowland Swetenham Trevor
63586, The Cheshire Regiment, Special Service Troops
Distinguished Service Order

In recognition of gallant and distinguished services in Burma.

L.G. 19.4.45

Temporary Major John James Dickson, M.C.
2/Lieut, W/Lieut, 96192, Territorial Commission, Sherwood Foresters, att 9th Royal Sussex §
Bar to Military Cross

In NE Burma

On 27th February 1945, Major Dickson was ordered to capture the feature known as Hill 800 near Myitson. This feature commanded the line of advance of the whole brigade, and captured enemy documents disclosed that the enemy attached great importance to its retention.

Major Dickson secured tactical surprise by attacking up a precipitous face, through dense jungle and avoiding the easier slopes which offered obvious lines of approach. The attack was met by LMG and sniper fire. Major Dickson, seeing that some men in the leading sections were wavering, owing to the barrage from our own guns falling short, at once went forward himself and became the spearhead of the attack. With cool courage and determination he personally led his company to the crest of the hill where the leading platoons were again held up by LMG fire from the far end of the ridge. Rapidly grasping the situation, he called for additional artillery fire and committed his reserve platoon to a left flanking attack. This attack was put in with such skill and determination that it met with instant success and the enemy fled, leaving one officer and five Jap other ranks on the field, together with an LMG, packs and other equipment which showed that the position had probably been at least a company one.

It was due to this officer's outstanding courage, initiative and superb leadership, combined with tactical skill of a very high order, which enabled the feature to be captured with the loss of very few casualties to our own troops.   *[L.G. 21.6.45]*

The Far East

Temporary Major John Hugh Stephenson Turnbull, M.C.
72893, The Gordon Highlanders, Special Service Troops
Bar to Military Cross

In recognition of gallant and distinguished services in Burma.
L.G. 19.4.45

Captain John Joseph Yelverton Dawson
W/Capt (Emer), 23351, No. 1 Commando
Military Cross (Immediate)

On the 31st January 1945, at Hill 170 near Kangaw Capt Dawson as Medical officer carried out his duties with exemplary courage and coolness throughout. He tended to wounded men who were still under heavy fire in exposed places, and helped to carry them to a shallow slit trench where he gave them further attention before evacuation, though still exposed to fire himself. The whole day long he moved about among the wounded showing complete disregard for his personal safety, and altogether dressed and evacuated 90 casualties most of whom he attended to under constant fire, in the forward area.   *[L.G. 19.4.45]*

Temporary Major John James Dickson
2/Lieut, W/Capt, 96192, Territorial Commission, 9 R. Sussex (from Sherwood Foresters), No. 5 Commando
Military Cross

N. Burma Campaign 1944.

On 10th November 1944 near Hpapan, Major Dickson was in command of a company ordered to attack and capture a strong enemy bunkered position on the banks of a river. The position contained a high proportion of machines guns and mortars, and it was obvious that Major Dickson was faced with a difficult task. This task he fulfilled with conspicuous skill and gallantry, both the planning and execution of the operation being a model of their kind. Leading the company himself he put in a most determined attack from the flank, rolling up the enemy position bunker by bunker and finally causing the remnants of the enemy to flee in disorder leaving behind them much new equipment. Major Dickson was always to the fore himself wherever the attack showed signs of slowing down, and by his personal example of courage and offensiveness ensured the success of the attack. On the following day, Major Dickson once more displayed exceptional skill and bravery when his company bumped the main enemy defences covering Pinwe. His company came under heavy machine-gun and shell fire, suffering casualties. In very trying circumstances Major Dickson exhibited a coolness and personal example of courage. [L.G. 22.3.45]

Temporary Major Dennis Ford
Captain, 124856, The Black Watch, No. 7 Commando
Military Cross

In recognition of gallant and distinguished services while engaged in Special Operations in South East Asia. L.G. 7.11 46

Temporary Captain John Garner Jones
TA W/Lieut, 92411, The Welch Regiment, S.S. Tps., att. No. 1 Cdo.
Military Cross (Immediate)

Arakan

On the night 22nd–23rd November this officer by a skilful night march crossed the Ton Chaung and surrounded a Japanese platoon in Hinthaya. He led his troop to the assault at dawn, achieving complete surprise. He drove the enemy from strong bunker positions. His troop killed six, wounded eight and took one live Jap prisoner. Capt Garner-Jones himself accounted for several of the enemy.

During this action he was everywhere exposing himself without the least regard for personal danger. He inspired his men by his courage and his sound tactics. After this success he withdrew his men without loss being himself the last to leave. [L.G. 22.3.45]

Captain Dennis Sydney Kerr
145403, W/S Captain (E.C.), No. 5 Commando
Military Cross (Immediate)

Arakan

At 1645 hours 23rd March 1944, during 5 Commando's attack on spur 383348, this officer led a determined attack by one of his sub-sections on a machine-gun nest which was captured despite fierce opposition.

Capt Kerr, concerned about the remainder of his force, then went down into the valley, to try and reorganise the troop. This he did under fire.

At 1715 hours this officer was severely wounded in the shoulder and leg and his arm was shattered. In spite of the pain and the fact that he was under fire he did not release his command and continued to issue orders calmly.

He successfully reorganised his men and his calm example and courageous devotion to duty undoubtedly saved the lives of many of his men. [L.G. 22.6.44]

The Far East

ACTING TEMPORARY CAPTAIN ERIC LANGLEY, R.M.
Temporary Lieutenant
MILITARY CROSS
For gallantry, skilful leadership and daring whilst serving with the Indian Army in the assault on Nyebon *(sic)* and Kangan *(sic)*.
L.G. 15.5.45

LIEUTENANT JOHN GEORGE LOUIS LARCHER
235098, Recce Corps, Att. No. 1 Commando
MILITARY CROSS (IMMEDIATE)
On 31st January 1945 at Hill 170 Kangaw Lieut Larcher was commanding a platoon which was ordered to reinforce the forward troop.

He carried out this task with considerable initiative and skill at a critical time without regard to his own personal safety. At this stage he exposed himself freely in order to rescue a number of wounded men. Later finding that the enemy were working round the right flank he immediately organised and led an immediate counter-attack which was successful and inflicted heavy casualties.
[L.G. 19.4.45]

LIEUTENANT RALPH WILLIAM NOBLE
265916, The Durham Light Infantry, Special Service Troops
MILITARY CROSS
In recognition of gallant and distinguished services in Burma.
L.G. 22.6.44

TY. CAPTAIN EDWARD ROBIN MCMURDO WRIGHT
EC 29, Indian Armoured Corps, Special Service Troops.
MILITARY CROSS
In recognition of gallant and distinguished services in Burma.
L.G. 22.3.45

LANCE SERGEANT ARNOLD WILLIAM SINCUP
4035009, K.S.L.I. att. No. 1 Commando
DISTINGUISHED CONDUCT MEDAL (IMMEDIATE)
Arakan 1945
On the 31st. January 1945 at Hill 170 near Kangaw L/Sgt Sincup was section Sgt of a platoon counter-attacking the enemy. When his platoon officer was wounded he took command of the two leading sections of his platoon and attacked an enemy post, personally killing five of the enemy of whom one was an officer. He then rallied the sections, evacuating five of his men who were wounded and made two attempts to bring in another wounded man who

was covered by enemy machine-gun and sniper fire. He then took up part of the defence of the forward right flank and by his leadership and personal example held this flank, helping with other troops to break up determined enemy attacks. He remained with his sections in this position constantly engaged with the enemy for ten hours, until relieved by another unit. [L.G. 19.4.45]

Ty. Company Sergeant Major Albert James Welsh
Ex.1217, Ty TSM, No. 42 RM Commando
Distinguished Conduct Medal (Immediate)

Arakan 1945

At Hill 170 near Kangaw on 31st January 1945, TSM Welsh's Troop were called up to reinforce No 1 Commando at a critical period when the enemy seemed likely to gain a footing o the crest of the hill. They were ordered to put in a counter-attack, which they did with great dash, the Troop Commander, the Platoon Commander of the leading platoon, and all but one of the forward section on the left soon being killed. TSM Welsh took charge and reorganised the troops, his remaining Platoon Commander by then also having been hit. Himself occupying a forward trench he repeatedly drove off counter-attacks with grenades and tommy gun fire until he was twice wounded. It was only after he had pulled out a number of casualties that he went back to the regimental aid post refusing a stretcher. His aggressive fighting spirit, complete disregard for his personal safety and inspiring leadership did much to hold together the remnants of his troop. (L.G. 15.5.45)

Private William Aird
3194769, K.O.S.B. attached No. 1 Commando
Military Medal (Immediate)

At Kangaw, Hill 170 (Map ref 515414, Myebon Sheet 1/25,000) on 23rd January 1945 Pte Aird was the bren gunner in a trench which bore the brunt of a fierce Jap night counter-attack.

Early on a grenade landed in the trench inflicting multiple wounds of the back to Pte Aird. He made no mention of his wounds and manned his bren gun awaiting the attack. His trench was continually assaulted for over two hours and every attack repulsed. In the morning one enemy officer and three other ranks were found dead 3 ft from Pte Aird's bren gun.

The position was under spasmodic MMG and mortar fire for five hours. Pte Aird completely regardless of his own wounds maintained his gun in action with a selfless courage and devotion to duty that inspired the men with him. [L.G. 19 4.45]

The Far East

PRIVATE EDWARD P. ALLEN
14627308, South Wales, No. 1 Commando
MILITARY MEDAL (IMMEDIATE)
Arakan 1945
On the 31st January 1945 on Hill 170 near Kangaw Pte Allen was No 2 on a Bren Gun of the forward platoon which was being heavily attacked. Early in the action he was completely deafened by a grenade burst, but he stayed with his gun until the No 1 was killed and the gun put out of action. Then on his own accord he moved around under heavy fire taking the place on several Bren's whose No 2's had been killed or wounded. Finally, although wounded, when a Pte was seriously wounded at his side, he carried him on his back despite heavy MMG fire to a place of safety.

MARINE WILFRED JOHN BARKS
Po.X.102116, No. 42 RM Commando.
MILITARY MEDAL (IMMEDIATE)
Arakan 1945
At Hill 170 near Kangaw on 31st January 1945, during a counter-attack by his troop when all three of his officers and his TSM had become casualties Marine Barks took charge of a party of Marines and with great determination held a sector of the positions gained against repeated attacks. He pulled out a large number of wounded and remained in charge until the evening, when the party was relieved. His self reliance and fighting spirit were a splendid example to the remaining men.
Recommended for immediate DCM, awarded MM.   (L.G. 15.5.45)

ACTING BOMBARDIER ERNEST BARNES
Gunner, P/Lance Bdr., 4748087, RA (S/L) att. No. 1 Cdo.
MILITARY MEDAL (IMMEDIATE)
On the 31st January 1945 at Hill 170 near Kangaw Bdr Barnes was an NCO in No 1 Platoon ordered to counter-attack on the right flank. The leading section of his platoon came under intense machine-gun fire and grenades, the officer and Platoon Sgt being hit immediately. In a short space of time most of the platoon were casualties and Bdr Barnes, though wounded in the thigh, took charge of the leading men, supervised the evacuation of the wounded, and then made a supreme effort to reach his Platoon Sgt who was severely wounded. Despite intense enemy fire he managed to reach his Sgt and drag him back some 20 or 30 yards. Owing to loss of blood from his wound he was then in need of support himself, he recovered slightly and when put on stretcher

refused to be taken back, got up and walked away saying that other men needed it more than he did.
Recommended for immediate DCM, awarded MM.   [L.G. 19 4.45]

MARINE AUBREY BERTRAM CHAPPELL
Ex 4371, No. 42 (RM) Commando
MILITARY MEDAL

Mne Chappell was a member of a small patrol of 42 Commando RM landed on the Jap occupied Elizabeth Island in the Bay of Bengal with the object of gaining information about a missing Naval officer and also capturing a prisoner.

They landed at 2200 hrs on 4th November and were to be taken off 5½ hours later.

On landing the patrol penetrated to the enemy headquarters in the village of Ondaw approximately four miles away. They were detected and a short engagement ensued during which at least three of the enemy [......] casualties without loss to the patrol.

During the withdrawal Mne Chappell as Bren Gunner was covering the rear, and by mischance became detached. On attempting to rejoin he was ambushed and realising that he was now cut off from the rendezvous he evaded capture by lying up in the jungle. In spite of his narrow escape Mne Chappell had clung to his bren gun, and his morale being undiminished, he decided to make best use of the day he must now spend on the island. With this in view he made his way to a commanding position from which he quickly realised that the information given the patrol relative to enemy strength on the island was quite incorrect. Mne Chappell counted 43 Japanese in one party and estimated the total strength at over 100. He also located a headquarters and a number of occupied positions.

That night he signalled from the rendezvous without result and from then on he endured five days of unremitting strain.

The enemy had been disturbed and was now suspicious and alert. Continually Mne Chappell changed his position, often avoiding discovery by a hair breadth, wet through, hungry and alone. Once whilst snatching a quick sleep he was disturbed by a nearby Japanese patrol obviously searching for him. He opened fire with his bren gun immediately and used his two grenades at short range but was wounded by a retaliatory Jap grenade, this made him decide to break off the engagement. On doing so he was shot in the left calf at 15 yards range by a Jap whom he promptly killed with his Colt automatic. He then managed to get away successfully.

The Far East

On taking stock he found that he had but seven rounds left for his bren and two magazines for the pistol. He had been wounded three times in the left leg (twice by grenade fragments) and once in the side. These wounds he treated with his field dressing. It had been raining almost incessantly and in spite of all efforts the bren gun was now very rusty. However his freedom from capture in this period was probably due to the terrible weather conditions, one patrol passing within a couple of feet of him in the pouring rain.

On the fifth night he made his way between two previously noted listening posts and stole a small sampan. This proved to be leaky. After almost 24 hours using an improvised paddle he sighted land and was promptly wrecked on some rocks, losing his weapons and boots. He managed to swim to shore and was by then utterly exhausted. In the morning he discovered that he was on another island. During the next three days he grew much weaker, became delirious and suffered from hallucination and by the tenth day his need for food was so great that he abandoned his former caution and finding a Burmese homestead he appealed for help. He was promptly betrayed by the Headsman and led into an ambush of six Japanese soldiers. During ten day of ever present danger without food and under appalling weather conditions Mne Chappell had shown daring, initiative and resource to the highest degree, retaining his weapons and his offensive spirit to the last whilst his devotion to duty and determination were in the highest tradition of the Service.

Prisoner of War 14th November 1944. (*L.G. 19.3.46*)

CORPORAL ROBERT WILLIAM CHRISTOPHER
5990123, Hertfordshire, HQ 1 Commando Bde
MILITARY MEDAL

1. This NCO maintained a consistently high standard of gallantry during the following Commando operations :—

(a) Sicily: When a Private: took part in actions near Cassibile, Torre Cuba and Agnone. In the last named he was recommended for a Distinguished Conduct Medal by his Commanding officer (Lt-Coll (now Brigadier) J. Durnford-Slater, DSO, RA).

(b) Italy: When a Lance-Corporal: took part in special Commando operations of a hazardous nature at Bova Marina and at Termoli. He showed indifference to his personal safety and great coolness under fire when acting as runner during five separate engagements.

(c) North-West Europe: When a corporal: landed with the leading wave of a Commando on D day and was in action for 2½ months. He was always a volunteer for any dangerous duty and throughout, his boldness and cheerfulness were outstanding.

(d) Burma: When a corporal: acted as a runner during Commando operations on the Arakan coast, notably at Myebon and Kangaw (Hill 170). At the latter engagement he was for twelve hours within grenade range of the enemy, who were making repeated attacks, regardless of losses. Corporal Christopher displayed his usual coolness under fire. He acted as guide in a difficult night relief and later, by personally directing the fire of one of our detachments, silenced enemy light automatic fire which had been causing casualties.

2. Corporal Christopher has taken part altogether in eight opposed landings with Commandos. He has shown indifference to danger during his service. Instances of his gallantry, typical of his conduct throughout, are given below :—

(a) At Agnone (Sicily) on 14th July 1943, Corporal Christopher was acting as a runner and twice succeeded in getting important messages to forward troops, under severe machine gun and mortar fire. On the second occasion he was under fire of a tank, firing an 88mm gun at a range of 250 yards. Later, during the withdrawal from a position he was the only man left with the second in command of the Commando, who was enabled, with his assistance, to rally eighteen stragglers and to take the offensive once more. There is little doubt that without his assistance most of these stragglers would have been taken prisoner. In fact, they were able to beat off a strong German patrol and to return safely to our lines.

(b) At Amfreville on 9th June 1945 a troop of No 3 Commando suffered heavy casualties during German attacks, which were followed by frequent and heavy shelling. The position was only half dug, and shells kept bursting overhead in the trees. Corporal Christopher exposed himself in fearlessly evacuating casualties. When one of the soldiers was half buried by part of a wall, which collapsed onto his slit trench, Corporal Christopher dug him out with his hands. This took a long time and was in the middle of a severe and accurate barrage. His conduct was a splendid example to the young soldiers present, few of whom had been in action before. It seemed almost miraculous that he was not hit on this occasion.

3. There can be few junior NCOs who have had such experience in action against the enemy in a Commando as Corporal Christopher, and none who have shown such indifference to personal danger. His services have not so far been rewarded, although he has been recommended by his Commanding officer once for a DCM and once for a 'Mention'. He is now recommended

for the periodic award of a Military Medal, in recognition of exemplary conduct on numerous occasions, in particular at Agnone in Sicily and at Amfreville in Normandy.   *(L.G. 29.11 45)*

PRIVATE JAMES THOMAS COKER
14604363, R. West Kent Regt Att. No. 1 Commando
MILITARY MEDAL (IMMEDIATE)

Arakan 1945

On the 31st January 1945, at Hill 170 near Kangaw, Pte Coker was No 2 on an LMG ordered to go forward to a weapon pit where the two previous men had been killed. His No. 1 on the gun was killed immediately after his arrival as the pit was under continual enemy fire. He took over the gun and continued firing. Two other men were sent to join him but were killed instantaneously. His Section Sgt then joined him in the trench manning the bren belonging to the two men just killed.

The Section Sgt was then killed and Pte Coker's bren put out of action. He immediately took over his Sgt's bren and continued firing. He was then joined by another man with a haversack of grenades and between them they enabled a bren gunner who had been cut off, to rejoin them. Throughout the day Pte, Coker showed great coolness and courage in face of great difficulties and was throughout regardless of his own safety.   *[L.G. 19.4.45]*

LANCE SERGEANT JAMES CROWE
313358 W/Cpl (A/L/Sgt.), Seaforth Highlanders, Att. No. 1 Cdo.
MILITARY MEDAL (IMMEDIATE)

Arakan.

At Hinthaya on 23rd November 1944, L/Sgt Crowe was commanding a sub-section in action for the first time in an attack on strongly held enemy positions. His tasks were to secure identifications and take a prisoner. When a hand grenade was thrown into an enemy trench and appeared to have disabled the occupants, this NCO rushed forward and pulled out one Japanese who died almost immediately. Another had been temporarily stunned. L/Sgt Crowe tackled him and after a hard struggle secured him with the aid of two of his men, preventing him from committing suicide.

During this engagement he was under constant fire from enemy machine guns and well concealed snipers. His coolness and determination in carrying out his tasks were an inspiring example to his sub-section and resulted in the capturing of a prisoner, who was in excellent physical condition, and has given valuable information.   *[L.G. 22.3.45]*

Acting Battery Sergeant Major John Joseph Downey
828326 WS Sgt, RA (Field) Att. No. 1 Commando
Military Medal (Immediate)

Arakan. 1945

On 23rd January 1945 at Kangaw Hill 170 (Map ref 515414 Myebon Sheet East 1/25,000) BSM Downey was in a key trench which was fiercely attacked for two hours by night.

Early on he was wounded with multiple grenade wounds of the back and sniper fire penetrating the base of his forehead and through the nose. All the occupants of the trench were wounded. He helped evacuate two casualties and withdrew. He then, although in great pain and under heavy MMG and grenade fire at point blank range, went forward and brought in a casualty wounded in both legs. He refused treatment for his wounds until all other casualties had been dealt with and remained in action until five hours later with the situation completely in hand he was ordered out of battle. *[L.G. 19.4.45]*

Temporary Corporal Ernest Fenton
Ex.1300, No. 42 RM Commando
Military Medal

Arakan 1945

During the Daingbon operation in Burma from 25th January to 1st February 1945, Cpl Fenton was in charge of the unit transport. For the whole of the period he was based at the foot of Hill 170 and continually volunteered to drive his truck from that feature to the beach and back with rations, ammunition and casualties, in spite of the fact that the road was under harassing fire. On one occasion another truck broke down in the road and Cpl Fenton immediately backed his truck along the road, which was being shelled at the time, and took the other truck in tow.

On the morning of 31st January 1945, after the enemy counter-attack, he brought up ammunition for the tanks which was urgently needed, although the shelling and sniping was still heavy, and was ever anxious to take his load as near to the scene of action as possible.

His personal initiative, coolness and determination in carrying out his dangerous duties both by day and night were and example to the other drivers under his command, many of whom had not been under fire before. *(L.G. 15.5.45)*

The Far East

WAR SUBSTANTIVE TROOP SERGEANT MAJOR JAMES [McI. McL.] FERGUSON
2318036, Cameronians attached No. 5 Commando
MILITARY MEDAL (IMMEDIATE)

Arakan 1945

This Warrant officer was in the action fought on Hill 170 on the afternoon of 31st January 1945.

Our own troops were being hard pressed by repeated strong enemy counter-attacks. The No 2 of a bren gun was knocked out by a grenade. TSM Ferguson immediately took over. The enemy was still pressing his attack and in order to prevent a break through TSM Ferguson leapt from his trench and flung grenades returning for more and again throwing them causing the enemy many casualties. He was then seriously wounded but still made attempts to fight on until forcibly evacuated.

Throughout the whole action he was cool, calm and resolute and by his fearless example he inspired the men around him.

[L.G. 19.4.45]

PRIVATE GEORGE MACDONALD GIBSON
2992911, No. 5 Commando
MILITARY MEDAL

Arakan

On 23rd March 1944 during 5 Commando's attack on Spur 383348 the sub-section, of which Pte Gibson was a member, was caught in the valley by enfilade fire from a MMG in a position on the hillside. Pte Gibson immediately volunteered to wipe out the post.

He climbed the hill and was about to open fire when he was attacked from the rear by two of the enemy. These he killed with his colt. He then emptied a bren magazine into the MMG crew at a range of 30 yards. The gun was silenced.

Shortly afterwards an enemy patrol of seven men passed within five yds of him. He again opened fire with his bren. None escaped.

By this time Gibson had lost contact and run out of ammunition. In trying to make his way back he was surrounded by a party of the enemy who closed in on him. He escaped by throwing himself down a gully where he lay until dawn. He rejoined his unit after first light.

Recommended for DCM, awarded MM. *[L.G. 22.6.44]*

Lance Sergeant John William Hedderman
VX.12728, 2/6 Aust. Inf. Bn, 3 Aust Div
Military Medal (Immediate)

In the absence of his platoon commander and platoon sergeant, L/Sgt Hedderman commanded 17 platoon D Company in the forward area covering the approach to the Lababia defences in the Mubo area from 20th June 1943 to 24th June 1943. His platoon was subjected to heavy LMG and mortar fire and were twice heavily attacked by the enemy. The platoon inflicted heavy casualties on the enemy and held their position.

L/Sgt Hedderman crawled forward with a telephone to within 80 yds of the enemy main party and directed our 3-in mortar fire with great success. On 21st June 1943 he assisted Pte Smith in carrying out Pte Meehan and Pte Wilson, who were both badly wounded.

This was done under very heavy small-arms and mortar fire, during which they were both very exposed. At approximately 1500 hrs on 21st June 1943 the right flank of 17 Platoon was seriously endangered by a large force of enemy using mortars and LMGs. L/Sgt Hedderman ran forward under this fire and, using an EY rifle, silenced a mortar and dispersed the enemy in that vicinity.

On 22nd June 1943 he crept forward under cover and killed the crew of an LMG with grenades from his EY rifle.

On 23rd June 1943, during the hours of darkness, he led a small patrol to located enemy weapon pits, where the patrol inflicted casualties with grenades and SMG fire, and caused the enemy to vacate this area.

Throughout the entire attack, L/Sgt Hedderman displayed great personal courage, initiative and leadership and controlled and handled his platoon coolly and efficiently. *[L.G. 7.10.43]*

Lance Corporal Thomas Henry Herbert
7265184, RAMC att. No. 42 RM Commando
Military Medal (Immediate)

Arakan 1945

At Hill 170 nr Kangaw on 31st January 1945 L/Cpl Herbert's Troop was committed to a counter-attack at a critical stage of the battle. The forward platoon immediately met with heavy casualties, the troop eventually losing all three officers and the TSM. L/Cpl Herbert repeatedly went forward under heavy fire to bring in and attend to the wounded; and ignoring a head wound which was bleeding freely, continued to work at high pressure for a period of over four hours until completely exhausted. His energy and

FUSILIER WILLIAM H. IRVING
6471335, RF attached No. 1 Commando
MILITARY MEDAL (IMMEDIATE)

Arakan 1945

At Kangaw Hill 170 (Map ref 515414, sheet Myebon 1/25,000) on 23rd January 1945, Fus Irving was in charge of the troop wireless set.

At midnight he had multiple grenade wounds of the back inflicted by an enemy grenade. Refusing treatment and evacuation he maintained communications all night. His set was hit three times.

His courage and devotion to duty enabled vital messages to be passed throughout the action. *(L.G. 19.4.45)*

ACTING TEMPORARY TROOP SERGEANT MAJOR GEORGE WILLIAM KEMSLEY
Temporary Sergeant, Ex 903, No. 44 RM Commando
MILITARY MEDAL

During operations with 33 Ind Corps between 11th March and 12th April 1944 Troop Sergeant Major Kemsley constantly commanded patrols with distinction. He invariably displayed outstanding qualities of leadership and his determination to close with the enemy inspired his men with confidence both in him and in themselves. On his own initiative he twice disguised himself as a native and reconnoitred enemy positions from a distance of nearly fifty yards, returning on each occasion with valuable information. *(L.G. 6.2.45)*

ACTING TEMPORARY TROOP SERGEANT MAJOR WILLIAM FREDERICK LUCAS
Temporary Sergeant, Ex.3508, No. 42 RM Commando
MILITARY MEDAL

During the last five years TSM Lucas has served in this unit with distinction, and became an outstanding SNCO.

In the last two years while engaged in the Far Eastern Theatre, he has on a number of occasions shown very great bravery and personal leadership of a high order.

Whilst landing in Myebon his landing craft was hit, wounding his troop Commander. TSM Lucas continued with the assault and showed great resourcefulness under very difficult conditions, until contact could be made. Whilst at Myebon he led a number of men to bring in the wounded from an Indian Battalion. The area at the time was under shell and small arms fire, and, although wounded himself, he completed the task of evacuating the wounded.

At all times, both in battle and training, he has been a very fine example to the younger NCOs and men. *[L.G. 6.6.46]*

Marine Peter Joseph Mellor
Po.X.112061, No. 42 RM Commando
Military Medal

Mne Mellor, throughout the period of the Unit's fighting in Burma, has shown himself a brave, reliable and resourceful fighter. Whilst at Kangaw he displayed very great courage and disregard for his personal safety and was directly responsible for saving the lives of a number of Indian Soldiers. He went forward himself under heavy fire and repeated shelling, and carried in three men. On the fourth attempt he was severely wounded in the head. He was ordered by his officer to remain where he was. He refused and managed to collect two more before loss of blood stopped further attempts. This man's leadership and example in a critical situation did more than all else to hold a position of eight men, six of whom were wounded. *[L.G. 6.6.46]*

War Subst. Sergeant Gordon L. Notley
7366507, RAMC attached No. 1 Commando
Military Medal

Arakan 1945

On the 31st January 1945 at Hill 170 near Kangaw Sgt Notley was Medical Sgt. He moved up to the forward troop just after first light, and on arrival he set to work, under fire, tending the wounded and organising their evacuation. With another Sgt he made three attempts to rescue a seriously wounded man who was lying in the open covered by an enemy sniper, only giving up when the wounded man was hit again and killed. On this occasion Sgt Notley deliberately exposed himself to the sniper's fire in order to carry out his job. Altogether Sgt Notley dressed some 20 men all of whom were exposed to incessant fire from the enemy. At 1400 hrs he was wounded in the eye while tending to a casualty. He refused a stretcher which was brought for him and though nearly blind walked back himself to the MDS. *[L.G. 19.4.45]*

The Far East

Private Leslie Cyril Olver
6286823, Buffs, No. 1 Commando
Military Medal (Immediate)

Arakan

At Hinthaya on 23rd November 1944, this young soldier in action for the first time, in his excitement got ahead of his sub-section. A party of some ten Japanese crossed his front. He engaged them with his TMC, wounding their leader who was an officer.

He then saw an enemy section post about 30 yards to his left manned by four men. He threw a grenade at them, stunning one, and then killed the other three with his TMC. This enabled his sub-section to capture a prisoner, who was not much hurt and who gave most valuable information.

His skill at arms and his dash were a magnificent example to the men of the sub-section.

Recommended for DCM, awarded MM. (L.G. 22.3.45)

War Substantive Sergeant Alexander Beverley Pirie
Ch.X.1178, No. 3 RM Engineer Commando
Military Medal

In Burma on 12th January 1945 Sgt Pirie was engaged in mine clearing operations on the landing beach at Myebon Peninsula.

Assisted by two NCOs he cleared fields of mines of a type hitherto unencountered in this theatre of war and unknown to them, with great coolness, devotion to duty and disregard for his own personal safety.

By his efforts many casualties were undoubtedly averted.

[L.G. 15.5.45]

Gunner Eric William Rabbitt
5884633, No. 1 Commando
Military Medal (Immediate)

Arakan

On 12th November 1944 at Alethangyaw (Sheet 1/25,000 Map ref 387271) the patrol of which Gnr Rabbitt was a member came under heavy small arms fire from the front and both flanks at close range when in open country.

When the officer in charge of the patrol, who was leading, was wounded, Gnr Rabbitt, who was his batman, doubled forward under intense fire with complete disregard for his own safety, applied first aid and attempted to drag the officer to safety.

With the subsequent assistance of other men of the patrol the officer was successfully evacuated.

Although in the open and under intense fire at short range throughout the action, Gnr Rabbitt, through his initiative and complete disregard for his own safety, set an example to the remainder of the patrol, which resulted in the wounded officer being saved from falling into enemy hands.

Gnr Rabbitt is 19 years of age and this was the first time he had been in action. [L.G. 22.3.45]

GUNNER STANLEY A. ROAST
11268880, RA (HAA) attached No. 1 Commando
MILITARY MEDAL

On the 31st January 1945 at Hill 170 near Kangaw, Gnr Roast was No 1 on the bren gun in the foremost weapon pit of his position which was constantly being rushed and grenaded. His No 2 on the gun was wounded early in the action, and two other men who subsequently came in to act as No 2 were either killed or wounded. Gnr Roast carried on firing on his own in spite of being on the forward slope by himself with a Jap MMG facing him only 20 yards away. He only withdrew when the battle had finished and his position was taken over by relieving troops. He had fired over seventy magazines. It was largely due to his high sense of duty that the position was not over-run. [L.G. 19.4.45]

TEMPORARY CORPORAL RONALD FRANK RUSSELL
Ch.X.3093, No. 42 RM Commando
MILITARY MEDAL (IMMEDIATE)

Arakan 1945
At Hill 170 near Kangaw on 31st January 1945, Cpl Russell was commander of a section which was ordered forward to reinforce troops of another commando who had suffered severe casualties. Under heavy fire from two machine-guns and four snipers and with numerous enemy grenades landing in his position, he re-organised his section who had suffered four casualties and drove off repeated enemy attacks. Although wounded twice he did not go back to the regimental aid post for medical attention until there was a lull in the battle two hours later. This corporal's cheerfulness throughout and inspiring leadership did much to restore a critical situation.

Recommended for immediate DCM, awarded MM. (L.G. 15.5.45)

The Far East

MARINE JACK SHAW
RM (Force Vipers)
MILITARY MEDAL

Padaung. 30th March 1942.
Lieut Fayle was Commander of the reserved platoon which was surprised at 0030 hrs by a large force of Japanese. He, with Cpl Winters, RM, and Marine Shaw, hid beneath a hut and inflicted casualties estimated twenty-five to thirty at very close range on the enemy, using a tommy gun, a bren gun, and grenades. Was charged twice and ordered to surrender, but crept out at 0430, and made his escape with his party, having run out of ammunition. Rejoined the launches six miles upstream at dawn. *[L.G. 9.3.43]*

LANCE CORPORAL HENRY THOMAS SNOW
Private, 7403421, RAMC attached No. 42 RM Commando
MILITARY MEDAL

Arakan 1945
At Myebon on 15th January 1945 L/Cpl Snow showed the greatest determination and devotion to duty.

When the troop to which he was attached came under heavy fire from three concealed machine-guns, the Commanding Officer, two Troop Officers and five other ranks became casualties in a very short time. While trying to rally a stretcher party, he was himself wounded in the arm which bled freely. When the Second in Command ordered him to the rear he refused saying he still had a good arm. He thereupon continued to organise the treatment of the casualties, refusing morphia so that he could carry on. He did not go to the regimental aid post until all the wounded had been evacuated.

His courage and tenacity was an inspiration in a most difficult situation and did much to steady the men.
Recommended for immediate DCM, awarded MM.   *[L.G. 19.4.45]*

PRIVATE GEORGE H. WEBB
14604144, Royal West Kent Regt attached No. 1 Commando
MILITARY MEDAL (IMMEDIATE)

Arakan 1945
On the 31st. January 1945 at Hill 170 near Kangaw Pte Webb was a member of the leading section of a platoon ordered to counter-attack on the right flank. They came under intense MMG and grenade fire. The platoon officer and platoon Sgt were mortally wounded and the remainder of his section became casualties. Unperturbed by the intense fire he showed great coolness and presence of mind supervising the evacuation of many wounded.

He succeeded in locating and evacuating all the casualties except his platoon officer and platoon Sgt. After being ordered to withdraw he volunteered to go forward once more and search for the platoon Sgt. After repeated attempts amid showers of enemy grenades he was persuaded to come back and stayed with the remainder of his platoon. Shortly afterwards a man was killed at his side in the act of throwing a grenade. Pte Webb picked up the grenade and threw it just before it went off. His courage and coolness the whole day were of a very high order. *[L.G. 19.4.45]*

WAR SUBST. SERGEANT THOMAS IVOR WILLIAMS
3909922, South Wales Borderers, 'B' Group Special Boat Section, No. 1 Commando
MILITARY MEDAL (PERIODIC)

On the night 16th–17th November 1944, Sgt Williams was the Number 2 of the leading foldboat which attacked an enemy motor boat on the Chindwin. Throughout the action he fired his TSMG with such accuracy that the enemy was forced to turn away as planned, towards the LMG. During the boarding, this NCO helped to bring his foldboat alongside with precision and efficiency, and on the return journey kept the enemy well covered.

On the night of 29th–30th November 1944, Sgt Williams was in charge of a bren gun in the bows of the assault boat ordered to attack the enemy off Kalewa. Throughout the attack Sgt Williams showed great coolness together with a high degree of accuracy, and used his initiative in such a way as to keep his gun firing continually until out of range. At all times throughout the period of operations this NCO worked extremely diligently and hard and showed marked ability and leadership. His continued cheerfulness, coupled with a willingness, was at all times a source encouragement to all ranks. *(L.G. 17.1 46)*

CORPORAL HARRY WINTERS
RM (Viper Force)
MILITARY MEDAL

Padaung. 30th March 1942.
Lieut Fayle was Commander of the reserved platoon which was surprised at 0030 hrs by a large force of Japanese. He, with Cpl Winters, RM, and Marine Shaw, hid beneath a hut and inflicted casualties estimated at Twenty-five to thirty at very close range on the enemy, using a tommy gun, a bren gun, and grenades. Was charged twice and ordered to surrender, but crept out at 0430, and made his escape with his party, having run out of ammunition. Rejoined the launches six miles upstream at dawn. *[L.G. 9.3.45]*

Miscellaneous Awards

C. R. HARDY
KNIGHT COMMANDER OF THE ORDER OF
THE BATH
L.G. 1.1.57

H. D. FELLOWES
COMPANION OF THE ORDER OF THE BATH
L.G. 1957

C. R. HARDY
COMPANION OF THE ORDER OF THE BATH
L.G. 10.6.54

J. C. HAYDON
COMPANION OF THE ORDER OF THE BATH
L.G. 1.1.48

P. W. C. HELLINGS
COMPANION OF THE ORDER OF THE BATH
L.G. 11.6.66

R. D. HOUGHTON
COMPANION OF THE ORDER OF THE BATH
L.G. 8.6.63

C. R. HARDY
COMMANDER OF THE ORDER OF THE
BRITISH EMPIRE
L.G. 19.10.51

TEMPORARY MAJOR LOGAN SCOTT-BOWDEN, M.C., R.E.
Captain, 95182, Corps of Royal Engineers.
DISTINGUISHED SERVICE ORDER
In recognition of gallant and distinguished services in the field.
L.G. 15.6.44

Commando Gallantry Awards of World War II

S. W. CHANT
OFFICER OF THE ORDER OF THE BRITISH EMPIRE
L.G. 10.6.54

E. E. ETCHES
OFFICER OF THE ORDER OF THE BRITISH EMPIRE
L.G. 1964

B. I. S. GOURLAY
OFFICER OF THE ORDER OF THE BRITISH EMPIRE
L.G. 13.6.57

J. C. HAYDON
OFFICER OF THE ORDER OF THE BRITISH EMPIRE
L.G. 8.6.39

R. D. HOUGHTON
OFFICER OF THE ORDER OF THE BRITISH EMPIRE
L.G. 7.1.49

G. POLLARD
OFFICER OF THE ORDER OF THE BRITISH EMPIRE
L.G. 1960

D. L. S. St.M. ALDRIDGE
MEMBER OF THE ORDER OF THE BRITISH EMPIRE
L.G. 7.1.49

P. J. BYRNE
MEMBER OF THE ORDER OF THE BRITISH EMPIRE
L.G. 11.6.60

TEMPORARY MAJOR P. CLEASBY-THOMPSON
Captain, 15067, Lancashire Fusiliers, Army Air Corps
MEMBER OF THE ORDER OF THE BRITISH EMPIRE
Military Division. On the celebration of His Majesty's Birthday.
L.G. 2.6.43

TEMPORARY CAPTAIN RICHARD PHILIP CARR, M.C., R.A.
90121, Royal Regiment of Artillery
MEMBER OF THE ORDER OF THE BRITISH EMPIRE
Military Division. In recognition of gallant and distinguished services in the field.
L.G. 29.1.46

Miscellaneous Awards

M. A. W. DAVIES
MEMBER OF THE ORDER OF THE BRITISH EMPIRE
L.G. 4.12.59

D. FORD
MEMBER OF THE ORDER OF THE BRITISH EMPIRE
L.G. 31.5.55

J. D. GIBBON
MEMBER OF THE ORDER OF THE BRITISH EMPIRE
L.G. 1.1.59

B. I. S. GOURLAY
MEMBER OF THE ORDER OF THE BRITISH EMPIRE
L.G. 1.1.49

A. D. LEWIS
MEMBER OF THE ORDER OF THE BRITISH EMPIRE
L.G. 1.6.53

P. W. C. HELLINGS
DISTINGUISHED SERVICE CROSS
L.G. 1940

MAJOR DENNIS LEOLIN SAMUEL ST. MAUR ALDRIDGE, M.C., R.M.
42 Commando
BAR TO MILITARY CROSS

Major Aldridge's outstanding gallantry throughout the battle of Port Said [Nov '56] was a byword in his Commando. Most strongly recommended for the award of the DSO.

On the 6th November in the assault on Port Said, this officer led the first wave of LVTs onto the beaches and captured the beachhead amidst a hail of fire from the front and right flank.

In order to be in a better position to direct operations, he stood on a high wall just clear of the beach and with the utmost coolness and with complete disregard for his own personal safety directed and encouraged the troops to their objectives, although being sniped at the whole time.

The sight of this officer, standing on his own in a very exposed position, was an inspiration not only to the first wave troops, but also to the subsequent waves as they beached. Throughout the 6th November he gave an outstanding example of leadership and courage which was largely responsible for the success of the operation.

On the 7th and 8th November, wherever there was rioting or sniping, Major Aldridge was in the thick of it, directing, encouraging inspiring others, with no thought for his own safety. *Recommended for DSO, awarded Bar to MC.*

Acting Captain Michael Hinton Webb, M.C.
Lieutenant, 242138, South African Forces, Special Service Troops
Bar to Military Cross

In recognition of gallant and distinguished services in the field.

L.G. 5.10.44

Captain Dennis Leolin Samuel St. Maur Aldridge, M.B.E., R.M.
41 Independent Commando Royal Marines
Military Cross

On 29th November 1950 Major Aldridge took over temporary command of 41 Commando when Lt-Col Drysdale was made force Commander of a force consisting of 41 Commando, United States Marines and United States Army who had orders to break through from Koto-Ri to Hagaru-Ri [Korea]. 41 Commando was in the centre of the convoy and throughout the day and early night was engaged in heavy fighting over ten miles of road. They were ambushed twice. Throughout the action Major Aldridge moved fearlessly up and down the column, encouraging the men and continuously exposing himself to fierce enemy fire.

This officer's calm demeanour, cheerfulness and quick decisions were an inspiration to the unit. It was largely due to his fearless leadership that so many of the unit did in fact reach Hagaru-Ri.

(L.G. 18.5.51)

Captain Peter Delap, M.B.
133538, Royal Army Medical Corps, No. 40 RM Commando
Military Cross

In recognition of gallant and distinguished services in the field.

L.G. 15.3.45

Chaplain the Reverend R. De Naurois
No. 4 Commando (French Army).
Military Cross

Not found in L.G. 1940–46

Miscellaneous Awards

TY. MAJOR RALPH DOUGLAS CAMERON MCCALL
Captain, 129038, Army Air Corps
MILITARY CROSS
In recognition of gallant and distinguished services in the field.
L.G. 5.10.44

CAPTAIN LAURENCE ERIC MACCALLUM
129561, The Manchester Regiment, Special Service Troops
MILITARY CROSS
In recognition of gallant and distinguished services in the field.
L.G. 5.10.44

TY. CAPTAIN AMBROSE JOSEPH MCGONIGAL
Lieutenant, 113419, Royal Ulster Rifles, Special Service Troops
MILITARY CROSS
In recognition of gallant and distinguished services in the field.
L.G. 2.3.44

LIEUTENANT IAN CHRISTOPHER DOWNS SMITH
108233, Royal Army Service Corps, Special Service Troops
MILITARY CROSS
In recognition of gallant and distinguished services in the field.
L.G. 2.3.44

TY. CAPTAIN MICHAEL WILLIAM STILWELL
Lt., 149313, Coldstream Guards, Special Service Troops
MILITARY CROSS
In recognition of gallant and distinguished services in the field.
L.G. 5.10.44

LANCE CORPORAL WILLIAM HOGGETT
2326631, Royal Corps of Signals, No. 2 Commando
DISTINGUISHED CONDUCT MEDAL
In recognition of gallant and distinguished services in the field.
L.G. 15.3.45

WARRANT OFFICER CL. II GEORGE FRANCIS HUTTON
6012900, The Essex Regiment, No. 2 Commando
DISTINGUISHED CONDUCT MEDAL
In recognition of gallant and distinguished services in the field.
L.G. 15.3.45

Commando Gallantry Awards of World War II

CORPORAL JOSEPH JACKSON
3781177, The King's Regiment (Liverpool), No. 2 Cdo.
DISTINGUISHED CONDUCT MEDAL
In recognition of gallant and distinguished services in the field.
L.G. 15.3.45

WARRANT OFFICER CLASS II ARTHUR SWINBURN
4855159, The Leicestershire Regiment, Special Service Troops, No. 50 Commando
DISTINGUISHED CONDUCT MEDAL
In recognition of gallant and distinguished services in the field.
L.G. 13.9.45

PRIVATE RONALD DOUGLAS BANKS
6451872, The Queen's Own Royal West Kent Regt, No. 3 Cdo.
MILITARY MEDAL
For gallant and distinguished services in the field.   *L.G. 10.6.46*

CORPORAL NORMAN ALAN BURFORD
5571232, Corps of Royal Engineers, No. 7 Commando
MILITARY MEDAL
For gallant and distinguished services in the field.   *L.G. 20.6.46*

GUNNER JAMES CLARK
402083, Royal Regiment of Artillery, No. 2 Commando
MILITARY MEDAL
In recognition of gallant and distinguished services in the field.
L.G. 13.3.45

RIFLEMAN RICHARD GILL
6846123, The Cameronians, Scottish Rifles, No. 2 Cdo.
MILITARY MEDAL
In recognition of gallant and distinguished services in the field.
L.G. 15.3.45

PRIVATE BERNARD J. HENDRY
5337785, The Royal Berkshire Regiment (Princess Charlotte of Wales's), No. 2 Commando
MILITARY MEDAL
In recognition of gallant and distinguished services in the field.
L.G. 15.3.45

Miscellaneous Awards

SERGEANT LEONARD PERKINS
2930945, Queen's Own Cameron Highlanders, No. 2 Cdo.
MILITARY MEDAL
In recognition of gallant and distinguished services in the field.
L.G. 13.3.45

WARRANT OFFICER CLASS II THOMAS WILLIAM WINTER
108938 CSM, RASC, SSRF 2 Para, SBS & SAS
MILITARY MEDAL
For gallant and distinguished services in the field. *L.G. 20.6.46*

E. T. LILLEY
BRITISH EMPIRE MEDAL
L.G. 1.1.52

BRIGADIER JOSEPH CHAMBERS HAYDON
Foot Gds §
LEGION OF MERIT, DEGREE OF OFFICER
Brigadier J. C. Haydon, Foot Guards, British Army, performed exceptionally meritorious service to the Allied governments from September 1944 to August 1945. As British Army member of the Washington Directors of Plans, he was charged with the responsibility of preparing plans to implement world wide strategy. His responsibility required close co-operation and co-ordination with the United States Joint Staff Planners. Brigadier Haydon displayed at all times the highest degree of co-operation and was imbued with the vital necessity of solving difficulties that arose to the mutual satisfaction of all concerned. This spirit pervaded in all his dealings with the United States Joint Staff Planners and contributed immeasurably toward resolving problems that at times seemed to present insurmountable obstacles. In addition to Brigadier Haydon's unique and invaluable ability to co-operate, his sound professional judgment and intelligent application of the principles of military strategy and tactics contributed in a large degree to the success of the Allied forces. *[L.G. 14.5.48]*

R. W. P. DAWSON
CROIX DE GUERRE
Not found in L.G. 1940–46

Commando Gallantry Awards of World War II

TEMPORARY CAPTAIN P. M. DONNELL
No. 47 RM Commando
CROIX DE GUERRE STAR
Not found in L.G. 1940–46

Escapes

LANCE SERGEANT RICHARD BRADLEY
5344190, Royal Berkshire Regt, No. 2 Commando
MILITARY MEDAL
and
PTE JAMES BROWN
2988949, (Ex Argyll and Sutherland Highlanders), No. 5 Cdo.
MILITARY MEDAL
and
LANCE SERGEANT ALFRED CLARENCE SEARSON
6403917, Royal Sussex Regt, No. 2 Commando
MILITARY MEDAL

After being taken prisoner at St. Nazaire on 28th March 1942, Bradley, Brown and Searson were sent to Germany. On 17th August 1942, using a stolen file, Brown, Searson and another prisoner of war cut through the window bars and escaped from Stalag VIII B. They had been at liberty for four days when they were caught as they slept in a wood.

Their second attempt was made at the beginning of October 1942; wearing overalls, old caps and rucksacks, they posed as civilian workmen, but their disguise was penetrated the next day. For punishment they were sent to stone quarries near Bunzlau, and when they refused to work, received instead nine days in the cells, prior to their return to the main camp. Although Brown succeeded in leaving Greiffenberg working camp in March 1943, he was arrested at Görlitz because the dye from his overcoat stained his face and neck. He was sent back to Stalag VIII B where he again met Searson who had in the meantime helped two other prisoners of war to leave a working camp at Sternberg, and had acquired money and clothing with a view to making another attempt. This took place in July 1943, from a factory at Freiheit-Johannesberg. Accompanied by Bradley, he travelled by train to Engen, and the two men were nearing the Swiss frontier when they were caught and once more returned to Stalag VIII B. Brown who had waited another month to acquire a civilian jacket, was detected as he was leaving the factory on 12th August 1943.

By October 1943 Brown, Bradley and Searson had completed their preparations for a combined effort. At this time they were employed at Wosswalda, and while the guards were having a meal the three men forced the door lock with a bent nail, walked to the

station, and travelling on slow trains reached Tuttlingen unchallenged. Completing the remainder of the journey on foot, they crossed into Switzerland near Hofenacker on 25th October 1943.
(L.G. 26.7.45)

PTE JAMES BROWN
(See under L/Sgt Richard Bradley.)

CORPORAL E. DOUGLAS
292793, Liverpool Scottish, No. 2 Commando
MILITARY MEDAL
and
PRIVATE V. HARDING
5189003, Gloucestershire Regt, No. 2 Commando
MILITARY MEDAL

We left Falmouth on the 26th March 1942 on a motor launch to take part in the raid on St. Nazaire. We were in the same party as L/Cpl Sims (S/P.G.(–)783) and were under the command of TSM Haynes. We arrived at St. Nazaire about 0130 hrs on 28th March and were landed on the breakwater just to the left of the old entrance to the basin. Our task was to attack the two 6-inch gun positions shown on the attached map. We attacked the positions from the rear, but found there were no guns there and returned to an arranged point at the entrance to the docks where Col Newman and seven or eight men had already gathered. Col Newman told us to fall in and await further orders. We remained at that point for about 25 minutes, being trapped by fire from 4-inch trench mortars and machine guns. During this time other people came in, including Major Copland, second-in-command, with two men. Major Copland was wounded in the neck, arm, and leg. Others to arrive were:— Capt Day (wounded in the lip), Capt Burns (wounded in the leg) and Capt Roy who had been on board the *Campbeltown* and who brought with him four or five men.

It was decided to make by way of the sheds for the re-embarkation point. (See attached map). On the way we were attacked with machine-gun fire from a house, but we threw hand grenades and two men with tommy-guns went in and cleared the house. By this time our party numbered about 70 in all. We were then attacked from the left of the house by about 30 Germans, firing automatic weapons. After we had repulsed them with tommy-gun fire, a naval man came along shouting the password and told Col Newman that, as our boats had been sunk, it would be impossible for us to re-embark. Col Newman then ordered us to

Escapes

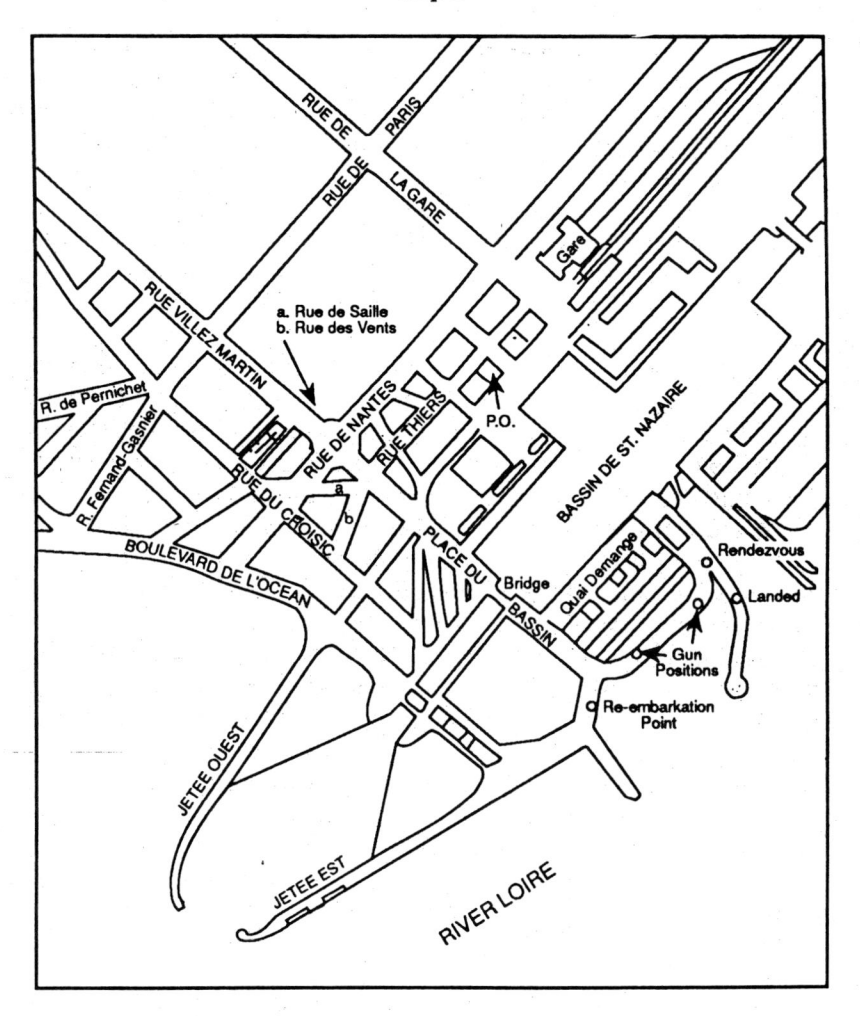

get back to England if possible, telling us not to give up while we had any ammunition left and to fight our way through the town.

Our section, in which there was only one wounded man (L/Cpl Grieve) was put out as point section. We made towards the Quai Demange, L/Cpl Douglas being in charge. On the way we wiped out a machine-gun post, and then walked westwards in the shadow of the buildings on the quay. As we were wearing rubber boots, we made very little noise and were not detected. At the corner of the sheds we came upon 150 or 200 German soldiers. We got into line and opened fire on them.

Those who survived ran. We continued up the Place du Bassin. As we crossed the bridge we were fired on. TSM Haynes was wounded in the neck, shoulder and arm, and Sgt Challington had a knee cap smashed. We saw Captain Day lying on the ground inside the girder of the bridge. There was a wire fence across the bridge with only one small opening. Machine-guns were trained on this opening, but we got through and continued up the street. We then reached a stationary ambulance and saw another ambulance turning slowly out of a side street behind it. We opened up on both vehicles with bren guns and tommy-guns and both the drivers were knocked out. There were no Germans inside the first ambulance. Sgt Challington hobbled over to the second ambulance and finished off the men inside.

Col Newman told us to carry on. We crossed a street junction into Rue Villez Martin. There were six in our party—TSM Haynes, Sgt Challington, a L/Cpl of the Guards, a full Corporal from a demolition party who was badly wounded in the leg, and ourselves. We came upon another ambulance and, though we suspected it might be a booby trap, we tried to start it, hoping to ride in it through the town. The engine would not start. By this time we had become isolated from the main party, who had turned left at the street junction and whom we could hear fighting down towards the harbour. We two took the lead of our party, and we all got into the doorway. A group of Germans shouted, 'Wer da?' We shouted 'Freund,' and they took no more notice of us but did not move away. We therefore opened on them with four tommy-guns, a bren gun and a rifle. Those we did not wipe out scattered. We continued over the junction of the Rue Desvents and Rue Thiers with the Rue Villez Martin. There were Germans coming down the Rue Villez Martin so we turned left into a back street (Rue de Saille). There we were fired on and the Germans shouted 'Commando surrender.' We got behind a road block and fired back. The Germans scattered.

We came out from behind the barricade and got into a bombed-out house to rest, putting up our bren gun in the entrance. We remained in the house till dawn when we began to hear Germans outside. The Sergeant wanted to get out, but we persuaded the others to 'lie doggo,' and we all got down into the cellar. There we dressed the wounded men with six shell dressings we had with us and gave them Horlick's tablets and water. During the day our whole supply of water was used up in washing the wounds of the injured men and giving them drinks. About 0700 hours two German sentries took up position outside the fence round our building and, looking up from the cellar, we could actually see them. There was also a workman walking on the boards above us, and clouds of dust came down when we moved. During the forenoon we heard the explosion on the *Campbeltown* which shook our building.

Escapes

We waited in the cellar till dark. At 1800 hours a German lifted the boards above us and looked down. We heard him say 'there are no British in the cellar' and the two sentries then left the gate. During the day Sgt Challington found some old clothes and he and TSM Haynes left about 2100 hours, dressed in them. The full Corporal who was badly wounded and intended to give himself up, left next. He was followed by the L/Cpl who was wounded in the back and who intended giving himself up to two gendarmes whom we saw on duty at the Police Prefecture across the street.

At about 2145 hours, some 20 minutes after the L/Cpl had left, we two came out of the building. We had left our equipment and gaiters behind us and had turned up our trousers at the bottom. We went up the Rue Villez Martin, but, as there were a good many German soldiers about—they were singing and we thought they might be drunk and therefore more inquisitive—we turned left and got into the Rue De Croisic up which we went to its junction with the Rue Villez Martin. We continued up the latter street and near a German barracks came to a road barrier on which there were two German sentries within about six feet of each other. It was impossible to turn back without arousing suspicion, so we slouched forward, dragging our feet on the ground to make as much noise as possible and so conceal the fact that we were wearing rubber boots. When we reached the barrier one of us (Douglas) said 'Bonne nuit.' The Germans said 'Bonne nuit' in return, and we walked through the barrier with the moon shining full on us. We walked on slowly until we were out of sight of the sentries and then ran like hell to some gardens where we got over a number of back walls. About 20 minutes later we heard firing and a hue and cry, and we assumed that the sentries had realised who we were.

After crossing a number of back gardens we reached open country through which we wandered for the next three days, travelling by night and sleeping in the woods by day. We tried to move north-east. About 0500 hours on Sunday 29th March, we went to a house and asked for food, but were told to go away. By this time we were very hungry, as we had finished our Horlick's tablets and the one emergency ration we had between us. We got into a wood round which there were dogs howling. One came up to the place where we were lying and smelt the head of one of us (Douglas). We saw a German's boots and trousers just outside our thicket. We lay quite still and the dog did not bark. It left, and we stayed in the thicket till night. After leaving the wood, we started walking, keeping off the roads. On the morning of 30th March, we went to a house and asked for water and food and were directed to another house where we were taken in. The lady of the house was a Frenchwoman who had lived for a number of years in the United States. She kept us for the night, fed us, gave us civilian clothes and 600 francs, and got us two old bicycles. That night (30th March) the lady's son in law told us there was still a machine gun firing from a cinema in the town and that the Germans could not get at it.

We left this house on the morning of Tuesday, 31st March on the bicycles with a young Frenchman, who took us to a spot near St. Lyphard and kissed us goodbye, but did not tell us where we were. We were dressed in corduroy trousers, sabots, and old coats. We had no maps and soon were completely lost. We kept on asking French people where the Germans were, and walked into Herbignac, which we left at once because we saw German guards on the bridge. We went round the east of the town and got to a place near Missillac, where an old Frenchman took us in and fed us and let us sleep in a barn (night of 31st March–1st April). He told us that if we were questioned, we were to say we were Algerians. We left this place on the morning of 1st April and made our way to a little village about five kms from La Roche-Bernard, where we found food and shelter for the night and got a map of the district from a wall calendar. We left on the morning of 2nd April and went to St. Gildas-de-Bois. There is a big German military establishment and hospital near there, and we saw a Gestapo control on the road. We avoided the control and returned to La Roche-Bernard and stayed at the place we had left in the morning.

On the morning of Saturday, 4th April we went via St. Dolay, Sevrac, Le Clandre and Le Derny to St. Emilien, where we were sheltered by an old Frenchman who agreed to put us up over Easter Sunday and Monday, when we would have appeared conspicuous had we travelled in our old clothes. We left on Tuesday 7th April, and, avoiding Mort because of the Germans there we went to Heric, Saffre, Rialle, Le Mars-La-Jaille, and round Cande to Segre and Châteauneuf-sur-Sarthe. We stayed the night at a small place near Châteauneuf. We did all our travelling on side roads. We had secured another calendar map, this time of the Angers district.

On 8th April we went on to La Fleche, Le Lude, and Broc (to the south of Le Lude). At Broc we went to a château owned by an Englishwoman, but the servant chased us away, and we spent the night in a barn. By this time one of the bicycles had broken down, and we were taking turns in using the other. On 9th April we got to a place south of Château-la-Valliere, where there is a château owned by Lord Halifax. We had intended going to this house, but were warned at a farm that it was being used by the Gestapo as a headquarters. After a meal at the farm we went on to Le Grand Ormeau. At a small cottage a lady whose son is a prisoner of war in Germany took us in and gave us shelter, food and baths, and washed and mended our clothes. She brought in the local schoolmistress who spoke English. The schoolmistress marked out our route to a place near Lengeis, and told us to go to the curé there. We did so, and told the curé, an ex-soldier of the last war, that we were British soldiers from St. Nazaire. He received us very well and gave us food, and wrote a note with his signature calling on all good French people to help us to get to unoccupied France. After providing us with four eggs and bread, he walked with us to Lengeis and arranged for the ferryman to take us over the ferry. We actually crossed with a number of German soldiers.

We went to Valleres to an address given us by the curé. We stayed the night there and then went on to Thilouze (12th April) where we were sheltered for a fortnight by people who would not let us go till they were certain of getting us across the Line of Demarcation. We worked on the farm at which we were staying, and our helpers in the village supplied us with books and frequently took us home to dinner. About the end of April we were taken by ponytrap to Ligueil, a Frenchwoman riding in front on a bicycle to make sure the villagers were safe. From Ligueill we were taken to the Line of Demarcation in a pony and trap covered with blankets. We stayed for a little at a farmhouse and then walked over with a girl and a Frenchman who has a farm on the Unoccupied side of the boundary.

We walked to Esves and then got the tram to Loches, where we were met by a friend of our helpers in the Occupied Zone. In Loches arrangements were made for us to visit Marseilles whence an organisation looked after our journey.

Corporal John Davie Coutts
4746052, Y.&LR, No. 52 ME Commando
Military Medal (Immediate)

Cpl Coutts was captured at Sphakia on 1st June 1941, moved to Maleme and then to Salonika. There were escapes nearly every day. The morning after a successful escape would be spent by the remainder on parade in the sun. Those caught escaping were not seen again.

One night the Germans decided to prevent any escapes by crowding the prisoners into the centre of the camp.

This suited the plans that Cpl Coutts and others had made that afternoon. They had noticed the opening of a sewer in the centre of the camp and had seen that it was wide enough for a man to crawl through. A Greek workman promised to take off the lid of another opening several hundred yards from the camp as soon as it was dark. They blocked the pipe from the latrines to the sewer and turned on all the taps there and in the wash-house and left them on all the afternoon.

The fact that all the prisoners of war had been pushed by the sentries to the centre of the camp provided an excuse for their presence by the sewer opening and Coutts and seven others climbed down and crawled along. It took them two hours. Cpl Coutts is broadly built and twice stuck in particularly narrow spots. The artificial washing down they had given it made a considerable difference to the conditions, but even so two of them passed out as soon as they reached the opening and fresh air. They waited till they came round and then split up into parties of two and three.

Cpl Coutts joined Cpl Ward and Tpr Nicholas. They knocked at the door of a house and were taken in. From there they gradually made their way down to Agion Oros peninsula, going north first to Langadas and then down through Evangelismos and Zagliveri receiving food and shelter wherever they stopped.

Tpr Nicholas got malaria badly and through weakness and lack of medical attention died on 7th October 1941.

Cpl Coutts and Cpl Ward stole a boat near Smerna and made for Imbros. Ten miles away bad weather forced them back. The effort was too much for Ward who died on 10th November 1941.

Cpl Coutts spent most of the winter in a hut he built on the hills. With spring, his strength began to return and he joined up with Lieut Thomas and Cpl Peacock in April.

On 5th April they got a boat at Klephtikon and sailed for Imbros. Bad weather forced them to go back. On 16th April they tried again from Nea Skete, but had to return as round the point a strong light was flashed on them and they heard voices.

They were joined by two Cypriots and a Greek officer on 2nd May 1942 and on the same day Pte Theodoros Georgiou, No. 4230, 232 Company RASC (who had been recommended for a DCM) reached them. On 4th May 1942 they left with him and arrived Turkey on 6th May 1942.

Cpl Coutts not only did an excellent escape, but in spite of the death of his two companions—which must have been hard blows to bear—his frustrated attempt to reach Turkey and his own personal weakness, he struggled on in Greece alone. Finally with L/Cpl Peacock and Lieut Thomas he made two more attempts to reach Turkey and only just failed owing to bad weather. He escaped thanks to sheer dogged courage. *(L.G. 24.9 42)*

Escapes

SERGEANT WILLIAM PATRICK DUFFY, M.M.
2568672, 1 SBS, 1st Bn SAS Regt & No. 8 Commando
MILITARY MEDAL

Sgt Duffy was a member of a party working behind the enemy lines on SAS operation 'Gain' in the area north of Orleans. On August 8th 1944, Sgt Duffy was captured by the enemy when his Commander Major Fenwick was killed, Sgt Duffy was knocked out, his jaw broken in two places, a bone in his leg broken and his right eye damaged. He was taken to hospital at Fontainebleau and later at Milly where he was the only Englishman in a ward with German wounded. Nobody spoke to him and he received next to no treatment. After about a fortnight he learned that the hospital was to be moved back to Germany the next day. With the help of a French girl who worked in the hospital, he managed to obtain the uniform of a German Medical Officer. About 1700 hrs the day before they were to be moved, seeing that the others in his ward were sleeping, he got into the uniform and slipped out of the ward. Unfortunately he had no boots but he managed to find the girl again and persuaded her to find him some. The boots he got were at least two sizes too small for him but nevertheless he squeezed into them and marched straight out into the court-yard where the enemy were loading trucks and ambulances for the move. Concealing his limp as well as possible he walked straight down the drive towards the gate. Here he had the alternative of trying to scale a high wall unseen or trying to continue his bluff past the two sentries at the gate who were armed with automatic rifles. He chose the latter course and walked straight down the middle of the drive and out of the gate. Once clear of the hospital grounds he slipped into a field and removed his boots which he could bear no longer. He then walked east for over thirty miles in his bare feet until he was found by the Maquis and looked after until the Allies arrived. His feet were so badly blistered when he was found by the Maquis that he was unable to walk further once he had stopped.

This is the second time that Sgt Duffy has escaped from an enemy POW Camp. In 1943 he escaped from the Italians in civilian clothes in similar circumstances. On both occasions his courage, initiative and daring have been an inspiration to his regiment who have been able to welcome back one whose qualities as a soldier both in and out of action are very greatly admired.
Recommended for DCM, awarded MM.   *(L.G. 22.3.45)*

Commando Gallantry Awards of World War II

Corporal Clifford Gregory Evans
4078107, South Wales Borderers, att. Special Service Troops, No. 1 Commando
Military Medal

(a) Capture.

I was captured alone on 3rd March 1943 while my unit was defending a height near Sedjenane (Tunisia). After capture I was made to work for two or three days by the Germans.

On 5th March I was sent to Perryville for interrogation by a German Officer who spoke very good English. He was particularly anxious to find out whether my unit had been transported to North Africa by sea or air, and at which ports we had embarked and disembarked. I told him we had come by sea, but that it had been dark both when we left and arrived and that I did not know the names of the ports. Our headquarters had been captured along with a number of secret documents and the German officer questioned me about casualties and promotions. I told him nothing that mattered.

After interrogation I was sent back to the front line where I was employed for three weeks removing English equipment which had been left behind in our withdrawal. On one or two occasions I was made to load mortar bombs for despatch to the German front line. During this three weeks behind the German front line I made one attempt to escape with Pte Duncan, Argyll and Sutherland Highlanders. We hid in a copse but were seen by Arabs. We moved to another copse, but Arabs saw us again and stoned us from high ground. Later they captured us, and handed us over to the Germans, from whom they collected a reward.

Shortly after this the British big push started. We were rushed back to Bizerta and handed over to the Italians. I was in Bizerta for two weeks.

(b) Camps in which imprisoned.

    Campo 98 (Palermo, Sicily), for about a month (May–June 1943)

    Campo 78 (Sulmona), (early June–mid-July 1943)

In Sulmona we were asked to volunteer for work. About 200 refused and were detailed for transfer to Germany. I was among this number. We were sent to Campo 53 (Macerata) where we spent one day and were joined by men from other camps, making a party of 2,000 altogether. From Sulmona we were sent to Germany by rail in cattle trucks. There were about 40 men to the truck. We were sent to

Escapes

Stalag IV B (near Munich).

Here I registered as a Corporal to avoid having to work. A Belgian in the camp put me wise to this. This was a French camp, in which there had been no British for some time. We were overcrowded and the place was so lousy that it was impossible to sleep at first. Later the Germans tried to improve conditions. I was in Stalag IV B for about three weeks, being moved to

Stalag VIII B (later 344) (Lamsdorf) (end August 1943).

After a month in hospital I volunteered for work, and early in October 1943 went in an NCO's working party to Adersbach (not traced) near Trautenau (Germany 1.100,000 Sheet 115, 6403. I intended to try to escape, but could not see any possible means, especially after the snow began in early November. I applied several times to return to the Stalag, but each time my application was turned down, as the party was supposed to remain six months on the job. During March 1944 there was much discontent on the party whose numbers had been reduced by sickness, and on 1st April 1944 we were sent to

Stalag VIII A (Görlitz) to which our party had been transferred from Stalag VIII B.

I volunteered for another working party from Görlitz and was sent to

Marschendorf (near Trautenau) on an NCO's party numbering about 100, mostly Warrant Officers. The party was working in a cigarette paper factory. Very few Germans were employed. It was popularly believed that the paper made in the factory was sent to Turkey where it was resold by the Turks to Britain. I remained only eight days on this party, being dismissed by the German foreman because I was not working hard enough at the labouring job which I was given after I had refused to work a machine. At this factory I met Dvr Siely, Cpl Verner, No. 3 Commando; two Australians and another Englishman. All these were dismissed with me. I discovered that Siely and Verner were interested in escaping.

5977, Dvr Walter James Seily, Div. Petrol Coy, 1 Div. N.Z.E.F.

I was captured in Crete on 1st June 1941, the day of the British capitulation to the Germans.

Galatos (Crete), three months in a temporary camp. Here conditions were very bad. I made three attempted escapes from this camp. On each occasion I got out through the wire with a friend and got in touch with Greeks who hoped to be able to get us away by boat. This, however, was difficult to arrange and on each occasion, seeing the reprisals taken by the Germans on Greeks who helped escapers, we returned to the camp.

Salonika, six weeks. From Salonika we were sent to Gerain in cattle trucks—40 men to each truck—with only four loaves of bread each for a journey which lasted about twelve days. My first camp in Germany was Stalag VIII B (Lamsdorf). I was here for seven months. From Lamsdorf I went to work on a building job at Novy Jicin (Meutitschein) in the Czechoslovak Protectorate south of Mauhristch-Ostrau. At Lamsdorf I had signed on as a Corporal to get on this party. In Novy Jicin I met a Czech girl who spoke English. She told me of the existence of a Czechoslovak organisation which might be able to help me if I could escape, but advised me to learn German and some Czech before I made a serious attempt. I did not escape from this party.

I was next employed at a sugar factory at Troppau (Germany 1:100,000 Sheet 127, 9333) from which there was no chance of escape. From Troppau I went to another party at Belton (not traced) in the same area, and to a third party at Stramberg, near [......] (eleven miles north of Olmütz). In the summer of 1943, no fewer than 32 prisoners of war escaped from Stramberg. I helped them all by getting maps from the Czech girl. I had intended going out myself, but on the day I had chosen for my attempt I was arrested by the Germans who had heard of my activities. The Commandant said he could not charge me with having helped my comrades to escape, but that he would charge me with being an agitator and influencing the men on the job. On this charge I received seven days cells.

I did my time at Jägernsdorf (Sheet 127, 7950) the headquarters of the guards in charge of the working parties in the district. Hauptmann Gross, who had sentenced me asked if after my sentence I would like to go out on a working party, as there was then an epidemic of typhus in the main camp. I agreed and just before winter set in in 1943 I was sent to Arboitskowando 399, at Oberwichstein (not traced). I had signed a paper promising to be a good boy, and not cause trouble.

First attempted escape.

I had been about a year and a half in Germany when I made my first attempted escape. After I had been about a week at Kommando 399 I escaped with a Londoner (Cpl Cushion). We filed a bar in a window in the billet at the Lager and got out. Four days later we were recaptured and taken to Jägernsdorf where I 'did' 14 days.

Escapes

Second attempted escape.

After I had served my sentence I was sent back to Stalag VIII B. A short time later I went out on a working party at a Holzwolle factory at Freiwaldau (Sheet 126, 4366). I was among those who came under suspicion when the factory and several adjoining farms was burned down, and in January 1944 I escaped with Cpl Verner, No. 3 Commando, Pte Ragan, the Buffs; and Sgt Wagstaff, a Canadian. We got out of a trapdoor in the theatre of our Lager. We went from Freiwaldau to Goldberg (not traced) by passenger train without identity papers. In this district we met a party of Czech partisans at Schönau (Sheet 103, 6454) with whom we spent about 24 hours. We told them that we intended to try to link up with the organisation about which the Czech girl had told me. The partisans fed us and conducted us to the railway station. They told us they had an Englishman with them, but they would not let us see him. We continued by train to Olmütz (Olomouc). Unfortunately, the map we had showed the German and Czech names of this town some distance apart, and when the train stopped at Olmütz we did not realise that we were already at our destination. As a result we were late in leaving the train and were stopped and arrested by the Gestapo. During this escape we wore Army overcoats and trousers dyed blue.

We were taken to Olmütz gaol, where we were interrogated. Ten days later we were transferred to Prague and spent eleven days in the Wehrmacht prison.

When captured I had inside my stocking a scrap of paper with the address of a communist living near Brno in Czecho-Slovakia. This scrap of paper was found. Lieut Miller, Royal Canadian Engineers, was in my cell in the Wehrmacht prison, and advised me what to do when interrogated, telling me not to reveal where I had got the address. We were all interrogated separately by Dr. Krüger, who was specially flown from Berlin to investigate our connection with the partisans. I was taken alone to the Gestapo headquarters in Prague for interrogation by Krüger. I was kept waiting for two hours before Krüger arrived with seven members of the Gestapo who all understood English. When he came in Krüger asked me to sit down. I refused, saying that they would 'belt' me if I did so, and that if they hit me I wanted to get in one at them. Krüger said to the others in German: 'We will have to change our tactics.' He then shook hands with me and said that he was an international lawyer and would get me out of the 'spot of bother' I had got into. Throughout the interrogation Krüger was very smooth, taking the line that he was trying to help me. He wanted to know where I had got the address, where I had crossed the frontier, and how I had travelled. I said I had found the scrap of paper in the corridor of the train. In the end he said I had cleared myself satisfactorily, and I was sent back to the Wehrmacht prison.

At the end of eleven days we were all sent back to Lamsdorf. For our escape we were sentenced to 21 days' cells, which we had already served.

After I had served my sentence, I volunteered for another working party and went to Marschendorf near Trautenau (Sheet 115, 6403). I had with me a copy of a foreign worker's Ausweis obtained in Lamsdorf, which I hoped to be able to get copied. On this party I met L/Cpl Evans.

L/Cpl Evans and Dvr Seily.

When we were sent back from Marschendorf to Stalag VIII A Verner, and we two each sold a battle dress and personal clothing such as jerseys and underclothing. The cigarettes we obtained for the clothing were bartered for chocolate which in turn was bartered with Serbians for civilian clothes. We were unable to obtain anything in the way of identity papers.

We chose a working party of NCOs and Privates which was engaged in railway repairs and based at Königshan (Sheet 115, 6916). We could not escape from the Lager at Königshan as the Unteroffizier in charge watched us too closely.

Attempted escape from Parschnitz.

After six days we were sent to work at Parschnitz (Sheet 115, 6704). On the journey we wore our civilian clothes under our uniforms. We had collected a store of biscuits, chocolate and cigarettes, which the other members of the party, all of whom were keen to help us to get away, carried for us in their pockets. Verner and we two each had an Italian military rucksack obtained in the Stalag from Italian prisoners of war. These rucksacks we left in a shed near our working place in the railway at Parschnitz, and a friend surreptitiously packed them with our food. We found later, however, that he had not had an opportunity of completing the packing and we were short on biscuits.

We were unloading a train and when it pulled into a siding at the station at Parschnitz to allow an express to pass, we three made for the shed. There were three Czechs in the shed, but we turned them out, removed our battle dresses, picked up our bags, and got out of the rear window.

We headed for Czecho-Slovakia, hoping to make contact with the Czechoslovak organisation of which Siely had heard on a previous attempted escape. We waited till nightfall in a wood near

Escapes

Parschnitz, and then got on to the railway track, along which we walked. On this walk we crossed the Czech frontier, which we knew to be patrolled by Grenzpolizei, but although we heard dogs we saw no sign of patrols. Next morning we reached the village of Schwadowitz (Sheet 115, 7400). We spent the day in a wood. In the evening an old woman, who told us there were no trains running, directed us to Eipel (Sheet 115, 7197). As we had had no bread since we set out, we went to a house at Eipel (after listening at the window to make sure the people were Czech). There were a woman and her daughter in the house. We told them we were British escapers and they appeared ready to help us. At this stage the woman's husband arrived, and we gathered that, while the wife was Czech, he was a Sudeten German. He said he would lose his head if he gave us food. The wife and daughter broke down and cried at this. We left the house quickly and, as we were very fatigued, we went to sleep in a haystack near the house. About 0300 hours 16 Czech policemen headed by one Gestapo man came along armed with bayonetted rifles and pistols, and woke us with shouts of 'Raus.'

We were taken to the gaol in Eipel. After a few hours we were moved to the Gestapo political gaol in Königsgrätz (Hradec Kralove), where we were detained for ten days. Here we were interrogated separately, by a civilian, through an interpreter, Siely being taken first. We had agreed beforehand that, in the event of capture, we should say that we were soldiers, that it was our duty to escape, and that we were heading for Italy. We were asked how we had obtained civilian clothing. We said we had got it from friends, and when we were asked for the names of these friends, we said they had been repatriated. We were well treated by the Feldwebel who seemed to be in charge of about 30 Gestapo men in the gaol. There were officers there, but we never spoke to them. Our interrogation seemed to be a joint one for the Staatspolizei and the Kriminalpolizei. Our fingerprints were taken.

From Königsgrätz we were sent to the Gestapo prison in Prague. The three of us were put into a cell across from which was another Englishman (Pte York, RASC), who had escaped from a working party attached to Stalag IV C (Colditz). We had been seven weeks in gaol. In the same prison were an RAF officer and a Czech pilot serving in the RAF. Later the RAF officer was sent back to Stalag Luft III, but the Czech was kept back. We never saw either of them.

Treatment was very bad in this prison. We had to be up at 0600 hours every day and had to scrub the floor of our cell. The food was damnable. At 0600 hours we got coffee and 150 grammes of bread; at 0900 hours a very thin soup; at 1600 hours coffee; and nothing more for the rest of the day. On arrival we had to stand facing the wall while our particulars were being taken, and those prisoners who did not clean their rooms got from one to four hours of this punishment. We also had to do everything at the double and had to do strenuous exercises, also at the double, in the prison yard. Siely refused to do the exercises. We complained and the Commandant was brought. We said that we had been sent in as political prisoners and that he did not know anything about our being soldiers. In the prison all prisoners are shaved once a week, by a barber who is allowed about one minute to shave each man and has to do 72 men with one safety razor blade. The SS guards threatened to knock us down when we answered them back. We saw them kick many prisoners, but we personally were never kicked. We stood on our dignity, and they showed respect for us. When we were entering the cell for the first time a Czech guard took a packet of cigarettes which Siely had managed to secrete during the search. When asked in Czech to return the cigarettes, the guard gripped Siely by the throat and later fetched an SS trooper who also gripped hold of Siely. The incident closed with the Commandant being fetched. We were eight days in the Gestapo prison and were not interrogated.

From the Gestapo prison we were transferred to the Wehrmacht gaol, also in Prague. Here we were put into a room with nine Russians and ten Englishmen. Conditions were very bad. There were only six straw paliasses in the room, which was lousy. The food was good, but short. The Russians were very generous and shared with us what they had. This gaol was also used for German deserters, of whom there were thousands including officers. We were here for ten days awaiting transport. We were not interrogated. All the other Englishmen left when we did.

We were sent from Prague to Stalag 344 (Lamsdorf) and spent 14 days in the Lager gaol. The Lamsdorf Commandant refused to try us as escapers, as we now belonged to Stalag VIIIA. In time RSM Sheriff, who is one of the finest Englishmen in Germany, got us transferred to the Straf compound, where we spent 21 days.

About 14th June 1944, we were sent to Görlitz, where we were interrogated and tried by the Gerichtsoffizier for escaping. We got 21 days' cells, which, however, we had already served.

Escape.

On our arrival at Stalag VIII A (Görlitz) we decided on a more serious attempt at escape, and realised that we would require to equip ourselves with identity papers. Before our previous attempt

Siely had left with a New Zealand friend the copy of the foreign worker's Ausweis. This Ausweis had been copied and used. Siely had now obtained, in the Straf compound in Lamsdorf, three much more up-to-date documents—a Dienstausweis, certifying that the foreign holder was in employment by a German firm; a Personalausweis (or identity certificate); and an Eisenbahnausweis, permitting the holder to travel by train. We now obtained copies of these documents for both of us, and also had the documents stamped with a replica of the Breslau police stamp. The Personalausweise bore photographs. (Siely had a proper identity card photograph. Evans's was cut from a larger photograph which he had had with him when captured). We managed to get, through a friend, from Frenchmen in the camp two civilian suits, and to have ourselves put on a working party near a railway line. A route to Stettin was worked out for us.

The working party was at a cement pipe factory at Münsterberg (Sheet 116, 3208) about 60 km from Breslau. This Privates' party numbered about 32 and was working about twelve hours a day. We went as NCOs and were detected straight away, which meant that we were closely watched. On the journey to Münsterberg we wore our civilian clothes under our battledress, and on arrival (8th July 1944) hid them in the straw of our paliasses. We worked for only a few days, and had trouble with the Germans because we were not working hard enough.

On 13th July we pulled a bar from the window of a wash house attached to our billet, which adjoined the factory. At 0500 hours on 14th July the guard came in to our sleeping quarters and shone the light in our faces to make sure we were there. At 0515 hours we got up, dressed (with our civilian suits under our battle dress) and went out to the wash house, crossing a corner of the yard to do so. The guard had not noticed the window from which we had removed the bar. In the wash house we took off our battle dress, which a commando was to take away at once so that the Germans should not know we had escaped in civilian clothes. We got out through the window, being partly screened by bushes from the guard who was patrolling the yard of our billet. We crossed a private garden, jumped a fence on to the road, and walked past the main entrance of the factory to the station. We each carried a small attaché case which we had obtained in the Stalag for 150 cigarettes. The train for Breslau left at 0555 hours, and we caught it with about two minutes to spare. We had no difficulty in getting our tickets, and did not have to produce our identity papers.

We had three hours to wait in Breslau and sat in a public park, where we ate our breakfast. We had brought a loaf and some

German margerine from the Lager so that if we had to eat in public—as for example, in the train—we should not be conspicuous. We had also brought French cigarettes to smoke on the journey, as we were travelling as Belgians. We re-booked to Frankfurt-an-der-Oder, leaving Breslau at 1000 hours. There was no incident on this stage of the journey.

At Frankfurt Siely was asked to show his identity papers when getting a ticket to Ederswalde. The girl booking clerk pointed out that the documents said that he was travelling to Stettin. When he complained that he wanted to spend the night with friends in Ederswalde, she produced the ticket. As Evans photograph was not as good as his, Siely produced his own card at another booking office and got another ticket for Ederswalde.

We arrived at Ederswalde about 2200 hours. On the journey Siely asked a German soldier if it was necessary to change on route for Ederswalde. The soldier said 'Parlez vous français?' Siely replied that he was Flemish and the soldier only told him in German that the train went direct to Ederswalde. We spent the night in the open near the Ederswalde aerodrome. It rained during the night.

At 0745 hours next day (15th July) we caught the train for Stettin, arriving without incident about 1100 hours. Leaving the station, which shows signs of bad bomb damage, some passengers showed identity cards. Others did not, and we followed the example of the latter. We crossed the Bahnhof Brücke but soon returned. We had no information about Stettin and walked all round the centre of the town. After a time we met two Poles who wore the P sign, by which we knew that they were not Germanised and therefore could safely be approached. Siely spoke to them in Polish, telling them who we were and asking to be taken to a brothel frequented by foreign sailors. The Poles showed us a brothel in the Kleinoder Strasse, but, as it was morning, the house was closed. The Poles then took us to a Swedish sailor whom we had watched coming off a ship at a quay near the Wesen Strasse. The sailor could not understand us, and we got no satisfaction from him.

At this time we noticed two Germans looking at us suspiciously, and we thought it would be a good time to get rid of our attaché cases. We left the two Poles and made our way on foot through the town to a public park probably north of the Westend See (Pharus Plan of Stettin C4). This was a big public park in which there is an SS barracks. Here we hid our cases.

We were now getting desperate, as it was raining and we had nowhere to sleep. We saw French workers who were obviously on their way back from work to their Lager, and followed them. Siely stopped one, saying 'Parlez vous anglais?' and showing a Stalag identity disc and a letter from home on a prisoner of war card. The Frenchman took us to his Lager, which is probably beside the building marked 'Stadtküche' on Fabrik Strasse (Pharus Plan, G4). He took us in and fed us.

There were about 20 Frenchmen living in the room into which we were taken. They fed and sheltered us for a week. By day we slept in the air raid shelters at the camp. At night we went into the town, accompanied by two Frenchmen, to visit the brothels and Gasthauser in search of a Swedish sailor. The two Frenchmen who accompanied us gave us French workers' papers. One of these men had been hiding in another camp from the Gestapo for a year. Both the men accompanied us to Sweden.

At the end of seven days (on 22nd July) we had to move to another French Lager at the Zuckersiederei adjoining the Neue Speicher (Pharus Plan, G8). We lived here in a bombed house, coming out at night to join the Frenchmen. One of them lived in the Lager while the other lived at the Opel Works, where he was employed.

On 22nd July we went out to Plughaven (Sheet 38, 7516) and had a look round the shipping, but could not get in touch with any Swedes. Siely and one of the Frenchmen then travelled one stop back towards Stettin on the tram, getting off when they saw ships flying the Swedish flag. Near here Siely met two Swedish sailors and on their way to church. He asked to see their papers and they produced their ships books. Siely immediately disclosed his identity, asked for help in getting on to a Swedish ship, and invited the sailors to go to the French lager to discuss the matter. One of the men spoke English. Evans and the other Frenchman now joined the party, and we all went back to the Lager at the Zuckersiederei. Here we said that if we were caught we would be shot; also that if they got us to Sweden, the Swedes could collect certain money. The English-speaking Swede said it would be very hard to get us on board.

For two nights this Swede came to the Lager and spoke with us. His ship was lying at the quay on the Stettin side of the Reine Werdermafen which is the port where Swedish vessels load coal. Their cargoes of iron-ore are discharged at the quay where the ship was lying. The ship was at the outer end of the quay and was anchored some distance off the quay. On the night of 24th July we went from the Lager to the landward end of this quay. After getting off the tram we hid in bushes beside the road till 2300 hours. Keeping to the bushes, we skirted the west side of the quay till we had reached the seaward end, still on the west side. (By doing this we avoided the watchman's post on the landward end of the quay and a Gestapo post further up the quay.) We were accompanied by only one of the Frenchmen. At the end of the quay the English-speaking Swede joined us, having swam from the ship—a distance of 400 or 500 yards—with a lifebelt for the Frenchman, who could not swim. The four of us then swam out to the ship which we boarded by a ladder let down by the other Swede. Next morning the boat moved to the coaling harbour and the first Swede went ashore for the other Frenchman, who got on board by using a Swedish passport.

The Swedes hid us in the air-shaft of the main funnel of the ship, entrance being gained through a cleaning manhole. In the air-shaft we had to lie on a ledge about a foot broad. As the chimney itself got red hot, the atmosphere in the ventilation shaft was stifling, and we were unable to eat the food which was lowered to us. We were, however, kept plentifully supplied with water. On one occasion Siely lost consciousness and fell to a wider ledge about 20 ft. below, hurting his head and arm superficially. After this our helpers were forced to report our presence to the Captain, and we came out early on the morning of 29th July, having been five days in the air-shaft.

By this time we were off Kalmar in Swedish waters. On learning we were English; the Captain said he would put us ashore in the pilot boat. This was done, and next day the local newspapers reported that two Englishmen and two Frenchmen had swum ashore from an unknown vessel. We were well treated by the police in Kalmar and allowed to report to the British Vice-Consul, who got us clothes and sent is to Stockholm. We arrived at the British Legation on 1st August   *(L.G. 9.11.44)*

GUARDSMAN J. FAIRCLOUGH
2619513, Grenadier Guards, No. 2 Commando & HOC
MILITARY MEDAL
and
PRIVATE F. TRIGG
6399046, Royal Sussex Regiment, No. 2 Commando
MILITARY MEDAL

We left our home port on 11th September 1942 and disembarked four days later. After the operation, which took place successfully on the night of 20th September, we climbed up to the huts behind Glomfjord power station. Captain Black then told the rest of us to climb the hill as best we could and get away. We divided into two parties, Smith, O'Brian, Christiansen, Fairclough and Trigg going up to the right and the others to the left. However Captain Black called Smith back to administer morphia to a man who had been wounded.

The four of us carried on for four hours up the mountain till 0600 hours 21st September when we reached the south side of a valley leading to Storglomvatnet Lake. We had abandoned our haversacks and everything but two Colts and our emergency rations. We had two compasses apart from the small compasses in the aid boxes. Christiansen had a large scale map.

The river was deep and rapid and we were on the wrong side of it as the Storglomvatnet lake blocked our way east. Christiansen managed to cross with difficulty but shouted to us not to follow him. He was in much stronger form than we were, he was as agile as a goat and was going strong when last we saw him again. He still had the map. We now had a compass between three of us, Christiansen having taken one with him. We were very tired and hungry and ate all our emergency rations in twenty minutes.

We went on down the south side of a valley and during the afternoon had to lie low because four Messerschmitts and a Heinkel came to look for us. In the evening we were able to cross the river where it reaches the lake and skirted round the north of the lake.

We walked all night and by Tuesday morning 22nd September we reached a road going north and south just to the south of South Bjeliaa Lake. It was an appalling journey through snow and blizzard 5,000 ft. up. On the road O'Brian approached a farm house and came out again with a parcel of food, bread, butter, cheese. After eating this we waded across the stream and up into the woods. O'Brian thought he saw four Germans and we hid in some rocks for an hour. We then marched up the hill (385417 GSGS 4090 K.14) and Sgt O'Brian lost the remaining compass. We continued, but the following evening we found we had gone round in a circle and dropped with exhaustion. We made a big fire and slept there all that night. O'Brian went down to a valley thinking he was going east. We followed him the next day 23rd September but never saw him again. We went to a second farm house at 1200 hours, where they fed us and gave us sandwiches for the journey. They pointed at the valley down which we had come as being the way to Sweden. We had, in fact, come down the valley we had previously gone up. We set off again up the same valley and climbed all that night. At the top we passed a woodman's hut. We climbed over to the other side of the mountain, but we were so exhausted that we went back to the hut which we reached at dawn 24th September We found some stale cheese, coffee and flour in it. Trigg made some doughnuts, fried the cheese and made some coffee. We slept until midday.

Despairing of getting to Sweden without help, we returned once more to the road intending to go to the farm again but got lost. We decided to follow the road north and came to another farm near South Bjeliaa Lake. The man who opened the door spoke English but was very frightened and said there was a German patrol on the road to the south. We carried on north along the road and after a few minutes the farmer followed us on a bicycle and told us to go to his parent's house which he pointed out east of the road. We went there and though they could not understand us, they fed us well and gave us some socks. Then the son arrived and said he would find a guide for next morning. He gave us a haversack each full of food and a bottle of milk. He took us a mile further up to another farm from where bedding, pillow and blankets were provided for us in a loft.

At 0500 hours 25th September he took us to the top of a hill, gave us a small compass on top of a pen and told us to march east. He drew a rough map showing the route to the north of a lake where we should see some telegraph poles. We were told to follow the line of these, but not too closely, as there was a hut nearby where there was thought to be a Quisling. When we got near the poles, we saw in the snow some tracks of commando boots which we followed but these came to an end and we never picked them up again.

When we got to the Mo–Bod road we had some trouble crossing the river. A motor cyclist passed by on the road, we ducked and were not seen. We eventually found a boat and crossed the river. We made a fire on top of the hill that night. It was very cold indeed with snow about six inches deep. We went to sleep but kept waking up with cold and making the fire up. The following dawn 26th September we again set out climbing a very high peak about 5,000 feet. It was sheer rock and we were scared, sometimes snow up to our chests. We eventually got down into a valley intending to keep to valleys in future. We followed this valley down to the Junkerdal–Craddis road. There we found a farm and they gave us food. It was at this farm that we met a man who was to guide us over the frontier. He took us to a friend's house a mile along the stream. There we had another feed and went to bed at 1500 hours. The guide went out to make arrangements to get us across that night.

He woke us up at 1800 hours giving us another meal and sandwiches. We left at 0900 hours and went up to his sister's house at Skiati. We had more food there at 2200 hours, and left at 2300 hours. The guide and his brother-in-law then accompanied us over the frontier and left us three hundred yards the other side. This was at 0230 hours, 27th September They told us to follow the telegraph poles for eight miles to some friends of theirs at Merkenes. The country here is very wooded and we could not have found this house unless we had been directed. We met nine Norwegian refugees here.

We were taken down the Lakes by motor boat and rowing boats to Jackvik where we stayed two days and were disinfected. This consisted of a Turkish bath, having our hair closely cropped, the hair scraped off our bodies and our clothes fumigated. Then we were taken to Jokkmokk where we were interrogated by a Swedish Intelligence Officer Lieut Levi. We said we had escaped from a prisoner of war camp in Norway. We afterwards discovered that there was no such camp for British prisoners of war but the Swedes did not ask too many questions. Orders then came from Stockholm that we were to be passed through immediately. We were taken to the Legation there and left by plane on 6th October arriving at Leuchars 7th October 1942. *(L.G. 7.1.43)*

PRIVATE V. P. HARDING
(See under Corporal E. Douglas.)

LANCE SERGEANT ALFRED CLARENCE SEARSON
(See under L/Sgt Richard Bradley.)

LANCE CORPORAL RICHARD WILLIAM SIMS
2033171, Somerset Light Infantry (Prince Albert's) attached to Special Service Brigade, No. 2 Commando
MILITARY MEDAL
and
CORPORAL GEORGE RUSSELL WHEELER
6899188, Royal Sussex Regt. attached to Special Service Bde..
MILITARY MEDAL

These two soldiers took part in the Combined Operation against St. Nazaire on the 27th March 1942. When it became clear that re-embarkation was impossible, they were instructed to fight their way into the new town in the hope of getting into the country. Early next day they succeeded in entering the new town, where they hid until midnight in a dried up drain underneath a house, which they later found to be next door to the German Kommandatur. In the moonlight they then made their way through the streets and into the open country, where, whilst hiding in a haystack they were discovered by a Frenchman, who took them to a farmhouse, where they were given food, clothes and money.

For the next fortnight they made their way towards the line of demarcation, being sheltered, fed and directed at the various farm houses at which they called. On the 13th April, they were conducted to the River La Creuse by the sister of a farmer who had previously sheltered them, and who was herself trying to escape from German occupied France. Dodging the patrols they succeeded in crossing the river in spite of the fact that the water came up to their chests and was flowing swiftly.

They had their clothes dried at a nearby farm and continued their journey south to Chaumussay where, at another farm, they received further hospitality in the form of food and shelter.

From here they went to La Bousse where they discovered a château, the owner of which was very pro-British. After giving them a good dinner and a room in his private suite, he gave them 200 francs and directed them to Châteauroux which they reached by bus.

As the bus was entering Châteauroux, they saw from a window a notice 'English spoken here' outside a cafe. They went in, and the owner who had previously lived in England found out the train times and fares to Toulouse for them, gave them wine and showed them where to buy bread. On the way to the bakers they met a Belgian boy of 16 or 17 who had been living in the refugee camp in the town and who asked whether he might accompany them. They consented to this, and with the Belgian, who bought the tickets for them, they took the train to Toulouse the next morning. In Toulouse they were put in touch with an organisation which arranged for their eventual return to this country. *(L.G. 29.9 42)*

PRIVATE F. TRIGG
(See under Guardsman J. Fairclough)

CORPORAL G. R. WHEELER
(See under Lance Corporal R. W. Sims.)

GUNNER MARTIN HENRY WINTERBURN
4801255, Royal Artillery, No. 6 Commando
MILITARY MEDAL

1. Capture:
I was captured at Mateur (Tunis) on the 19th or 20th December 1942. I was wounded in the elbow.

2. Camps in which imprisoned:
Transit Camp in Sicily.   December 1942.
Campo 70 (Fermo).   December 1942–March 1943.
Campo 65 (Bussetto).   March–September 1943.

Escapes

Stalag VIII B (Lamsdorf)	15th September 1943. (Germany 1:100,000, Sheet 117, 6703).
Also working parties at:	
Blechhammer (Silesia)	February 1944. (Sheet 117, 1981).
Oppeln	March 1944. (Sheet 117, 9615).

3. Attempted Escapes:
(a) From Blechhammer. In February 1944 I was with a working party employed at an oil refinery at Blechhammer (Sheet 117, 1981). I had no papers, so meant my escape to be in the nature of a reconnaissance for future attempts. I escaped with a man named 'Texas,' an American deserter from the USA Navy, and now in the South African Forces. We were jumping trains, and 'Texas' fell off and was injured. Later he was caught and taken back to Stalag VIII B, where he was given 14 days' cells. I was caught at Oppeln (Sheet 117, 9615), taken to the prison there, and questioned by the Criminal Police. Then I was taken back to Blechhammer, and confined in a dark cell for 30 days. On release, I was put in a labour battalion, (Kgf-U-Dau, Bn 21). I refused to work saying that I was a Corporal, and was sent back to Stalag VIII B. In March 1944 I was sent to work at a stone quarry near Oppeln.
(b) From Quarry near Oppeln. I stole civilian clothes, and traded chocolate and cigarettes with the guards for money. About the middle of March 1944 I got away from the quarry and hid in the woods till darkness fell. I travelled by train from Oppeln to Breslau (Sheet 104, 3264), and in Breslau I managed to steal a bicycle on which I rode to Frankfurt-an-der-Oder (Sheet 66, 6901). I left the bicycle outside the city, and went by train to Stettin (Sheet 38, 7021). I was arrested in the station, and sent back to Stalag VIII B, at the end of March 1944.

4. Escape:
In Stalag VIII B I managed to obtain an Ausweis with photograph and temporary identification papers made out in the name of Marcel Flamming. I was to pose as a Belgian electrician, and to travel openly as a foreign worker. I had myself sent to a working party at Oppeln, on 5th June 1944, while I was still awaiting trial for the previous escape. I worked at the warehouses of a civilian food distribution centre, belonging to the firm of 'Rigol Waluga.' I met two other men who were planning to escape, one of whom was awaiting Court Martial. We bought civilian clothes from a Pole at Oppeln, and sold our few valuables, some food and cigarettes to the guards for German money. I had about 300 Rm. out of which I

paid the Pole for my clothing. We had obtained suitcases, which we hid in the bath-house.

On 25th June 1944 we went to the baths, which were situated out of sight of the sentry position, and changed our clothes. We had stolen the key of the postern and walked out, making our way to the station where we bought tickets for Breslau (Sheet 104, 3264). I was going to Klagenfurt (Austria) (Italy 1.250,000 Sheet 7B, D 28) and the others to Cologne (Germany 1.100,000 Sheet 94B). At Breslau we changed trains and separated. I travelled on the Berlin–Vienna express via Breslau, Oppeln, Ratibor (Sheet 127, 1250), Moravska-Ostrava (Czechoslovakia, 1:75,000, Sheet 4060) to Vienna (Germany 1:250,000, Sheet 0 49, X 49). I could understand and speak enough German to pass muster when asked for papers on the train.

I arrived in Vienna at about 0820 hrs on 26th June 1944, and changed from the Sudbahnhof to the Ostbahnhof, where I took a ticket to Klagenfurt. I had time to spare, so went by tram into the city, where I was caught in an RAF raid and had to spend 1½ hours in a shelter. I noticed considerable damage in an area which was cordoned off.

My train left at about 1100 hours. There was no control on this train, but a civilian woman questioned me and asked where I was going. My papers appeared to satisfy her. I arrived at Klagenfurt in the evening, and went into the hills, where I destroyed my papers and spent the night. I was heading for the Loibl Pass on the Austrian–Yugoslav border (Italy 1:250,000, Sheet 7B, D 26) and reached the River Drava (Sheet 7B, D 27) towards evening on 29th June 1944. There was a railway bridge and a foot-bridge across the river, both of which were guarded. The river was about 300 yards wide and fast flowing, with built-up banks. I kept the bridge under observation until dark, when I entered the river. The strong current carried me downstream a long way before I was able to cross to the far side.

Next day I met a French prisoners of war working party. An old man noticed the tattoo marks on my hands, and I declared myself as an English officer and asked for the Partisans. He said they were about twelve miles away, but later I found that they had gone into the hills after blowing up some bridges.

For two days it poured with rain, and I asked for help at a farmhouse. They directed me to a Gasthof near the Loibl Pass where I found a girl who spoke English. She had worked in Baker Street, in London, and I had difficulty in convincing her of my status, as I had told her I came from London, from the King's Cross district, which I know only vaguely. She wanted me to give myself up, and said she would inform the police. I saw a patrol in the distance, so took myself off to the hills.

That night the rain drove me to look for shelter and I hid in a shed attached to the Gasthof. When I awoke the girl had brought me bread and milk, and told me to leave at once. She gave me directions for crossing the pass. In the mountains I was fired on by a patrol, but got away unhurt. After dark I was hidden under a bridge in the valley, by some Slovene woman and later at night the daughter of one of the women took me to the Yugoslav Partisans. I had no means of identifying myself, but as I recognised the Partisans' weapons, battledress, and gas capes as being British, they seem satisfied.

We had fights with the patrols, and later I met two British Intelligence Officers, an English S/Ldr. RAF, and two Corporals of the Royal Corps of Signals. I spent two days with them, in the district south of Ljubljana (Yugoslavia) (Italy 1.250,000, Sheet 7B, D 31) and wanted to stay there, but a wireless message ordered me to go to Italy. I was guided by a Russian girl, and after two days we met a patrol of British, American and Russian officers and men, who sent me on with a runner. Fifteen days later I reached liberated territory and went on alone to Toplice (Yugoslavia 1:250,000, Sheet Y2, D 88), where I met a Captain (Hussar Regiment) who kept me for three days. I was then sent by lorry to a point about 50 miles from Toplice, with some American Air Corps personnel. We joined some New Zealand and American air crews, and were flown to Bari on 25th July 1944. From there we went to Naples and sailed for U.K. on 29th July 1944 arriving at Liverpool on 13th August 1944. *(L.G. 1.3.45)*

Bibliography

BUCKLEY, C.. Norway The Commandos, Dieppe: *HMSO*
CHANT-SEMPILL, S.. St. Nazaire Commando: *Book Club Associates*
CUNNINGHAM, ADMIRAL A.: A Sailor's Odyssey: *Hutchinson*
DUPREY & DUPREY: The Encylopedia of Military History: *Harper & Row*
DURNFORD-SLATER, BRIG.: Commando: *Kimber*
FERGUSON, B.. The Watery Maze: *Collins*
HMSO: Combined Operations 1940–1942: *HMSO*
LADD, J.: Commandos and Rangers of WWII: *MacDonald & Jane*
LEWIN, R.: Rommel As Military Commander: *Batsford*
MASON, D.. Raid on St. Nazaire: *MacDonald*
MELLOR, J.: Forgotten Heroes—The Canadians at Dieppe: *Methuen*
PHILLIPS, C. E. L.: The Greatest Raid of All: *Heinemann*
PHILLIPS, C. E. L.: Springboard To Victory: *Heinemann*
REYBURN, W.. Rehearsal For Invasion: *Harrap*
ROBERTSON, T.. The Shame & The Glory—Dieppe: *McClelland & Stewart*
ROSKILL, S. W., CAPT.. The War At Sea—Vols. I, II: *HMSO*
ST. GEORGE-SAUNDERS, H.. The Green Beret—The Story of the Commandos: *Michael Joseph*
ST. GEORGE-SAUNDERS, H.. The Red Beret—The Story of The Parachute Regiment 1940–1945: *Michael Joseph*

Commando Gallantry Awards of World War II

Index

Name	Rank	Unit	Award	Page
Abbott, J. H. R.	Gnr	3 Cdo	MM	41
Adderton, V	Pte	3 & 14 Cdo	MM	41
Addington, R. T. C.	Capt	13 (HAC) Regt RHA, 5 Cdo	MC	231
Aird, W.	Pte	KOSB att 1 Cdo	MM	272
Alderson, J.	Capt	Seaforth, SS Tps	MC	194
Aldis, A. G.	Cpl	RM	MM	94
Aldridge, D. L. S. St M.	Maj	41 Indep Cdo RM	MC	290
———	Maj	RM 42 Cdo	Bar to MC	289
———			MBE	288
Allen, A. J.	Lt	RM	MC	231
Allen, E. P	Pte	S Wales, 1 Cdo	MM	273
Allen, H. R.	Cpl	Provost Coy RMAA & Cdo Bde	MM	126
Allen, M. R. H.	Capt	Black Watch att 9 Cdo	MC	140
Allender, J.	Pte	1 DWR, 6 Cdo & SBS	MM	42
———	Sgt	1 DWR, 6 Cdo	Bar to MM	68
Amesbury, A. E.	Tpr	44th Recce Regt, 2 Cdo	MM	159
Anchor, J. R.	L/Cpl	Gren Gds, 2 Cdo	MM	94
Andrews, A. M.	L/Cpl	Lond Rifle Bde, 3 Cdo	MM	69
Angus, D. C.	Capt	RM, 40 (RM) Cdo	MC	84
Anscombe, A. E.	CSM	30 Bn RM	MM	238
Appleyard, F	Mne	7 Bn RM	MM	126
Aslett, A. R.	Brig	72 Inf Bde, SS Bde HQ	DSO	266
Avery, H.	Sgt	27 Bn RM	MM	239
Aylett, B. McG.	Sgt	40 (RM) Cdo	MM	159
Baker, A.	L/Cpl	Grenadier Guards, 1 Cdo	DCM	63
Balloche, F	Sjt	10 (Inter-Allied) Cdo, att 4 Cdo	MM	42
Banks, R. D.	Pte	RWK, 3 Cdo	MM	292
Barks, W J.	Mne	42 RM Cdo	MM	273
Barnes, E.	Bdr	RA (S/L) att 1 Cdo	MM	273
Barnes, G.	CSM	Gren Gds, 8 Cdo & 1 SBS	MM	95
———	CSM	SBS	Bar to MM	93
Barnett, D. S.	Capt	RM	MC	141
Barr, E.	Cpl	HLI, 11 Cdo & 2 SBS	MM	95
Bartholomew, P I.	Lt-Col	Som LI, 3 Cdo	DSO	227
Barton, B. J.	Capt	Recce Regt, RAC, SS Tps	DSO	136
Barton, H.	L/Sgt	Manch Regt, 9 Cdo	MM	160
Bassett-Wilson, P	Lt	R Innis Fus, SS Tps	MC	141
Beadle, I. N. N	Maj	45 RM Cdo	MC	194
Beadle, J. C.	Lt	RM, Land Forces Adriatic, 40 RM Cdo	MC	84
Beattie, J. S.	Cpl	R Scots, 1 Cdo	MM	69

Commando Gallantry Awards of World War II

Name	Rank	Unit	Award	Page
Beaven, H. F. G.	CSM	RM, 40 & 45 RM Cdo	MM	240
Bennett, H.	TSM	40 & 45 RM Cdo	MM	240
Berrisford, P. J.	Sgt	RA (Fd), att 6 Cdo	MM	95
Bevan, G. R.	Mne	RM	MM	42
Bircher, C. A. D	Lt	SAUDF	MC	194
Black, G. D.	Lt	S Lancs Regt	MC	116
Black, J. W.	TSM	48 (RM) Cdo	MM	241
Blackwell, A.	L/Cpl	S Lancs Regt, 1 SS Bn & SOE	DCM	64
Blair, D. A.	Capt	Seaforth Hldrs §	MBE	139
——	Maj	5 Bn Seaforth Hldrs, 11 Cdo	MC	231
Blake, A. L.	Maj	HQ 2 SS Bde (RM), SB 94, 45 RM Cdo	MC	84
Blake, J. P.	Capt	RM	MC	141
Blunden, C. H.	Cpl	4 Cdo	MM	42
Blunden, S.	Cpl	See Blunden, C. H.		
Bolden, S.	L/Cpl	Camerons (12 Cdo), 1 Cdo	MM	117
Booth, J. H.	Cpl	Seaforth Hldrs, 1 SBS	DCM	89
Bostock, T.	L/Cpl	S Lancs, 9 Cdo	MM	160
Bradley, J. W. E.	Capt	SS Bde, 13th Corps, 40 RM Cdo	MC	141
Bradley, R.	L/Sgt	R Berkshire Regt, 2 Cdo	MM	295
Bradshaw, L. C.	Mne	RM	MM	43
Bray, H. A.	Capt	2 Dorsets, 5 Cdo	MC	31
Breen, T. E.	Mne	40 RM Cdo	MM	43
Bremner, G. C.	Sgt	1 Lond Scot, SBS & 8 Cdo	MM	96
Brittlebank, J.	Bdr	RA, 3 & 8 Cdo & 1 SBS	DCM	65
Brodison, S. J.	CSM	R Irish Fus, HOC, 12 & 10 Cdo	MM	43
Brooking, W. M. J.	CSM	30 Bn RM	MM	241
Brown, A.	Sgt	45 RM Cdo	Bar to MM	200
Brown, J.	Pte	Ex A&SH, 5 Cdo	MM	295
Brown, R. H.	L/Sgt	Lond Scot, 2 Cdo	MM	69
Brownfield, J. E.	Sgt	48 RM Cdo	MM	242
Bryan, G. J.	Lt	RE, 9 & 11 Cdo	MC	85
Bryce, C. K.	Cpl	47 RM Cdo	MM	200
Bullock, D. C.	Cpl	41 RM Cdo	MM	161
Burford, N. A.	Cpl	RE, 7 Cdo	MM	292
Burgess, S. C.	Mne	48 RM Cdo	MM	201
Burn, M. C.	Capt	KRRC, 2 Cdo	MC	31
Burt, H.	Capt	Norfolk, SS, 4 Cdo	MC	194
Burton, F. G.	L/Cpl	45 RM Cdo	MM	242
Butler, H. H. C.	Cpl	S Lancs Regt, 1 SBS & 11 & 9 Cdo	MM	70
Butler, R. H.	L/Sgt	R Norfolk Regt, 1 Cdo	MM	44
Byrne, P. J.	Sgt	3 Bn Irish Gds, 4 Cdo	MM	243
——			MBE	288
Calder, H. W.	Pte	RAMC, 40 RM Cdo & HOC	DCM	151
Callf, L. S.	Capt	RWK, 9 Cdo	MC	141
——	Capt	RWK, 9 Cdo	Bar to MC	139
Cameron, R. A. C.	Capt	9 Cdo	MC	142

Index

Carr, E. L. K. A.	Capt	RA, 4 Cdo	MC	214
Carr, F. A.	Sgt	RE, 5 Cdo	DCM	36
Carr, R. P.	2Lt	52 ATk Regt, RA	MC	31
——	Capt	RA	MBE	288
Challington, W A.	Sgt	Cameron Hldrs, 2 Cdo	DCM	37
Chant, S. W	Lt	Gordon Hldrs, 5 Cdo	MC	32
——			OBE	288
Chapman, K. H.	Pte	Beds & Herts Regt, 3 Cdo	MM	161
Chappell, A. B.	Mne	42 (RM) Cdo	MM	274
Charlwood, H.	Mne	46 (RM) Cdo	MM	243
Christie, T. J.	Lt	R Signals, 1 Cdo Bde Sig Tp	MC	232
Christopher, R. W.	Cpl	Beds & Herts, HQ 1 Cdo Bde	MM	275
Churchill, J. M. T F	Capt	2 Manch Regt	MC	32
——	Lt-Col	Manch Regt, 2 Cdo	DSO	136
——	Lt-Col	Manch Regt, 2 Cdo	Bar to DSO	79
Clapton, J. F	Lt	Cameronians, 6 Cdo	MC	233
Clark, J.	Gnr	RA, 2 Cdo	MM	292
Clark, R. T	Cpl	48 RM Cdo	MM	201
Clarke, S. C.	Pte	3 Cdo	MM	44
Cleasby-Thompson, P	Maj	1 Bn Para, AAC, 2 (Para) Cdo	MC	60
——	Maj	Lancs Fus, AAC	MBE	288
Coates, J. G.	Capt	Int Corps att HQ SO(M) 10 & 30 Cdo	DSO	82
Cogger, D. J.	Lt	RM	MC	195
Coker, J. T	Pte	RWK att 1 Cdo	MM	277
Cole, R. W.	Cpl	41 RM Cdo	MM	161
Convery, J. J.	Sgt	40 RM Cdo	DCM	152
Cooper, C.	Sgt	2 Bn Cheshire Regt, 40 RM Cdo	MM	70
Cooper, D. E.	Fus	Lancs Fus, 2 Cdo	MM	162
Cooper, J. M.	L/Sgt	2 Bn Scots Gds, SAS Bde	DCM	90
Cooper, S.	Sgt	46 RM Cdo	MM	202
Copland, W C.	Maj	S Lancs Regt, 2 Cdo	DSO	29
Coulson, L. N.	Maj	DLI, 4 Cdo	MC	233
Courtney, G. B.	Capt	RWK, SBS	MBE	59, 60
Courtney, G. B.	Maj	RWK, SBS	MC	61
Courtney, R. J. A.	Capt	Q Westminster Rif (KRRC) SBS	MC	86
Coutts, J. D.	Cpl	Y&LR, 52 ME Cdo	MM	301
——	L/Sgt	Y&LR, 52 ME Cdo	Bar to MM	199
Cowap, D. H.	Lt	RA (Fd), 1 Cdo	MC	61
Craft, A. J.	Pte	3 Cdo	MM	44
Cramer, J.	L/Cpl	RAMC, 9 Cdo	MM	162
Cregan, J. C. F.	Capt	RAMC, 41 RM Cdo	MC	195
Cretney, F. G.	Mne	30 Bn RM, 30 RM Cdo	MM	243
Crooks, J.	Sgt	41 RM Cdo	MM	127
Crooks, R. J.	Sgt	N Somerset Yeo, 52 Cdo	DCM	91
Crowe, J.	L/Sgt	Seaforth Hldrs, att 1 Cdo	MM	277
Cunningham, H.	L/Cpl	RAMC, 4 Cdo	MM	218
Cunningham, J.	Dvr	3 Cdo	DCM	37
Cunningham, W	Capt	41 RM Cdo	DSO	124
D'Arcy, E. J.	Capt	RAMC, 9 Cdo	MC	143

327

Name	Rank	Unit	Award	Page
Daniels, S.	L/Bdr	RA (Fd), 9 Cdo	MM	163
Darlington, K. C.	Pte	Border Regt, 12 Cdo	MM	118
Davidson, D. M.	Capt	SWB, att SS Tps	MC	62
Davies, M. A. W.	Capt	Northamptons, 9 Cdo	MC	143
—			MBE	289
Davis, T.	L/Sgt	KOYLI, 6 Cdo	MM	71
Davison, J. C.	Cpl	RAC, 3 Cdo	MM	164
Dawson, J. J. Y.	Capt	1 Cdo	MC	269
Dawson, R. W. P.	Lt-Col	Loyals, 4 Cdo	DSO	192
—			CdG	293
Day, S. A.	Capt	R Signals, 2 Cdo	MC	32
De Naurois, The Rev R.	Chpln	4 Cdo (French Army)	MC	290
De Nobriga, D. J.	Sgt	Q Westminsters, 2 Cdo	DCM	66
Deacon, W. G.	Sgt	RM	MM	244
Dean, R. F	Sgt	3 RM HAA Regt	MM	127
Deery, S.	Sgt	R Innis Fus, 12 Cdo	MM	45
Delap, P.	Capt	RAMC, 40 RM Cdo	MC	290
Denham, J. S.	L/Sgt	Sherwood Foresters, 3 Cdo	MM	165
Dexter, J.	Capt	RM	MC	234
Dickson, J. J.	Maj	9 R Sussex, 5 Cdo	MC	269
—	Maj	S Foresters, att 9 R Sussex §	Bar to MC	268
Dobbs, C.	Sgt	S Staffs, 6 Cdo	MM	244
Dockerill, A. H.	L/Sgt	RA, 1 Cdo	DCM	38
Donnell, P. M.	Maj	47 RM Cdo	DSO	227
—	Lt-Col	47 RM Cdo	CdG	210
—	Capt	47 RM Cdo	CdG Star	294
Douglas, E.	Cpl	Liverpool Scot, 2 Cdo	MM	296
Dowling, J.	Cpl	DLI, 3 Cdo	MM	127
Downey, J. J.	BSM	RA (Fd) att 1 Cdo	MM	278
Dransfield, G. D.	Dvr	RASC, 2 Cdo	MM	96
Duffy, W. P	Sgt	1 SBS, 1 Bn SAS Regt & 8 Cdo	MM	303
—	Gdsm	Gren Gds, 1 SBS, SAS & 8 Cdo	Bar to MM	68
Duggan, J. F.	Mne	RM	MM	96
Dunbar, W.	Sgt	A&SH, 11 Cdo & 1 SBS	MM	71
Duncan, G. I. A.	Capt	Black Watch	MC	86
—	Lt	Black Watch	Bar to MC	62
Dunn, E.	Capt	RM	MC	214
Dunne, P R. R.	Capt	R Horse Gds, att SS Tps	MC	144
Durnford-Slater, J. F.	Lt-Col	3 Cdo	DSO	115
—	Lt-Col	RA, 3 Cdo	Bar to DSO	123
Durrant, T. F	Sgt	RE att Cdo	VC	24
Easton, N. K.	Capt	46 RM Cdo	MC	234
Ecrepont, E. W.	Capt	RM	MC	144
Ellis, D. C.	Cpl	2 SBS & 6 Cdo	MM	72
Ellis, W. E.	L/Sgt	47 RM Cdo	MM	202
Ellwood, W. C.	L/Sgt	Essex Regt, 2 Cdo	DCM	153
Emsley, R.	Mne	47 RM Cdo	MM	202
England, J. P.	CSM	43, 46, & 47 RM Cdo	DCM	216

Index

Name	Rank	Unit	Award	Page
Ephraums, M. J.	Capt	RM	MC	124
Essex, N. A.	Maj	RM	MC	235
Esther, R. W. W.	Sgt	47 & 42 RM Cdo	MM	219
Etches, E. E.			OBE	288
Etches, W. W.	Lt	R Warwicks Regt, 3 Cdo	MC	33
Evans, C. G.	Cpl	1 Cdo	MM	304
Evans, J.	SQMS	Welsh Gds att SBS	BEM	104
Evans A. W.	L/Sgt	Royal Fus, 3 Cdo	MM	202
Fairclough, J.	Gdsm	Gren Gds, 2 Cdo & HOC	MM	314
Farquhar, J. K.	Pte	Seaforth Hldrs, 9 Cdo	MM	165
Feebery, C.	SSM	1 SAS Regt, 8 Cdo 1 SBS & SAS	DCM	66
Fellowes, H. D.	Lt-Col	Att. 42 RM Cdo	DSO	267
——			CB	287
Fenton, E.	Cpl	42 RM Cdo	MM	278
Fenwick, J. L.	C/Sgt	45 RM Cdo	MM	245
Ferguson, J. McI. McL.	TSM	Cameronians att 5 Cdo	MM	279
Fielding, W G.	2Lt	1 Bn R Irish Fus, 6 Cdo	MC	145
Findley, F G.	SgtMaj	RASC, 6 Cdo	MM	97
Finney, W	Tpr	4 Cdo	MM	45
Fitzpatrick, M. B.	Cpl	RAC, 3 Cdo	MM	118
Flower, R. T	Capt	RM	MC	214
Flunder, D. J.	Capt	48 RM Cdo	MC	214
Flynn, J.	L/Cpl	KOSB, 3, 4, & 7 Cdo	MM	46
Foot, J. P	Lt	Dorset Regt	MBE	60
Foote, J. W.	H/Capt	Cdn Chpln Svcs, R Hamilton LI	VC	25
Ford, D.	Maj	Black Watch, 7 Cdo	MC	270
——			MBE	289
Forfar, J. O.	Capt	RAMC, 47 RM Cdo	MC	215
Franks, B. F M.	Lt-Col	2 SAS Regt, SAS Bde & 1 Bde	DSO	30
Franks, B. F M.	Maj	R Signals (Mx Yeo), HQ SS Bde	MC	145
Fraser, A. J.	WO2	RAC, att Raiding Forces	BEM	104
French, R. D.	Sgt	43 RM Cdo	MM	97
——	Sgt	RM, 43 RM Cdo	Bar to MM	158
Fynn, F W.	Maj	3 Bn Lond Scot att 12 Cdo & 3 Cdo	MC	116
——	Lt-Col	Lond Scot Inf, 8 Cdo	Bronze Star	189
Gadsden, D. R.	Mne	47 RM Cdo	MM	203
Gallon, T. C. D.	Sgt	43 RM Cdo	MM	97
Gardner, D. H. G.	Sgt	47 RM Cdo	MM	203
Garner Jones, J.	Capt	See Jones, J. G.		
Gelder, J. W.	L/Bdr	RA (Coast), 2 Cdo	MM	98
Gibbon, J. D.	Capt	Border Regt, 46 RM Cdo	MC	235
——			MBE	289
Gibson, G. M.	Pte	5 Cdo	MM	279
Gibson, R. R.	Lt	Cheshire Regt, SS Tps	MC	146
Gill, R.	Rfn	Cameronians, 2 Cdo	MM	292
Goldstein, I.	Lt	SAUDF	MC	195

Goodall, W.	L/Sgt	Border Regt, att 6 Cdo	MM	98
Gorman, J. J. T	Cpl	40 RM Cdo	MM	166
Gornall, J.	Gnr	RA, Cdo, 11 Cdo	MM	166
Gourlay, B. I. S.	Capt	RM, 43 RM Cdo	MC	86
—			MBE	289
—			OBE	288
Gray, A.	Fus	R Fus, 2 Cdo	MM	166
Gray, P. E.	L/Cpl	King's Regt, SS, 6 Cdo	MM	203
Gray, T M.	Lt-Col	46 (RM) Cdo	MC	195
—	Lt-Col	46 RM Cdo	DSO	228
Gray, W. N.	Maj	45 RM Cdo	DSO	192
—	Lt-Col	45 RM Cdo	Bar to DSO	226
Green, N.	Mne	45 RM Cdo	MM	204
Griffin, J. A.	Mne	47 RM Cdo	MM	204
Groves, E. R. C.	L/Cpl	RASC, 2 Cdo	MM	167
Hadfield, J. W.	Mne	41 RM Cdo	MM	167
Haines, G. E.	TSM	E Surrey, 2 Cdo	DCM	38
Halley, J.	S/Sgt	RAMC, BMA Force 281	BEM	105
Hambleton, A.	Capt	RM	MC	235
Harden, H. E.	L/Cpl	RAMC	VC	225
Hardey, R. G. K.	Capt	HLI, 6 Cdo	MC	196
Harding, V P.	Pte	Glosters, 2 Cdo	MM	296
Hardy, C. R.	Lt-Col	46 RM Cdo	DSO	228
—	Lt-Col	46 RM Cdo	Bar to DSO	191
—	Brig	RM, 3 Cdo Bde	2nd Bar to DSO	266
—			CBE	287
—			CB	287
—			KCB	287
Harrington, J. L.	L/Cpl	RUR, 2 Cdo	MM	46
Harris, I.	Cpl	45 RM Cdo	MM	246
Harrison, A.	Cpl	RASC	BEM	105
Harrison, A. H.	L/Sgt	RE, 6 Cdo	MM	246
Harrison, T.	Sgt	45 RM Cdo	MM	105
Hatton, C.	L/Sjt	East Lancs Regt	MM	204
Hausmann, F S.	Dvr	RASC, 2 Cdo	DCM	91
Haw, The Rev R.	Chpln	47 & 45 Cdo	DSC	230
Hawkins, K. S.	CSM	40 RM Cdo	MM	168
Haydon, J. C.	Brig	SS Bde	Bar to DSO	113
Haydon, J. C.			OBE	288
Haydon, J. C.			CB	287
Haydon, J. C.	Lt-Col	2 Bn Irish Guards	Bronze Star	53
Haydon, J. C.	Brig	Foot Gds §	LofM	293
Hazell, J. H.	Mne	46 RM Cdo	MM	248
Head, C. S.	Capt	RA, 3 Cdo	MC	124
Hedderman, J. W.	L/Sgt	2/6 Aust Inf Bn, 3 Aust Div	MM	280
Hellings, P. W. C.	Maj	40 RM Cdo	MC	146
—			DSC	289
—			CB	287
Henderson, J. P. L.	Maj	RE, SS Tps	MC	146
Hendry, B. J.	Pte	R Berks Regt, 2 Cdo	MM	292

Index

Herbert, R. G.	Pte	5 Northamptons, 3 Cdo	MM	46
——	Sgt	3 Cdo	DCM	116
Herbert, T. H.	L/Cpl	RAMC att 42 RM Cdo	MM	280
Heron, J. G.	Lt	2 Dorsets, 5 Cdo	MC	33
Hodgson, G.	L/Cpl	Black Watch, 3 Cdo	MM	205
Hodkinson, J.	L/Sgt	Lancs Fus, 9 Cdo	MM	168
Hoggett, W.	L/Cpl	R Signals, 2 Cdo	DCM	291
Honey, P	Pte	Cameron Hldrs, 2 Cdo	MM	47
Hook, R. S.	Chpln	43 RM Cdo	MC	146
Hooper, R. H.	Capt	King's Regt, 2 Cdo	MC	125
Hope, W M.	Sgt	40 RM Cdo	MM	168
Hopkins, F. W.	Pte	3 Cdo	MM	47
Hopkins, L. W.	L/Sgt	Mx Regt, 9 Cdo	DCM	153
Hopson, D. C.	Maj	RAC, 3 Cdo	MC	196
——	Maj	RAC, HQ 1 Cdo Bde & 3 Bde	DSO	229
Horsefield, H.	Sgt	47 RM Cdo	MM	205
Houghton, R. D.	Maj	HOC, 40 RM Cdo	MC	34
——			OBE	288
——			CB	287
Howard, J. D.	L/Cpl	RAMC, 2 Cdo	MM	99
Hubbard, S.	CSM	Worcs Regt, 3 Cdo	DCM	237
Hudspith, J. C. D.	Capt	43 RM Cdo	MC	86
Hughes, G. W. S.	L/Cpl	RAMC, 9 Cdo	MM	169
Hughes, J. H.	Mne	7 Bn, RM, SBS	MM	128
Hughes, R. G.	Cpl	DCLI, 3 Cdo	MM	128
Hugill, J. A. C.	Lt	30 Cdo	DSC	193
Humble, W. McC.	L/Cpl	QO Cameron Hldrs, 2 Cdo	MM	170
Hunter, T. P	Cpl	RM att SS Tps, 43 RM Cdo	VC	133
Hunter-Gray, J. S.	Lt	RA, 4 Cdo	MC	216
Hurwitz, S. M.	Sgt	22 Cdn Armd Regt (CGG)	MM	248
Hutton, G. F	WO2	Essex Regt, 2 Cdo	DCM	291
Irving, W. H.	Fus	R Fus att 1 Cdo	MM	281
Jackson, H. C.	Sgt	S Staffs, 9 Cdo	MM	171
Jackson, J.	Cpl	King's Regt , 2 Cdo	DCM	292
James, C. V.	Capt	R Signals, SS Bde, 2 Cdo	MC	147
James, W. T. B.	Lt	Welsh Regt, 4 Cdo, 47 RM Cdo	MC	197
Jenkins, W. G.	Lt	43 RM Cdo	MC	148
Jennings, T A.	Pte	Beds & Herts, 3 Cdo	MM	206
Johnson, G. A. T. W.	Cpl	40 RM Cdo	MM	171
Johnson, J.	Cpl	Gordon Hldrs, 12 Cdo	MM	48
Jones, B. V	Mne	23 LAA Bty, RM, 2 RM AA Regt	DCM	92
Jones, C.	Sgt	Cameron Hldrs, 2 Cdo	MM	48
Jones, G.	Sgt	5 (I) RM Bty	MM	206
Jones, H.	Mne	4 Cdo Bde Sig Tp.	MM	220
Jones, J. G.	Capt	Welch Regt, SS Tps, att 1 Cdo	MC	270

Name	Rank	Unit	Award	Page
Kay, J. N.	C/Sgt	2 RM Armd Sp Regt	MM	207
Keat, E. C. B. S.	Lt	RAMC, 6 Cdo	MC	235
Keep, R. W.	Maj	W Yorks att 2 Cdo	MC	87
Kemp, G. L.	Sgt	48 (RM) Cdo	MM	220
Kemp, P. M. McI.	Maj	Int Corps, 62 Cdo	DSO	83
Kemsley, G. W	TSM	44 RM Cdo	MM	281
Kendall, H. R. F	Sgt	DWR, 6 Cdo	MM	248
Kendrick, P. G.	L/Cpl	RAMC, 47 RM Cdo	MM	207
Kennen, The Rev H.	Chpln	45 & 46 RM Cdo	DSC	230
Kerr, D. S.	Capt	5 Cdo	MC	270
Keyes, G. C. T	Lt-Col	R Scots Greys, RAC	VC	58
Khytovitch, E.	L/Sgt	RE, 6 Cdo	MM	72
Kieffer, P.	Capt	IA Cdo with 4 Cdo	MC	197
King, E. G.	L/Sgt	3 Cdo	MM	129
King, L. S.	Cpl	SS Gp Signals RM	MM	48
King, P F.	Lt	DCLI, 4 Cdo	MC	236
King, R.	L/Cpl	RAMC, 9 Cdo	MM	172
Kinnear, E. A.	Sgt	40 RM Cdo	MM	173
Kirkhope, W. A. F	Sgmn	R Signals, SS Bde Sig Tp, 2 Cdo Bde.	DCM	154
Knowland, G. A.	Lt	R Norfolk Regt (att Cdo)	VC	263
Komrower, A. G.	Capt	Lancs Fus, 3 Cdo	DSO	138
Lander, G. D.	Sgt	27 Bn RM	MM	249
Lane, G. H.	Lt	Buffs, 10 (IA) Cdo	MC	34
Langley, E.	Capt	RM	MC	271
Larcher, J. G. L.	Lt	Recce Corps, att 1 Cdo	MC	271
Lassen, A. F. E. V. S.	Maj	General List	VC	134
Laynon, F W.	Mne	47 RM Cdo	MM	220
Leach, J. E.	Pte	See Leech, J. E.		
Lee, J.	Maj	RM	MC	197
Leech, J. E.	Pte	Beds & Herts, 3 Cdo	MM	174
——	Sgt	Beds & Herts, 3 Cdo	Bar to MM	200
Lees, J. S.	CSM	41 RM Cdo	MM	250
LeGrand, C.	L/Cpl	10 (IA) Cdo (Belgian Tp)	MM	221
Leicester, B. W.	Brig	RM	Bar to DSO	213
Lewis, A. D.	Lt-Col	Dorset, 6 Cdo	DSO	230
——	Lt-Col	Dorsets, 6 Cdo	CdG	261
——			MBE	289
Lewis, H. H.	L/Sgt	R Signals, 3 Cdo	MM	174
Leyland, S. J.	L/Sgt	Welch, 3 Cdo	MM	174
Lilley, E. T.	L/Sgt	3 Bn Coldm Gds, 3 Cdo	MM	72
——			BEM	293
Lister, W.	L/Sgt	Border Regt att 6 Cdo	MM	99
Litherland, H.	Cpl	47 RM Cdo	MM	250
Littlejohn, R. R.	Lt	Black Watch, SS Tps	MC	198
Livingstone, R. P	Maj	RUR	MBE	60
Long, D. B.	Lt	Lancs Fus, 9 Cdo	MC	148
Long, M.	Capt	9 Cdo	MC	149
Loraine, P P	Pte	Essex Regt, 6 Cdo	MM	49
Lovat, The Lord	Lt-Col	Lovat Scouts	DSO	30
Lucas, W. F.	TSM	42 RM Cdo	MM	281

Index

MacCallum, L. E.	Capt	Manch Regt, SS Tps	MC	291
MacDonald, W	Mne	47 RM Cdo	MM	207
Mackenzie, R. G.	Capt	RM	MC	198
Malcolm, G.	CSM	40 RM Cdo	MM	175
Mallorie, H.	CSM	46 RM Cdo	MM	251
Mann, R.	L/Cpl	4 Cdo	MM	49
Manners, J. C.	Lt-Col	RM	DSO	138
Marshall, L. G. B.	Capt	RM	MC	149
——	Capt	RM	Bar to MC	140
McCall, R. D. C.	Maj	AAC	MC	291
McCarthy, P F.	L/Sgt	4 Cdo	MM	50
McCarthy, R.	L/Cpl	RAMC, SS Tps	MM	207
McDonough, T	Gnr	4 Cdo	MM	50
McGonigal, A. J.	Capt	RUR, SS Tps	MC	291
McGregor, A. McK.	Sign	SS Bde Sig Tp	MM	208
McKay, L. L. A.	Capt	SAUDF	MC	198
McPherson, G. McG. F.	L/Sgt	Black Watch, 9 Cdo	MM	176
McVeigh, P	L/Sgt	Loyals, 4 Cdo	DCM	217
Meakin, T.	CSM	28 Bn RM	MM	251
Mellor, P J.	Mne	42 RM Cdo	MM	282
Merritt, C. C. I.	Lt-Col	S Saskatchewan Regt	VC	26
Mills-Roberts, D.	Maj	Irish Guards	MC	35
Moore, E. L.	Capt	RAMC, SS Tps	MC	125
Morgan, F C.	L/Cpl	R Fus, 2 Cdo	MM	73
Morgan, T	C/Sjt	41 RM Cdo	MM	176
Morland, P. D.	CSM	S Lancs Regt, 2 Cdo	DCM	92
Morris, L. J.	L/Cpl	Lond Irish, 2 Cdo	MM	73
Morris, M. F	Cpl	1 RE Cdo	MM	74
Moulton, J. L.	Lt-Col	RM	DSO	193
Mulcahy, T J.	L/Bdr	RA (Coast), 2 Cdo (RA (Coast))	MM	100
Mullard, S. J.	Sgt	Cameron Hldrs, 4 Cdo	MM	222
Murray, W.	Cpl	41 RM Cdo	DCM	125
Musgrove, L.	Sgt	41 RM Cdo	MM	222
Musk, R. L.	Sgt	RE	BEM	106
Myram, A. E.	Sgt	Som LI, Indep Coy Gibraltar, 2 Cdo	MM	129
Nash, D. J.	Cpl	Worcs Regt, HOC, 12 RM Cdo	MM	50
Neale, P W J.	Capt	RM	MC	236
Newman, A. C.	Lt-Col	Essex Regt att Cdo	VC	27
Nicholl, J. E. C.	Capt	RA, SS Tps	MC	149
Nicholls, C.	Mne	RM	MM	100
Nicholson, D.	Mne	48 RM Cdo	MM	223
Nicklin, N. C.	L/Sgt	R Signals	BEM	106
Nightingale, F L.	Cpl	41 RM Cdo	DCM	218
Noakes, W. J.	Sgt	45 RM Cdo	MM	252
Noble, R. W.	Lt	DLI, SS Tps	MC	271
Notley, G. L.	Sgt	RAMC att 1 Cdo	MM	282

Commando Gallantry Awards of World War II

O'Brien, J. P	Capt	RM	MC	150
O'Brien, R.	L/Sgt	R Berks, att 2 Cdo	DCM	117
———	Sgt	R Berks Regt, 2 Cdo	MM	177
O'Flaherty, D. W. V P.	Lt	RA	DSO	115
O'Reilly, J. M.	L/Sgt	Irish Gds, 8 Cdo & SBS	MM	100
Ogden-Smith, B. W.	Sgt	E Surrey Regt att 2 SBS, SS Bde	MM	51
———	Sgt	E Surrey Regt, Copps §	DCM	39
Olver, L. C.	Pte	Buffs, 1 Cdo	MM	283
Osborne, V A.	L/Cpl	Welch Regt, 3 Cdo	MM	208
Packer, M. C.	Sgt	RM	MM	223
Palmer, E. C. E.	Lt-Col	RM	DSO	213
Palmer, E. E.	Cpl	40 RM Cdo	MM	101
Pantall, R. W.	Bdr	RA (Fd), 3 Cdo	MM	177
Parkin, D.	CQMS	R Signals	BEM	107
Parkinson-Cumine, R. N.	Capt	RM	MC	88
Parsons, C. D.	Sgt	Beds & Herts, 2 Cdo	MM	178
Parsons, G. A.	Lt	Som LI, SS Tps	MC	150
Paton, C. W	Mne	4 RM Eng Cdo	MM	252
Patrick, N.	Cpl	40 RM Cdo	MM	178
Peachey, F	L/Sgt	S Lancs. Regt, 2 Cdo	MM	179
Peachey, V.	L/Sgt	S Lanc R, 2 Cdo	Bar to MM	158
Perkins, L.	Sgt	QO Cameron Hldrs, 2 Cdo	MM	293
Perrott, K. R. M.	Capt	RM	MC	198
Phillips, C. F.	Lt-Col	RM	DSO	193
Pickering, K. R.	Sgt	43 RM Cdo	MM	101
Pirie, A. B.	Sgt	3 RM Engineer Cdo	MM	283
Pollard, G.	Sgt	169 LAA Bty RA, 57 LAA Regt RA, 3 Cdo	MM	74
———	2Lt	3 Cdo	MC	150
———	Lt	RA, 3 Cdo	Bar to MM	193
———			OBE	288
Pomford, D.	Cpl	S Lancs Regt, 1 SBS	MM	101
———	Sgt	S Lancs Regt, 1 SBS	Bar to MM	93
Pooley, J. B. V	Capt	RA, SS Tps	MC	125
Porteous, P. A.	Maj	RA	VC	28
Portman, I.	L/Sgt	SS Bde, 2 Cdn Div, 4 Cdo	MM	51
Preece, F	Tpr	101 Troop, 2 SBS	DCM	39
Preston, M. L.	Capt	SAUDF, seconded to RM	MC	151
Pryor, F. W.	Cpl	41 RM Cdo	MM	179
Pymm, A. L.	Cpl	47 RM Cdo	MM	253
Rabbitt, E. W	Gnr	1 Cdo	MM	283
Rae, W.	Sgt	S Staffs, 6 Cdo	MM	75
Ralphs, E.	Pte	S Lancs Regt, Special Raiding Sqn & 7 Cdo	MM	179
Randall, R. C.	Sgt	Cameron Hldrs, 2 Cdo	DCM	40
Raynor, F	Mne	30 Bn RM	MM	254
Reace, G. A.	WO2	Att. 9 Cdo	DCM	155
Reid, W.	C/Sgt	41 RM Cdo	MM	180
Rennie, W	Mne	46 RM Cdo	MM	254

Index

Name	Rank	Unit	Award	Page
Riches, I. H.	Lt-Col	RM	DSO	139
Rigg, P	Pte	RAMC, 3 Cdo	MM	180
Roast, S. A.	Gnr	RA (HAA) att 1 Cdo	MM	284
Roberts, C. W.	Sgt	RM	DCM	93
Robinson, D. A.	Capt	RA, SS Tps	MC	63
Rogers, J. G. A.	L/Sgt	Cameron Hldrs, 2 Cdo	MM	101
Rowbottom, T. F	Lt	RM	MC	237
Rozen, B. J.	L/Cpl	10 Cdo att 2/6 Queen's R Regt	MM	181
Rudge, W. F	Sgt	S Lancs Regt, 2 Cdo	DCM	156
Rushforth, J. N.	Maj	RM	MC	198
Russell, R. F.	Cpl	42 RM Cdo	MM	284
Ruxton, A. F	Capt	RUR	MC	35
Ryalls, K. J.	Mne	48 RM Cdo	MM	223
Saberton, E. C.	L/Cpl	43 RM Cdo	MM	181
Scanlon, G.	L/Cpl	RAMC, 4 Cdo	MM	208
Scantlebury, J.	Cpl	Mx Regt, 1 Cdo	MM	75
Scott, A.	Pte	Camerons, 9 Cdo	MM	181
Scott, T F.	Cpl	QO Cameron Hldrs	GM	89
Scott-Bowden, L.	Maj	RE, att 2 SBS, SS Bde	MC	35
——	Maj	RE	Bar to MC	231
——	Maj	RE	DSO	287
Scullion, J. P	Cpl	RM	MM	255
Searle, C. F.	L/Sgt	9 Cdo	DCM	157
Searson, A. C.	L/Sgt	R Sussex Regt, 2 Cdo	MM	295
Selwyn, J. J.	Capt	13/18 R Hussars, RAC	MC	36
Sharples, D. J.	Sgt	27 Bn RM	MM	255
Shaw, J.	Mne	RM (Force Vipers)	MM	285
Sherwood, J. B. B.	Sgt	RASC, 8 Cdo & 1 SBS	MM	76
Simister, C. A.	Cpl	RAMC, 2 Cdo	MM	182
Sims, R. W.	L/Cpl	Som LI att SS Bde, 2 Cdo	MM	317
Sincup, A. W.	L/Sgt	KSLI att 1 Cdo	DCM	271
Smale, K. W. R.	Lt	RM	MC	36
Smith, C. W	L/Cpl	RAMC, 43 RM Cdo	MM	102
Smith, H.	Sgt	40 RM Cdo	MM	182
Smith, I. C. D.	Lt	RASC, SS Tps	MC	291
Smith, T	L/Cpl	S Lancs Regt, 2 Cdo	MM	102
Smith, W. T	Sgt	RASC, 3 Cdo	MM	183
Snow, H. T	L/Cpl	RAMC att 42 RM Cdo	MM	285
Southworth, J. C. H.	L/Sgt	SWB, 1 Cdo	MM	76
Spears, T.	Sgt	RAMC, 3 Cdo	MM	129
Spencer, P.	Capt	RM	DSO	214
Stevens, T. M. P	Capt	RM	MC	198
Stewart, J. C.	Fus	R Welch Fus, 1 Cdo	MM	77
Stilwell, M. W.	Capt	Coldm Gds, SS Tps	MC	291
Stockdale, W. R.	TSM	RA, 4 Cdo	DCM	40
Stokell, C. L.	Sgt	RM	MM	224
Stratford, H. E.	Capt	RM	MC	125
Stringer, E.	Cpl	41 RM Cdo	MM	184
Stringer, J. C.	Sgt	48 RM Cdo	MM	209
Stuart, R.	Cpl	45 RM Cdo	MM	256
Style, D. C. W.	Capt	Lancs Fus	MC	36

Name	Rank	Unit	Award	Page
Summers, R. A. L.	Sgt	KRRC att SBS	MM	102
Swinburn, A.	WO2	Leics Regt, SS Tps, 50 Cdo	DCM	292
Sykes, J.	L/Cpl	45 RM Cdo	MM	256
Tailyour, N. H.	Lt-Col	RM	DSO	230
Tanswell, J. W	CSM	41 RM Cdo	MM	257
Tasker, P H.	Capt	RAMC, SS Tps	MC	199
Taylor, G.	L/Sgt	RA, 3 Cdo	MM	130
Terry, J.	Sgt	RA, 11 Cdo & SAS	DCM	67
Thomas, R. F.	Pte	Glosters, 3 Cdo	MM	257
Thompson, J. E.	Capt	SWB, SS Tps	MC	199
Thompson, N.	Sgt	RE, 6 Cdo & 2 SBS	MM	77
Thomson, J.	L/Sgt	KOSB, 9 Cdo	DCM	157
Thwaytes, J. W	L/Cpl	RAMC, SS Tps	MM	209
Tibbles, H.	Pte	Border Regt, 6 & 12 Cdo	MM	258
Tickle, F. B.	L/Cpl	RAMC, SS Tps	MM	209
Tilney, W. E.	Sgt	41 RM Cdo	MM	184
Tomlinson, R.	WO2	RA (Fd), 2 Cdo	MM	184
Tomsett, C. P	S/Sgt	RE	BEM	107
Towler, D.	Mne	45 RM Cdo	MM	258
Trevor, K. R. S.	Lt-Col	Cheshire Regt, SS Tps	DSO	268
Trigg, F.	Pte	R Sussex Regt, 2 Cdo	MM	314
Tucker, E.	Sgt	RE	BEM	108
Turnbull, G. H. S.	Capt	Gordon Hldrs, SS Tps	MC	63
Turnbull, J. H. S.	Maj	Gordon Hldrs, SS Tps	Bar to MC	269
Tyman, F P	Mne	40 RM Cdo	MM	185
Usher, F G.	Cpl	40 RM Cdo	MM	185
Vardy, T.	Mne	46 RM Cdo	MM	259
Verri, A.	Cpl	R Berks, 2 Cdo	MM	103
Wadge, E. E.	L/Cpl	3 Cdo	DCM	238
Wakeling, J. D.	Maj	RM	MC	88
Waldie, R. G.	Capt	KOSB, SS Tps	MC	151
Wall, P H. B.	Maj	RM	MC	237
Walsh, E.	L/Sgt	Irish Gds, SS Tps	MM	209
Walsh, F	Sgt	A&SH, 9 Cdo	MM	185
Walton, D. H.	Maj	RM	MC	199
Warnock, J.	L/Cpl	AAC	MM	77
Waugh, W	Cpl	A&SH, 9 Cdo	MM	186
Webb, G. G. H.	Capt	RA	Bar to MC	31
Webb, G. H.	Pte	RWK att 1 Cdo	MM	285
Webb, J.	L/Cpl	RAMC, 2 Cdo	MM	187
Webb, M. H.	Capt	S African Forces, SS Tps	Bar to MC	290
Welsh, A. J.	CSM	42 RM Cdo	DCM	272
Wham, J. H.	Cpl	R Scots, 3 Cdo	MM	187
Wheeler, G. R.	Cpl	R Sussex Regt att SS Bde.	MM	317
White, E. G.	Cpl	3 Cdo	DCM	117
White, H. V. H.	Capt	2 SBS	MC	63
White, J. E.	L/Sgt	Gren Gds, 2 Cdo	MM	130
White, W. H. A. R.	L/Cpl	3 Cdo	MM	52
Whitfield, G. F.	Capt	Recce Corps, RAC, SS Tps	MC	151

Index

Wickson, L. C.	Sgt	Beds & Herts Regt, 2 Cdo	MM	52
Wilkins, G. R.	L/Sgt	Lond Scot, 9 Cdo	MM	188
Wilkinson, A. D.	Capt	RM	MC	151
Wilkinson, J. W.	L/Sgt	Bedfs & Herts, 3 Cdo	MM	188
Williams, J. A.	Pte	KSLI, 1 Cdo	MM	78
Williams, T. E.	Capt	RM	MC	237
Williams, T I.	Sgt	B Gp SBS, 1 Cdo	MM	286
Wilmott, H.	Sgt	AAC	MM	78
Winter, T. W	WO2	RASC, SSRF 2 Para, SBS & SAS	MM	293
Winterburn, M. H.	Gnr	RA, 6 Cdo	MM	318
Winters, H.	Cpl	RM (Viper Force)	MM	286
Wither, R. J.	Sgt	41 RM Cdo	MM	209
Wood, J. H.	Mne	48 RM Cdo	MM	259
Wood, N. P.	Maj	RM	MC	216
Woodiwiss, A. F	Cpl	Queen's R Regt, 2 Cdo	MM	53
Worrall, F. G.	Sgt	RA, C Bn Layforce, 11 Cdo	MM	103
Worthington, F A.	Sgt	R Sussex Regt, 6 Cdo	MM	260
Wraith, W.	L/Sgt	KOYLI, 6 Cdo	MM	260
Wright, E. R. McM.	Capt	Indian Armd Corps, SS Tps	MC	271
Young, P	Capt	Beds & Herts Regt	MC	116
——	Maj	Beds & Herts Regt, SS Tps	2nd Bar to MC	139
——	Maj	Beds & Herts Regt	DSO	30

Note .

§ Award was won while serving with a unit other than Commando.

DESIGNED AND SET IN
CASLON 11 POINT LEADED 1 POINT
WITH 30 POINT FOR DISPLAY
BY
LANGLANDS EDITION
LOUGHBOROUGH